Music in American Life

*A list of books in the series appears
at the end of this book.*

MILTON BROWN
and the Founding of
Western Swing

MILTON BROWN
and the Founding of
Western Swing

CARY GINELL

With special assistance from
Roy Lee Brown

UNIVERSITY OF ILLINOIS PRESS   Urbana and Chicago

Publication of this book was supported by
grants from the John Edwards Memorial Forum
and the Sonneck Society for American Music.

This book is printed on acid-free paper.

Library of Congress Cataloging-in-Publication Data

Ginell, Cary.
    Milton Brown and the founding of western swing / Cary Ginell ;
with special assistance from Roy Lee Brown.
        p.   cm. — (Music in American Life)
    Discography: p.
    Includes index.
    ISBN 0-252-02041-3
    1. Western swing (Music)—History and criticism. 2. Brown,
Milton. I. Brown, Roy Lee, 1921–   . II. Title. III. Series.
ML3541.G56   1994
781.642–dc20   93-29364
                                                        CIP
                                                        MN

For the Brownies

Contents

Acknowledgments

This book would not have been possible without Roy Lee Brown. As the Brown family's historian, Roy Lee is the only living person who could have related the basic facts about the lives of Milton Brown, the Brown family, and the Musical Brownies. In addition, he was able to steer me to sources of information and corroboration that I would not have been able to find on my own. From the moment I met him, I have found Roy Lee to be a scrupulously honest partner, observant, analytical, and a meticulous researcher. Roy Lee Brown's goal was to find the absolute truth and tell his story to the world. His dogged determination rubbed off on me during my five years of researching this book, and I am indebted to him for his trust in my abilities and devotion to a subject that started as a curiosity but ended as a labor of love.

After writing each chapter, I sent it to Roy Lee for approval and/ or corrections. We agreed to include verbatim transcripts of my interviews, not only to render faithfully the personal memories of our subjects but also to bring the times alive.

Roy Lee Brown was also responsible for the preservation of most of the photographs used in the book as well as their identification. Other sources for photographs are noted in the captions. I would especially like to extend a hearty "thank-you" to Marvin "Robby" Robinson, who gave generously of his time and resources to preserve, restore, and duplicate pertinent photos and documents presented in the book.

Jimmy Thomason of Bakersfield, California, has been one of my strongest supporters as well as a western swing pioneer in his own right. I treasure my many visits with him at his home and during our mutual trips to Fort Worth each spring. His sharp memory and articulate comments were invaluable additions to the book as well.

Fort Worth music pioneer Roscoe Pierce helped organize my yearly sojourns. He alerted possible subjects to my impending arrival and was the driving force to "git it all together."

Research assistance came from many sources. I would like to personally thank Bob Pinson of the Country Music Foundation, Glenda Stone of the Stephenville Public Library, Linda Brown Allie, the staffs of the Fort Worth Public Library and the Amon Carter Museum, Bill Crawford, Gene Fowler, Charles Wolfe, Barber's Book Store in Fort Worth, John I. Taylor, Kevin Coffey, "Big Jim" Sarver, Hank Harrison of the Witte Museum in San Antonio, and Jack Gordon, Chris Evans, Mike Price, and Earl Moore of the *Fort Worth Star-Telegram* for their valued and much appreciated efforts.

Back home, D. K. Wilgus and Eleanor Long of the Folklore and Mythology Program at UCLA read through the entire manuscript, adding and removing commas, making pertinent comments, gently scolding me for grammatical errors, and providing moral support to "keep plugging." Their wisdom, counsel, and praise have meant the world to me.

Folklorist Ed Kahn helped me understand and communicate more clearly Milton Brown's role in the founding of western swing. Ed's sage advice and passionate belief in the importance of my work helped get me through the difficult periods when I wondered whether the book was indeed worth all the effort I was putting into it.

Judith McCulloh of the University of Illinois Press is responsible for bringing the story of Milton Brown to fruition. In the years since I first proposed the book to her, she has been an undaunted voice of support and encouragement. Her enthusiasm and confidence in the project enabled me to pursue every lead, tie up every loose end, and polish the manuscript until it shone. My thanks to her, to her assistant, Margaret Sarkissian, and to copyeditor Pat Hollahan for their efforts.

The initial stimulus for my interest in western swing came from a run-down record store in Santa Monica, California, called the Jazz Man Record Shop. Its longtime owner, a bearded, sixtyish curmudgeon/record-collecting genius named Don Brown, was "den father" to a group of weekly derelicts known cumulatively as the Saturday Crowd. Arriving at the shop each Saturday, the regulars attended the weekly social get-togethers with religious fanaticism, playing old 78s, swilling beer, arguing, challenging, laughing, theorizing, and eventually initiating me as an honored member (code name: Paladin). The shop closed its doors forever in 1983 and Don retired. He died two years later. To this day, the Orphans of the Jazz Man meet monthly to continue the traditional Saturday get-togethers. They include Darlene Brown, Mark Cantor, Lawrence Cohn, Eugene "Gentleman Gene" Earle, Alan Franklin, John "The Fox" Fraser, Bill Givens, Don Gray, Ed Guy, Barry "Dr. Demento" Hansen, Michael

Helwig, Ed Kahn, Mike Kieffer, Donald Lee Nelson, Harvey Newland, Bill Olson, Alan Roberts, Pat Shields, and John "The Bugg" Tippet. Thanks for the camaraderie, guys, and save an E+ gold box Vocalion for me.

My friend Hank Penny taught me volumes about country music
history and about life as well. His outrageous sense of humor, consummate professionalism, and inordinate faith in my abilities helped
me believe in myself.

Mike and Kay Dorrough generously made available the video equipment I used to document all of the interviews and jam sessions during my trips to Texas. They are preservationists of the highest order,
and my respect and affection for them cannot be overestimated.

My parents provided me with immeasurable support that can
never be repaid. Their faith in my ability kept me going and it was
comforting to know there was always a willing ear at the ready
when I needed it. To Mom and Dad: I don't know what I'd do without you.

Although I did not meet my wife Gail until after the manuscript
had been completed, she read the book with great interest and provided valuable editorial assistance in the many rewrites and revi-
sions. My life would be meaningless without her love and understanding.

On a smaller scale, our dogs Sparkle and Angel provided tacit approval of all that went on.

Finally, I want to thank the people of Texas; not only the musicians and other informants who graciously and magnanimously
helped untangle the knotted history of the Musical Brownies but all
of the folks I met along the way, in restaurants, gas stations, libraries, record stores, book stores, antique shops, Dairy Queens, and radio stations. Your friendly smiles and eagerness to make me feel at
home showed me a lot of the legendary southern hospitality. This
book may be for the world, but it is especially for you, because it
was people like you who discovered and appreciated Milton Brown.

Cary Ginell

I owe a lot of thanks to many people for their contribution to this
book. Without their help and knowledge, we could not have made
the book as complete as it is. I obviously cannot attempt to list all
who have helped, but I must publicly give credit to a few.

First, I give thanks to my father and mother, who were great Chris-
tians and who taught me to try to be the best person I could be. My

father always said, "A man's word is his bond," and I have always tried to abide by this principle.

Next, I owe a lot to my brother Derwood. He gave me information about the Brownies down through the years that I would not have had otherwise. Many incidents and facts I would not have known if he had not related them to me. I'm sad to say that Derwood never received credit for the key role he had with the Brownies band. Not one to seek recognition or draw attention to himself, Derwood just beat the heck out of his guitars and sang his music with the ability God gave him, without fanfare.

A special thanks to Marvin "Robby" Robinson. His interest and support went an extra mile in the creation of this book!

Thanks also to my cousin Preston Hook for information and memorabilia that he contributed, which would have been otherwise unavailable.

I also would like to give thanks to Ellen, my wife of fifty-five years, for her support and help. Her ability to compose letters that I had to write and doing the typing of these letters and all the other secretarial work are deeply appreciated.

Now my thanks and appreciation to Cary Ginell, who deserves much credit for his many years of labor and extensive research. He was determined not to just take my word as fact for any information I gave him, or information of others who he interviewed. Cary searched for documented proof in the form of letters of bygone years and old newspapers as well as visiting courthouses, libraries, and vital statistics bureaus. Good job, Cary.

Finally, I ask forgiveness of many friends and relatives whom I have not found space to mention here. I do offer sincere thanks. Without your help, this book would not have been possible.

God bless all!

Roy Lee Brown

Introduction

Fort Worth, Texas
June, 1983

John Bruce "Roscoe" Pierce took a satisfying sip from his morning "eye-opener," a glass of half water and half Early Times, and called out, "Hey, Boots, you wanna go out?" A chunky, affable dachshund ambled into the kitchen and headed for the back screen door and waited. Pierce, guffawing at the dog's comical walk, opened the door, and Boots scooted outside in search of mythical feline adversaries.

Roscoe Pierce is seventy. In his performing days in the 1930s and 1940s, Bruce Pierce was tall and skinny with thinning blond hair, prominent ears, and an infectious wide grin. Today, the grin remains, although he has put on some weight over the years. His moon-shaped face is now augmented by a pair of thick Coke-bottle-bottom eyeglasses, making his expression even more humorous. The nickname "Roscoe" was given to Pierce by country personality Bob Shelton (of the Shelton Brothers) while both were members of the Sunshine Boys, a popular string band in Shreveport and Dallas. Roscoe was a barefooted hillbilly character Pierce portrayed with the Flying X Ranch Boys, a group that appeared on early Fort Worth television. Roscoe was fond of saying, "I'd a been the first person seen on TV in Fort Worth if it wasn't for President Truman beatin' me to it. Ha!"

Before World War II, Pierce was one of the best tenor banjo players in Texas. His early experiences included a brief stint with the Light Crust Doughboys and Blackie Simmons's Famous Blue Jackets, the latter a string band that entertained during Texas's centennial celebration of 1936. Pierce also appeared on a handful of recordings with the Sunshine Boys and with Cliff Bruner's Texas Wanderers. His banjo playing on these numbers is instantly recognizable: a steady 2/4 beat punctuated by syncopated half-step chops.

For two years, Roscoe Pierce had been my door opener. I had met him while doing research for an album reissue of recordings made by Ocie Stockard and the Wanderers, a Fort Worth string band of the 1930s. From my home in Los Angeles, I made contact with Stockard, a retired bartender living in Fort Worth. During my vacation that spring I flew to Texas, hoping to meet him in person and learn something about the bands that flourished in Texas during the early days of western swing. Ocie Stockard was a charter member of Milton Brown's Musical Brownies, a band that seemed to be the focus of universal reverence among musicians in Texas. Stockard, apparently unsure of my motives, invited Roscoe over to sit in on the interview as security. Many of the musicians I later interviewed were also suspicious of my reasons for traveling fifteen hundred miles just to talk to some old-timers who used to make phonograph records a half-century ago.

The interview with Stockard led to completion of the album. But I was not finished with Texas. My curiosity had been aroused, and the next year I returned to try to track down other musicians. Roscoe offered his assistance, inviting me to stay in his comfortable home and save money on motels.

Roscoe Pierce lived in a two-bedroom brick house in Fort Worth's suburb of Forest Hill, five miles southeast of downtown. After his retirement (Roscoe was a traveling salesman for an electronics company after his music days ended) he lived with his wife, Elizabeth, who had passed away several years before I met him. Now it was just Roscoe and Boots, although Roscoe's son Ronald had moved his family into the house next door.

Each year after our initial meeting, Roscoe graciously offered his home to me as headquarters. I spent many hot days sitting with Roscoe at his cluttered kitchen table, heaped with old correspondence, photographs, Musician's Union directories, and remnants from Riscky's Barbecue lunches. With the air conditioner roaring behind us, we traced Roscoe's contemporaries and drove out to interview them, the farthest trip taking us to DeBerry, Texas, about twenty miles from the Louisiana border, to visit with Grundy "Slim" Harbert, another member of the Sunshine Boys. Roscoe had not seen Slim in twenty years; their reunion was particularly poignant, for the formerly jovial Harbert had developed Alzheimer's disease and was visibly failing.

Roscoe Pierce soon became much more to me than simply a temporary landlord and tour guide. He and many other musicians I met became my friends. I discovered in time that Texans are initially suspicious of outsiders, but soon the famed southern hospitality rises to the surface and they open their hearts and homes to you. I have never met more generous, friendly, and loyal people in my life, and my heart aches as much as theirs whenever I get word from Roscoe that their number has been decreased. It is unfortunate to lose a source of information, but it is tragic to lose a friend. Time and time again in later years I would return to my interview videotapes and relive my brief associations with some of the musicians who have since died: Darrell Kirkpatrick, Sam Graves, Lefty Perkins, Tommy Camfield, Buster Ferguson, J. B. Brinkley, Fred Calhoun, Ocie Stockard, and Wanna Coffman.

Today, Roscoe and I were going out to the small town of Aledo to visit with Roy Lee Brown, the surviving brother of the late Milton Brown, leader of the Musical Brownies.

Along with other Texas-based string bands, including the Light Crust Doughboys, Bill Boyd's Cowboy Ramblers, and Bob Wills's Playboys (later, Texas Playboys, after their move to Oklahoma), the Musical Brownies was one of the Southwest's most popular musical organizations. Milton Brown was an original member of the Light Crust Doughboys before forming his own group in 1932. The Musical Brownies helped trailblaze western swing in the mid-1930s by establishing its repertoire and instrumentation. They popularized it by using radio as a promotional medium and through their extremely successful regional dances. The Musical Brownies' broadcasts, personal appearances, and phonograph records had a tremendous influence on southwestern musicians, including Bob Wills, who is commonly given credit as the "father of western swing." Unfortunately for widespread recognition of his role, Milton Brown died tragically, from injuries suffered in an automobile accident in April 1936, cutting short his career at the peak of its popularity and influence. He was only thirty-two years old. But the seeds of western swing as an independent musical subgenre of country music had already been planted. In the years after Brown's death, further developments in western swing were popularized by groups such as Roy Newman and his Boys, Cliff Bruner's Texas Wanderers, Jimmie Revard's Oklahoma Playboys, a new generation of Light Crust Doughboys, and eventually, Bob Wills and his Texas Playboys.

I was researching Brown's music for the purpose of providing liner notes for an album reissue of the Brownies' records made for Bluebird in 1934. Roy Lee Brown and Roscoe Pierce had known each other since the 1930s, and it was Roscoe who called Roy Lee and arranged time for an interview.

As he locked up the house, Roscoe made sure Boots was safely inside and we got into my rented Buick Regal for the journey to Aledo.

As a seasoned veteran of the Los Angeles freeway system, I was confident that I could handle anything Texas would throw at me. By now, however, I felt fortunate to have Roscoe along as I tried to sort out the Lone Star logic that produced two Highway 35s and another highway (Interstate 820) that travels in all four directions of the compass in a loop around Fort Worth.

"Get on that damn Loop 820, going WEST," said Roscoe. His speech is peppered with salty language and Justin Wilsonisms: I recognized "helllla yes!!" and "I guarantold you" from Wilson's Cajun cooking program on public television.

Loop 820 took us to the westernmost side of Fort Worth, where it merges with Interstate 30. Continuing west on 30, we were soon out of the Fort Worth city limits. Civilization dissipates quickly outside cities in Texas. There is no gradual progression from bustling downtown to suburb to outskirts as there is in California. No sooner did we make the transition to Interstate 30 than we found ourselves in the country. The highway gave way to a flat, sometimes gently rolling eight-lane slab of concrete. On either side of the freeway, Texas extended to the horizon in an endless expanse of green farmland and oak trees. The sky is bigger in Texas; there are no mountains like those with which I had become familiar in California. Without mountains framing the sky, the sun lasts longer before it disappears beneath the horizon in a blaze of melted reds and oranges. Oblivious to this splendor, Roscoe signaled me to exit and we got off the freeway, crossed over, and found ourselves on a fast two-lane road that immediately began dipping and curving as it headed into the small town of Aledo, population one thousand.

My portable cassette machine was playing recordings of old Milton Brown 78s as we drove through the quiet town. Roscoe sang along with "Some of These Days," "Darktown Strutters' Ball," and other favorites of his while I noticed changes occurring in the landscape. The flat expanse had now given way to rolling hills and plunging valleys thick with oaks and cedar trees. As the road narrowed I could almost see the Brownies' bus rattling down one of the dirt roads, kicking up wakes of red Texas dust, a bass fiddle strapped to its roof, the driver squinting into the fading daylight for some signs of a dilapidated dance hall, roadhouse, or high school.

There were large black spots on the road, which was just drying off after a Texas thunderstorm. To my surprise, the spots were moving. "Tarantulas," Roscoe stated matter-of-factly. "Rain always makes 'em come up to dry ground." I maneuvered around them and began thinking of the man we were going to see. Roy Lee Brown, Milton's youngest brother and the sole survivor of the Brown family. Roy Lee was eighteen years younger than Milton, a disparity wide enough that Milton could easily have been Roy Lee's father. I wondered if Roy Lee was old enough during the Brownies' glory years to remember anything at all.

"I've known Roy Lee since he was just a little bitty kid," said Roscoe. "Didn't get to know him personally for a while, but he changed strings for Derwood up on the bandstand at Crystal Springs when he was a teenager." I had heard a lot about Derwood, the middle brother, whose guitar rhythm was so insistent, even violent, that an extra person was hired to accompany the Brownies to change the strings on Derwood's guitar when one snapped. A fresh guitar was always waiting in the wings for Derwood's frantically gesturing hands; the transaction took place on countless occasions each night.

The road crossed a narrow bridge and began to rise. At the ridge the road leveled out to reveal a neat row of several well-built brick homes, separated by networks of chain link fencing. "Third house on the left," said Roscoe. I nodded and pulled into the gravel driveway of the third structure, stopped at the gate, and honked the horn. A man was sitting on the front porch in an old-fashioned metal tubing patio chair. As he arose and started to head for the gate, I noticed a shingle hanging directly above him over the front door, stating simply "Brown." He approached the gate with two dogs barking at his heels. "Sandy, Dingo, be quiet now!" he commanded. I drove in after he opened the gate and parked in front of the house. Roy Lee Brown closed the gate and walked to where we had parked, arriving in time to help Roscoe laboriously climb out of the car. "Whaddya say, Bruce?" said Roy Lee, extending a hand. "Not too much, Roy Lee," said Roscoe with a grunt as he got out and straightened up. "I'm a-used to my old Cadillac, got no use for these damned small cars, ha haaa!" It was then that I noticed the remarkable resemblance between Roy Lee Brown and his famous older brother Milton. His smile was as warm as Milton's, whose familiar visage I had seen in a few dim photographs. The hair was wavy and dark with streaks of gray, although Roy Lee was already in his early sixties.

"You must be Cary," Roy Lee said as he turned to me, extending a hand. "I appreciate your interest in Milton. I've seen some of those albums you've done for Texas Rose and you're the first person to get things right about the Brownies. Hope y'all can stay for supper. Ellen's fixin' it right now. It'll be ready by the time we're finished with the interview."

The recording equipment was set up on the back porch and we

began the interview. It was not long before I realized that Milton and Derwood Brown were not the only remarkable brothers in the family. Roy Lee's attention to detail and photographic memory recalled people and incidents that I thought would have been lost forever through the passage of time. Although he was only a teenager when the Musical Brownies were performing and recording, Roy Lee was a self-described "big-eyed, big-eared kid" who listened attentively as his brothers talked around the supper table with their parents. He traveled with the band for two glorious summers in 1935 and 1936 as its band boy/string changer and still had vivid memories of people and places he had seen fifty years before.

Roy Lee and I developed a rapport from the very beginning, testing each other's knowledge with questions about people, songs, and incidents. To me, this was history, but to Roy Lee it was nostalgia. His mind held a scrapbook of images and conversations triggered by a lifelong idolization of his brother, Milton Brown. While I had anticipated some elements of bias, Roy Lee's recollections were fair and he generously gave credit where credit was due. Long after my videotape supply was exhausted, we continued talking about Milton Brown and his Musical Brownies. Over a Texas-sized supper of homemade poor boy stew and corn bread, with vanilla ice cream for dessert, Roy Lee expressed a desire to have his memoirs preserved. When he showed me the memorabilia he had saved over the years—family photographs from the turn of the century, letters from Milton to dance hall owners, and assorted playbills and newsclippings—I decided that his was a story that must be told. Bombarded by this plethora of primary documents, most of which had never been examined by scholars, I began to question Milton Brown's relatively minor role in the history of western swing. Roy Lee Brown must have sensed my fascination with the subject, because we soon agreed to write a book about the Brown family and the beginnings of western swing. Each summer after that initial meeting I returned to Aledo to probe Roy Lee's mind, interview musicians and friends of the Browns, trace leads through fading newspaper clippings and eye-straining microfilm, and listen over and over to the old recordings of Milton Brown and the Musical Brownies.

The story of Milton Brown is much more than the story of a band that made records sixty years ago. It is the story of a man with a vision, a man whose love for people and whose instinct for entertaining drove him to cast aside traditions in one ambitious move after another. His ideas were bold, his actions swift. Milton Brown's innovations were all accomplished with the personal magnetism evident in other music pioneers such as Jimmie Rodgers, Louis Armstrong, and Elvis Presley.

However, I soon learned that this is also the story of an American family, a family that limped into the twentieth century on their hands and knees in cotton fields, surviving as sharecroppers until their eldest son began his climb out of misery and despair to the pinnacle of his profession, only to see the Depression threaten to wipe out everything and everybody. The Brown family witnessed and participated in the beginning of the end for rural, isolated Americans, a microcosm of a changing, expanding way of life as they moved from rural Stephenville to the quickly growing metropolis of Fort Worth.

Finally, this is the story of the Musical Brownies, a group of extraordinarily talented musicians who were able to merge their abilities into one music-making machine that became the envy of all who saw and danced before it. Although every fan of the Brownies will say that people came to Crystal Springs to see Milton Brown, it was Milton's band that established the sound and rhythm admired for so many years by southwestern musicians.

The Musical Brownies pushed the boundaries of hillbilly music to their outermost limits in the mid-1930s. None of the Brownies, except for Jesse Ashlock, an unabashed admirer of Bob Wills, owed specific allegiance to any country musician. Milton Brown himself was one of the few singers in the country field before World War II who did not categorically name Jimmie Rodgers as a prime influence. All the musicians who knew Milton and heard him sing say that Milton set his own style, never copying anyone. If anything, his energetic vocals, affecting recitations, and Roaring Twenties "hotcha" style suggest Ted Lewis or Cab Calloway on jazz tunes and Fred Astaire on Tin Pan Alley songs. Although he never played an instrument, Milton used his voice as a jazz instrument, improvising around the melody, much as Bing Crosby was doing with Paul Whiteman's Rhythm Boys. With Milton Brown's arrival, the focus of Texas string bands changed from the fiddle to a singer. This change proved revolutionary to Texas rural music. It was the first in a series of similarly dramatic factors introduced by Milton Brown that combined previously disparate traditions into a new, exciting brand of music.

Similarly, the Musical Brownies' fiddler, classically trained violinist Cecil Brower, idolized jazz great Joe Venuti, the chief influence on most western swing fiddlers in the 1930s. Whatever folk traditions Cecil Brower learned, he got from Ocie Stockard, Jesse Ashlock, or Cliff Bruner, three rurally trained fiddlers who learned to play "hokum" with the Brownies.

Steel guitarist Bob Dunn and pianist Fred Calhoun were also products of the Jazz Age. Calhoun played in the barrelhouse, left-hand-heavy rhythm style of Bourbon Street, while Dunn created an entirely unfolklike sound based on the wails of trombones à la Jack Teagarden.

Ocie Stockard, though rurally trained on the fiddle, adapted his knowledge for the tenor banjo. His heavily accented 2/4 beat, which began as a modified Dixieland 4/4 rhythm, became the basis for all rhythm sections in western swing bands until drums arrived on a widespread level during World War II.

Derwood Brown's primitive, violent guitar rhythm and lurching single-string solos suggest the early work of Teddy Bunn, who played with the Washboard Rhythm Kings before becoming a member of the Spirits of Rhythm.

The Brownies' repertoire deemphasized traditional country music in accordance with this jazz-oriented interplay between the musicians and the vocals; and with their focus on current popular numbers, classic city blues, and sophisticated jazz instrumentals, the band totally transformed hillbilly music in Texas.

Visually, the Brownies resembled big-city jazz bands, the group members nattily attired in splendid hand-tailored suits with neckties and no hats (the western/cowboy element did not enter western swing until the late 1930s, triggered by such groups as the Sons of the Pioneers).

These elements—performance style, repertoire, and visual presentation—all contradict contemporary impressions of the nature of western swing. Yet on the infrequent occasions where Milton Brown is given credit as a pioneer, it is as a talented but forgotten figure of early country music. Although his influence cannot be overestimated, Milton Brown has been placed in a category in which he did not belong during his lifetime. In the early years of western swing's evolution, the genre bore little similarity to country music. "Hillbilly music," as it was known then, meant artists such as Gid Tanner and his Skillet Lickers, Uncle Dave Macon, and the Carter Family, along with homespun radio programs like WSM Nashville's Grand Ole Opry and WLS Chicago's National Barn Dance. The performers on these shows learned much of their material from traditional folk sources. As musicians, they were generally self-taught and rarely read music. If they knew anything at all about blues or jazz, they looked down on them as inferior, alien sounds. The Brownies would have felt more comfortable in the small jazz clubs of Europe, playing alongside Django Reinhardt and the Quintet of the Hot Club of France, than in checkered overalls on the stage of the Grand Ole Opry.

In their day, the Brownies' sound was so new that radio stations and newspapers had trouble tabbing the group with a descriptive label. Advertising cards sometimes listed the Brownies as a "string orchestra," while the *Fort Worth Press* called them a "fiddle band." An October 1933 issue of the *Fort Worth Radio News* displayed a picture of Milton Brown with the caption "King of the Hillbilly Bands." When the Brownies were signed to Decca late in 1934, their records were to be incorporated into its new 5000 series, which was labeled "Hill Billy."

Although the Brownies' audience consisted chiefly of country people, Milton Brown knew that in order to expand his popularity beyond the rural community, he would have to sell his music to urban audiences. But he was never able to escape the image of being head of a hillbilly band, despite occasionally adding horns to his group.

Bands in Texas were separated into two generalized categories: string bands and horn bands, the determining factor being the lead instrument in each group. The Musical Brownies, which always featured a fiddle playing lead and usually dominating the instrumentation, was called a "fiddle band" or "string band." At the same time, the Brownies learned much of their material from phonograph records or radio programs featuring "horn bands," jazz bands from New Orleans or Chicago that were dominated by the clarinet (Johnny Dodds), trumpet or cornet (Louis Armstrong, King Oliver), and trombone (Kid Ory, Jack Teagarden). In most cases, Milton Brown simply transferred the melodic lead to the fiddle. It was the dominance of this instrument that kept the Brownies conveniently placed in the "string band" category, despite the improvisatory nature of their music.

A less apparent factor that led to the labeling of the Brownies as a hillbilly band was the persona of Milton Brown himself. Hailing from the rural town of Stephenville, Milton was the son of a sharecropper who remained poor much of his life. However, Milton Brown was never ashamed of his roots and refused to deny his rural heritage and the friendships he developed with country people. Despite exhibiting the exterior of an urban dandy (new cars, fancy clothes, fast women always at the ready), Milton remained a country boy at heart. Likewise, Milton may have sold his band's talents short by continuing to play smaller venues when he might have been able to attract the larger, more sophisticated audiences that frequented Fort Worth's Lake Worth Casino ballroom or equivalent facilities in nearby Dallas. By playing Crystal Springs, Milton even had Fred Calhoun convinced that his was just another string band. As a KTAT pianist, Calhoun had learned about the Brownies through a visiting jazz group from Chicago and doubted the group's belief that he would fit in with the band.

Until World War II, western swing remained a Texas phenomenon, with its sphere of influence extending mainly to Oklahoma, Arkansas, and Louisiana. Exceptions to this general rule were evident in other parts of the United States during the Depression. In Virginia, Norman Phelps's Virginia Rounders played pop, blues, and jazz tunes with improvised take-offs by fiddler Earl Phelps and banjoist Ken Card. The Rounders' banjo-heavy string band sound differed in its emphasis of the first and third beats as opposed to the Brownies' Dixieland influenced two-four beat.

In Alabama, Montgomery-born Hank Penny modeled his Radio Cowboys directly after the Brownies' Decca recordings, covering tunes such as "The Hesitation Blues" and penning lyrics to Bob Dunn's "Taking Off."

The Prairie Ramblers brought elements of western swing to radio audiences in Chicago and New York beginning in 1933. Noted for their musical versatility and the fine left-handed fiddle playing of Tex Atchison, the Ramblers were also important for showcasing the vocal talents of such western radio stars as Gene Autry and Patsy Montana. However, their success was chiefly as a radio and show band and not as a touring dance band.

Ed Woodfin, representative for Brunswick Records in Florida, Alabama, and southern Georgia, reported enthusiastic sales in black neighborhoods for records by the Dallas string band led by pianist Roy Newman. Woodfin noted specifically the popularity in Miami of Newman's 1934 recording of "Drag Along Blues."

But despite these regional rumblings of western swing's slow expansion, the music remained restricted to its birth state and areas covered by Texas and Oklahoma radio stations. Even Bob Wills, who organized his first band in September 1933 (a full year after the Musical Brownies were formed), struggled for most of the 1930s. Beginning in Waco, Texas, he moved to Oklahoma in 1934, first to Oklahoma City and then to Tulsa. Wills's first recording session with his own band did not come until September 1935, by which time Milton Brown had already produced three sessions, amassing fifty-four recorded sides. During the mid-1930s Wills was by no means successful nor well known beyond the territories covered by Tulsa's KVOO, his home base from 1934 until 1941.

When he died in the spring of 1936, Milton Brown was at the

threshold of effecting changes created that might have resulted in thrusting western swing into a different direction than that taken by his successors. His impatience with the wearisome routine of touring and the endless series of one-nighters was evidenced by his anticipation of the Texas centennial, his hoped-for relocation to Houston, and his prospective promotion of his band via motion pictures and musical short subjects. These developments would have surely taken Milton Brown and his music into new, uncharted territory. But his death ended his plans, and others took western swing on a different course of development.

With Milton's death in 1936, other bands vied for the position of preeminent string band in the Southwest. The Texas Wanderers, led by Brownie alumnus Cliff Bruner, picked up where the Musical Brownies left off and became a phenomenal draw in the southeastern portion of the state, first in Houston and then in Beaumont. Bruner's band included musicians such as Bob Dunn and Leo Raley, the latter introducing the crisp sound of the amplified mandola, which often supplanted Bruner's fiddle as lead instrument. Bruner's 1938 recording of Floyd Tillman's "It Makes No Difference Now," featuring vocalist Dickie McBride, became one of western swing's earliest smash hits.

While Bob Wills continued to struggle in Oklahoma, the Brownies were influencing bands throughout the Southwest. Groups such as Jimmie Revard's Oklahoma Playboys and Bill Boyd's Cowboy Ramblers shamelessly covered recordings popularized by the Musical Brownies. Even Bob Wills drew much of his material from the Musical Brownies' repertoire. Songs such as "Right or Wrong," "St. Louis Blues," and "Corrine Corrina" were recorded first by Milton Brown and then by Wills's Texas Playboys. For the remainder of the 1930s, Wills's recordings consisted of fiddle tunes, cover versions of popular jazz standards, and up-tempo blues, all staples of the Musical Brownies' catalog. To these Wills added instrumentals featuring steel guitarist Leon McAuliffe and Jimmie Rodgers songs sung by Rodgers fan Tommy Duncan. It was not until 1940 that the repertoire established by Milton Brown began to change, as the cowboy image fast becoming associated with the genre resulted in newly composed songs befitting this western flavor.

Other bands incorporated other regional musical heritages into the constantly mutating music. Adolph Hofner added Bohemian-flavored polkas and schottisches favored by the German immigrants of central Texas, Happy Fats LeBlanc adapted the sound to his Cajun swing band, and south Texas groups such as the Tune Wranglers and

Revard's Oklahoma Playboys added cowboy tunes and Mexican folksongs. In addition to repertoire, Wills incorporated other elements of the Musical Brownies' sound into his group, as did other string bands in Texas and Oklahoma. These included smooth vocals, two fiddles playing in harmony, jazz piano, amplified instruments, slapping of the string bass, and improvised take-offs. However, it was the influence of Wills's training as a breakdown fiddler that redirected western swing toward country music in the late 1930s.

Even Bob Wills's trademark holler did not predate Milton Brown. Roy Lee Brown recalled that his brother Milton had been hollering long before he met Wills and he continued this practice with the Light Crust Doughboys. Although Milton Brown and Bob Wills both developed hollers, they were noticeably different. Wills's was a folk holler, derived mainly from his experiences in medicine and minstrel shows. Milton Brown's hollers served more as jazzy exclamation marks (similar to those used by Fats Waller), rarely more than a few words in length ("Yowsah, Yowsah!" "Tickle them ivories, boy!" "Papa cal-houn!!") and generally used to punctuate a soloist's take-off without really drawing attention from it. For both Milton Brown and Bob Wills, it is likely that their respective hollers were simply manifestations of enthusiasm rather than being derived from any singular source.

By 1940, many of the early western swing bands that had been emulating the Brownies were no longer active, having disbanded due to the lingering effects of the Depression. Yet Bob Wills continued on, appearing in western films such as *Take Me Back to Oklahoma,* starring Tex Ritter, and *Go West, Young Lady,* with Glenn Ford and Ann Miller. It was only after Wills's relocation to California and subsequent appearances in other westerns opposite Charles Starrett and Russell Hayden that western swing's transformation was complete. Before, the "western" element had been merely geographical. Now, it had become a reflection of the cultural West exhibited by cowboy movies, with appropriate music rounding out the effect. With his profound showmanship, Bob Wills was able to establish himself as western swing's ambassador and introduce Milton Brown's creation to the rest of the country. Wills's ability to exploit the western phenomenon enabled him to survive the war years and emerge with his most popular band ever in the late forties.

Much of Bob Wills's success has been attributed, justifiably, to his engaging personality and ability to entertain. However, a factor that contributed equally to his long-standing fame was his remarkable longevity. Wills was one of the few southwestern bandleaders who escaped the stranglehold of the Depression and continued as a performer into the 1940s. His career as a western swing personality lasted thirty-nine years, until a stroke felled him at his final recording session in December 1973. Wills's ability to stay visible and active during his career established him as the most familiar and the most successful representative of western swing, and, to many, the one most responsible for creating it. In comparison, Milton Brown's brief, three-and-a-half-year career with the Musical Brownies is all the more remarkable when one considers that Brown's innovations permanently influenced the genre.

As Wills became the music's most popular figure, his own innovations and personal style were added to Milton Brown's handiwork. Band sizes increased, with horns and drums successfully introduced. (Milton Brown experimented with these instruments in 1935, but determined that his public preferred the smaller string band sound.) The role of the amplified steel guitar, introduced by Bob Dunn, changed as Leon McAuliffe gained popularity with his reworking of "Guitar Rag," a 1923 guitar solo by black Louisville musician Sylvester Weaver. McAuliffe's masterpiece, entitled "Steel Guitar Rag," was recorded with Wills's Texas Playboys in Chicago in September 1936. This record established the amplified steel guitar as a melodic lead instrument in western swing, whereas Bob Dunn used it mainly to imitate the sounds of a jazz trombone.

Bob Wills's appearances in "B" westerns necessitated a steady supply of newly written cowboy and western-oriented compositions. Songwriter Cindy Walker was responsible for many enduring classics in this mode, including "Dusty Skies," "Cherokee Maiden," and "Miss Molly." Where Milton Brown had kept current by recording cover versions of best-selling popular songs, Bob Wills abandoned these in favor of atmospheric and evocative songs from the silver screen.

Wills himself became an accomplished songwriter. Assisted by vocalist Tommy Duncan, he created a bevy of soon-to-be classics, including "Time Changes Everything," "Stay a Little Longer," and "New San Antonio Rose." The latter was covered in 1941 by pop sensation Bing Crosby and eventually reached million-selling status, propelling Wills to national fame. Wills was fond of saying that Crosby's recording took him "from hamburger to steak." In connection with the change in repertoire, the spit-and-polish, suit-and-tie image established by Milton Brown gave way to cowboy hats and western garb associated with the themes conveyed in western films.

The geographical expansion of western swing in the early forties can be attributed to several factors. One was the breaking down of the regional barriers that surrounded western swing during the Depression. Economic restraints had kept Texas bands from traveling too far from their respective home bases. Transportation was generally limited to buses and automobiles. Air travel was out of the question financially, although the Light Crust Doughboys did have their own aircraft, funded by Burrus Mill. Even trains were too expensive to transport a six or seven piece band from city to city or from state to state. The only time the Musical Brownies ever used train travel was when they went to Chicago in January 1935, for their first recording session for Decca. In that instance, the record company paid for their transport.

Another factor that had kept western swing bands close to home in the early days was the need to play daily radio broadcasts at centralized studios. Radio was barely into its second decade when the Musical Brownies played their first program on Fort Worth's KTAT, and in the 1930s, radio was chiefly a live medium. Contrary to today's practices the three major record companies (RCA Victor, ARC, and Decca) believed that radio airplay detracted from sales of phonograph records. All of the Musical Brownies' releases on Bluebird and Decca included the phrase "not licensed for radio broadcast" imprinted on their labels. Although the policing of radio stations for the purpose of reporting the airing of "canned music" to ASCAP was a cumbersome and inexact science, phonograph records still were secondary to personal appearances in terms of promotional value and were rarely heard on radio stations. The prevalence of electrical transcriptions would not come until late in the decade, an advancement that freed many string bands to tour farther afield.

In addition, the rise of coin-operated jukeboxes enabled dance hall owners to dispense with the more expensive practice of hiring a band to entertain customers on a nightly basis. By the late thirties, jukeboxes had become popular additions to these clubs.

Low phonograph record sales during the Depression was another factor that helped restrict the geographical dissemination of western swing. During his lifetime, Milton Brown never achieved a national hit record, nor did he ever write a hit song. But by the time he died, his sound had already been established, and bands throughout the Southwest were using the Musical Brownies as their model.

World War II itself helped break down the regional barriers that prevented western swing's expansion, as defense plant bound draftees helped spread the music westward. The migration of Dust Bowl weary families to more promising prospects on the West Coast also helped this dissemination process. By this time, the music created by Milton Brown had changed, with Spade Cooley leading orchestras playing the music now known for the first time as western swing.

As the dust of these new and sweeping developments settled, Milton Brown and his Musical Brownies were all but forgotten by the American public. There was no body of original compositions that was being performed by the newer groups spearheaded by the Wills influence. The Brownies' visual presentation had been altered to the extent that the music Milton Brown created was now forever linked to the western image associated with its most successful hit songs. Most importantly, the music now focused upon the personality and magnetism of Bob Wills, much as it had focused on Milton Brown during the Brownies' heyday. Bob Wills and his fiddle were the chief attractions, with his band acting as supporting players.

*   *   *

The question of what western swing actually is and how it can be defined has been contentious in recent years, as more attention has been directed toward the genre and its development. Many scholars and historians have attempted to assign defining factors to the music, which resulted in contradictions and inconsistencies when applied to specific groups from different musical eras. For instance, it is difficult to include both the Musical Brownies and Spade Cooley's orchestras of the late forties and early fifties in the same category, given the stylistic differences between the two groups. The Brownies played mainly jazz, both in instrumental execution and in repertoire choice. Cooley's orchestra played western and cowboy songs from arranged charts, in the manner of swing bands such as those led by Tommy Dorsey or Glenn Miller. Their repertoire consisted mainly of original compositions, whereas the Brownies performed chiefly cover versions of pop and jazz standards. The western element combined with a structural similarity to the reigning swing bands of the forties, resulting in Cooley's self-ascribed sobriquet as the "King of Western Swing."

However, if one looks at western swing as a continuum, it is easier to understand the disparity between Milton Brown's string band jazz of the 1930s and Spade Cooley's carefully orchestrated symphonic swing of the late forties. Today, each group falls into the same musical category, a category that simply did not exist during Milton Brown's lifetime.

Western swing can be divided into four distinctive periods, each headed by a single individual who provided the impetus to influence his successor and draw inspiration from his predecessor. It is interesting to note that in each case, the repertoire and style of western swing reflected the popular taste in music typical of its era. This versatility and ability to adapt to the times is a hallmark of a sturdy, enduring musical genre.

The first era of western swing was led by Milton Brown, whose Musical Brownies provided the model that was copied by aspiring string bands, mainly in Texas and Oklahoma. Milton Brown converted traditional Texas fiddle bands into dance bands designed to entertain in dance halls as opposed to individual homes. He first added vocals, jazz take-offs, and a more pronounced rhythm section, expanding the size to as many as five instruments. Later, he added amplified instruments and piano. By the end of the 1930s, bands grew even larger, and were beginning to experiment with horns and structured arrangements. This development paralleled that of swing, which was also experiencing an increase in sophistication and orchestra size.

The second era was led by Bob Wills, who drew from his experience playing under Brown's influence to add elements of his own to the music and expand it geographically to the West Coast. Wills took the parallel to swing orchestras further, incorporating entire horn sections, consisting of trumpets, trombones, and saxophones. Wills's recording sessions just prior to World War II even deemphasized the role of the fiddle as lead instrument. By 1940, recordings such as "Big Beaver" and "New San Antonio Rose" made western swing virtually indistinguishable from the swing of Benny Goodman and Glenn Miller.

After World War II, the torch was passed to Spade Cooley, the chief attraction of the third era. Cooley's orchestras brought the fiddle back into focus as the central instrument in western swing, going so far as to feature a trio of fiddles playing melodies and structured arrangements. Cooley added instruments such as accordion and harp to the mix, while still relying on steel and electric guitars for take-offs. For the first time, the music was given the label "western swing," as part of a promotional campaign with Cooley as its model. Horn sections disappeared and only the occasional trumpet remained from the glory days of Bob Wills's big swing bands of the early forties.

The fourth and final era cemented western swing's heretofore peripheral association with country music. This was due to the success of Hank Thompson and his Brazos Valley Boys, a band that had a remarkable string of hit recordings for Capitol Records in the 1950s. Thompson's contribution to the development of western swing lay in his combining the postwar sound of Spade Cooley with the phenomenally successful "honky-tonk" sound of the 1950s, triggered by such country vocalists as Hank Williams, Lefty Frizzell, and Faron Young.

The key link in the chain that began in the 1930s with Milton Brown is Bob Wills. Although he did not create western swing, Wills nevertheless was indispensable in perpetuating the genre and adapting to its various stages of development. As the only bandleader who participated in each of the four eras of western swing, he emerged as its most recognized celebrity. Even after western swing's heyday ended with the coming of rock and roll in the late 1950s, Wills continued to change with the times. He attempted, albeit unsuccessfully, to combine western swing with rock and roll in the late fifties ("So Let's Rock") and, even more absurdly, with early sixties dance trends ("Buffalo Twist").

Charles Townsend's landmark biography of Wills, *San Antonio Rose,* one of the very first serious studies of a major country music figure, included much outstanding research. Townsend also drew frequently upon Ruth Sheldon's *Hubbin' It,* a romanticized biography of Wills that was privately published in 1938. This book, while valuable for its colorful stories of Wills's early life (most of which were related to the author by Wills himself), is nevertheless highly questionable as a competent historical source. Based on his reading of the available evidence, Townsend credited Wills with the leadership role in the initial stages of western swing, reduced Milton Brown's role to that of a one-time subordinate, and gave no credit at all to Spade Cooley and Hank Thompson for their respective contributions.

Since Townsend's account appeared, there has been considerable fresh research on western swing. This new scholarship supplements his pioneering efforts and provides a much fuller perspective on the intricate origins and development of the genre. Bob Wills surely deserves his inclusion in the Country Music Hall of Fame, though not as the originator of western swing but as its longest surviving proponent. Many other bandleaders and musicians deserve similar recognition for their contributions. Cecil Brower, for example, should receive equal credit with Wills for his influence as western swing's first and most important fiddler. Until now, Brower has remained a minor figure, noted more for his television appearances with Jimmy Dean and Red Foley in the 1950s and 1960s than for his pioneering recordings with Milton Brown, Bob Wills, Roy Newman, and others.

Bob Dunn's steel guitar revolutionized popular music, not just country music. Marvin Montgomery, who has led the Light Crust Doughboys through more than fifty years of stewardship of the genre, deserves wider acclaim as well.

The true scope of Milton Brown's leadership in founding western swing has also become clear, as interviews with key musicians with seminal bands throughout Texas and Oklahoma attest, and as primary sources such as newspaper articles, photographs, and correspondence confirm. He developed the repertoire and instrumentation and then augmented these factors by constant experimentation. He took musical risks, adapted to the times, and wasn't afraid to try something new. These accomplishments warrant his inclusion in the Country Music Hall of Fame alongside pioneers such as Bill Monroe, Hank Williams, and Jimmie Rodgers. As time passes, fewer and fewer people will have heard of Milton Brown, and his induction into the Hall of Fame will grow less likely.

Yet Milton Brown's legacy lives on in musicians like Johnny Gimble, a fiddler in the mold of Brownies Cecil Brower and Cliff Bruner, and groups such as Asleep at the Wheel. It lives in the modern western swing styles of people like Merle Haggard and George Strait. Strait's number one recording of "Right or Wrong" in 1984 brought knowing smiles to the faces of Fred Calhoun and Ocie Stockard, for they remembered when Milton Brown introduced this pop tune to western audiences in steamy dance halls a half-century before. The heady mixture of black and white music the Brownies brought about anticipated by two decades the similar mixture in Memphis that gave rise to Elvis Presley and rockabilly. Milton Brown's struggle for airtime in the 1930s and all the politics involved, and the story of how a hot new music had to struggle against the entrenched powers, just as rock and roll did, will certainly strike a modern chord.

The country folk who saw Milton Brown and his Musical Brownies perform are disappearing. Even those with sharp memories now find these images beginning to fade as more than fifty years have passed since Milton Brown sang his last song in a Fort Worth hospital room. His remarkable Musical Brownies apparently were never captured on film, never made the *Billboard* best seller lists, and, save for two brief recording ventures to Chicago and New Orleans and occasional dances in southern Oklahoma, never left Texas. But sixty years later, the impact Milton Brown had on country music is still felt—and will be felt as long as people dance in claustrophobic dance halls and honky-tonks or tap their feet to some long-forgotten, wistful melody from a dim past.

Milton Brown
and the Founding of
Western Swing

ONE

Stephenville

(1903–18)

In May 1855 a party of thirty pioneers led by John M. Stephen arrived in what is now Erath County, Texas, and began selecting sites on which they hoped to build their homes. Erath County had been first mapped by a land surveyor named George B. Erath from Waco, Texas.[1] After riding horseback up the Bosque River to an area about four miles northeast of Lingleville, he returned to his neighbors with glowing reports of the tall grass, fertile land, and unsettled country. Ten years later, Stephen, Erath, and a Dr. W. M. McNeill decided to move permanently to the area on the north banks of the Bosque, naming the new community after Stephen, who had acquired a large tract of land where the town is located. Stephenville in 1855 had become the westernmost settlement on the Bosque. Stephen himself arranged to have land donated for the building of a county courthouse and lots for his fellow settlers and several churches in return for naming the town after his family. When George Erath surveyed the county in 1856, the area was officially designated Erath County, with Stephenville as the county seat.[2] The original town of Stephenville consisted of twenty-five one-acre blocks of land surrounding the public square, where the courthouse was finally completed in 1893.

Stephenville grew slowly in its early stages at mid-century, with the surrounding farmlands growing faster. The fertile soil and good weather conditions attracted farmers and stockmen from the East as cotton and cattle became the chief commodities in the area. The city government of Stephenville was officially established in 1889, the same year the first railroad line arrived in town. Before the railroad, supplies had to be hauled from Alexander in wagons drawn by oxen and later by mules. Other supplies came from as far away as Waco and Dallas. The Texas Central Railroad had actually been the first line to be extended to that part of Texas, arriving in Alexander in 1875 and Dublin in 1879. But the Fort Worth and Rio Grande line was the first to come into Stephenville, reaching the town in 1889, by way of Cresson, Granbury, Tolar, and Bluff Dale. This event was celebrated with great fanfare, as were similar happenings in other towns of the Old West. The regular departures and arrivals of the trains became special occasions for residents of Erath County.[3]

Two miles east of town, off what is now Texas Highway 377, lay a community known as Smith Springs. The town, if it could be called that, consisted of a schoolhouse and two churches, one Baptist and one Methodist. There were farms scattered in the region between there and Stephenville. Smith Springs does not exist today, nor do many of the current Stephenville residents recall the town at all, although there is a Smith Springs Road that runs through where the community used to be located.

Sometime in the early 1890s, a family arrived in Stephenville on the Fort Worth and Rio Grande line from northwestern Arkansas. The family was led by a Civil War veteran named James Franklin Brown and included his wife, Belva, and their six children. When he arrived in Stephenville, James Brown was in his mid-forties. He had enlisted in the Confederate army at the age of sixteen, running away from home shortly after Tennessee seceded in June 1861 to join Robert E. Lee's thousands of followers, bent on fighting off the hated Yankees.

After the war, Brown moved to Arkansas, where he married Belva Pope. The couple lived near the railroad stop at Potts Station in Polk County, located in the northwestern sector of the state. The Browns had three girls (Lilly, Etha, and Etta) and three boys (Joe, Malley, and Barty). It was the youngest son, Barty, who later became the father of Milton, Derwood, and Roy Lee Brown, the three brothers who would witness and participate in the birth of Texas swing music some fifty years later.

Barty Lee Brown was born on the farm near Potts Station, Arkansas, on February 6, 1881. His father probably gave him the middle name of Lee in honor of General Robert E. Lee.[4] Barty Brown was also known as "Bart," although on formal occasions he used his initials "B. L." At just five feet two inches tall, Barty was called "Shorty" by both friends and denigrators. But despite his small stature, Barty Brown was not at all somebody who could be bullied, excelling at relay races in Stephenville.

Barty's athletic ability would eventually be passed down to his sons, who used these talents in different ways. Milton excelled in team sports while in school, starring on the football and basketball teams. Younger brother Derwood became a feared pugilist and a crafty street fighter. This talent would become handy in later years when he had to deal with would-be toughs at Crystal Springs and other dance halls during the rough-and-tumble Depression.

By the turn of the century, Stephenville was still a frontier town. Farmers such as James Brown and, later, his son Barty drove wagons and team into town from Smith Springs to buy supplies. Even so, the Wild West was slowly disappearing in Erath County, although there were still reminders of the old ways, specifically frontier justice. Until it was cut down in 1910, a live oak tree stood near the southeast corner of the square in Stephenville. Known as "the hanging tree," it had a large limb extending toward the north and about twenty feet above the ground. In the early days men often dangled from the end of a rope tied to this limb, usually cow and horse thieves who had been tried on the spot and immediately hanged.

With the advent of motor vehicles and paved highways, small towns such as Smith Springs began to disappear. Travel between larger towns became easier and faster as the more affluent Texans began purchasing automobiles in greater numbers after 1910. The mule, horse and buggy, and wagon were soon phased out, as were work horses with the arrival of the tractor. Small towns, which at the turn of the century had typically supplied such necessary services as a post office, general store, blacksmith shop, church, and a gin, soon began to dry up because of advances in modes of transportation. Gradually, big farming took over little farming, and many families moved to larger towns, further depleting small communities such as Smith Springs.

As soon as the Brown family had settled in Smith Springs, they enrolled their children in grade school. One of Barty's brothers, Joe, died in his teens of unknown causes. James Brown worked as a farmer until his death sometime around the turn of the century. While in grade school, Barty Brown met a young girl from Stephenville named Martha Annie Huxford. Known by her middle name, Annie was born on January 11, 1883, in Texas. Her father had come to Texas from his home state of Iowa, where he had met Annie's mother.

ROY LEE BROWN: "My maternal grandparents owned a farm, two and a half miles east of Stephenville, adjacent to Highway 377. They raised a little cotton and corn. They also had several head of cattle, horses, chickens, and pigs. I believe my grandmother had a little vegetable garden. She had a huge dishpan that she washed dishes in, and after she finished washing the dishes and scalding them (hot water came from a kettle of water, boiled, on a kerosene stove), she would take the pan of dishwater outside and throw it to the pigs. They would almost inhale it. When I hear the term 'slopped it up like a pig,' it reminds me of grandmother and her pigs.

"Speaking of my grandparents naturally reminds me of their home out there in the country. Grandmother cooked on a kerosene stove, and for light, they had to use kerosene lamps. The house had a large back porch that was used as a utility room instead of a patio as they would use it today. On the patio they had a separator and a cooler, among other odds and ends—all useful of course. The separator was used to separate the whole milk from the cream. This was a machine similar to an ice-cream freezer. My cousin Lena Faye and I would take turns cranking the handle to get the milk separated. Grandmother would churn the cream and make butter. There would also be something left over that resembled what we call yogurt. Grandmother called it 'clabber.' It was very tasty with cold cornbread as a snack. The cooler was the equivalent of a refrigerator. There were no icemen to bring ice so they had to improvise as best they could, hence the cooler. This was a sort of chest which was open at the top, draped with a piece of wet cheesecloth. The trick was to keep the cloth wet and the breeze blowing over it would cool the chest."

On November 23, 1899, Mr. B. L. Brown, eighteen, and Miss Annie Huxford, sixteen, were married by J. D. Jackson, ordained minister of the gospel in Stephenville. The two quit school and Barty went to work as a sharecropper. Farmers in Stephenville as well as in nearby towns such as Fort Worth, Weatherford, and Lingleville farmed mostly cotton.[5]

Stephenville's first cotton mill, the Cotton Seed Oil Mill, was built out of rock and commenced operation in about 1892. Eventually, the cotton mill was converted to accommodate peanuts, which were easier to process than cotton. The Cotton Compress began operation about 1894 in the northern part of Stephenville. In the early part of the twentieth century, Barty Brown and other sharecroppers from Smith Springs would load up their wagons with the unprocessed cotton, hitch their team to the wagons, and drive through town to the compress, where through sheer force and steam a bale of cotton could be squeezed down to a more accommodating size for shipping. Barty worked long hard hours in the cotton fields to provide for his new bride. Before long, they had their first child. A beautiful little girl with a round china doll's face and apple cheeks, Era Lee Brown was born on June 29, 1901. A little more than two years later, Annie Brown gave Era a baby brother.

Milton Brown (left) as a baby, Stephenville, Texas, early 1904. Standing beside him is his older sister, Era. Courtesy Roy Lee and Ellen Brown.

The Brown family poses solemnly for the photographer's camera, Stephenville, 1914. From left: Milton, age ten; father, Barty; sister, Era; and mother, Annie. Milton's older sister Era would die suddenly four years later at the age of sixteen, an event that triggered the family's move to Fort Worth. Courtesy Roy Lee and Ellen Brown.

Born around midnight on September 7, 1903, the boy was delivered by Dr. L. N. Miller and was named Willie Milton Brown. In his
haste, Dr. Miller entered his own surname into the county record instead of "Milton." By the time the official certificate was filed with
the county clerk of Erath County on September 10, the middle name
had been corrected. Throughout his life, Milton Brown celebrated
his birthday as September 8, claiming that his actual birth occurred
at some unspecified time close to midnight. Milton never gave his
first name as "Willie." He preferred the more dignified William and
signed his checks Wm. Milton Brown. (Willie had been the middle
name of Milton's maternal grandfather, Charles Willie Huxford. Annie Brown also had a brother named Willie Huxford, who lived in
Stephenville and eventually helped move the Brown family to Fort
Worth in 1918.)

Although times were hard in those first years of the twentieth century, Barty and Annie Brown did all they could to send their two children to school. They knew that a good education was the only way
to keep from spending a lifetime in the cotton fields. That life was
already showing its effects on Barty, who now had four mouths to
feed instead of just two. Milton and Era attended Smith Springs
school, which included children in grade school as well as young
men and women of high school age. Both were bright students, developing outgoing personalities at an early age. They were insepara-
ble and were popular with their classmates.

ROY LEE BROWN: "My dad's cousin, who lives in Rendon just outside
of Fort Worth, told me that when Milton was just a small boy, Mom
and Dad came to see her daddy and mother in Rendon. While my
folks were there they went to Burleson. In downtown Burleson they
were walking down the street when my Uncle Lee Pope, my grandmother's brother, told some friends that Milton could sing. Milton
was about seven or eight at the time. So the people there asked Milton to sing for them, which he did. And they started to pitch pennies and nickels at him. I guess this was one of the first times Milton
sang for money [laughs].

"Milton had a love for singing all his life. He and Era started singing together right from the start and they both loved to sing and entertain people. Wherever Milton was, it was said there was always a
song."

ELLEN (MRS. ROY LEE) BROWN: "When Milton was twelve, he was strick-
en with appendicitis. Barty Brown had no transportation and there
was no hospital in Smith Springs or Stephenville at the time so he

had to take Milton to Dallas by train for an appendectomy. Before boarding the train, several of Barty's friends came to the depot to see them off. Charlie Mefford said, 'Boys, I feel real sorry for Barty—in fact, five dollars' worth. How about the rest of you?' Each one then emptied his pockets and gave Barty all they had. Barty never forgot his friends' kindness.

"On the way to Dallas, Milton's appendix ruptured and he became gravely ill. As soon as they reached the hospital, they had to rush him immediately into surgery.

"Milton withstood the operation all right, but several days later, the incision became abcessed and it was necessary to operate on him again and have the infection treated. Although Milton was not yet out of the woods, Barty refused to believe that his first son would not pull through. It was as if he virtually willed Milton to recover. No doubt it helped that Barty was a praying man.

"Barty also refused to leave Milton alone. He merely settled down in the one chair in the room and prepared to wait until Milton was out of danger. A nurse informed him that he would not be permitted to stay, but Barty would have none of that. He had no intentions of leaving whatsoever. The nurse insisted and raised her voice. He raised his louder at her. Finally, the nurse went swishing out and returned with an orderly who pointed at the door and said, 'Out!' Barty replied simply, 'Nope.' This went on for several minutes until the orderly said, 'If you don't get out of here, I'm going to throw you out that window!' Barty said, 'You're probably big enough to do it, but I'll guarantee you one thing: you'll go out with me!' Barty expected the orderly to call the police, but instead, the orderly left. He evidently saw that Barty was determined to stay and that's precisely what he did.

"The next day Barty decided to go outside for a stroll. Milton was out of danger by now and Barty had become restless and missed Annie and Era. So he walked to a five-and-dime store to buy some little trinket for Milton. At that time, America was going through 'Chaplin mania.' Charlie Chaplin was a household name and children as well as adults loved the Little Tramp. At the five-and-dime, Barty bought a small glass replica of Chaplin wearing his black derby, baggy pants, and cane, leaning against a barrel of tiny candies. Milton was delighted when Barty gave it to him and it became one of his favorite keepsakes. To this day, although it has a chip in it, it still is considered a treasure in our household."[6]

The entertainment center of Stephenville was known as the

Stephenville Jokey Yard. It was originally started around 1860 and continued as a hub of activity until about 1930. The Yard covered all of Block No. 15 in the original town of Stephenville, and each first Monday of the month was Trade Day. Most of the trading involved horses, mules, and livestock, but anything and everything was traded at the Jokey Yard on Trade Day. In addition, the Jokey Yard was where traveling medicine shows set up shop on their way through Texas. Carnival barkers sold bottles of tonic guaranteed to cure anything. Usually, however, by the time the user discovered that the elixir did little more than get him drunk, the sellers were long gone and the guarantees were discovered to be worthless. Appearing at various times at the Jokey Yard was Harley and Billie Sadler's tent show. Sadler, a renowned showman in the early twentieth century, was a consummate entertainer who incorporated more than the hawking of tonics into his programs. The melodramas, romances, plays, and musical numbers he performed invariably utilized his engaging personality and glib tongue.

Another magnetic personality, the famous Buffalo Bill Cody, also played the Stephenville Jokey Yard, setting up his rodeo and Wild West Show for the farmers. The famous "Booger Red," whose real name was Samuel T. Privett, a well-known rider of outlaw horses, made appearances in Stephenville as well. For a thirty-year period beginning in 1890, Privett was considered the best bronc rider in America.

Young Milton Brown may have picked up elements of his stage presence from shows such as these, because in later years he utilized the tent-show patter in his performances with the Musical Brownies. The best example of this affinity for the patter of the carnival barker is on the Brownies' recording of "Wheezie Anna" (Decca 5342-B), which tells of the girl whose feet are "big as ships," measures "nineteen-seven 'round the hips," and who has "sixteen double chins which flap around each time she grins." Milton's patter on this recording, delivered with the familiar bravado and singsong aplomb of an accomplished tent showman, exhibits his familiarity with this now extinct period in American vaudeville. "ALLLL-RIGHT, folks, come on over, come down just a little bit closer please! We're going to introduce to you the big fat lady, the fattest lady in all the land, known as Wheezie Anna! She's so fat, the menagerie uses her skirt for a tent, ladies and gentlemen! Come on down just a little closer! Get your tickets on the right and have them ready! One more show on the platform and we're going to turn you into the tent, ladies and gentlemen!"

We do not know definitively whether Milton actually attended the vaudeville shows and carnivals that passed through Stephenville, but considering other ways of absorbing what was to become an urban-influenced musical education, this would seem to be a possible early source of inspiration. In pre-radio Texas, the chief means for disseminating songs was through oral tradition in the home or church, the increasingly ubiquitous phonograph, and from broadsides. The more affluent Texas families were able to afford a piano, the standard household instrument until the guitar became popular in the 1930s. Street singers also provided some influx of repertoire outside the immediate area, but there is no evidence that Milton Brown ever knew any of these people either in Stephenville or later when the Browns moved to Fort Worth.

The early vocal repertoire of Milton Brown when he was growing up in Smith Springs probably consisted of sacred tunes learned in church and sentimental ballads such as "Barbara Allen" learned from his parents. Although his father played the fiddle, Milton never showed an interest in any form of musical expression other than singing.

On September 29, 1915, Annie Brown gave birth to a second son. This one was named Melvin Derwood. The spelling of Derwood's name has generally been D*u*rwood. However, people who knew Derwood as a member of the Brown family usually pronounced his name "Dairwood." On the Musical Brownies' recording of "Down by the O-H-I-O" (Decca 5111-B), Milton can be heard saying "Pick it out, Dairwood," in introducing a guitar break by his brother. After Milton's death, when Derwood became the financial manager for the Brownies, their checks bear the signature "Derwood Brown," as does correspondence from Derwood's later years. It is apparent that Derwood preferred his name spelled with the unconventional *e* although "D*u*rwood" was used more often.[7]

Like his older brother, Derwood was called by his middle name. There has been no evidence that anybody called him "Melvin," just as there has been no indication that Milton was ever called "William" or "Willie."

Derwood was as different from Milton as two brothers could get. Although they were similar physically (with Derwood tending to be heavier), it was the difference in their personalities that stood out. Both were outgoing and made many friends, but Derwood was the more aggressive of the two.

ROY LEE BROWN: "Milton was impossible to get mad. He was so even-tempered that even if he did get mad, you'd never know it. He just got along with everybody. Some people were jealous of him but he'd tell them off in a way that they just couldn't hold it against him. Derwood was just the opposite. He'd tell you off right out and if you didn't like it, he'd fight you."

The job of watching over little Derwood fell to Era. At fourteen, the eldest Brown child was developing into a pretty young woman, and baby Derwood adored his older sister. In May 1918, Era suddenly became ill. Within a week she died. The cause of Era's death is a mystery, although Annie Brown told Roy Lee that it might have been spinal meningitis or encephalitis, diseases that claimed many lives in rural Texas in the early part of the twentieth century.

According to the Erath County Death Record, Vera [*sic*] Brown died of unknown causes on May 14, 1918, aged 16 years, 10 months, 15 days. She was buried the next day at Smith Springs Cemetery. A local newspaper printed a brief notice acknowledging the death of "a daughter of Bart Brown" and stating that the girl "had suffered about a week from an illness which physicians were unable to diagnose." It also noted that the girl was a pupil at Smith Springs school and was "an unusually bright student."

Era's death hit the Brown family hard. They had expected wondrous things from their two oldest children and now their first-born was gone. The close-knit Brown family felt they had to find a way to deal with their grief.

ROY LEE BROWN: "Era was going with a fella named Alf Wooley at that time and they were slated to get married. My mother told me that Era and Milton both loved to sing right from the very start. Era sang with Milton at schoolhouses and churches all the time. She told me how full of life Era was and how she and Milton were a whole lot alike. They both went to school at Smith Springs. She was just sixteen years old when she died and it just about killed my parents and Milton. She and Milton were real close. I don't know much about the cause of her death other than the fact that my mother said they had to hold her down on the bed when she died. She was scratched by a cat about a week or so before she died so some people thought it might have been rabies but I don't know for sure. My mother said that when my sister died, Derwood would toddle over to Era's door and cry. Derwood was too small to remember any of this, but my mother said that Era took care of Derwood a lot."

ELLEN BROWN: "Barty was devastated. Era Lee was 'Papa's girl' and had been the apple of his eye. Mrs. Brown, although heartbroken herself, was the strong one during this crisis. It was she who picked up the pieces and put them together again. Fifteen-year-old Milton, who had been so close to his sister, was a tremendous help, his mother told me. She said that he was sweet and caring and did all he could to help ease the pain all the family felt."

ROY LEE BROWN: "My parents buried Era at Smith Springs Cemetery, about half a mile from my grandparents' home place. Today, we rarely ever go to Stephenville without stopping at the cemetery, which is located on the eastern outskirts of Stephenville. Most of the time we took hoes and rakes and maybe a saw, to clean off the cemetery lot.

"My folks talked often about missing Era after she died and that's the main reason why they left Smith Springs. They were grief stricken about her death and also, farming wasn't good. They figured a change in scenery would help them forget. Fort Worth was the largest, closest town and my dad thought he could get work there. So my dad and my mother's brother Will Huxford went to Fort Worth, got jobs, and then came back to Stephenville to bring the rest of the family to Fort Worth. It was maybe a few months after Era's death that they moved."

Milton never talked about his sister. All the information about Era came secondhand from Annie Brown through Roy Lee and Ellen Brown. Annie told Roy Lee that Milton grieved over Era's death for a long while, never really getting over it. In Fort Worth, Milton's best friend was Roy McBride, whose sister Maebelle became Milton's surrogate sister. Maebelle was dating her future husband Harry Fowler at the time and Harry remembered Milton's devotion to her.

HARRY FOWLER: "He always looked after Maebelle. He called her 'Sis.' One night we went out to Crystal Springs like we usually did on Saturday nights to dance to the Brownies. And for some reason, I guess I may have been outside talking to some people I knew or whatever, Maebelle went in first—without me. Well, Milton was standing at the door and he stopped her and said, 'Maebelle, who are you with?' So she kidded around with him and said, 'Why, Milton, I'm by myself tonight.' And he turned her around and said, 'Well, Sis, you get back on that bus and go on home!' Then I came in and we all had a good laugh about that. Milton took it well; he never let anything get to him. He was really a swell guy."

By this time, Barty Brown had switched from cotton to peanut farming. An attack of boll weevils in Stephenville had destroyed much of the cotton crop, despite the use of poison to combat the pests.[8] As a result, many farmers switched to peanuts, while others raised livestock. Milton's uncle Will Huxford and Barty Brown hitched up their wagon and drove the sixty hard miles to Fort Worth. Having had experience as peanut farmers, they had no trouble getting positions with the Bain Peanut Company.

And so it came to pass that in the summer of 1918, Barty and Annie Brown, their children (Milton, fourteen, and Derwood, two), and the Huxfords arrived in Fort Worth, Texas, to start a new life.

TWO

The Harmony Boy

(1918–25)

The Browns and the Huxfords encountered a rapidly changing Fort Worth when they arrived there in the summer of 1918. World War I would end soon and the city would play an important role in its denouement. Fort Worth had been selected as an ideal site for the training of military personnel in 1917, when Major General Charles G. Norton, heading a local committee, recommended that the community of Arlington Heights be converted to a military training ground. A total of 4,285 acres were utilized for this purpose, with 1,410 going toward the base itself. Fort Worth was an ideal location because of its readily available crop supply and railroad transportation. After the United States' entry into World War I on April 6, 1917, the army had established a supply base in Fort Worth's Tarrant County for units serving in Mexico. The training camp, named after Alamo hero Colonel James Bowie, became one of four such army posts in Texas. By the end of the war, Camp Bowie had trained 100,000 men.[1] Adjacent to the camp, the military constructed a two-lane brick road, which was named Camp Bowie Boulevard. The Camp Bowie/Arlington Heights area, on the west end of town, was also the home of the Bain Peanut Company, Barty Brown's new employer.

The influx of army personnel was only one reason Fort Worth became one of Texas's big boom towns in the years following World War I. By 1918, Fort Worth had become the "Wild Cat Center" of the oil industry. "Wildcatting" was the term applied to the myriad independent prospectors of oil in the Southwest, many of whom established the forerunners of today's major oil companies. The Gulf Oil Company refinery was built in Tarrant County in 1911, followed by the Magnolia Petroleum Company (now Mobil) refinery in 1915. Texas oil became a critical wartime resource, with millions of barrels contributing to the war effort. With the help of the centrally located railroad facili-

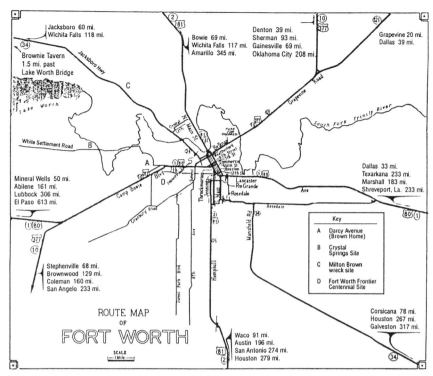

Fort Worth, Texas, in 1937. This map shows key landmarks in Milton Brown's life, as well as major highway routes traveled by Fort Worth musical groups.

ties, gushers in nearby Ranger (1917), Burkburnett (1918), and Des-demona (1918) attracted refinery and pipeline companies such as Tex-as Producing and Refining, Montrose Oil and Refinery, Star Refining, Baltic Refining, Home Oil and Refining, Sinclair Refining, Texaco, Humble Oil and Refining, and Cosden Petroleum. The wildcatters also attracted investors in the oil stock exchange, with an open-air stock emporium being established in downtown Fort Worth at Seventh and Taylor streets. Today the site is the home of the *Fort Worth Star-Tele-gram,* one of the leading Texas newspapers.[2]

The Lake Worth area, located to the northwest of downtown, be-came one of Tarrant County's most attractive recreational facilities. The lake itself was created by the impounding of the waters of the west fork of the Trinity River in 1914, at a cost of one million dol-lars. Of the 5,302 acres consumed by the development, 2,779 acres were used for a park, in which were built a casino with a dancing pavilion, a bathing beach, and sites for carnival attractions. In 1917, the city built a forty-mile road meandering around the lake. Lakeside cottages became romantic attractions for vacationers in the 1920s.[3]

Of the three Fort Worth radio stations established before the Depression, two were opened in 1922. WBAP, owned and operated by the *Star-Telegram,* was the first, signing on from the Blackstone Hotel in May. Later that year, KTAT began broadcasting from the Trinity Life building downtown.[4] WBAP became the first radio station to feature a "barn dance" program, when on January 4, 1923, an hour-and-a-half-long program of square dance music was directed by an old-time fiddler and Confederate veteran named Captain M. J. Bonner, who later would become acquainted with Derwood Brown. The enthusiastic response to this and to other similarly hillbilly-oriented broadcasts predicted the success of barn dances begun elsewhere in succeeding years (WLS's National Barn Dance in Chicago in 1924 and WSM's Grand Ole Opry in Nashville in 1925 being the two notable examples).[5] The third radio station, KFJZ, began broadcasting in 1927 from Meacham's Department Store on Main Street. KFJZ took over KTAT's facilities when the latter station moved to the Texas Hotel around 1933.

The 1920 census placed the population of Fort Worth at 106,482. Many of these people were newcomers, like Barty Brown, Will Huxford, and their families, attracted by the booming oil industry and the prospect of improved living conditions in this increasingly urban metropolis. The sleepy community of Smith Springs had never consisted of more than three hundred residents, most of them farmers. Like many other farm families, the Browns did not own their own piece of land. The future for such families was understandably bleak, and many sought to escape the drudgery of farm work by moving to the bigger towns and cities. If erstwhile peanut farmer Barty Brown yearned to forget the agonizing distress of losing his cherished daughter, the bustling, expanding Fort Worth area was the remedy. In Fort Worth, the third Brown son was born.

ROY LEE BROWN: "My family settled near the west side of Fort Worth near the Bain Peanut Company where my dad and uncle went to work. Bain was located behind an old Chevrolet building and my dad walked to work from where we lived. My dad worked for Bain Peanut for twenty-five years, beginning in 1918. He did a little bit of everything there over the years. The farmers would bring the peanuts in from the fields and sell them to Bain Peanut Company with the shells still on them. Bain had machinery to shell the peanuts. Sometimes my dad worked the machinery. After the peanuts were shelled, they would ship them out to different companies for roasting. They didn't do any roasting at Bain Peanut. Dad never did any of the picking because only women did that. He would run the machinery. Sometimes my dad would test the peanuts that the farmers brought in to see what grade they were. The better the grade the more money they would bring in. Peanuts were graded by inserting a twelve-inch long tapered hollow chute which was pointed on one end into sacks of peanuts loaded on a truck. When the chute was full, you would then shell the peanuts to see how they would grade out. Later on, when my dad's health got bad, he became a watchman. Even when he was working he would watch on Sunday, when he was the day watchman. He worked seven days a week because that's how bad off we were. And for all that work, he made about fifteen dollars a week.

"Dad rented a house down in the 2700 block of Oakland Street, just west of a Montgomery Ward store. I was born in that house on February 27, 1921. In 1922 they had a big flood and Bain Peanut and Montgomery Ward were flooded when the levees on the Trinity River broke. A man that worked at the water works came down and helped evacuate us before the water came. We spent the night at his house. After that, we moved to the 3400 block of West Seventh Street.

"Milton was enrolled in West Side High School, which was located on the corner of West Lancaster and what is now University Drive. Later it was renamed West Van Zandt and became a grade school. When that happened, Milton transferred to Arlington Heights High."

The earliest record of Milton Brown at Arlington Heights High School dates from 1923. Even though Fort Worth was a quickly growing city with many job opportunities in various industries, the 1920s were still a time of struggle for the Brown family. As a teenager, Milton helped pay the bills by quitting school for months at a time, working with his father at Bain Peanut beginning in 1923.

ROY LEE BROWN: "It took him a while to graduate because he had to help provide for the household. As a result, he didn't graduate until he was twenty-one years old. You see, usually, when the crops came in, country people had to take their kids out of school to harvest the crops. School was never really essential to anyone back then, but my parents insisted that he stay in school. They always said that having a diploma was needed to get a good job. Graduating from high school back then was like graduating from college today. Very few people in our area went to college."

Milton Brown continued his singing when the family arrived in Fort Worth in 1918. Barty Brown played breakdown fiddle for house dances, and on occasion Milton would tag along and sing popular songs of the day. A friend of the family remembered some of these house dances.

JOSEY LACY: "I met the Brown family back in 1918 when they came to Fort Worth. I was living over on Oakland Street and we used to go to home dances at their house, my house, and my sisters' homes. All of our friends loved to square dance and round dance. Milton was the singer and he sang lots of beautiful songs. I only associated with him closely at dances, but we knew and loved him. My husband just idolized Milton."

Despite being introduced to an environment totally alien to what he had been used to in Stephenville, Milton Brown made friends easily and quickly. His best friend all during the 1920s was Roy McBride. Born in Rotan, Texas, on August 4, 1906, McBride and his younger sister, Maebelle, lived near the Brown family residence on West Seventh Street.

ROY LEE BROWN: "I was named after Roy McBride, who was Milton's best friend. My mother was going to name me Lee Roy, but Mrs. McBride insisted my mother put the Roy first [laughs]."

MAEBELLE MCBRIDE FOWLER: "We moved to Fort Worth in 1913 when I was three years old. My dad worked in a grocery store that was right across from the Montgomery Ward building on West Seventh. We were living in that area when Roy Lee was born in 1921. We lived in one block and they lived in the next. In those days we didn't have paved streets. Just dirt roads. In the evening, the whole neighborhood would get out and play in the streets. That's when Milton and Roy first got acquainted out there. They'd play ball and hide and seek, and eventually they started singing together. Ohhh, did those two love to sing! And they'd just sit on the front porch of our house and sing to whoever walked by. We had an old Victrola, just about the only one in the whole neighborhood. And all the kids would congregate around our house and listen to Milton and Roy sing along with the Victrola. I remember one time when Milton must have been

The Browns were living in Fort Worth when this picture was taken in 1923 while they were visiting Stephenville. Top: Annie, Milton, Barty. Bottom: Derwood and Roy Lee. Milton, at nineteen, was starting his first semester at Fort Worth's Arlington Heights High School. *Courtesy Roy Lee and Ellen Brown.*

Barty Lee Brown (right), father of Milton, Derwood, and Roy Lee, was an accomplished breakdown fiddler who often entertained at house dances in Stephenville and later in Fort Worth. Seated is family friend Silas Anderson. The photo was taken in the early 1950s. Courtesy Roy Lee and Ellen Brown.

about fourteen or fifteen. My mom always kept my hair in curls. And I just wanted to get a haircut so I talked her into letting me get one. So when I came home, Roy and Milton were there like always. And Roy took one look at me and said 'If you're not the awfulest looking thing I ever saw!' And of course I just boo-hooed all over the place. Well, Milton came over and patted me on the head and said, 'That's all right, Maebelle. We'll just let Roy think you're ugly. I don't. I'll keep you for my sister.' I had known that he had lost a sister but he never really talked about her that I can remember. But to him, I was always 'Sis.'"

When he was attending school, Milton Brown was a class leader. Burning with ambition, he joined and excelled in just about every activity the school had to offer. For three successive years beginning in 1923 Milton was a member and officer (secretary-treasurer) of the Hi-Y Club. He was also a member of the Knight Hawks and president of the Curtain Club, Arlington Heights' dramatic club, whose purpose was "to develop the dramatic talent of its members and to provide entertainment." It consisted of eighteen charter members with no new members being admitted until one or more dropped out.

Milton also excelled at high school athletics, becoming a starter on the school basketball team and a star end on the football squad. The 1924 school yearbook, the *Yellow Jacket,* had this to say about "Brownie": "Milt was always on the jump; he could always break through and get his man. Brownie was very quick at diagnosing a play and at acting accordingly. This youngster received a pass and ran forty yards for a touchdown against Laneri."

Milton starred again in his senior year, when Arlington Heights went 5-1 to become the Class B city champions. The 1925 *Yellow Jacket* anticipated his graduation with regret.

As if he did not have enough to do, Milton was also pep squad leader. The 1925 class yearbook shows a spirited Milton Brown in mid-yell, both fists clenched, cheering his team to victory. Alongside him is his pep squad partner and girlfriend Augusta Pearl Barton. Considering the future of its young cheerleader, Arlington Heights' football cheer possessed a double meaning:

> You haven't got the pep,
> You haven't got the jazz,
> You haven't got the team
> That our school has!
>
> Your pep! Your pep! You've got it, now keep it!
> Dog-gone it, don't lose it! Your pep! Your pep!

Milton Brown's popularity in high school was also shown by the inscription beneath his name in his senior yearbook. Next to a photograph of a studious-looking tuxedo-clad Brown, with hair slicked back from his handsome face, was the inscription: "We call him the 'Harmony Boy' with never a discord in all the days we have known him."

ROY LEE BROWN: "Milton was always harmonizing with other people in his school, but even so, I think that nickname 'the Harmony Boy' had another meaning because he was so easy to get along with in addition to having a good voice. Mom and Dad were really proud of his abilities in school and in sports. It was a big status symbol even then. Milton became vice president of his class. He had to drop out from time to time because he took school seriously and when he was in school it was a full-time job for him."

A classmate, red-haired Elizabeth Mauldin, remembered Milton Brown as a high school idol.

ELIZABETH MAULDIN FRENCH: "I graduated with Milton in 1925. I actually had known him since the eighth grade when he first came to Fort Worth. In that last year he was the most popular boy in school. He was congenial and warm and everybody was crazy about him. It was his personality that made him so popular with boys and girls alike. It wasn't just the popular, good-looking girls, but ALL the girls. He paid attention to everybody equally. I remember he was always on a program singing. His musical ability just came naturally I guess. I sang with him in the chorus. He had a beautiful tenor voice back then.

"And he belonged to a lot of the school organizations. He belonged to the debating club and the Curtain Club. Now the Curtain Club was really the school's most important organization. The people that were in it were usually the more affluent students. Milton was invited to join because he was so good at drama and acting. He was always very aware of his social status because his family was so poor. Maybe this made him try harder. There were maybe two or three levels in Arlington Heights' graduating class. If you had money, well, you were in that top class. Milton didn't, but he was immaculate and clean and all the teachers just loved him. He was a gentleman, not a smart aleck like some other boys in school. And I remember him being real good at English and history. I never knew anybody that didn't like Milton Brown."

Milton's girlfriend during the 1924 school year was Margaret Templeton. It is not known what eventually caused the relationship to end but the class yearbooks furnish evidence that Milton and Margaret were "the class couple." The 1924 yearbook aimed some good-natured ribbing at certain members of the class:

Can You Imagine: Wilmore Tipton—saying something.
Ratliff Grey—not saying "I did so-and-so."
Bozeman Gilder—with his hair combed.
Stanley Carter—not imitating the "Humming Bird."
Margaret Templeton—without Milton Brown.
Milton Brown—without Margaret Templeton.

The "School Prophecies" segment projected the whereabouts of alumni ten years afterward, in 1934: "A couple of weeks later we went to Los Angeles. Here we met Mrs. Milton Brown, who will be remembered perhaps as Miss Margaret Templeton. She told us that her husband had become a millionaire through his marvelous invention of 'The Noiseless Automobile Horn,' and that they and their twin children, Willie and Tillie, were living in a luxurious mansion on Terrace Drive, across the street from the Marmaduke Van der Block's."

In 1924, Milton collaborated with one Valeria Gordon on a song entitled "The Heartsick Blues." Milton, who penned the words to the song, gave it to Margaret before they broke up sometime that year. A broadside of the song offers no evidence as to whether or not it was ever published or copyrighted. Although she later married a man named Bobby Noyd, Margaret kept the piece of sheet music until 1976, when she presented it to Roy Lee Brown's wife Ellen. Milton's lyrics were typical of the sentimental songs popular during the 1920s, and show a stylistic similarity to the classic city blues of Bessie Smith.

The Heartsick Blues

I know a gal she lives in Tennessee,
And she was a heart breaking fool;
She went down to Memphis looking for her man,
She said he had disobeyed her rule;

She thought she had him strong,
So she just fooled along;
Then he went away one day,
And when she came home, she found her papa gone
You can hear her say:

> Oh I'm so lonely, yes, I'm so lonely,
> I don't know what to do.
> I feel so worried, I feel so worried,
> Honey it's all over you.
>
> Just since you left me, just since you left me,
> I realize I got my dues,
> But if you don't come home, I'm gonna lose my mind,
> If I don't lose those heart-sick blues.
>
> She didn't think she loved him, 'til he went away
> Then she saw where she was wrong.
> She didn't get to see him, just to ask him to stay,
> So fooled around too long,
>
> Now she just cried and moans, and wishes him back home
> She is weeping all the time,
> She writes him every day, and at the end of every line,
> This is what she says:
>
> (repeat chorus)

Milton Brown's occasional attempts at songwriting indicate an early interest in pursuing music as a serious career potential. However, his subsequent actions show that what Milton wanted most from his life was to lead a band. Songwriting continued to play a part in this ambition, but Milton's intention had never been to become a writer.

About the time Milton broke up with Margaret Templeton, he began seeing another classmate, Augusta Pearl Barton. Roy McBride was dating his future wife Glenna during Milton's final semesters at Arlington Heights.

GLENNA MCBRIDE: "Pearl was a real sweet girl. And smart, too. She came from a real good family, the Bartons. Her daddy was in real estate. She was also a brilliant girl; what we called a 'high class' girl. Now I don't mean she was stuck up or anything, but she had been raised with plenty. She wasn't rich but she wasn't as poor as we were. They lived out in Arlington Heights on Clover Lane and Milton went with her a long long time. In fact, Milton and Pearl went to our wedding, mine and Roy's."

ROY LEE BROWN: "Milton used to bring Pearl Barton by the house when I was a little kid and I thought she was just about the prettiest thing I ever saw. I thought they were going to get married but they never did. She was very popular too—all everything in school. But Milton wasn't ready to settle down. He had his eye on a career and was afraid the marriage might have interfered in this. I think he already knew he wanted to sing for a living and make music his career. He knew that marriage and musicians don't mix well. Being on the road takes time away from married couples and there are always other women around, what we called 'celebrity chasers.' So anyway, Pearl eventually married Larry Cox, who played minor league baseball with the Fort Worth Cats. They left Fort Worth and the last I heard of them, they were living in Austin."

When Milton graduated from high school in 1925, he continued living with his parents and two brothers in the house on West Seventh Street.

ROY LEE BROWN: "We moved around a lot. I remember my mother said that we lived in every one of those duplexes at one time or another except one of them. We lived in the 3300 block of Camp Bowie Boulevard in the first year I went to kindergarten. That Christmas, Derwood got a mandolin and I got a cowboy suit. Derwood didn't like the mandolin so Milton got him a ukulele. Later on I got a ukulele and Derwood got a guitar and he went off from there. In the beginning Derwood taught himself, although he got a few things from other musicians."

The 1920s was a boom period for America, and Fort Worth was experiencing increasing prosperity and opportunity. The boundaries of Fort Worth itself were expanding, too. Between 1909 and 1928 the city grew from 16.83 to 61.57 square miles. The communities of Arlington Heights, Niles City, Riverside, and Polytechnic were added in 1922. A third radio station, KFJZ, started broadcasting in 1927 in Meacham's Department Store. The Eighteenth Amendment to the Constitution, which prohibited the manufacture, sale, and transportation of intoxicating liquors went into effect in 1920, beginning the era now known as Prohibition.

Milton Brown was now out of high school. At the age of twenty-two, he was ready to tackle the world head-on. He did not yet know what direction his talents would take him, but he knew that he wanted to make his living in music.

THREE

Peanuts, Cigars, and Aladdin Lamps
(1925–30)

After Milton Brown graduated from high school in 1925, he divided his time between singing and working for Bain Peanut with his father. The Fort Worth city directory had listed Milton as a "laborer" for Bain since 1923. In his spare time, Milton, together with best friend Roy McBride, sang for established organizations and businesses, although rarely were they paid for their efforts. Around 1927, Milton left Bain Peanut and worked for Harkrider and Keith Produce Company delivering produce in the company delivery truck.[1] Roy McBride found work with the Rock Island Railroad as a machinist. He had married the former Glenna Davis in 1926 and needed a full-time job to support his new bride.

Sometime late in 1925 or early in 1926, Milton wrote his second composition. Entitled "Old Man Snow," the song was based on a bizarre multiple murder that had just occurred in Stephenville, resulting in sensational press coverage in papers throughout Erath and Tarrant counties. On November 27, 1925, an itinerant woodchopper named F. M. Snow methodically butchered his wife, mother-in-law, and stepson in cold blood. He then tried, rather carelessly, to hide the evidence, which was soon uncovered by the local authorities. What made this murder case of unusual interest was the fact that, in a rather ghoulish procedure, the head of the decapitated stepson was placed on public view so that members of the local community might seek to identify it. Snow was eventually convicted of the atrocious deeds and electrocuted early in 1926.[2]

Milton Brown found the tale of F. M. Snow intriguing and wrote a song about it in a style that resembled that of other event songs written by the Reverend Andrew Jenkins and noted "citybilly" songwriters Frank Luther, Carson Robison, and Bob Miller:

Old Man Snow

It was down in Erath County
Where the farmers are true and good.
There happened there a tragedy
They never thought it would.

A farmer was coming from hunting,
'Twas nearly time for bed,
And in a darkened cellar,
He found a young man's head.

He took it into Stephenville,
A town we all know well,
To see if it was this town
Where the beheaded boy had dwelled.

They advertised in papers
In nearly every state
To see if they could find someone
Who knew the young man's fate.

One farmer said "I think so,
In fact I nearly know,
It is the stepson of the man
We all here know as Snow."

Well, the policemen went out to see him
One cold December day.
They wanted to find that man called Snow
Just to see what he would say.

They walked right in the front door
To make themselves at home,
And in the open fireplace
They found some human bones.

When at last they caught him,
Well, he confessed it all:
"I killed my wife and stepson,
Also my mother-in-law.

"I don't know why I did it,
But the killings have been done."
And now the public's waiting
To see if he'll be hung.[3]

In 1927 Milton and Roy McBride added a third voice to their vocal group, calling themselves the Rock Island Rockets. Ellis Fagan, who worked with McBride at the Rock Island Railroad roundhouse, sang baritone to Milton's first tenor and Roy's second tenor. By this time, Milton had left Harkrider and Keith and got a job as a salesman for the Henry Lowe Cigar Company, a business that distributed Dutch Master, Lovera, Henry George, and Samuel I. Davis cigars, in addition to assorted candies. Milton's job with Lowe entailed traveling throughout the greater Fort Worth area delivering consignments of cigars to local merchants and general stores. In addition to making deliveries, he approached prospective clients and added them to his regular route. Although he was a salaried employee, Milton received a commission on each sale that he made, which enabled him to save some money after contributing to the household.

ROY LEE BROWN: "When he was with Lowe Cigar Company, Milton tried to sell Lovera cigars to one place, I forget where it was. The guy that ran this place told Milton they didn't need any Loveras. Well, Milton figured that they didn't carry Loveras so he decided to create a demand for them. So he gave Fagan a dollar and had him go into that store and ask for a dollar's worth of Lovera cigars. A few minutes later, Fagan came out of the store with a dollar's worth of Lovera cigars! What Milton didn't know was that the guy had gotten them from some other salesman [laughs]. But, with this job, Milton figured out ways to get what he wanted; he was always figuring angles. I guess you could call Milton a flatterer. You needed that to be a good salesman and Milton did well with Lowe."

With a steady job under his belt, Milton began accumulating a wardrobe of suits, usually purchased at Hy Myer's clothiers in Fort Worth, with whom he always kept an open account.[4] He realized that a big part of being a successful salesman was appearance, and from that point on, Milton Brown never appeared in public without being neatly attired. The trio of Milton, Roy McBride, and Ellis Fagan usually dressed in tuxedos when performing under a variety of names at functions sponsored by such organizations as the Elks or Lions clubs.

ROY LEE BROWN: "This trio that Milton was in had no regular name. They went by whatever name fit their purpose. My first remembrance of Milton singing on the radio was when he, Roy McBride, Fagan, and a fellow named Driscoll sang on WBAP radio for the police force in the public relations department. When they did that, they called themselves the Police Quartet. Driscoll worked for Texas Electric. When they worked for the police department, they would

Milton Brown, about the time of his graduation from high school, Fort Worth, 1925. Courtesy Roy Lee and Ellen Brown.

The three Brown brothers, standing in front of their Darcy Avenue home in Fort Worth, late 1920s. From left: Milton, Roy Lee, Derwood. Courtesy Roy Lee and Ellen Brown.

Milton Brown (left) poses with best friend Roy McBride and Roy's new bride, Glenna, in 1927. Courtesy Roy Lee and Ellen Brown.

The earliest known photograph featuring Derwood Brown (right) playing guitar. Derwood is about twelve or thirteen in this picture, which was taken in the late 1920s. Boyhood friend Tommy Echols is playing the Hawaiian guitar. Echols would become a member of Derwood's Musical Brownies in the 1940s. Courtesy Roy Lee and Ellen Brown.

Milton Brown's first professional photograph was as lead singer for a vocal trio that performed at various functions in Fort Worth. Billed here as the Three Yodeliers, the trio changed its name to suit its purposes. From left: Milton, Roy McBride, Ellis Fagan. The photograph was taken during the summer of 1927. Courtesy Harry and Maebelle Fowler.

The original Light Crust Doughboys, KFJZ radio, Fort Worth, late 1930 or early 1931. The group was sponsored by Light Crust flour, milled by the Burrus Mill and Elevator Company. From left: Bob Wills (fiddle), Truett Kimzey (announcer), Milton Brown (vocals), Herman Arnspiger (guitar). Courtesy Roy Lee and Ellen Brown.

get policemen's badges so they could get into picture shows or get a discount on certain merchandise. I don't know for sure if they got much in the way of gratuities for this. It was just something they loved to do. They would sing anywhere for any price: churches, schoolhouses, wherever they could make a dollar. I remember when Milton first went on the air, there were only one or two radios on our block. But the people who lived next door to us had a radio and we would go over there and listen to the Police Quartet.

"I remember when they performed at schools, churches, etc., they sang a song called 'Two Little Girls in Blue.' As they sang the song there were two little boys in suits that stood on the right side of the stage up front. On the left side of the stage were two little girls dressed in blue that stood to the front of the stage. The singers were back a ways from the front of the stage. I would be one of the boys and I must have been six or seven then. We wouldn't do anything except look at the audience. Wendell Bryant was one of those boys who stood next to me several times and he is a lifelong friend of mine. Most people thought we were brothers. Wendell reminded me that an old man with white hair sat in the middle of the stage in a rocking chair, rocking while they sang the song."

GLENNA MCBRIDE: "Those boys used to practice all the time and Lord, they used to keep me up half the night with their singing! They'd all get polluted and Roy wouldn't get home 'til no telling when. I'd be waiting at the door for him. Oh, lordy mercy, did they sing! They sang barbershop mostly, but they also sang other songs like 'Were You There When They Crucified My Lord' and also 'I Want a Girl Just like the Girl That Married Dear Old Dad' [laughs]. Milton would sing lead, Roy would sing tenor, Fagan sang baritone, and Driscoll sang bass."

ROY LEE BROWN: "One guy I worked with said he and his wife were sound asleep with their windows up one night. There wasn't any air conditioning then. And they heard this singing outside. So they looked outside the window and there were Roy and Milton and somebody else serenading them. In the middle of the night [laughs]. I guess they didn't care where they sang or for whom. They just loved it. I remember them singing a few sad songs like 'Please Mr. Conductor, Don't Put Me off the Train.'"

Milton Brown's vocal group rarely, if ever, used any instrumental backing. Roy Lee Brown remembered Ellis Fagan's telling him that Milton would always "pitch" the key before they started singing. On occasion, they would have a piano accompaniment, but not very often. They sang uncomplicated, three-part-harmony barbershop vocals. The fourth member, who we know only by his surname Driscoll, was added when the occasion demanded. Unfortunately, there is little evidence to compare them with any contemporary vocal group. It is important to understand that even at this early stage in his musical career, Milton Brown's vocal style was set. He spent these few years expanding and developing his repertoire. Some historians have made attempts to categorize Milton's singing style, comparing it to one singer or another, the most likely comparison being made to jazz/pop bandleader Ted Lewis. However, as with other western swing pioneers, the key to the establishment of the genre was repertoire, derivative at first, and then becoming increasingly self-rejuvenating and original. Milton was comfortable with his own voice and even though he was keenly aware of many popular artists (including Jimmie Rodgers), he never assimilated any of these styles. He was simply western swing's first song collector, drawing from his own sources of "oral tradition" (records and radio) much as A. P. Carter assimilated folksongs for the Carter Family.

The earliest known newspaper recognition of Milton Brown as a performer appeared in the *Fort Worth Press* on September 26, 1927. The item is a rather inconspicuous listing of entertainers scheduled to perform at Arnold Park on Friday, September 30, including the names of Ellis Fagain [*sic*], Roy McBride, and Milton Brown.[5]

In February 1928, a photograph appeared in the *Press* that showed Milton Brown, Roy McBride, and Ellis Fagan, dressed in tuxedos and looking like men-about-town. Calling themselves the Three Yodeliers, the trio was scheduled to participate in the Odd Fellows Jubilee Minstrel at the Central High School auditorium the following Friday and Saturday. According to Roy Lee Brown and Glenna McBride, the group's repertoire at that time was restricted to barbershop harmonies and popular songs. It is not known whether the group performed at minstrel shows, although Milton did appear with Bob Wills in such programs several years later.

ROY LEE BROWN: "At that time, Milton was yodeling on a few songs. This is why the group was occasionally called the Three Yodeliers. Milton had a good falsetto voice, which he used from time to time. One of his favorite songs that he did was 'I Ain't Got Nobody,' in which he'd yodel. This was early in his career; he didn't do much yodeling in later years because he didn't want to sound too much like Jimmie Rodgers. Milton had respect for Rodgers but he didn't particularly like his songs."

The photograph used to publicize the Three Yodeliers was shot in a professional studio early in 1928. Roy McBride presented his mother with a copy on April 8 of that year. It was becoming apparent that Milton was serious about a career in music.

During this period, Milton continued to accompany his father to local house dances. Since these occasions were more oriented toward dancing, Milton did not sing the same songs as he did with his vocal group.

In addition to performing for the police department and various local organizations with his vocal group, it is possible that Milton Brown became associated with the Burrus Mill and Elevator Company as early as 1928. Glenna McBride remembered Roy's telling her that he and Milton had advertised Light Crust Flour. There is no record of Roy McBride ever having been a Light Crust Doughboy,[6] though in 1933 he was hired by W. Lee O'Daniel to work at Burrus Mill when cutbacks during the Depression forced the Rock Island Railroad to lay him off.

GLENNA MCBRIDE: "My husband worked for O'Daniel during the Depression. He delivered flour from about 4:00 in the morning until 7:00 at night, and he only made twelve dollars a week. After he got laid off at the railroad, he did everything he could to find work. There wasn't any welfare then. If you didn't have people to help you, you starved."

Considering Milton Brown's inclination to help his friends, it is possible that McBride got the delivery job through Milton; and since the Light Crust Doughboys were not officially organized until 1930, Glenna McBride's recollections would seem to indicate that the quartet which included Milton Brown and Roy McBride had been employed by Burrus Mill at an earlier date.

This evidence points to 1927 as the year Milton seriously began to consider music as a potentially lucrative career. School was behind him, he had a good job as a salesman, and he had formed a singing group that was being advertised on radio and in newspapers, receiving good response from the various organizations it played for. It was also the year that Derwood Brown, guitar in hand, began following his older brother around town.

ROY LEE BROWN: "Derwood was about twelve when he started running around with Milton to these house dances and different places. He was playing the guitar by then and had played with a friend of his named Tommy Echols. Tommy played Hawaiian guitar while Derwood played standard. When he played with Tommy, Derwood always played strictly rhythm, unless there was another guitar player around who played rhythm with them. Then Derwood started going around with Milton, playing house dances mostly on the west side of town but occasionally on the South Side. They'd pass the hat at these house dances and Milton and Derwood would make maybe a couple of dollars a night. Actually, Milton did not make anything, only the instrumentalists would. Dad would go with them sometimes and play the fiddle. A couple of dollars may not seem like much money now, but back then, a quarter was like five dollars now, maybe even ten. When they passed the hat, most of the people put in a quarter. I don't remember anyone putting in more than a quarter, but they'd put in less, maybe a dime or fifteen cents. There would never be more than two musicians that played these house dances, aside from Milton, who never got paid. Milton never played an instrument that I know of. He just went along to these places so he could sing.

"In 1928 or '29 Captain M. J. Bonner, an old-time fiddle player in Fort Worth, asked Derwood to go to Mississippi with him and play guitar at an old Confederate reunion and fiddle contest. I don't remember the town in Mississippi where they went, but Mama and Dad decided to let Derwood go with Captain Bonner, who was well liked and respected in town. So, Derwood and Captain Bonner hopped the train and went to Mississippi for the reunion. They won some money in the fiddlers' contest but I don't remember just how much. Derwood was a very good accompanist for breakdown fiddle players. He was doing a lot of bass runs by this time and had excellent rhythm. They were in Mississippi several days and took in some of the sights while they were there.

"When Derwood got back home, he told us about a battle that he saw on the Mississippi River between the Coast Guard and some rumrunners. He said that the rumrunners were trying to bring their boat full of booze up the Mississippi, and when the Coast Guard intercepted them, a gun battle broke out. The Coast Guard used machine guns on the rumrunners' boat and the bullets cut it in half as if a saw had gone through it. After that, the rumrunners just gave up and they were arrested. That was very exciting for a thirteen- or fourteen-year-old boy like Derwood, and I was real excited to hear about it, too."

The audiences that the vocal group sang for were different from the house dance crowd. By the late 1920s, Fort Worth had become a bustling, urbanizing city. Between 1920 and 1930, its population ballooned from 100,000 to 160,000 people. Dance bands were popular in the 1930s and ornate dance halls such as the Casino by Lake Worth catered to patrons from the growing communities which surrounded the city.

ROY LEE BROWN: "The Jacksboro Highway crossed Lake Worth on its way to the town of Jacksboro. Casino Beach was located just after you crossed the bridge heading northwest. The Casino was what we called a 'swanky' place and only horn bands played there. Bands like Paul Whiteman's, mostly. The Casino had a boardwalk and a roller coaster which was called the Thriller. Milton lost several hats on the Thriller. The hats would blow off his head while he was riding it and he would never be able to find them [laughs]. They also had motor boat rides and a big pleasure boat out in the middle of the lake where they had gambling."

But in the 1920s, very few of the transplanted country folk (such as the Browns) attended dances at the Casino, preferring instead the informal house dances, where the host would "roll up the carpet," as one popular song stated, and invite the neighbors over to dance.[7] Despite their characterization as "roaring," the twenties hardly roared at all for the rural immigrants of Fort Worth. Work was hard to come by, wages were low, and people usually had to find ways to entertain themselves without spending much money. Admission to downtown dance halls was too costly. Moreover, Prohibition limited liquid refreshment to nonalcoholic beverages. At the smaller neighborhood get-togethers, home brew was plentiful and admission was usually free. Milton Brown sought to combine the excitement of the urban dance hall and its hundreds of dancing couples with the down-home family atmosphere of the local house dance.

ROY LEE BROWN: "Here in Fort Worth, there was a group of families that had these dances, and they'd take turns playing at each others' houses. This occurred usually on Saturday nights. They would roll back the carpet or the linoleum, sprinkle a little corn meal on the floor, hire a fiddle and guitar player, and they'd have a dance. Most of it was square dancing, but there were a few waltzes and sometimes a round dance or a two-step. Sometimes they called the two-steps 'rags.' Dad was a country musician and he liked breakdowns.

Real country songs. He later became a big fan of Roy Acuff. There wasn't too much singing at these house dances, except when Milton came in and sang. They had no amplification, so Milton would bring in one of these megaphones. He didn't own one, but sometimes the people at the house dance would have one. He was always trying to make sure the dancers could hear the music."

A longtime Fort Worth resident remembered attending house dances with the Browns.

JOSEY LACY: "We danced at Everett and Louise Evans's home on Washburn, and also the homes of Mr. and Mrs. O. B. Bentley and Mr. and Mrs. Wiley. The Bentleys lived out at the White Settlement on Burton Hill Road and also over on West Vickery. Let's see, we danced in the home of John Hoyle and also Charlie Glassie. It was like a big family affair and everybody certainly enjoyed them. Milton's father and Derwood played for several years in these home dances. We had them from about 1918 up until about 1930."

ROY LEE BROWN: "In 1928 we moved to a house at 3419 Darcy Avenue. Darcy was a little short street about two blocks long that ran parallel to Camp Bowie Boulevard. It was bordered by West Seventh Street on the north and Camp Bowie on the south. Milton was still living with us then, even though he was twenty-five years old. Back then, nobody could afford to live separately like they can now. So, until you got married, you lived with your family."

Milton divided his time between selling cigars for Henry Lowe Cigar Company, singing with his vocal group, and attending house dances with his family. Many times, after a singing engagement was finished, Milton would appear at somebody's home, where Barty Brown and Derwood or some other musicians would be playing, and either join the dancers or sing a few songs for the crowd.

On October 24, 1929, the nation's economy was staggered by the collapse of the stock market. The industrialized East felt the impact immediately, as losses of life savings and bankruptcies became commonplace. However, business in the Fort Worth/Dallas area remained relatively stable until the winter of 1932–33. The Texas oil industry continued to pump at full capacity and agricultural setbacks were minimal. Tarrant County statistics showed only 2.3 percent unemployment in 1930, due mainly to the burgeoning oil industry and Fort Worth's rapid construction of new buildings.

Despite the delayed impact of the Depression on Texas, Milton Brown suffered immediately from its effects. In the late fall of 1929 Lowe Cigar was forced to cut back and Milton was laid off. After that, he supported himself solely on moneys received from his singing engagements. Milton also began to rely more on his fourteen-year-old brother Derwood, now his accompanist, as they traveled from house to house, playing and singing at neighborhood house dances and other social events.

ROY LEE BROWN: "I remember the Christmas after Milton got laid off, I was the only person that got a Christmas present from him. He came home and gave me a shirt that he had bought. He had been working steadily for Henry Lowe and had accumulated quite a few clothes: dress clothes, suits, and that nature. One night, Milton and Derwood went into a house on the South Side and there was a fiddler and a guitarist playing. Milton and Derwood knew practically everyone there so they went on in and were real sociable with everybody, as they always were. Everywhere Milton went, people wanted him to sing. I don't know if somebody asked him to sing this particular time, but he got up and sang 'St. Louis Blues' with the fiddle player and the guitar player. Well, the fiddler turned out to be Bob Wills and the guitar player was Herman Arnspiger. This led to a relationship and the four of them—Milton, Derwood, Bob, and Herman—started getting different places to play. The vocal group broke up about this time because Milton had a band in mind and not a singing group. So when he met Bob and Herman, he simply replaced the other singers with the two instrumentalists and he became the only vocalist. Milton, Bob, Herman, and Derwood did the same type of programs and played at the same places as the trio did: schools, lodges, etc.

"As far as I know, Milton was never hired just to sing for these house dances because the people could never afford to pay more than two musicians. But Milton made money elsewhere by making appearances at schoolhouses and doing special programs, first with his vocal groups, and later, with Bob Wills and Herman Arnspiger. When he and Derwood joined up with Bob and Herman, Milton would get jobs for them at a schoolhouse or maybe a church. Although Milton booked the jobs, he wasn't the leader of the group and neither was Bob Wills. There was simply an informal agreement by the members of the band as to where they would play. They never made enough to have a salary; they just split up whatever they made evenly among themselves."

James Robert Wills was born on March 6, 1905, in Limestone County, Texas. His family tree included a variety of musicians, mostly fiddlers. As Wills was fond of saying in later years:

BOB WILLS: "Both grandfathers were fiddlers, my dad was a fiddler, nine uncles were fiddlers, and five aunts. I guess it kind of runs in my blood!"

As a boy, Jim Rob (he would not be known by his middle name until he came to Fort Worth in 1929) learned many traditional Texas fiddle tunes from his father, John, a statewide champion fiddler. John Wills and the legendary A. C. "Eck" Robertson became friendly rivals in Texas fiddle contests. Wills's early life was nomadic, the restless youngster hopping freight trains and traveling from town to town as he struggled to earn a living. As with other Texas musicians, such as Ocie Stockard, Wills earned money as a barber, and in 1929, he arrived in Fort Worth looking for work. While playing in minstrel and medicine shows, he met guitarist Herman Arnspiger, and the two became close friends. The minstrel show experience helped Wills develop his exuberant stage presence, which would emerge after he formed his first band in Waco in 1933. It also expanded his musical repertoire, which had up to then consisted mainly of waltzes and breakdowns he had learned from his father. The rowdy city blues of Bessie Smith and Emmett Miller became staples in the Wills repertoire, and Wills patterned his own vocal style after that of Miller and other minstrel performers.[8]

During the time he lived in Fort Worth, Bob Wills lived a meager existence, often living from hand to mouth. His winning personality earned him many friends, and he was often able to translate his fiddling talents into small change, playing occasional house dances like those frequented by the Browns and other local musicians.

ROY LEE BROWN: "Bob was very poor at that time and had just gotten married and had a new baby daughter. According to J. B. Brinkley, Bob was so poor that he only had one pair of pants. He used to wash them out every night, hang them up to dry, and put them on again the next morning.[9] When Milton and Bob teamed up, Milton gave Bob one of his suits to wear. Milton wasn't rich or anything, but compared to Bob he was."

HARRY FOWLER: "The first time I ever saw old Bob Wills was when he came down to our house. Milton had brought him over there. When

Bob sat down, I could see that he had a hole in the bottom of each shoe. Great big holes, too. I never will forget that [laughs]."

Wills and Arnspiger had only recently teamed up, playing at various house dances and medicine shows as the Wills Fiddle Band. After Milton and Derwood Brown joined the group, the name Wills Fiddle Band was dropped. As with Milton's vocal group, the name of the band was changed often, depending on the party who hired them. Milton presumed that it would be advantageous to a sponsor to have the band's name promote its product. Until they got a job promoting Aladdin Lamps on WBAP later that year, the band had no formal name. The job promoting Aladdin lasted only a few months, and during that time the group was known as the Aladdin Laddies.

ROY LEE BROWN: "Bob hadn't been in Fort Worth long when he met Milton and Derwood. He worked up there at the barber college on Weatherford Street and was playing medicine shows doing blackface comedy. Back then, medicine shows were all the go. They'd come into town and have their little stage set up and they'd sell their patent medicine for a dollar a bottle. They sold boxes of candy and gave away prizes and also had contests now and then.

"I entered one of these contests at a medicine show once. It was a cracker-eating contest. I guess about eight boys got up on the stage at this medicine show, which was set up at West Seventh and what is now University Drive. The people that ran the show put some crackers in front of each contestant and the first one to eat all his crackers and then whistle would be the winner. Well, I ate the crackers real fast all right, but for the life of me, I couldn't whistle whatsoever. I lost.

"After the contests were over they'd put on a show for the people. They used to have outdoor park movies, too. We'd go to those and if we were lucky enough to have a nickel, we could get a candy bar or a cold drink. Milton did several medicine shows with Bob Wills. It was never the group, just Milton and Bob. Milton did it to help Bob out because Bob didn't have any money at all back then. Milton would act as Bob's straight man. Bob would be in blackface and Milton would just wear a suit like he always did. The only time I ever saw Bob Wills in blackface was after they had done a medicine show and Dad and Derwood were playing a dance at the Evanses over on Washburn Street off of Montgomery. After the medicine show was over, Bob and Milton came out to this house and Bob still had his blackface makeup on."

J. B. BRINKLEY: "Bob was doing blackface at medicine shows with a banjo player named Frank Barnes. Frank played the only five-string banjo I ever saw with a tin head on it. Boy, you didn't need no amplification on that thing [laughs]! Bob was doing blackface and one of the things they'd do at this medicine show was when Frank Barnes was doing his spiel. He was Bob's 'straight man,' so to speak. So Bob would come out front and Frank would say, 'What was that big noise I heard over at your house last night?' Bob would say, 'Ooh, dat wuz my maw and my paw, fightin'!' Frank would say, 'Who *was* your maw and paw?' And Bob would answer, 'Dat's whut dey wuz fightin' about [laughs]!" And Bob also did some dancing, tap dancing. They called it 'buck and wing' then."

ROY LEE BROWN: "Back in those days, there were amateur contests and fiddlers contests. I remember one time Bob and Herman entered a fiddlers contest on KFJZ. Bob was playing house dances at that time and he thought he could get all the people at the house dances to vote for him when the time came. I understand that the prize was fifty dollars. So Bob and Herman bought a bunch of penny postcards, brought them to the house dance, and gave several to each family there. And that's how they won, by getting these people at the house dances to send in all these cards. My parents sent in four or five themselves. So Bob and Herman won that contest, not necessarily because they were better than the other contestants, but because they got more cards sent in to the station. So with the fifty dollars, Bob and Herman bought themselves brand new suits and a pair of shoes. Back then you could buy a real fine suit for ten dollars. Maybe even seven and a half. Shoes would be a dollar and a half to two dollars.

"After they won that contest and started playing together and making a little money, Derwood and Milton would take me swimming with them on Sunday afternoons. We'd go over to the pool at Forest Park and swim. I remember one particular time, Milton, Derwood, Bob Wills, and I went over to Forest Park in Milton's car. Bob didn't have a car of his own yet but Milton did. Bob didn't have much of anything at that time so he spent quite a bit of time at our house as well as other people's houses, especially on weekends. Bob lived with his wife, Edna, and their little baby girl, Robbie Jo, in a two-room house on the corner of Elmwood and South Main. This one Sunday, Bob was at our house and Milton suggested we all go to Forest Park for a swim. They told me I could come along so the four of us went on out there. I remember them talking about girls all the way over to the park [laughs]!

"After Milton and Derwood teamed up with Bob and Herman, Milton booked a regular engagement at the Eagles Hall lodge in uptown Fort Worth. It was located on Fifth Street between Houston and Main. The hall was upstairs and the group played only on Saturday nights. The house dances were still going on at this time because I remember my mother and dad took me to the Glassies' house, right off of West Seventh Street, right close to the peanut factory. After Milton, Bob, Derwood, and Herman got through at the hall, they'd come out to these house dances, because they would last longer than the Eagles Hall dance would."

The basic group that played the Eagles Hall in 1930 included Milton Brown, Bob Wills, Herman Arnspiger, and Derwood Brown. However, other Fort Worth musicians sometimes sat in with the band. The size of the Eagles Hall ballroom allowed for more musicians than the smaller house dances. Through his contacts at the Eagles Hall, Milton was introduced to other local musicians, among them fiddler Red Steeley, guitarist Clifton "Sleepy" Johnson, and guitarist/banjoist Ocie Stockard.

A. L. "Red" Steeley was known as one of the finest breakdown fiddlers in the Dallas/Fort Worth area. Steeley's partner was a guitarist named J. W. "Red" Graham, who also played five-string banjo and mandolin. Steeley and Graham came to Texas from Alabama as children, meeting in Arlington, then just a small town halfway between Dallas and Fort Worth. They had been playing together since 1909 and had become renowned in the Fort Worth area. The pair had a successful radio program on WBAP in the late 1920s, one of the earliest regular programs featuring hillbilly musicians. As the Red Headed Fiddlers, Steeley and Graham recorded ten instrumentals for Brunswick Records in 1928 and 1929.[10]

ROY LEE BROWN: "When Dad and Derwood played for dances, Red Steeley and a guitar player [probably Red Graham] would also play on occasion, as did Bob Wills and Herman Arnspiger. My mother and dad went to a house dance nearly every Saturday night somewhere in Fort Worth. Red Steeley was much in demand for these dances, more than anyone else that I knew. I would hear the grown-ups talk, and most of them preferred Red because he was one of the best breakdown fiddlers around, if not the best. If they couldn't get Red, then they would get Bob Wills or Dad. They used Bob a lot until he started playing with Milton at the Eagles Hall and other functions. The people liked Bob personally and they also felt sorry for him because he had a wife and baby and didn't have enough to eat much of the time.

"Milton didn't work the house dances with any of the duos but he would sing with them when he was there. There wasn't any demand for a singer in any group then. Milton started that when he and Bob teamed up. Instead of having a fiddle all the time, you had vocals occasionally. I remember several times when Milton, Derwood, Bob, Herman, Red Steeley, Jesse Ashlock, and others would get together on a Sunday afternoon at someone's house just to play and sing. No dancing was done, they would just play for each other.

"I don't know if Milton and Red ever did any schools or gigs together but most likely they did a few. Derwood also may have played with Red. I would hear about Red Steeley every now and then but I never did see him that I know of after the house dances ended."

Clifton Johnson, nicknamed Sleepy because of his droopy, perpetually sad-eyed expression, was born in Llano County, Texas, on February 25, 1911. His widow, Sally, remembered meeting Sleepy in 1932. They were married in 1934 and spent forty-two years together before his death shortly after performing at the Bob Wills Day festivities in Turkey, Texas, in 1976.

SALLY BEARD JOHNSON: "Sleepy's mother died shortly after he was born so he was raised mostly by an aunt and uncle. He left them when he was about fourteen and came to Fort Worth. He had a sister who lived on the South Side. He went to school over at Poly for a while but he had to quit and go to work to support himself. One of his first jobs was working at Rockefeller's hamburger joint. I don't know how old he was when he started playing music, but he lived in Denton for a while with his brother, who was a painter. Sleepy took up the paint trade there, which is what he did in later years. When he came to Fort Worth there were little bands all over the country. Sleepy's sister was married to a man named John Dunnam, who worked for the fire department."

CLIFTON "SLEEPY" JOHNSON: "When I first came to Fort Worth, my brother and I played the first radio program that was ever played with a string band, and that was out here at the old Camp Bowie, when they had a camp out there for soldier boys. We broadcast from a square dance out there. I was fourteen years old.[11] Actually, the band was just fiddle and guitar. Then we had what we called the Firecracker String Band here at Firehall No. 14. It was several firemen and I [who] played

with them. It was many, many years ago, and as I said, there was a fort
out there at the time and they had square dances in this big building
there. Of course that was our first chance to broadcast and we didn't
even know what was going on, hardly. It came out over WBAP. I'm
sure WBAP has some records that this Firehall No. 14 String Band did.
A few years later Bob Wills came along and they had the Aladdin Lamp
program. That was a paid program."[12]

ROY LEE BROWN: "There was a country club just off of Camp Bowie
Boulevard called Meadowmere and it had a big old building where
dances and shows were held. One time, Milton, Derwood, Bob, Herman, and maybe Sleepy played a dance there and Mom and Dad took
me to hear them. We rode the streetcar to the end of the line, which
was the 5200 block of Byers Street, and walked the rest of the way
to Meadowmere. It was a big old barnlike place with a stage and box
seats up high around the place like an opera house."[13]

One of the musicians who played with Sleepy Johnson in the Firecracker String Band was probably John Dunnam. Roy Lee Brown,
also a fire fighter in later years, worked with John Dunnam and remembered playing breakdowns with him at the fire hall. It was Dunnam who approached the Aladdin Lamp company and arranged for
them to sponsor the band on WBAP. The group that became the Aladdin Laddies for several months in 1930 included Dunnam, Milton
Brown, Bob Wills, Sleepy Johnson, Herman Arnspiger, and Derwood
Brown.

ROY LEE BROWN: "The Aladdin Laddies program was started by John
Dunnam. He got the Aladdin Lamp company to sponsor the show
over on WBAP. Aladdin Lamps were similar to Coleman lamps, they
were kerosene lamps. John got Milton, Derwood, Bob, Herman, and
Sleepy to play it. They were on just once a week, on a Tuesday or
Wednesday night from eight to eight-thirty. A station announcer at
WBAP did the commercials for Aladdin Lamps. Back then, musicians
never said anything on the air unless they were asked something by
the announcer. Until Milton started his own band, the station announcer would make all nonmusical announcements. When Milton
started the Brownies, he began announcing his own dance dates. As
far as I know, he was the first to do this.

"John Dunnam played fiddle occasionally with the group on the
radio. They had two fiddle players: John [Dunnam] and Bob Wills.
They never played twin fiddles because neither was good enough to

play harmony. About all John could do was play breakdowns, same as Bob. The Aladdin Laddies used the same theme song that the Light Crust Doughboys used later on: 'We're the Aladdin Laddies from WBAP.' Milton got it from a record by a colored group from Tennessee. He then changed the words so he could get a copyright on it."

The Aladdin Laddies' theme song later became the theme for the Light Crust Doughboys and also for Bob Wills's groups beginning in August 1933. The record Milton Brown adapted was "Eagle Riding Papa" by the Famous Hokum Boys, a black group that featured Mississippi country blues singer/guitarist Big Bill Broonzy. The Hokum Boys played "rent party" songs, up-tempo numbers with a heavy ragtime influence laced with risqué lyrics. Broonzy was in the middle of a transitional period. His style was changing from that of Texas blues shouter Blind Lemon Jefferson to the intricate jazz of Lonnie Johnson. "Eagle Riding Papa" was recorded at the Hokum Boys' first session, in New York City on April 9, 1930. Broonzy was joined by rhythm guitarist Frank Brasswell and pianist "Georgia Tom" Dorsey. Milton Brown loved the happy, lively rhythm of the Hokum Boys and in 1936 recorded the flip side of "Eagle Riding Papa," "Somebody's Been Using That Thing," with his Musical Brownies.[14] The recording date of the Famous Hokum Boys' recording helps us date the creation of the Aladdin Laddies. If the record was released in May, we can assume that the Aladdin Lamp sponsorship began sometime in May or June, lasting through the summer months of 1930.

ROY LEE BROWN: "Right about the time when Milton and Bob joined up, Milton met Will Ed Kemble. Will Ed owned Kemble Brothers Furniture Company, which was located on Throckmorton Street between Bellknap and Weatherford in downtown Fort Worth.[15] The Aladdin Laddies and later the Doughboys and the Brownies used to rehearse up in his store. It was a real nice store. I don't remember ever going in there when they were rehearsing, but I do know that they had a mezzanine floor that they would use and maybe that's why Will Ed let them do that. Maybe some of the customers liked to come and watch them rehearse. They also sold a lot of phonograph records there. The only place you could hear records was on the radio, but a lot of people didn't have radios yet. We had an old wind-up Victrola and I remember Milton bringing home that record of 'Eagle Riding Papa.' Phonographs were more prevalent than radios back then."

The Aladdin Laddies was basically the same group of musicians that played every Saturday night at the Eagles Hall on Fifth Street. This band, which numbered anywhere from four to seven people (including Milton, who only sang), now became the largest string band ever to play in Fort Worth. In the 1920s "string bands" generally consisted of two instruments, usually fiddle and guitar. These musicians played house dances and occasionally high schools and churches, much as Barty Brown did in Stephenville at the turn of the century. At house dances in Fort Worth, the old country dance tunes and breakdowns began to mix with popular numbers played by the larger dance orchestras. As the crowds increased in size, so did the string bands. By the end of the decade, many string bands were numbering three and four members. Milton Brown became a link between the rural and urban audiences by introducing vocals to string bands. During his appearances at the Eagles Hall, he introduced many of the popular tunes he had performed with his vocal quartet to the other musicians. In turn, Bob Wills incorporated breakdowns and waltzes from north Texas, which he had learned from his father.[16]

As the size of the dance halls increased, it became apparent that more instruments were necessary to accommodate the noisier crowds and larger facilities. Milton Brown had used a megaphone to amplify his vocals since the early 1920s and he continued to do so until the public address system was introduced sometime in 1930. One instrumental change at this time became the first of many significant modifications in traditional string band music in Texas during the 1930s: the abandonment of the tenor guitar in favor of the tenor banjo. The tenor guitar and tenor banjo both had four strings and were tuned identically. However, the crisper, louder sound of the tenor banjo became an ideal rhythm instrument during this critical transition period in Texas music. In time, the addition of other instruments like the piano and amplified guitars rendered the tenor banjo unnecessary. But until World War II, it was a standard ingredient in the early makeup of western swing bands. J. W. Graham had played five-string banjo in his duets with Red Steeley, but the five-string began to be phased out as the New Orleans jazz influence invaded east Texas. The man most responsible for this transition was one of the key pioneers of western dance bands and a future Musical Brownie: Ocie Stockard.

OCIE STOCKARD: "I was born in a little old town called Crafton, Texas, on May 11, 1909. My middle name is Blanton. Crafton was about sixty-five miles northwest of Fort Worth. When I joined the Brownies, we recorded a fiddle tune I had written called 'Crafton Blues,' which Cecil Brower played.[17] Crafton was a real small town, which had maybe two or three stores and a post office. Eventually, they moved the post office out and Crafton sort of disappeared. You can't even find it on the map anymore. Chico is about the closest town to where it used to be, about seven miles the other side of Bridgeport.

"We didn't have electricity on our farm in Crafton. We didn't even have running water. We had to cut our own wood to cook and heat the house with and we had windmills to draw water. We used to wash our clothes by catching rainwater in the wells. We had a windmill which was attached to a pump and if the wind was blowing, you could pump it and get water from the well.

"When we needed groceries, we generally had to go to Bowie. I remember my dad used to hook up the wagon in the morning and drive out there. It was an all-day trip to Bowie and back. I used to go into Bowie with my dad to get groceries and when I'd get there, I'd see those barbers cutting hair with those fancy ceiling fans and everything and I thought to myself: 'Ocie, there ain't no life for you in Crafton. These barber fellers have really got it made [laughs]!' So I decided to become a barber. Ain't nothing I could have done out there in the country. I quit school and took a barbering course in Wichita Falls. After I got out of barber college, I worked a while in Bowie.

"While I was in Bowie, I learned to play the guitar. My sister, who was four years older than me, was going with a guy who was a pretty good guitar player. So he taught me chords and I soon knew that if you could play chords, why, you could play just about anything you wanted to. I started playing country dances when I was ten years old. My dad taught me how to play breakdowns on the fiddle although he never played at dances. Instead, I would play with this rancher up there in Bowie.

"I barbered for a while in Wichita Falls, and while I was there, I took fiddle lessons from a lady who was playing a show up there. I remember she taught me to play 'My Blue Heaven.' She played real fine and said that she'd teach me to play. She wasn't a fiddle player, she was a 'violin' player.[18] So I learned enough from her to be able to read music and play lead. I wasn't very good at first because I never got to practice much. In Wichita Falls, that guy who taught me guitar had a little band. The banjo player in that band was named Jack Garrett and he taught me to play tenor banjo. I learned all three instruments—guitar, banjo, and fiddle—and the three of us played a few dances and private parties in Bowie. We'd make maybe four or five dollars apiece. Then in Wichita Falls, I played tenor banjo with them on stage Wednesday and Saturday nights. I did that for a while and then came to Fort Worth in an old Model A Ford. The road that came down to Fort Worth from Wichita Falls was just a little old two-lane road back then. Most of it wasn't even paved.

"When I got to Fort Worth I took a job as a barber down at Robin's Barber Shop on Twenty-fourth Street out on the North Side. And you know, that place turned out to be a musician's hangout! One day a guy came by who wanted to start a band. The guy's name was Clifford Gross. He came from Bowling Green, Kentucky, and played real good breakdown fiddle. Cliff wanted to get a band to play on KTAT and came to the barbershop to get me to play with him. But he wanted me to play tenor guitar. I had never played tenor guitar before but I told him okay. I remember it was a Friday when he came by. As soon as he asked me, I went into town and got a chord book and studied it whenever I wasn't working. By Monday I was ready and we went on the air as the High Fliers at noon on KTAT. This was probably about a year after I got to Fort Worth.[19]

"Clifford Gross was the leader of the High Fliers and he played fiddle. Claude Davis was the mandolin player. I lived with him for about a year. I met my wife through Claude. Claude couldn't play choruses [improvised take-off solos]. He played a big old tater bug mandolin. Herman Arwine played guitar and I played tenor guitar. Cliff got us the program on KTAT and we all took a bus out to the radio station to do the show. We didn't have a sponsor but we had spot announcements. I believe we had a whole hour, from twelve o'clock noon until 1 P.M. every day. The announcer was a guy named Zack Hurt who had one eye out. He had a motor and wrapped a piece of leather around the thing. Then he cranked it up and made that airplane noise that started our program. Then he'd move it away from the microphone like it was taking off. Zack is the one that named us the High Fliers."[20]

John Bruce "Roscoe" Pierce was a young musician who met Ocie Stockard at Robin's Barber Shop in Fort Worth. He was born in Blanchard, Oklahoma, on January 1, 1913, and came to Fort Worth in 1929 from Springtown, Texas, a small town in Parker County, northwest of Fort Worth.

ROSCOE PIERCE: "I came to Fort Worth with Raymond DeArman, who I met while I was living in Springtown. Raymond and I both met Ocie at that barber shop. I was out there on the North Side and had been in that barber shop before. I took in all that good picking that they did. I remember the Hataway boys; boy, could they pick the guitar. Finger-style like Merle Travis did later on. Ira was the oldest and he was the main picker. Raymond found that barber shop first and got me to go down there with him one day. He told me there was good fiddlers and stuff down there. I started out playing when I was about sixteen, playing one-room country dances. We'd clear everything out of one room and put it in the hall and then we set up a dance floor. They'd throw meal or sawdust on the floor and we'd dance."[21]

OCIE STOCKARD: "When we had those dances, we'd have a bookkeeper: somebody to call out the names of the people who could dance in the next set. See, there wasn't enough room for more than four couples to dance at one time so we had this lottery. People would pay one time to get on each set. They could pay again to get in on another set if they wanted to. Some of them wanted to do square dances, some old-time waltzes, some schottisches, some round dances. So the bookkeeper would put your name down and also what kind of dance you wanted to do. Mostly people like the old-time waltzes."

ROSCOE PIERCE: "The first string band I remember when I came to Fort Worth in 1929 was the High Fliers. They played pretty good music but they didn't play what we call western swing today. They didn't have anybody who could play take-off choruses. Ocie didn't do that until he joined Milton Brown."

Ocie Stockard became an unofficial member of the band that played the Eagles Hall in 1930. In addition to his role with the High Fliers, Stockard joined Wills, Arnspiger, and the Browns, playing regular dances at the East Front Dance Hall on Wednesdays, Fridays, and Saturdays (East Front Street later became East Lancaster).

ROY LEE BROWN: "My mama and dad carried me over to that East Front Dance Hall one time and I saw Milton, Derwood, Bob, and Herman playing. Sleepy Johnson and Ocie Stockard were also there. That night, a fire started on the back stairway. We all evacuated the building, and after the fire was put out, everybody went back inside and continued the dance [laughs]!"

It was at the East Front Dance Hall that Milton Brown met Ocie

Stockard. Stockard was playing tenor banjo on that occasion and Milton complimented Ocie on his superb rhythm.

OCIE STOCKARD: "I met Milton over at this place upstairs on East Front. Bob and I and Herman and Sleepy Johnson were playing for a dance. I was playing banjo at the time. I remember there wasn't any P.A. system there. No speakers at all. And people were dancing around in that old hall. That was also the first time I met Bob Wills. Well, Milton came in and sat in with us and sang through a megaphone."[22]

In the fall of 1930 Milton Brown was singing with the Aladdin Laddies on radio station WBAP and appearing with the unnamed group of Fort Worth musicians at the weekly Saturday night dances at the Eagles Hall lodge. Having been a salesman and radio performer for several years now, he realized the power of radio in promoting personal appearances. However, the Aladdin Lamp program was of no help to him because any announcements during the show were limited to advertisements of Aladdin products. The Eagles Hall dances were successful, but Milton longed for a larger place where he could play more frequently than one night a week. When the Aladdin Lamp program went off the air, he began searching for another spot on the radio. And then he found Crystal Springs.

Crystal Springs was the name of a multipurpose entertainment facility located four miles northwest of downtown Fort Worth at 5336 White Settlement Road. It was run by Samuel C. Cunningham, a large, jovial, cigar-chomping gentleman known until the end of his life as Papa Sam.[23]

When Milton Brown first met Sam Cunningham or paid his first visit to Crystal Springs is not known. But sometime in the late fall of 1930, Milton arranged for the group that was playing at the Eagles Hall to play dances at Crystal Springs.

ROY LEE BROWN: "Right about the time Milton got the Crystal Springs job, Will Ed Kemble steered them to KFJZ for an audition for a radio program. Derwood had just turned fifteen and he was still in school, otherwise he would have played the audition. So it was just Milton, Bob Wills, and Herman Arnspiger who went."

The young man who auditioned the trio at KFJZ was Al Stricklin, who later earned a reputation as a piano player with Bob Wills. Stricklin was working at the station so he could earn a few extra dollars for his struggling family after quitting school because of the Depression.

The trio began their audition with "Who Broke the Lock on the Henhouse Door." After they played several more numbers,[24] KFJZ's chief engineer, Truett Kimzey, who was also in attendance, decided that the boys might do well advertising local products. Kimzey suggested Light Crust Flour as a possible sponsor and took the idea to the general sales manager of the Burrus Mill and Elevator Company, which milled Light Crust. The manager's name was W. Lee O'Daniel.

FOUR

We're the Light Crust Doughboys from the Burrus Mill

(1930–32)

Wilbert Lee O'Daniel was born in Malta, Ohio, on March 11, 1890. After working for several midwestern milling companies, he arrived in Fort Worth on July 4, 1925, to work as sales manager for the Burrus Mill and Elevator Company. O'Daniel had many grandiose plans for expanding the market for Light Crust Flour but this required a much larger mill than the one president J. Perry Burrus had built on Front Street by the Texas and Pacific Railroad siding. Burrus promised O'Daniel that he would indeed build a new, modern facility if O'Daniel increased sales figures.

W. Lee O'Daniel has been described as the quintessential salesman, one who could "sell iceboxes in Labrador or snowshoes on the Equator." Although his methods were often suspect, his results were always remarkable. After a short time, O'Daniel increased Light Crust Flour sales by 250 percent, which resulted in a promotion to general manager.[1] Truett Kimzey had apparently witnessed Light Crust's increase in advertising and approached O'Daniel on behalf of the band.

W. LEE O'DANIEL: "One day in 1930 a group of jobless musicians came in to see me. They had a suggestion for hooking up flour advertising with a musical radio program, using songs that would have a homey appeal to ordinary middle-class people, and it all sounded pretty good to me."[2]

Kimzey returned to KFJZ and told Milton, Bob, and Herman of O'Daniel's willingness to sponsor the group, and they got busy assembling a repertoire and rehearsing for the programs. The Doughboy program was to go on the air at 6:00 A.M., before any regular an-nouncers were on duty at KFJZ. Announcing would be handled by Kimzey himself, who would read blurbs and announcements on be-half of Light Crust Flour provided for him by O'Daniel. It was Truett Kimzey who dubbed the group the Light Crust Doughboys.

The date of the first Light Crust Doughboys broadcast is unclear. It has been generally assumed it took place in early January 1931. However, this date—"around January 1, 1931"—was only an estimate that O'Daniel gave arbitrarily during a lawsuit he filed against Bob Wills in 1933 for deceptive promotion.[3] The *Fort Worth Press,* in a story on O'Daniel, interviewed Truett Kimzey, who estimated that the initial broadcast had taken place during the fall of 1930. The ear-liest mention of Light Crust Flour in the *Fort Worth Press* radio logs was on Wednesday, November 12, 1930, when a program by the "Light Crust Minstrels" was listed on KTAT from 7:45 to 8:15 A.M. The Wednesday listing appeared three more times: on November 19, December 3, and December 17. Whether this program featured Mil-ton, Bob, and Herman is unknown, but it does show that Light Crust Flour was sponsoring a program in the fall of 1930. Sometime be-tween December and the spring of 1931, Light Crust moved their program to KFJZ and the Light Crust Doughboys were born.

It was KFJZ engineer Truett Kimzey who uttered the words that became synonymous with western swing in the 1930s and 1940s: "The Light Crust Doughboys are ONNN the air!!" With this, Bob Wills plucked the first two strings on his fiddle and Milton Brown sang the Doughboys' theme song, which they had first used when they were known as the Aladdin Laddies. By this time, Milton had rearranged the Famous Hokum Boys' "Eagle Riding Papa" to accommodate Light Crust Flour. The first section was used to start off each program:

> Now listen everybody from near and far
> If you want to know who we are
> We're the Light Crust Doughboys
> From the Burrus Mill
>
> If you like the way we play
> Listen while we try to say
> We're the Light Crust Doughboys
> From the Burrus Mill
>
> And all night long,
> We're going to sing this song
> If you get this song,
> You can't go wrong (and how!)

> We wear a smile and make things bright
> We'll make you happy from morn 'til night
> We're the Light Crust Doughboys
> From the Burrus Mill

The Doughboys closed each program with the following words to the song:

> Now we never do brag, we never do boast
> We sing our songs from coast to coast
> We're the Light Crust Doughboys
> From the Burrus Mill

> If you like our song, think it's fine
> Sit right down and drop a line
> To the Light Crust Doughboys
> From the Burrus Mill

> And I'll declare, you'll get it there
> And if we have some time to spare (somewhere)

> Sometime when we're down your way
> We'll drop in and spend the day
> We're the Light Crust Doughboys
> From the Burrus Mill

After the theme song finished, Milton Brown began singing a popular prison ballad entitled "Twenty-one Years," a recent creation of New York "citybilly" songwriter Bob Miller. In the song, the singer took the blame for an unstated crime that had actually been perpetrated by his sweetheart.[4] "Twenty-one Years" was a perfect song for Milton Brown because it enabled him to use the warm, convincing delivery he had perfected since singing with his sister Era in Stephenville fifteen years earlier. He knew that this quality was what attracted people to him and it was for this reason that he abandoned his vocal group when he met Bob Wills and Herman Arnspiger. He needed a dance band and the kind of vocals with which country people could identify.

After the song finished, Bob Wills led the group in the familiar fiddle breakdown "Chicken Reel." Wills was best at breakdowns. Milton hollered all the way through this one, urging on Bob and Arnspiger, the latter beating out the rhythm on his standard guitar. Although hollering became one of Bob Wills's trademarks, it is evident from his recordings that he did not, or could not, holler while he was playing fiddle. It was not until he added more instruments capable of playing the melody that he began to interject the "aaah-ha's" that later made him famous. With a three-man group, where Wills had to carry the melodies of popular tunes and blues during entire instrumental pieces all of the time, he remained silent. An intriguing photograph of the Light Crust Doughboys appeared in newspapers after W. Lee O'Daniel became their announcer. It showed O'Daniel, Sleepy Johnson (who had replaced Arnspiger in 1932), Wills, and Milton Brown, with Milton's mouth wide open in an apparent holler, eyes ablaze. The viewer is immediately drawn to Milton, more than the urbane O'Daniel and the handsome accompanists Wills and Johnson.

When "Chicken Reel" concluded, announcer Truett Kimzey welcomed the audience and read one of O'Daniel's blurbs, after which the Doughboys played "a few Jimmie Rodgers yodeling numbers."[5] When Kimzey asked the listening audience for comments, KFJZ was deluged with hundreds of letters within a few days, a remarkable phenomenon considering the limited power of KFJZ's transmitter. At 250 watts (100 after sunset), KFJZ, located at 1370 kilocycles on the AM dial, was the least powerful of Fort Worth's three radio stations. Owned by local businessman Ralph Bishop, KFJZ opened in 1927. As astute a businessman as W. Lee O'Daniel was, it is surprising that he would select the weakest possible radio station to broadcast the Light Crust Doughboys. However, in the beginning O'Daniel was unsure of the group's drawing power. He disliked "hillbilly music" intensely, and it was not until much later, when he discovered the Doughboys' immense popularity, that he became their most ardent supporter. It is not known how much O'Daniel paid per program for sponsoring the Doughboys since the first edition of *Variety*'s radio annual did not appear until the 1937–38 broadcast year. At that time, after the Depression had eased a little, KFJZ's sponsorship rate was $48 for a half-hour of programming, compared to $125 at KTAT, and $250 at WBAP, the powerhouse at the Blackstone Hotel. It is likely that O'Daniel did the best thing for Burrus by "experimenting" with the Doughboys on KFJZ, where they would do the least amount of financial harm should they fail.

After a few weeks, O'Daniel canceled the program. His dislike of the music the band played superseded his usually acute business sense. Milton pleaded with him and Kimzey presented the bags of mail the station had been receiving on behalf of the Doughboys. Finally, O'Daniel relented and put the boys back on the air, with the stipulation that Brown, Wills, and Arnspiger each work at Burrus Mill.

After rehiring the group in 1931, O'Daniel built a special practice room for the band inside the mill, complete with a record player and a large selection of all the latest releases.[6] The group was required to practice at the mill for eight hours each day for the nightly broadcasts, which were carefully scripted, focusing more and more on O'Daniel's poetry and recitations. The length of rehearsal time was mainly for Bob Wills's benefit, as it took him a great deal of time to learn new material.[7]

ROY LEE BROWN: "They were making fifteen dollars a week. Milton was a salesman, Bob drove a truck making deliveries, and Herman worked in the plant. This was part of the agreement they made with O'Daniel that they'd work that way. But as soon as they got the studio and started rehearsing, they stopped working at the mill. O'Daniel started booking them at stores, parks, and other places to play, so they didn't have time to work in the mill. He got them all these white uniforms with a chef's hat and they'd go around in this car that had a platform on the back. The three of them (four when Derwood went along) would crowd around that platform and they'd play from the back end of that car. Light Crust always had a booth every year at the stock show. They would make hot biscuits (out of Light Crust flour, of course) and serve them with butter to the people while the band played. And they always had a crowd. They continued that same format after Milton left them."

O'Daniel's skepticism was unwarranted. The Light Crust Doughboys were an instant success. Light Crust Flour sales rose almost as fast as the flour itself, and O'Daniel decided to take the Doughboys on the road. Their first engagement was probably for the state bakers' convention in Galveston in March 1931. O'Daniel chartered a bus, had Kimzey wire it for sound, and took the band down to the Gulf. Will Ed Kemble went along, as did Derwood Brown, who was now an unoffical member of the group, playing rhythm guitar.

"It was the first time that a sound truck had been used for such a purpose, and the lads stole the show in Galveston. Crowds swarmed about the long white bus not only in the seacoast city but in towns visited enroute."[8]

Kimzey was still the announcer for the group, although O'Daniel and several other Burrus Mill salesmen attended the convention in Galveston. Upon returning to Fort Worth, O'Daniel decided to buy a bus of his own. It was actually an automobile, a seven-passenger white Packard. Signs were mounted on it that read "Eat More Bread, Your Best and Cheapest Food" and "Patronize Texas Industry and Texas Agriculture and Prosperity Will Return." The vehicle, dubbed "Prosperity Special," soon became a familiar sight in towns such as Mineral Wells, Weatherford, and Waco.

As the Doughboys' fame spread, W. Lee O'Daniel slowly realized the potential advertising power he had at his fingertips. Although he was not a singer nor a musician, O'Daniel was an accomplished orator. He and his wife Merle were also good at composing poetry. Sometime late in 1931, the Light Crust Doughboys were scheduled to go on a goodwill tour with the Fort Worth Chamber of Commerce. Truett Kimzey was unable to abandon his duties at KFJZ, so O'Daniel volunteered to replace him. In Weatherford, O'Daniel announced the program for the first time and completed the tour. Immediately, he moved the program to WBAP, leaving Kimzey behind.

WBAP was Fort Worth's most powerful radio station, booming 50,000 watts throughout the Southwest. From its meager beginnings as a five-watt radio station in March 1922, WBAP expanded quickly in the 1920s, increasing its power first to 500 watts, then 1000, then 1500. It broadcast the Democratic presidential convention that nominated Alfred E. Smith for president from Houston in June 1928. Four months later, WBAP increased its power to 50,000 watts, the maximum allowed by the Federal Radio Commission.

With this instant explosion of power, O'Daniel assumed the role of Doughboys announcer permanently. He also wrote heartrending lyrics, all of them based on popular melodies. On Shreveport, Louisiana's KWKH, the Shelton Brothers had achieved success with a song called "Just Because." With the help of Milton Brown, O'Daniel slowed the tempo down, changed the time signature to 3/4, and wrote one of Texas's most enduring anthems: "Beautiful Texas." Milton was given no credit for his role in the writing of the song or for any other contribution he made to the band. As popular as the radio program became, Milton Brown never made more than fifteen dollars a week while he was employed by Burrus Mill. However, he often made much more than that playing dances at Crystal Springs each Saturday night.

ROY LEE BROWN: "The program on the radio was one thing. The dances were extra, kind of like part-time jobs. Milton ran the dances, and until O'Daniel came along, he ramrodded the radio program too. I'm sure they all discussed together what tunes they were going to do for the program while Truett Kimzey was the announcer. But O'Daniel picked the tunes after he became their program director. Milton would then program the show and balance it out. He'd start off with a fast tune and then play a slow one, etc. But O'Daniel was now the boss of the Doughboys. After he got in there announcing, he told them what to play and what not to play. And he wanted these tear-jerking, don't-send-my-boy-to-prison-type songs. Or my-old-gray-haired-mother songs. Now I'm not knocking those, they're good, too. But that's what he wanted. Old folk-type songs. He wrote 'My Own Sweet Darling Wife,' which is really 'When the Bloom Is on the Sage.' He also wrote 'Put Me in Your Pocket,' which is 'When Irish Eyes Are Smiling.' And of course, Milton helped him put new words to 'Just Because,' which became 'Beautiful Texas.' O'Daniel used some other tune for just about every song he ever wrote. He was good with poetry but he couldn't write a melody if his life depended on it.

"In the beginning, Mr. O'Daniel would come into the studio and check to see how everything was going with the program. And the band tried to get him to say a few words on the air. When he did, he liked it so much that, well, he just took over the announcing. And he got to be one of the finest philosphers and orators around. He had a pleasing personality and I guess the band members liked him. But then he got kind of cantankerous about them playing dances at Crystal Springs. He also would rarely give them credit on the air as to who they really were. I don't know whether he ever called Bob Wills anything at all but he called Milton 'The Boy with the Golden Voice.' That's what he would say when he introduced him. He'd say, 'Now here's the Boy with the Golden Voice to sing this next song.' Later on he got to where he would mention their names more."

Longtime Brownie fan and Texas resident A. B. Gilbert recalled seeing the Light Crust Doughboys during one of their tours.

A. B. GILBERT: "I was born in 1913 in Santo. That's about fifty miles west of Fort Worth. My cousin and me had been to Fort Worth on horseback and we saw these musicians in town doing a show from this car. We slept out on the prairie there and then the next day we came on back and when we got to Weatherford, we saw O'Daniel and these three musicians again. The musicians was in the back seat of whatever kind of a car it was they used and there was a picnic goin' on. Governor 'Straw Hat' Bill Murray of Oklahoma was the speaker. They needed some entertainment so the Doughboys went out there. We followed alongside the car as they rode out there and that was the first time I talked to Milton and Bob. They had a platform there and there were chairs set up, so we stayed and listened to the entertainment. Milton sang 'On My Farm in Oklahoma Where the Red Red River Flows.' We knew the song as mentioning Louisiana but I guess Milton changed the words because the governor of Oklahoma was there.

"'Round where I grew up we had fiddle, guitar, five-string banjo, and mandolin music. We had country dances all right, but nobody sang. We never heard of anybody singing at a dance until Milton started singing.

"Later on, the Doughboys had a booth at the Fat Stock Show on the North Side. They had bales of hay laid around so people could sit down and watch the show. Two or three times a day they played a fifteen-minute program for the people."

ROY LEE BROWN: "I heard Derwood and Milton talking to Mama and Dad about the trips they used to take as Doughboys to the small towns around Fort Worth. O'Daniel paid for the Doughboys' meals while they were on the road. Most of the places they went to had fruit stands set up along the roadside between towns at certain times of the year. O'Daniel used to tell the bus driver to stop at these fruit stands and he would buy a bunch of overripe bananas for the boys to fill up on so they wouldn't eat so much when mealtime came.

"Neither Milton nor Bob did any announcing then. You wouldn't even hear Bob's voice at all on the air. Milton did all the singing and hollering. It was real early in the morning. They'd be on at 6:00 so they could sell all the Light Crust Flour and corn meal to the country people before they got out into the fields."

Teenager Jimmy Thomason was an enthusiastic lad living in Waco, about ninety miles south of Fort Worth. Whenever the Doughboys traveled south, they stopped at Waco for a show, making guest appearances on radio station WACO. Thomason later recorded with Waco's Doug Bine and the Dixie Ramblers, the Shelton Brothers, and other early Texas string bands. He vividly recalled his early impressions of Milton Brown and the Light Crust Doughboys.

JIMMY THOMASON: "In those days, to sell that flour, they had to do a lot of PR work. They drove down to Waco in a car with the sound system on top. It wasn't a bus. Whoever they knew in town, they'd go over there and broadcast from the car. Well, they were over in East Waco and they parked in front of our postman's house. And we went down there and, sure enough, there was Bob Wills, Milton Brown, and Herman Arnspiger. O'Daniel was the master of ceremonies. One of the first songs I remember Milton doing was that deal, 'Crazy 'bout Nancy Jane.' I remember that very well. I also remember the smile on Milton's face. He sure seemed to be enjoying that work. Wills looked like a human dynamo at that particular time. He

The Light Crust Doughboys, KFJZ radio, Fort Worth, late 1930 or early 1931. From left: Milton Brown (vocals), Derwood Brown (guitar), Truett Kimzey (announcer), Bob Wills (fiddle), Herman Arnspiger (guitar). Derwood, fifteen, was a recent addition to the group. Courtesy Marvin Montgomery.

The High Fliers, KTAT radio, Fort Worth, c. 1930. Seated, from left: Claude Davis (mandolin), Clifford Gross (fiddle), Ocie Stockard (banjo). Standing, from left: Ramon DeArman (bass), Herman Arwine (guitar). Gross and DeArman would later join the Light Crust Doughboys while Stockard became a charter member of the Musical Brownies. Courtesy Ocie Stockard.

The Light Crust Doughboys, on the road for the first time, March 1931. During this trip, Burrus Mill general sales manager W. Lee O'Daniel replaced Truett Kimzey as the Doughboys' new announcer. Standing in front of the bus, from left: W. Lee O'Daniel, Blaine Thompson (Burrus Mill sales manager), unknown, Herman Arnspiger (guitar), Bob Wills (fiddle), Milton Brown (vocals), Derwood Brown (guitar), unknown. Courtesy Roy Lee and Ellen Brown.

The Light Crust Doughboys, out of uniform but still dapper men-about-town, Fort Worth, 1931. From left: Milton Brown, Derwood Brown, Bob Wills, Herman Arnspiger. Courtesy Roy Lee and Ellen Brown.

The Light Crust Doughboys, broadcasting from the home of W. Lee O'Daniel on WBAP, Fort Worth, 1932. From left: Clifton "Sleepy" Johnson (guitar), Bob Wills (fiddle), Milton Brown (vocals), W. Lee O'Daniel (announcer). Sleepy Johnson is wearing the sweater of the recently fired Herman Arnspiger. Courtesy Roy Lee and Ellen Brown.

The Fort Worth Doughboys, c. February 1932. In conjunction with the release of their first record for Victor, the four members of the Light Crust Doughboys had this picture taken, sans their Doughboy uniforms. From left: Sleepy Johnson (guitar), Bob Wills (fiddle), Derwood Brown (guitar), Milton Brown (vocals). Courtesy Roy Lee and Ellen Brown.

enjoyed it so much. I got to thinking, 'Man, these guys get to do this every day!' We listened faithfully to the Doughboys after they got on WBAP. It came on at noon, just the right time, when people were home having lunch. And that radio would be on. Even if your radio wasn't working, you could listen to your neighbor's because his was up high enough anyway [laughs].

"And Milton was the idol of every boy in Waco. Radio was popular, period. That was all you had back then. You went to school activities, you went to church, and you listened to radio. I remember the first radio that my daddy bought. You talk about having to hock the family jewels to get it, we did. I don't know what it cost, but I will never forget that thing. It didn't matter what we heard either. We just had to sit on one end and hear somebody else on the other.

"I can remember the thirties, 1931 and 1932 when they were paying my uncle to plow his cotton under. Instead of harvesting the crop. You remember that tune they used to sing on the Opry? 'Eleven Cent Cotton and Forty Cent Meat'? It was worse than that back there. We used to say that you couldn't raise a fight in Waco with a barrel of whiskey and a bunch of iron workers. That's how slow it was. We couldn't raise nothin'."

Another fan of the Light Crust Doughboys was Ernie "Red" Varner, who later became an accomplished guitarist. Varner first heard Milton Brown sing with the Doughboys when he too was living in Waco.

RED VARNER: "The year was 1931. Somehow, the word reached us, me and my friend Roy Armitage, that the Light Crust Doughboys were coming to town and would be playing a program from, at that time, Waco's only radio station, WACO. Someone at the station told us to come on up and take in the show. We could sit just outside the broadcasting room and view the performers and the master of ceremonies through the large double-paned picture window. You could see windows like that one in all of the large and small radio studios of the time. There was something—something indefinable, I guess, about watching someone perform in front of a microphone and knowing that hundreds, maybe thousands of people are out there listening.

"The moment finally came. There they were, in the flesh, standing there right before us, dressed to the nines and ready to play for the listening audience as well as for those of us just outside the window who would see and hear the program. On violin, there was Bob Wills; on guitar, Herman Arnspiger, who until recently was always

'Herman Ironspiker' to me. That's the way I heard it. The singer was Milton Brown. The announcer was W. Lee O'Daniel. A moment for tuning, a word of introduction just after the 'on the air' light came on, and they were off and running. It was a grand program. Roy and I agreed that we had never heard anything like it. This was the first time that he or I had been that close to musicians who played full time for a living."

MARVIN "ROBBY" ROBINSON: "We lived in the same block as the Browns. There was a twelve-, thirteen-, fourteen-year difference between my age and Milton's. He was a young man-about-town and I was just a kid. So we were not what you might call 'runnin' mates.' I was born in 1918 so Derwood was more my age than Milton was. I remember that Derwood was runnin' around with the boys that were the big bullies.

"I first heard Milton on the radio in 1931. That's when I was living in Riverside. I was going to Riverside High School and was thirteen or fourteen years old. By this time I was well into country-type music. This new type of music got rid of that other type. 'Cowboy Jack' and a bunch of those that were strictly cowboy. I don't like this modern jazz, but Milton sang the kind that I liked. After he hit the air there was nothing to compete with him. The closest that come to it was down on West Seventh Street at the Melrose. They had three different singers that would come down there in person but they were doing what was being done in those days: songs like 'Utah Carroll' and 'Cowboy Jack.' At that time, Milton was getting the publicity in the Doughboys. I didn't know Bob Wills was the fiddle player or even that Derwood was the guitar player. But I just loved Milton's brand of music."

In addition to barnstorming for Light Crust Flour, Milton Brown and the band continued to play dances every Saturday night at Crystal Springs. O'Daniel had nothing to do with the group's dance engagements and constantly worried about what those "disreputable establishments" would do to Light Crust Flour's reputation. The Light Crust Doughboys' repertoire as the Doughboys differed greatly from what was played at the dance halls. On the radio, with W. Lee O'Daniel in charge, songs were limited to those with "high moral character," meaning old-time ballads about mother, home, religion, and family. Milton Brown sang these tunes with great affection, but he knew that people also wanted more up-to-date numbers, especially at dances. During rehearsals at Will Ed Kemble's furniture store, the Doughboys listened to all the latest 78 rpm recordings, which Kemble sold. Through these records, Milton expanded his vocal repertoire to include popular and jazz tunes, some of which he had learned while with his vocal group in the late 1920s.

Because of O'Daniel's objections, the Doughboys were not allowed to promote their dances on the radio. When that became evident, Papa Sam Cunningham had flyers printed up and distributed around town. On these flyers, Cunningham stressed dancing, but also informed the public that Crystal Springs, located "four miles out on the White Settlement Road," was available for swimming and fishing as well ("Get your minnows at Crystal Springs"). One flyer included a poem that identified members of the Doughboys band:

> Crystal Springs the place to play,
> Join us friends and help us stay.
> The way to stay and always play
> Is keep your booze and drunks away,
> Bring your friends and families here
> Dough Boys Band you will like to cheer.
>
> Brown will sing and the strings will ring,
> Dough Boys Band plays everything.
> Sleepy cries and wipes his eyes,
> And plays his banjo mighty wise.
> Brown and Ocie, young and gay,
> Their guitars, they sure can play.
> This thought we have for you tonight.
>
> This cake of soap we hand you tonight,
> We hope will keep you clean and right.
> Right is what we mean to say,
> Please keep your drunks and booze away.
> Dear friends come and treat us right,
> And have no passing out at night.

From the very beginning, Mr. and Mrs. Samuel C. Cunningham insisted on stressing a family atmosphere at Crystal Springs. There was never an age restriction at the dance hall, and children often were seen dancing or sitting at tables while their parents danced. Warnings to drinkers to stay away were included on most announcements, and Cunningham's son Henry, an imposing figure at well over two hundred pounds, was the first in a series of bouncers Papa Sam employed to keep order. Respect for the neighborhood, sparse as it was, was also foremost in Papa Sam's mind. The bottom of the above flyer had one final piece of advice: "Friends, when you leave at night, please leave quiet—That'll treat our neighbors right."

To further emphasize the atmosphere of clean, down-home fun, Papa Sam handed out a free cake of soap to each dancer, a custom celebrated in his poem.[9]

Four musicians were mentioned in the poem: Milton Brown, Sleepy Johnson, Derwood Brown, and Ocie Stockard. The inclusion of Stockard and the exclusion of Bob Wills from the flyer is a mystery. At no time, according to Roy Lee Brown, did the band play without Wills's fiddle, nor was Stockard used to replace Wills or augment the band on fiddle, although Ocie was an accomplished breakdown fiddler. Stockard and Johnson's instruments were inadvertently transposed in the poem. Ocie played strictly tenor banjo by this time, and was still a regular member of the High Fliers. Sleepy Johnson played tenor guitar, although he too played fiddle with a later aggregation of High Fliers in Oklahoma City.

With the success of the Light Crust Doughboys in 1931, string band music took a quantum leap in popularity. KFJZ's High Fliers added June Eldon Whalin to play bass fiddle. Late that year, O'Daniel moved the Light Crust Doughboys program to WBAP at 12:30 in the afternoon. On KTAT, another string band started broadcasting: the Southern Melody Boys. More than any other early radio band, the Southern Melody Boys started the change in direction for Texas string bands from hillbilly to jazz. An original member was Kenneth Pitts, who later became popular with the Light Crust Doughboys. Pitts and boyhood friend Cecil Brower were the group's violinists:

KENNETH PITTS: "I was born December 15, 1913, in a wide place in the road called San Simon, Arizona. My dad was a bricklayer and traveled around everywhere. We came to Fort Worth in 1919 when I was about five or six years old. We got a little old apartment over on Bessie Street. Finally my dad bought and renovated a house over on East Terrell. We lived there a few years and then moved on out to Glenwood. My mother and I lived a lot of different places after the family broke up in about 1927.

"We were living over on Terrell St. and I used to buy those little tin whistles down at Woolworth and play up a storm on those things. Somebody brought an old cornet around the house and I got a hold of that thing and started experimenting with it and finally started playing some tunes on it. My mother and dad noticed that and decided to start giving me music lessons. I started with old Wylbert Brown who lived right around the corner. I started taking violin lessons with him in the early twenties right before we moved to Glenwood. In a year's time I was playing very complex tunes. I used to play with the Lions Club and all those things. Wylbert played with the Haywire Fiddle Band. Me and Cecil Brower both grew up playing together. We were in the Junior Harmony Club. We called it the Juvenile Delinquents' Harmony Club [laughs]. It was through taking lessons with Wylbert that I met Cecil. I remember we used to play a tune called 'The Juggler.' We'd get on stage and had costumes on and play that thing. Cecil always outplayed me a bit, in some ways. He didn't study on it like I did and didn't really know as much about it but he could play without having to practice hard and I couldn't. I still have to practice like a demon to keep going. Anyway, Blanke Sorrels used to run an orchestra and I played in it and anything I could get my hand on to continue playing."

Wylbert Brown was born in Missouri in 1894, but he taught violin in Fort Worth from just after World War I until 1939, when he moved to Hollywood. No relation to Milton or the Brown family, Wylbert Brown was an original member of the WBAP studio orchestra and the original, all-male gospel singing group, Bewley's Chuck Wagon Gang (not to be confused with the Carter family quartet, also known as the Chuck Wagon Gang). He also played in the orchestra of the Southwestern Exposition Fat Stock Show and Rodeo and the Paul Whiteman Orchestra for four years. Looking forward to the Texas centennial of 1936, Brown copyrighted the words to "The Eyes of Texas" in 1928, hoping that it would be selected as the state song.[10] Less than a year before his death on February 2, 1987, at the age of ninety-two, Wylbert Brown spoke via telephone from his home in Roseburg, Oregon, about his years in Fort Worth:

WYLBERT BROWN: "I had several classes teaching violin and Kenneth Pitts was my second student. I used to take Fritz Kreisler arrangements of classical solos and boy, would he play them! I also taught Cecil Brower and Buck Buchanan. All three later played with the Light Crust Doughboys. What I taught Kenneth and Cecil mostly was the classical method of bow handling. Most hillbillies had no technique in bowing at all. Kenneth was real good. Those two were so talented, they could have picked up anything I taught them and played it. I led a group orchestra and a string quartet and Kenneth and Cecil were in the quartet. Cecil was a lot more spunky than Kenneth, and I taught him to use the 'tremolo mute.' This was a small spring with a ball bearing attached to it. You'd put it on the bridge of the fiddle and when you bowed, it would produce a vibrating sound like it was being played under water. I used it when I went to

Hollywood to play trick violin in concert.[11] Kenneth was better at playing double stops but they were both exceptionally good harmony players. They learned to play harmony with each other right from the start. I knew that they were also playing in the hillbilly bands, although they weren't aware that I knew. They were hiding it from me [laughs]!"

Cecil Brower was born in Bellevue, Texas, located near Bowie, about sixty miles northwest of Fort Worth, on November 28, 1914. The only child of Vera and Hubert Brower, Cecil moved with his family to San Pedro, California, near the port of Long Beach, when he was still a boy. From there the family moved to Fort Worth in 1924. Cecil graduated from Polytechnic High School and also attended Texas Christian University, where he majored in music. His father was in the navy before becoming a city detective in Fort Worth. Unable to play any musical instrument, Hubert Brower vowed that his son would learn to play *something*. So Cecil began taking violin lessons from Wylbert Brown along with fellow student Kenneth Pitts.

KENNETH PITTS: "Finally, when I graduated from high school, I started to get into the Southern Melody Boy thing. That was in 1931. Cecil was the driving force that got us together but it was one of those things that just kind of happened. The original Southern Melody Boys were Cecil Brower and I, Bob Wren, and Burk Reeder. Burk played guitar and Bob played tenor banjo.[12]

"In that band, I started to play 'fiddle' as opposed to 'violin.' The difference was stylistic. I played 'fiddle' out of necessity. I learned some of those old breakdowns and played them. We didn't play hoedowns with the Southern Melody Boys, we played all popular music. And played it in a good violin style. We were quite well known in this part of the country for our duet work, Cecil and I. We could get a good sound in tune because of our training. I don't like to criticize the guys that grew up playing country music but frequently they don't play in tune. But Cecil and I played exactly right on pitch. All the time.

"There used to be a root beer stand across the street from William James School on Nashville. They got us up there to play and to draw the customers in and we made about fifty cents a night commission. We played up at that thing, which kind of got us started. This was sometime in the summer of 1931. I graduated high school in February 1931. Somebody called from WBAP even, and we played there too. Just to do it, we didn't get paid anything. We played a root beer stand up on North Main, too, Ace's Root Beer stand. Tommy Duncan used to play guitar and sing up there a lot.

"Anyway, Burk Reeder got cancer and died and we replaced him with Hubert Barham. Then he moved over and played bass and Raymond DeArman joined about that time. Our theme song was 'La Golondrina,' an old Mexican folk tune. That was the song that made us famous. Everybody recognized that immediately when we came on. We played a lot of the sweet stuff, but we also played some jazz. Whatever was popular. I remember one of our big deals was 'Tiger Rag.' I remember when 'Sweet Georgia Brown' came out, we latched onto that one in a hurry.[13]

"There was an old jazz tune called 'Business in F' that we used to play. It wasn't much of a tune for a fiddle band really. We had a little arrangement that made it go pretty well.[14] I played some take-off choruses but Cecil was the main thrust on that. He had more of a knack for it than I had. He always had that fine tone coming through which made anything he played sound better than me."

The introduction of jazz to string band music did not belong solely to the Southern Melody Boys. Bit by bit, group by group, Fort Worth musicians were learning ways of combining popular tunes with old-time country songs, all played on traditional folk instruments. Milton Brown began singing popular and jazz songs in the 1920s and continued performing them with the Light Crust Doughboys, although neither Bob Wills nor Herman Arnspiger could play take-off choruses. The Southern Melody Boys, with Cecil Brower and Kenneth Pitts leading the way, became the first string band to feature improvised solos, patterned after the work of jazz violinist Joe Venuti.

KENNETH PITTS: "Part of the theory is that we really didn't have brains enough to leave it alone. In a way we should have left it alone because it wasn't the music for us. 'Business in F' wasn't right for a fiddle band. 'Tiger Rag' was all right for us to play. Of course 'Sweet Jennie Lee' or 'Sweet Georgia Brown' lent themselves well to Cecil taking a chorus or me doing one.

"We played at some residences and they'd take up a collection and give it to us. Sometimes we'd make two or three dollars. Most time, less. But that was like making forty dollars now. We played some clubs in Dallas once, too. Dorothy Lamour was singing there with some bandleader.[15] We made about $4.50 apiece that night. That was good money.

"On the other hand, there was an old place out on the North Side that we played at and not one customer would come in for hours at a time. Then somebody would see somebody coming down the road and we'd say 'Strike up a tune! There's a car coming [laughs]!' Boy, times were hard then. My mother and I got down to the time when we didn't have any money or food in the house at all."

The Southern Melody Boys were heard on KTAT as far away as Waco, where Red Varner and his friend Roy Armitage decided to attend a broadcast by the popular group by traveling to Fort Worth.

RED VARNER: "The year was 1932. Roy Armitage and I had come to Fort Worth from Waco one step above the shanks-mare or thumb-in-the-air method. We had used the services of a Depression-time business: the Texas Travel Bureau. If you owned an automobile and were making a trip of twenty-five to fifty miles or more, you could drop by the bureau and maybe pick up a paying passenger. If they had someone there who was going in your direction, chances were good that your expenses would be covered at least as far as gasoline and oil were concerned. Fare for ninety or a hundred miles was maybe a dollar, two at the most per person.

"The Texas Travel Bureau driver put us in Fort Worth in time to visit two radio stations that day. We would hear the Southern Melody Boys on KTAT and the High Fliers on KFJZ. When we walked into the KTAT studios, the Southern Melody Boys were in the midst of preparations for that day's broadcast. Someone in the studio noticed us standing outside the viewing window. I don't remember how we knew it was Cecil Brower who came out to speak to us, but it *was* Cecil. He made sure that we were comfortable, made sure we could see everything and everybody around the microphone, said something like, 'Hope you enjoy the program,' and went back into the studio. Enjoy the program we did! It was not often that musical groups of that kind sound so well rehearsed. And certainly it was not often that you could find two violinists playing two parts that had the sound of written preparation. We heard from one source and then another that Kenneth Pitts was responsible for the writing and that he and Cecil worked on what was written until it flowed like the spoken lines of a fine actor who has the knack of sounding like he is ad-libbing just as he would in ordinary, everyday conversation. Most of the two-fiddle teams that we heard in those years sounded like they were faking every note they played.

"The musical programs offered by the Southern Melody Boys always showed careful preparation. The way they played together showed a deep interest in music and a love for what they were doing. If you listened to the Southern Melody Boys, you were hearing music played well.

"When we visited the High Fliers at their program, Ocie Stockard was playing the fiddle. On that day, I noticed that he held the bow with the fourth finger of his right hand tucked next to the frog between hair and stick with the four fingers draped over the stick. I don't know why he held the bow that way. Seven years later when I finally met him, he was playing violin in a five- or six-man group and holding the bow in the normal position. I never got around to asking him why he held the bow that way. Herman Arnspiger was the guitarist that day. He had left the Light Crust Doughboys and played for a while with the High Fliers. The High Flier reception was as courteous and cordial as that of the Southern Melody Boys. They invited us into the broadcasting room. Chairs were provided and we watched the show in an atmosphere of friendly welcome and comfort. I still appreciate that kind treatment. Maybe they realized that our interest was genuine. Roy and I agreed that we had had two very pleasant visits with two groups of fine people."

In February 1932, a recording team from the Victor recording company in New York City arrived in Dallas to make records. Eli Oberstein, director of artists and repertoire, led the expedition and immediately contacted the local radio stations to procure talent for the sessions. The main attraction for Victor was the famous Blue Yodeler, Jimmie Rodgers, despite the fact that Rodgers had fallen upon hard times. His health was failing and his record sales had dropped dramatically because of the Depression.[16]

Other artists who recorded at the Jefferson Hotel in Dallas ranged from Shreveport's Jimmie Davis, then a Jimmie Rodgers imitator singing bawdy country blues tunes, to the black blues singer "Rambling" Willard Thomas.

Will Ed Kemble heard Victor was in town, and it was probably he who suggested that the Doughboys record.[17] On February 9, 1932, the Light Crust Doughboys, then consisting of Milton Brown, Sleepy Johnson, Bob Wills, and Derwood Brown, recorded two takes each of two tunes which were credited to Milton: "Sunbonnet Sue" and "Nancy Jane." The Victor logs described the vocals as by "Milton Brown and the Orchestra."[18] Roy Lee Brown remembered Milton and Derwood coming home after the session was over and excitedly telling their family that they had met the great Jimmie Rodgers.

The Victor logs and subsequent record releases on Victor and Bluebird of the two titles listed the group as the "Fort Worth Dough-boys." The reason for renaming the group for the purpose of this session is open to speculation. Wills, Johnson, and Derwood Brown all told Wills biographer Charles Townsend that the change was "due to Burrus Mill policy."[19] However, it is also possible that the name was changed by Milton Brown, who did not want to cause trouble between the band and W. Lee O'Daniel. It is unlikely that O'Daniel would have allowed the singing of the risqué "Nancy Jane" on the Doughboys' radio program, with its rather salacious references to the effects produced by the girl in the title, although Waco resident Jimmy Thomason recalled Milton singing the song at personal appearances with the Doughboys. O'Daniel may not have been present on those occasions. Opposed to anything that smacked of loose morals, O'Daniel kept tight control on the Doughboys' repertoire on their radio program and would undoubtedly have rejected any association of Burrus Mill with "that type" of music.

Milton Brown and W. Lee O'Daniel may have agreed that if the group recorded, they should do so under another name. However, Milton may have changed the name deliberately without O'Daniel's knowledge in order to copyright his own compositions. Several months later, on June 9, 1932, Milton filed a copyright for the Light Crust Doughboys' theme song, which he called "The Fort Worth Doughboys from WBAP."[20] This move proved to be fortuitous, because it enabled Milton to thwart O'Daniel's attempts to sue Bob Wills for using the Doughboy theme song when Wills formed his own band in Waco in 1933.

Also, we do not know whether W. Lee O'Daniel was really interested in recording in 1932. If he was, he would certainly have used some of his own compositions, as he did when the Light Crust Doughboys recorded under their own name for Vocalion in October 1933. Burrus Mill, like most other businesses during the Depression, was struggling and needed any kind of publicity it could get. Royalties on a recording, even if it were just the Doughboys' theme song, would have had a definite, positive return for the company, considering the popularity of the radio program and the group.

When the recording of "Nancy Jane" and "Sunbonnet Sue" was released, a flyer promoting the record (Victor 23653) was issued. Printed by the Texas Radio Sales Company on Commerce Street in Dallas, it featured a photograph of the "Fort Worth Doughboys": Milton and Derwood Brown, Bob Wills, and Sleepy Johnson, making no mention of W. Lee O'Daniel or Burrus Mill. It was one of the few times the Doughboys were photographed without O'Daniel in the picture. Underneath was the caption "New Victor Artists, but old time favorites on Radio Station W.B.A.P. every day from 12:30 to 12:45 o'clock noon, and 6:45 to 7:00 Tuesday, Thursday and Saturday evenings. Don't fail to hear their first Victor Record. It will convince you what Texas Boys can do." All four musicians are beaming confidently, even the usually stoic Sleepy Johnson, and all are neatly dressed in matching suits and ties. When promoting Light Crust Flour, the Doughboys usually dressed either in sweaters with their initials on their sleeves and the Light Crust logo (a lyre) across the chest or in gleaming white uniforms with caps bearing the words "Light Crust Doughboys." It is unlikely that W. Lee O'Daniel had any knowledge of what his employees were doing.

The Victor record released by the Fort Worth Doughboys is the earliest example of Milton Brown's singing and the earliest released example of Bob Wills's fiddle playing.[21] On the records, Wills sticks to the melody and utters a sound only when Milton is singing. On "Nancy Jane," Milton sings the verses while Bob and Derwood provide the harmony vocals on the refrain. Derwood's heavy rhythm on guitar is evident on both tracks, with Sleepy Johnson playing tenor guitar. Milton, Derwood, and Bob all provide hollers on "Nancy Jane," although Milton's are the most audible. Since there was only one microphone present, it would have been necessary for Bob and Derwood to back away from the mike when Milton was about to sing. Both Bob and Derwood's hollers are faint but evident. Milton seemed to have stayed close to the microphone, and his hollers included the words "Oh, Nancy!" (twice), and "Ah ha, she's killing me!" Bob utters two "aaah-ha's" and two "haa's" and Derwood says "Oh, Nancy!" once. On the original record of "Nancy Jane" by the Famous Hokum Boys, Big Bill Broonzy hollers "Aww, do it!" and "Aww now!" during instrumental breaks, sounding very much like Milton would two years later. There are no hollers on "Sunbonnet Sue," which runs at a more sprightly tempo with heavier rhythm by Derwood.

Although the group did not realize it at the time, the style we now call western swing was going through a critical transitional period. In comparing the Fort Worth Doughboys' record to other contemporary string band recordings in the Southwest, one can make several observations. First and foremost is the presence of a vocal, not just any vocal but a sophisticated, smoother sound, more associated with the big city than the dry, dusty sound of cowboy vocalists such as Carl T. Sprague or Jules Verne Allen. Even Dallas's Marc Williams,

"IMITATING"?

whose sobriquet was "the Cowboy Crooner," had a style closer to that of the type of singer Vernon Dalhart was imitating rather than the jazz/pop singers Milton Brown resembled. Singers such as Williams, "Peg" Moreland, and Fort Worth radio personality Cecil Gill were little more than balladeers, Texas's folksingers, who borrowed neither style nor repertoire from pop or jazz sources.

Before the Doughboys' arrival, Texas string bands were predominantly instrumental groups.[22] Some of the few vocals that existed were by Prince Albert Hunt, whose harsh singing style was nearly unintelligible. Aside from Hunt's recordings, vocals on Texas string band records were virtually nonexistent. Thus, the appearance in 1932 of a string band with not only a featured vocalist but one with an uptown, jazzy sound was not just an anomaly, it was unheard of. The effect Milton Brown's vocals had on singers and string bands in the Southwest was nothing short of revolutionary.

The second remarkable aspect of the Doughboys' record is the rhythm, which was heavier, emphasizing the off-beat. Both Derwood Brown and Sleepy Johnson would later develop their talents further to include take-off solos and improvised runs. However, on "Nancy Jane" and "Sunbonnet Sue" there is still no improvisation, one ingredient that marks a major difference between string band music and western swing. The reason I cannot consider this record *the* first western swing recording is, ironically, the presence of Bob Wills himself. Although considered by many to be the father of the genre, Bob Wills could not play jazz. On the Fort Worth Doughboys' sides, Wills plays melody, without variation. Wills's fiddle on these two sides exists as the one holdover from the Texas string band tradition. Every other aspect of the recordings—jazzy vocals, syncopated rhythm, and repertoire—was entirely new.

BULLSHIT

The Fort Worth Doughboys' record is also singular because it provides us with the only recorded evidence of Milton Brown and Bob Wills performing together. For whatever reason—his abilities as a fiddler, the band's decision about its sound, or the recording company's preferences—Bob Wills restricted his performance to melodies. In later years, Wills always had on hand at least one accomplished violinist to play the jazz he loved.[23]

On February 22, 1932, the sixteen-year-old Derwood Brown got married. His bride, Opal Grace Towery, was a student at Stripling High School, where Derwood met her. The new member of the Brown family was petite (about five-foot-two) and dark-haired. Derwood quit school and supported his new wife by playing dances with the Doughboys at Crystal Springs, where Opal became a regular patron. Although he was unofficially a regular member of the Doughboys and played their radio program on WBAP, Derwood was not a paid employee of Burrus Mill. Now having a wife to support, Derwood asked Milton to see if W. Lee O'Daniel could put him on salary.

ROY LEE BROWN: "So, Milton went in and talked to O'Daniel. Now, this wasn't an easy thing to do because none of the Doughboys ever had enough nerve to talk to O'Daniel except Milton. And he said, 'Mr. O'Daniel, I have a family to take care of and I need more money than what you're paying me.' Each member of the Doughboys was getting fifteen dollars a week. Derwood wasn't paid anything. Crystal Springs was his livelihood. Milton had me, Dad, Mama, Derwood, and Derwood's wife, Opal, to support. Plus, Dad didn't even work half the time anymore. I think maybe Opal was pregnant at the time, too.

"Well, O'Daniel was adamantly against the Doughboys playing dances. Period. He complained about it all the time. He didn't want them to play those places because they were considered beer joints and they had dancing there and no respect for religion and all those other things. He may have thought that it might give Light Crust Flour a bad name if people knew the group was associated with those places. I don't even think O'Daniel ever went out to Crystal Springs. Milton didn't want to quit playing dances because he could see a future there. But Milton decided that for the sake of his family, he'd try and make a deal with O'Daniel. So he went in and asked for a raise. I don't think he specified an amount. He just asked for a raise for himself, not for the band. He also asked O'Daniel to give Derwood a job. In return, he told O'Daniel that the Doughboys would quit playing dances altogether and spend all their time working for him. So O'Daniel said, 'Well, Milton, let me think it over.' And Milton went home and started to prepare for O'Daniel's answer.

"Milton figured that if he had to quit playing dances, he might as well get something out of it. Derwood needed to play dances because unless O'Daniel gave him a job, he would have to find work elsewhere."

Milton Brown made his proposal to W. Lee O'Daniel early in September 1932. The Depression was at its nadir and Milton knew that if O'Daniel turned him down (as he fully expected), then he would have to make a decision to leave the security of the regular paycheck he was receiving from Burrus Mill and strike out on his own.

After three years of Herbert Hoover, the United States was also in the mood for a change. Running for reelection, President Hoover was opposed by the smiling, confident, ambitious Democratic nominee from New York, Governor Franklin Delano Roosevelt. In a campaign speech in Georgia, Roosevelt said that "the country demands bold, persistent experimentation. . . . Above all, try something." Milton Brown, another bold innovator with a confident, smiling, charismatic presence, probably never heard Roosevelt's words that day. But he no doubt would have agreed with them. As he anxiously waited for O'Daniel's response to his offer, Milton busily prepared for the consequences. Within several months, America would witness the explosive effects of the progressive innovations of the New Deal. In the city of Fort Worth, Texas, in a small house on Darcy Avenue, singer Milton Brown discussed with his parents a smaller revolution, a revolution that would have little effect on the country as a whole, but a powerful and lasting effect on American music.

FIVE

How Do You Do, We're Here
to Sing to You

(1932)

Milton Brown fully expected W. Lee O'Daniel to turn down his request to raise his salary and hire Derwood as a full-time member of the Light Crust Doughboys. Since his earliest days singing with his sister in Stephenville, Milton had wanted to be an entertainer and lead his own band. But his vocal talents needed the backing of musicians capable of complementing the kind of music he wanted to perform. Unfortunately, that was exactly the kind of music that W. Lee O'Daniel detested: music made for dancing. After nearly two years with the Light Crust Doughboys, Milton realized that not only was O'Daniel controlling the Doughboys' repertoire but now he was threatening to stop him from playing dances, where Milton would often make many times his weekly salary as a Doughboy. As he and Derwood waited for O'Daniel's decision, Milton half hoped the tyrannical flour salesman would reject his proposal.

ROY LEE BROWN: "Finally, about a week after Milton asked for a raise, O'Daniel called him back into his office, and he told him 'All right, Milton, I've been thinking about your situation and here's what I'll do for you. I'll raise you up to $25 a week. But I cannot use Derwood.' Milton thought for a moment and said, 'Well, in that case, I want to turn in my resignation. I'll give you a week's notice.' So Milton played out the week and did his last program for the Light Crust Doughboys on a Saturday morning. He was one of the few people who parted on good terms with O'Daniel. O'Daniel could have hired Derwood if he had wanted to, but he couldn't see the need for it. Not knowing music, he could not see the benefit Derwood brought to the Doughboys by singing harmony behind Milton, playing lead guitar, and also providing good rhythm.

"The following Monday afternoon, Milton went on the air with the Musical Brownies. He already had his band set up. He figured O'Daniel wouldn't give Derwood a job."

The last Light Crust Doughboys broadcast on which Milton Brown sang was probably Saturday, September 17, 1932, on WBAP. The earliest appearance in the *Fort Worth Press*'s radio listings of the Musical Brownies was on the following Monday, September 19, when they played a special evening program on KTAT. Shortly after, the listings for their regular noon show began.

ROY LEE BROWN: "They had that evening program for a little while and then moved to the noon hour, six days a week. For a while they played Sunday afternoons at about 4:00. I would go to a western movie on Sundays and when I would get out, I would go straight to KTAT and listen to the program. Usually I had a friend with me."

W. Lee O'Daniel, confident that the Doughboys could survive without their popular vocalist, was cordial and fair to Milton when he resigned. In addition to allowing him to play out the week, O'Daniel gave Milton one week's extra pay. Milton's replacement in the Doughboys was Thomas Elmer "Tommy" Duncan, a singer and guitarist who was well known at Robin's Barber Shop, where Ocie Stockard had worked. For a time, Duncan worked as a pants-presser behind a counter at the rear of the shop. Before joining the Doughboys, Duncan also frequented the Ace High Root Beer stand on the North Side, singing and yodeling Jimmie Rodgers songs and playing guitar. He left the Doughboys with Bob Wills for Waco in 1933, beginning a long and fruitful relationship as Bob's lead vocalist.

The other two members of the Light Crust Doughboys, Bob Wills and Sleepy Johnson, remained with O'Daniel, although it is likely that Milton invited them to leave the Doughboys and join his band.[1] Sleepy was a good musician but was more of a country fiddler than what Milton was looking for. Similarly, Bob Wills, an otherwise excellent breakdown fiddler, was incapable of doing the two things essential to jazz performance: improvising and playing in meter.

ROY LEE BROWN: "I have heard a lot of things over the years about both Bob and Milton wanting to lead the Doughboys and that was why they split up. Now it's true that they both wanted to lead a band, but that wasn't the reason they split up. Milton always considered Bob his close friend and likewise with Bob. Milton would never have done anything to hurt Bob. He liked Bob a whole lot and despite what people have said, there was never any conflict between the two of them from what I could see. Usually Bob was willing to go along with anything Milton wanted to do. I remember the first automobile Bob Wills had in Fort Worth. It was an open, four-door Model A Ford with curtains on it. It was used, but it was new to him. As soon as he got it, he, his wife Edna, his daughter Robbie Jo, me, and my cousin, Henrietta Huxford, went for a ride together. Bob and Edna lived in the 3100 block of West Seventh Street in one side of a duplex. My uncle Henry Huxford and his two daughters lived in the other side. This was after the Doughboys were going and Bob had the money to buy a car."

If not for his devotion to his family, Milton might have left the Doughboys sooner. Although he never doubted his ability to lead his own band, the security of the fifteen dollar weekly salary as a Light Crust Doughboy restrained him, until Derwood's recent marriage forced the issue.

The full impact of the Depression hit Tarrant County in the late months of 1932, just when Milton Brown was starting his band. The construction boom of the late 1920s had finally worn itself out, and when that failed and Fort Worth officials began laying off city employees, the whole economy collapsed. City employees who were allowed to keep their jobs gratefully accepted 25 percent pay cuts rather than be laid off. Shelters for impoverished children were established near Lake Worth as the entire community pitched in to raise funds for the hungry. By November, county road funds were exhausted and the trade unions cut employees' wages by 20 to 30 percent. The soup lines and Hoovervilles, which Fort Worth residents had seen only on newsreels, now became frightening realities. Burnett Memorial Park became a regular gathering spot for hundreds of unemployed and destitute men and women. In addition, the winter of 1932–33 was particularly harsh. The homeless were forced to seek shelter anywhere they could: from school basements and crowded welfare centers to ramshackle tents and park benches. People had long since given up looking for work and instead were merely trying to survive.

ROY LEE BROWN: "I don't remember seeing the soup kitchens in Fort Worth or the 'Hoovervilles.' But my mother fed many a person who came to the back door for a handout during that time. My family didn't feel the Depression like most people did, at least until Milton died. Milton and Derwood were making good money playing music at that time and Milton lived at home. Fortunately, we made it through that period pretty good."

Soon after the formation of the Light Crust Doughboys, Derwood Brown met a young man from the small town of Roanoke, Texas, named Wanna Arvin Coffman. Born on August 10, 1911, the lanky Coffman began his musical career by playing Hawaiian-style steel guitar.

WANNA COFFMAN: "Derwood and I started running around together when he was still in high school. We used to go and fool around up at WBAP all the time. Ol' Joe Kaipo was a friend of ours at WBAP. He was a real good steel guitarist and taught me and Derwood some Hawaiian tunes.[2] Anyway, I was out there in the country in Roanoke one day and Derwood came out there and invited me to come to WBAP to play a fifteen-minute program with him. I didn't ask him how much it paid because it didn't matter to me. I was just glad to play on the radio. I played steel guitar at that time. Derwood would sing in addition to playing guitar but I never did sing much. So me and ol' Derwood had a program on WBAP about three days a week. Then we'd go out and play these little ol' house parties where you'd sit in the corner like they used to do in these square dances. We played old Hawaiian tunes like 'Hilo March' and 'Song of the Islands.' That's about all I knew back then. Eventually, Derwood invited me out to their house for supper and that's how I met Milton."

In addition to his brother Derwood, Milton recruited three other Fort Worth musicians to round out his band, which he named "Milton Brown and his Musikal Brownies."[3] They included High Flier Ocie Stockard, Derwood's friend Wanna Coffman, and a seventeen-year-old fiddle player named Jesse Ashlock.

ROY LEE BROWN: "Jesse was a young kid that hung around with Bob and Milton but mainly with Bob. He was a much better fiddle player than Bob for the songs Milton wanted to do. He played the more modern stuff;[4] Bob couldn't play jazz, just melodies and breakdowns. Then Milton got Ocie Stockard from the High Fliers to play tenor banjo. For the final member, I heard Milton tell Mama that he was going to use Wanna Coffman to play bass fiddle. And she said, 'What in the world do you want with a bass fiddle?' And Milton said, 'Well, it will add to the rhythm.' Then she asked about the bow and Milton said,

The earliest known photograph of the original Musical Brownies, September 1932. The sweaters were later replaced with stylish suits. Top, from left: Derwood Brown (guitar), Jesse Ashlock (fiddle), Ocie Stockard (banjo). Bottom, from left: Milton Brown (vocals), Wanna Coffman (bass). Courtesy Ocie Stockard.

A cartoon promoting the Brownies' regular morning radio program on KTAT, sponsored by Globe Laboratories, manufacturers of vaccines for animals, c. fall 1932. Despite the image portrayed in the caricature, Milton Brown never performed in western outfits. Courtesy Roy Lee and Ellen Brown.

'Mama, he's not going to use the bow, he's going to slap it. He'll use the bow only on waltzes.' I don't know where Milton got the idea to do that, but he always was rhythm-minded. The Doughboys never used a bass fiddle at all. The only instruments they had were a fiddle and guitar, or maybe two guitars when Derwood played with them."[5]

Wanna Coffman remembered being surprised at what his new benefactor had in mind.

WANNA COFFMAN: "Derwood came out to the house in Milton's '30 model Ford, and he said, 'I want you to go to work with Milton. He's going to organize a band.' I said, 'Well, what am I going to play?' He said, 'Bass fiddle.' I said, 'I ain't never had a bass fiddle in my hand in my life, Derwood!' But then I got to thinking. The four strings on a bass are like the last four strings on a guitar: G-D-A-E. Same thing. Now I was good on the guitar; I could play chords real good. So I learned how to play a bass in an hour. And I never had had one in my hand before! Milton wanted me to pick and slap it right off. I had blood running out of my fingers for a while. It was kind of awkward at first. I was used to using those picks on the steel guitar which I had on two fingers. So at first I tried to pick it that way. Well, I saw that wasn't going to work so I just stretched my fingers out. It didn't take me long to learn how to pull those strings out and get a tone out of them. I still have a corn right here from years of bass playing. I didn't have my own bass when Derwood came out to get me. Eventually we went out to a hock shop on Main Street. And we found one: an old beat-up thing. The neck had been broke off of it and it had a wire on the top where the keys are which went right down to the bridge. That wire actually held the neck on! That was the only bass we could find in Fort Worth. I didn't give but fifteen dollars for it. So I played on it the best I could for a couple of months. Then I took it out to Old Man Stamps and he fixed the fingerboard and repaired two or three cracks that were in it."

ROY LEE BROWN: "The High Fliers had a bass fiddle that was being played by June Whalin. But he was bowing it, not slapping it like Milton wanted Wanna to do. Derwood told me that when the Brownies started, Wanna borrowed the bass fiddle from the High Fliers to play their radio program. The High Fliers got a little peeved about this borrowing after a while, so Milton got Wanna one of his own. Wanna would play at least one number on steel guitar on every radio program until Bob Dunn came along in 1934. Wanna had a National, all-steel-bodied guitar and he only played Hawaiian numbers. He was good, too. Back then, everybody that played steel guitar played Hawaiian-style. Nobody even dreamed about playing what Bob Dunn later played."

OCIE STOCKARD: "Wanna slapped his bass first. Actually he slapped at it. Then, after a while, he learned how to pick it more. Derwood played rhythm at first; he didn't do any take-off choruses in the beginning. The melody would either be played by Jesse or sung by Milton. Jesse was one of Bob's friends and he tried to learn to play breakdowns like Bob. I never taught Jesse anything; he had his way of doing things. Nobody could tell him anything.

"When Milton started his band, I left the High Fliers. Elmer Scarborough took over the band and Pat Trotter replaced me. Elmer played tenor banjo and Pat was a good hot fiddle man. Milton wanted me to play tenor banjo with his band. We'd been playing together out at Crystal Springs for a long time already so he knew me well enough. We played mostly on Saturdays and Sundays, sometimes Thursdays; Milton, Bob Wills, and me. I was with the High Fliers but I sat in with them occasionally."

Milton Brown's first fiddle player, Jesse Thedford Ashlock, was born in Walker County, Texas, on February 22, 1915. The Ashlocks were a musical family, with nearly all of Jesse's six brothers and sisters playing instruments. Brother Jim Ashlock taught Jesse to play breakdowns when Jesse was only eight. In 1926 the family moved to Fort Worth, where, in 1930, he met Bob Wills and Milton Brown. Although he was never a regular member of a string band until he became a Musical Brownie, the feisty Ashlock played with members of the Light Crust Doughboys and the High Fliers at such Fort Worth establishments as Crystal Springs and the Cinderella Roof. Eventually, Ashlock and Wills became close friends, with Jesse shadowing Bob, carefully watching and learning Wills's technique. In time, he became a first-rate breakdown fiddler.[6]

KTAT, the number two radio station in town after powerhouse WBAP, had been undergoing changes before the Musical Brownies made their debut. On Friday, September 9, 1932, the *Fort Worth Press* reported the appointment of a new commercial manager for KTAT by the Southwest Broadcasting Company. Howard Davis, formerly commercial manager at WIL in St. Louis, Missouri, was described as "redheaded and a dynamo of energy."[7] The Southwest Broadcasting Company was one of the earliest regional radio networks in the United

States. At the time of the acquisition of KTAT, the SBC owned three other radio stations: WACO (Waco), KOMA (Oklahoma City), and KTSA (San Antonio), in addition to being affiliated with KTRH (Houston), WRR (Dallas), KGKS (Amarillo), and KGKO (Wichita Falls), creating a veritable blanket over Texas and Oklahoma. Until W. Lee O'Daniel formed the Texas Quality Network in 1934, the SBC was the Southwest's most powerful network. Howard Davis's enthusiasm for the acquisition of KTAT was reflected in his statement that the ten-year-old radio industry was "still in its infancy" and by his stated intent to spend half of his time at the KTAT studios on the sixteenth floor of the Trinity Life Building, located at the corner of Seventh and Main streets in downtown Fort Worth.

Several weeks later, Howard Davis appointed a new program director at KTAT, Marvin Bennett. A seasoned announcer, Bennett had most recently worked as program director for KFYR in Bismarck, North Dakota, where he had sponsored radio personality/singer Hazel Johnson, featured on the cover of *Radio Digest* magazine.[8] Bennett would become the Musical Brownies' first announcer. His handsome, mustachioed face would be featured opposite Papa Sam Cunningham's on early Crystal Springs flyers promoting Brownies dances. It was apparent that with the addition of a new manager and new program director, KTAT was ready to take on a new string band such as the Brownies, even without a sponsor.

With the threat from W. Lee O'Daniel eliminated, Milton Brown went into high gear, using his radio program and his dance engagements at Crystal Springs to promote each other. Now that the Brownies were making personal appearances, Milton decided they needed some kind of uniform to separate them from the other bands. The Light Crust Doughboys had worn white jackets with hats only when they went on goodwill tours promoting Light Crust Flour. When the band members played dances, it was not as representatives of Burrus Mill, so they wore coats and ties. At appearances on WBAP, they usually wore sweaters with their initials sewn on the sleeves. Through his contacts with Fort Worth clothiers, Milton had five brown sweaters made up, with "Musical Brownies" sewn on the back and the figure of a "brownie" running up the chest in front.

Papa Sam, realizing that the KTAT program amounted to free advertising for Crystal Springs, began distributing four-by-six-inch postcards inviting the public to come "Dance at Crystal Springs, the Home of Milton Brown and his Musikal Brownies, Tuesday, Thursday, Saturday, and Sunday nights." The cards also encouraged customers to "hear the Brownies over KTAT Daily from 12:00 Noon to 1

P.M." and provided friendly reminders that "We do not take the advantage of our Customers on any Birthday or Holiday Dances—Our Prices are always Men, 40 cents—Ladies, 10 cents. Visit Us and Feel at Home. Watch for Opening of Our Swimming Pool."

By this time, prime time in radio for string bands had moved from 6:00 A.M. to the noon hour.[9] When the Brownies began broadcasting, Fort Worth at lunchtime featured a barrage of string band music, with the High Fliers, the Musical Brownies, and the Light Crust Doughboys each broadcasting simultaneously on KFJZ, KTAT, and WBAP, respectively. Waco fiddler Jimmy Thomason summed up the feelings of many aspiring Texas musicians upon first hearing the Brownies on KTAT.

JIMMY THOMASON: "I used to get up at 6:00 to listen to Milton when he was with the Doughboys. I didn't want to hear anybody else if I had Milton Brown. Bob Wills didn't do the things to me that Milton did, musically. Then, when Milton pulled off from the Doughboys and got on KTAT, man, I'll guarantee you, that was something! Jesse Ashlock was the first hot fiddler I'd ever heard. When I heard Jesse, and that band, with that beat, that 'Milton Brown Beat,' as we called it, why, that changed my entire outlook on music. I knew then that I wanted to play. I'd just been piddling around here in Waco, but when I heard that Brown beat, that was my incentive right there.

"I remember Tommy Duncan going with the Doughboys too. In the beginning, when Tommy joined them, I thought the Doughboys would fold up. This was how pro–Milton Brown I was. I didn't think they could operate without Milton. Then about two days after he joined, he laid an Emmett Miller thing on them. And Bob and Tommy would do the talking deal at the front of 'I Ain't Got Nobody' and to me, that's what sold the Doughboys to their audience. So, as soon as they did that, now we've got a new ballgame. Milton had his dance band and the Doughboys had a show band."

ROY LEE BROWN: "The Brownies were on KTAT every day at twelve o'clock noon except Sunday. Milton went on at noon because he figured people were on their lunch hour and could get to a radio while they had their lunch. Back then, there was no air conditioning. So all the windows in the houses were wide open during the summertime. I remember walking home and I'd walk down the street and never miss a tune. I might pass a house that had another program on, but by the time I got to the following house, there was Milton again. I've had lots of people tell me that they'd run home from school real fast at lunchtime so they could turn on the Brownies. At noontime that's what you heard. Now, you couldn't find anybody that would admit to it, but on the street you could hear it all day long. String bands. After that would finish you'd start to hear other types of music.

"See, that type of music was considered 'common.' Not sophisticated enough. Simple music. The same thing went for Crystal Springs. You couldn't find hardly anybody who would admit going to Crystal Springs, but you could go out there and see all types of people. You could find the rich out there, the poor, and everybody in between. But the majority of the people that went out there could barely afford the price of admission."

With the new band came a new theme song. The Light Crust Doughboys were still using Milton's variation on "Eagle Riding Papa," so when he decided to start his own band, Milton adapted one of his own compositions, "Sunbonnet Sue," which the Doughboys had recorded for Victor in February.

JIMMY THOMASON: "I'll never forget it. Ol' Jesse Ashlock would hit that thing and they'd be off and running at a hundred miles an hour!"

After Jesse played the introduction, Milton and Derwood Brown stepped up to the KTAT microphone and sang the words that would, for the next three and a half years, establish Milton Brown and his Musical Brownies as the Southwest's most sensational string band:

> How do you do?
> We're here to sing to you
> Our songs both old and new
> How do you do?
>
> We hope it's true
> That before we are through
> We'll chase away your blues
> How do you do?

After performing for an hour and making brief announcements of the Brownies' upcoming dances at Crystal Springs, Milton and Derwood sang the program's closing lyrics:

> Now we must go
> Our time is up you know
> You'll hear us to-mor-row
> On radio;

> We'll do our best
> To sing all your requests
> Just write and let us know
> For we must go.

ROY LEE BROWN: "I heard the first program Milton did. We didn't have a radio so we had to go next door to hear it. They were the only people on the block that had a radio."

Unfortunately, there is no evidence of recorded examples of these early Brownies radio shows. The only known transcription of Milton Brown announcing his programs was dubbed off a Brownies broadcast in 1935. Roy Lee described it.

ROY LEE BROWN: "I had a little transcription that somebody made during Milton's program when they were on WBAP. It was just a home recording off the radio. The announcer introduced Milton like he was introducing a speaker to an audience and then Milton came up and said, 'Mr. Chairman, Ladies and Gentlemen, it is a pleasure indeed to come before you to make this announcement,' and then he went ahead and told the people where the band was going to be appearing that week. I kept that record and played it until it wore out. Then it lay around the house until it finally got lost. I remember Milton bringing that record home himself. He said some guy had recorded it off the radio program on WBAP."

The initial response to the program was phenomenal. Requests began to pour in by the hundreds, despite the fact that KTAT's signal was inferior to rival station WBAP's. The Light Crust Doughboys continued with their program, but now many WBAP listeners who were Milton Brown fans switched their dials to 1240 kilocycles to listen to the Musical Brownies. Throughout their tenure on KTAT, the Brownies were without a sponsor. However, many local businesses, impressed by Milton Brown's smooth delivery as the group's announcer, requested that he read commercials for their products.

ROY LEE BROWN: "On that first program, they played the theme song and then the announcer came on and told who they were: Milton Brown and his Musical Brownies. I don't think they even did any commercials on that show. They didn't have any one sponsor. They had a bunch of sponsors. Globe Laboratories had them do a show each morning at seven o'clock except Sunday for a short while.

Globe was a laboratory out there on the North Side that made vaccines for animals. The band was still the Musical Brownies but when they did that show for Globe they called themselves 'Milton Brown and the Globe Trotters.' It was about a fifteen-minute program and lasted maybe six months."

A hilarious cartoon advertising the Globe program showed a smiling Milton, decidedly out of character in checkered shirt, cowboy boots, and hat, holding a syringe in his left hand, a hip flask conspicuously tucked snugly into a rear pocket of his jeans. When Milton sold Sal-O-Mint toothpaste, he went by the name of Milton "Sal-O-Mint" Brown. This practice went on as long as the Brownies played on KTAT. *Fort Worth Press* radio listings during April 1934 show segments by Milton Brown and his Highland Brownies and Milton Brown and his Iron Men. These constituted the first fifteen minutes of the Brownies' regular noon broadcast. At 12:15 the listings reverted back to the regular Musical Brownies name. By using partial sponsorship, Milton was able to attract money for KTAT, yet still retain the autonomy he needed to freely plug his dances.

Although the Brownies' programs had regular spot announcements, Milton never actually read them himself. That job went to station announcer Marvin Bennett. Other announcers who read spots and made other generic announcements on Brownies' programs included Mike Gallagher and Marshall Pope.

ROY LEE BROWN: "Milton got a certain amount of money for doing those spot ads. Sometimes, they'd be on the air for an hour and a half strictly because they had so many spot announcements. But the show wasn't sponsored by any one company like the Light Crust Doughboys were. When he moved from KTAT to WBAP in 1935, he didn't know that he was going to get paid for the program as well. I heard him tell Mama that he didn't realize that when he went over there that he was going to get paid to go on the air. He started on the radio with the idea that he would use the program to advertise his dances. Then he got a check for that first week for all the spot ads that were on and he knew he had something special."

The songs the Brownies performed on their program showed an immediate change from the staid hillbilly numbers W. Lee O'Daniel programmed for the Light Crust Doughboys. Milton continued singing some of the heart-tugging "weepers" like "The Prisoner's Song" and "Twenty-one Years" and the Texas anthem "Beautiful Texas." But now he was able to sing more jazz tunes and blues. Two of Milton's favorites, the Mississippi Sheiks' "Sitting on Top of the World" and "Corrine Corrina," would become popular at Crystal Springs, and the Brownies would record them at their sessions for Bluebird in 1934.

WANNA COFFMAN: "We used to go up on the second floor of Will Ed's furniture store and practice the tunes we wanted to learn. He had a piano and hauled it up there and we learned a whole lot of our tunes off of records that Will Ed sold up there. We'd keep playin' it over and over until Milton got all the words. Sometimes we'd stay up there three, four hours a day. Nobody would bother us. Some of those records we could listen to one time and know it right off. The rhythm wasn't too hard to get a hold of but sometimes Milton had trouble getting the right words. Some of those records you could hardly understand what they were saying. I think Milton tried to copy Cab Calloway when he sang 'Four or Five Times.' There were a lot of 'hi-de-ho's' in it [laughs]."

The band members were still getting used to each other, but, from the very start, the rhythm was there. With only Jesse Ashlock playing the melody, this left the other three musicians, Derwood Brown, Wanna Coffman, and Ocie Stockard, to create an unshakeable pulse. They would become the backbone of the Brownies' sound, the largest strictly rhythm section in a string band up to that time. Derwood Brown's rhythm was so insistent that it caused a tremendous strain on the strings of his guitar. Milton had to hire an extra person, usually a boy in his early teens, to keep a freshly strung guitar handy to give to Derwood when he broke a string.[10]

WANNA COFFMAN: "That was the funniest thing I ever saw. He played harder rhythm and broke more strings than anybody I've ever seen or heard of. He played too close down to the bridge. If he'd have gotten up over that sound hole, that wouldn't have happened so much. And then if that wasn't bad enough, he'd get the stiffest pick he could find, and just beat the hell out of that guitar! My brother Horace fixed strings for him for a long time after Milton died. And Derwood kept him busy sitting there fixing strings. Sometimes he had three guitars. Derwood wouldn't play more than two tunes without breaking a string [laughs]."

A. B. GILBERT: "I remember they used to make fun of Derwood on the air. They'd call him 'Chubby Break-a-String Brown.'"

Milton was happy that the Brownies' sound was jelling so quickly, but he was still not satisfied with a four-piece band. He was looking ahead to the time when the band would start playing larger venues. He knew this would happen because the regular dances at Crystal Springs were so popular that word was getting around the countryside that the Brownies were the band to dance to and Crystal Springs was the place to dance. KTAT's signal enabled Milton's announcements about Crystal Springs to reach a 100–150 mile radius around Fort Worth. But then, Milton thought about the people within the listening range of KTAT who could not afford to drive or take a train to Fort Worth for his dances. In addition, the Brownies were free three to four evenings per week. The engagements at Crystal Springs were rarely more than thrice weekly, with the heaviest attendance on Saturdays and Sundays. Within a few weeks after the Brownies' debut on KTAT, Milton began to look around for another fiddle player. He also thought about increasing the volume of his orchestra. One banjo (Ocie's) was enough, and he also had a bass and a guitar. What he needed now was an instrument that would be loud enough to take the place of several rhythm instruments, yet still be able to take jazz choruses. On a cold Thursday night in the late fall of 1932, the answer to Milton's problem walked into Crystal Springs.

SIX

Take a Chorus, Mister Calhoun!
(1932–33)

On a wintry evening at the Crystal Springs Dancing Pavilion in the late fall of 1932, a mustachioed piano player named Fred Calhoun pounded out his first notes with the popular Fort Worth string band called the Musical Brownies. At that precise moment, the several hundred couples who stopped dancing and turned their heads to identify the source of the unfamiliar sound became a part of history because then—if any one event can be said to mark the beginning of a new style—western swing was born. In the years since the Brown family moved to Fort Worth, Milton Brown had spearheaded the transition in traditional dance music in Texas from two instruments providing musical entertainment for a handful of rural families to an organized, disciplined jazz band, performing for hundreds of dancers from a variety of backgrounds.

Previously, Milton had introduced vocals and a larger rhythm section, and had expanded the musical repertoire. With the addition of a piano, played by a bona fide experienced jazz musician, he took the first drastic step away from convention. Other innovations were still to come, but the key addition to the Musical Brownies was the man who would be forever known as "Papa" Calhoun.

Born in the small north Texas town of Chico on November 30, 1904, Frederick E. Calhoun came from a family of piano players, although he himself started on drums.

FRED "PAPA" CALHOUN: "My father played, I guess, every instrument there was. He played stringed instruments: banjo, fiddle, and guitar. And then in the city band he played trombone, trumpet, bass; whatever they needed, he played it. And he also played some piano. My older brother Paul was a fine piano player. Back before I was old enough to be playing, he was already playing with dance bands. He was five years older than me. My mother and sister played piano too. I had two sisters. One was killed in an accident.

"I learned to play drums first with Paul. We'd play these little house parties and dances and I'd play drums and he'd play piano. When I was about sixteen, I had a ten-piece dance band. I played drums in that too. 'Course we were a horn band, we weren't using fiddles. But we had a Dixieland tenor banjo playing rhythm, see. Drums, saxophone, clarinet, trumpet, slide trombone. Jazz band. We played Dixie arrangements. This was when I was living in Oklahoma. I finished high school there. But that was a good band. They had musicians in there that could read those arrangements.

"We did Dixieland tunes like 'Muskrat Ramble,' 'Darktown Strutters' Ball,' 'King Porter Stomp,' things that were popular 'long about then. We'd play a lot of swing stuff like the Louisiana Five was playing back in those days. We also liked Red Nichols and Bix Beiderbecke.

"'Long about 1929 or '30 I moved to Decatur, Texas, and went to work in a mill. A friend of mine worked in a flour mill and I went to work for him. So I organized a band there, too. It was a regular horn band with just about the same setup: saxophone, trumpet, clarinet, tenor banjo, trombone, and a bass horn. Sousaphone.[1] Well, our piano player was a school teacher, and when school was out, he left. And we didn't have another piano player in town. I was teaching a boy how to play drums, he was a nice little drummer, learning to play pretty good. We had a dance coming up there Saturday night at the club there in Decatur, so I went up there and woodshedded.[2] I knew how to make a few chords. So when we went out to play the dance that night, I played piano and put this kid on drums. I never did go back to playing drums [laughs]! I started to chord around, then I started to hit a few little licks, and it just kind of came naturally to me, I guess. So that's how I got started playing piano, by necessity. If it hadn't been for that night I might still be playing drums.

"Shortly after that, I came to Fort Worth and got a job playing solo piano on KTAT three times a week. They were thirty-minute programs. The station manager, Marvin Bennett, announced the show and for some reason, he called me the Colonel from Kentucky. So we talked a pitch, you know, read commercials, and he'd ask me about horseracing in Kentucky.

"A group called the Three Jacks came in from Chicago to do a program on KTAT. They were a singing group with guitars and were big up there at the time.[3] That particular day they were scheduled to follow me and they asked if I would sit in as a guest artist on their program. So I said, 'Yeah, I'll sit in with you.' So I went in and played the program with them. When we got through they said, 'Hey, how about going with us, we're going out to Crystal Springs.' I said, 'Crystal Springs, where's that?' They said, 'Out on the edge of town there on White Settlement Road. Milton Brown and the Brownies play out there and they got a *fine* beat. You'd enjoy playing with them.' I said, 'Aww, I don't want to mess them up, they're a string band, aren't they? I've never played with a string band.' They said, 'Well, they've got the rhythm, you'll like it.' Anyhow, they talked me into going out there.[4]

"I remember this was on a Thursday night. It was wintertime and there was snow on the ground. So we got in their car and went on out there. And I'll tell you, they had a full house. On a Thursday in bad weather. That shows you how good Milton was going even then. Well, we went on inside and had some coffee at the hamburger stand there,[5] and I told Jack Stone, he was the head of the group, 'Hey, they do have good rhythm, don't they?' He said, 'Yeah, they sure do.' So we listened for a while longer and he said, 'How about sitting in with them?' I said 'No, I don't think so, Jack. I'll only mess them up.'

"I kept on drinking coffee and then I saw ol' Stone go down to the bandstand and say something to Milton. Milton leaned down off the bandstand, nodded his head, and then he went over to the piano they had on stage, pulled the lid off, took a towel and started wiping off the keys [laughs]! I knew right then that I was going to have to play.

"Milton got up to the microphone and said to the crowd, 'Ladies and gentlemen, we have a guest artist tonight. He's very talented and he's known as the Colonel from Kentucky on KTAT. He's going to sit in with us on piano.' So now I had to. So I went up there and Milton said, 'What do you want to play?' I said, 'How about "Nobody's Sweetheart," do you fellas know that?' He said, 'We sure do.' We took off on that thing; Jesse took a chorus and Milton sang. And then Milton said, 'Take a chorus, Mister Calhoun!' That's what he said. So I took a chorus on it. Then the next tune we played was a Paul Jones.[6] After that we played 'Tiger Rag.' The people started to look at us kind of funny and some of them had stopped dancing. Milton said, 'Take a chorus, Mister Calhoun!' So I took some doublehanded licks, played real fast and fancy. And when we finished that tune, EVERY-BODY had quit dancing and was all ganged around the bandstand. They'd never seen a piano in a string band before. I always played with my back to the audience so I didn't see what was going on. When I finally turned around I looked at Milton and said, 'Say, what's going on, what's the trouble?' Milton said, 'They're just watching you play.' I thought maybe there had been a fire or something!

Opal Grace Towery, sixteen, and Derwood Brown, seventeen, about the time of their marriage, February 1933. Courtesy Roy Lee and Ellen Brown.

Milton Brown and his Musical Brownies, early 1933, taken in the studios of KTAT, Fort Worth, shortly after the addition of pianist Fred "Papa" Calhoun and fiddler Cecil Brower. From left: Wanna Coffman (bass), Marshall Pope (KTAT announcer), Milton Brown (vocals), Jesse Ashlock (fiddle), Fred "Papa" Calhoun (piano), Cecil Brower (fiddle), Ocie Stockard (banjo), Derwood Brown (guitar). Courtesy Cary Ginell.

A Crystal Springs promotional photo advertising its most popular attraction, c. 1933. Standing, from left: Fred Calhoun, Cecil Brower, Jesse Ashlock, Wanna Coffman, Derwood Brown, Ocie Stockard. Seated, from left: Henry "Babe" Cunningham, Milton Brown, "Papa" Sam Cunningham. Papa Sam is listed as "manager." This refers to his role as proprietor of Crystal Springs, not to any official capacity as a representative of the Brownies. Courtesy Roy Lee and Ellen Brown.

FORT WORTH RADIO NEWS

Published each Friday for the Benefit of Radio Fans

VOLUME 1
NUMBER 3

Fort Worth, Texas, Friday, October 6, 1933

Eugene Rhinehart, Editor
913 W. 2nd St. Phone 2-8747

NEWS FROM WBAP

Jack Pearl, the modern Baron Munchausen and one of radio's most popular comedians, is returning to the air to resume the weekly tall stories which endeared him to millions of listeners last season.

The comedian, assisted by his indispensable associate, Cliff Hall, as "Sharlie," will be heard for half an hour each Saturday night over WBAP beginning at 8:00 o'clock Saturday, October 7.

* * * * *

Early morning listeners to WBAP are familiar with the entertaining songs of Cecil Gill, the Yodeling Country Boy, who is heard daily except Sunday at 6:45 a. m. Cecil is a veteran radio performer, and has a wide variety of numbers which he fills requests from his many listeners. Immediately following this program, WBAP offers 15 minutes of snappy syncopation by the Sunrise Rhythm Makers, who play rhythmical interpretations of popular selections—both old and new.

* * * * *

Lovers of organ music are always near their radio at 8:30 each morning for the "Between Us" program broadcast by WBAP. This program features the organ solos of Billy Muth, playing in the Worth Theatre. The leading soloist heard also on this program is Preston Fowler. Selected poetry is an occasional feature of this period, and the poems are read by Parker Wilson.

* * * * *

The Jewel Gems, popular orchestra heard over WBAP, daily except Sunday at 9:00 a. m., have had a swift and complete rise to popularity with the Southwest radio audience since their premier some three months ago. This group is composed of musicians with a world of stage and radio experience, and their tuneful and novel interpretations have made them prime favorites. In addition to several vocal soloists who assist the orchestra, a male trio is often featured.

* * * *

W. Lee O'Daniel and His Doughboys left this week for Chicago and the World's Fair. Consequently they will not be heard in their usual programs during the next two weeks over WBAP. The Doughboys' chief object in going to Chicago, according to Mr. O'Daniel, is to record some of their original compositions for the Brunswick Company. The availability of these records to the thousands of Doughboys' listeners will be announced upon their return.

* * * *

A feature of the WBAP Saturday program this fall will be the broad-

HILLBILLY ARTIST

MILTON BROWN

Log of North American Broadcasting Stations

Call	Location	Freq.	Call	Location	Freq.
KABC	San Antonio, Tex.	1420	WABC	New York City	860
KEX	Portland, Ore.	1180	WBCN	Chicago, Ill.	870
KFAB	Lincoln, Neb.	770	WABZ	New Orleans, La.	1200
KFDM	Beaumont, Tex.	560	WACO	Waco, Tex.	1240
KFI	Los Angeles, Cal.	640	WAPI	Birmingham, Ala.	1140
KFJZ	Fort Worth, Tex.	1370	WBAP	Fort Worth, Tex.	800
KFLX	Galveston, Tex.	1370	WJBT	Chicago, Ill.	700
KFUL	Galveston, Tex.	1290	WDAG	Amarillo, Tex.	1410
KFXR	Oklahoma City, Okla.	1310	WDAH	El Paso, Tex.	1310
KGFG	Oklahoma City, Okla.	1370	WDSU	New Orleans, La.	1250
KGFI	Corpus Christi, Tex.	1500	WEAF	New York, N. Y.	660
KGKL	San Angelo, Tex.	1370	WBCN	Chicago, Ill.	870
KGKO	Wichita Falls, Tex.	570	WFAA	Dallas, Tex.	800
KGO	San Francisco, Cal.	790	WLIB	Chicago, Ill.	720
KGRS	Amarillo, Tex.	1410	WHAS	Louisville, Ky.	820
KJR	Seattle, Wash.	970	WHO	Des Moines, Ia.	1000
KMAC	San Antonio, Tex.	1370	WJBO	New Orleans, La.	1420
KMOX	St. Louis, Mo.	1090	WJR	Detroit, Mich.	750
KNOW	Austin, Tex.	1500	WKY	Oklahoma City, Okla.	900
KNX	Los Angeles, Cal.	1050	WLAC	Nashville, Tenn.	1470
KOA	Denver, Colo.	830	WLW	Cincinnati, Ohio	700
KOMA	Oklahoma City, Okla.	1480	WMAQ	Chicago, Ill.	670
KONO	San Antonio, Tex.	1370	WOAI	San Antonio, Tex.	1190
KPO	San Francisco, Cal.	680	WOC	Davenport, Iowa	1000
KPRC	Houston, Tex.	920	WOWO	Fort Wayne, Ind.	1160
KRLD	Dallas, Tex.	1040	WPG	Atlantic City, N.J.	1100
KSL	Salt Lake City	1130	WRR	Dallas, Tex.	1280
KSTP	St. Paul, Minn.	1460	WRVA	Richmond, Va.	1110
KTAT	Fort Worth, Tex.	1240	WSB	Atlanta, Ga.	740
KTHS	Hot Springs, Ark.	1040	WSM	Nashville, Tenn.	650
KTLC	Houston, Tex.	1310	WTAM	Cleveland, Ohio	1070
KTRH	Houston, Tex.	1120	WTAW	College Station, Tex.	1120
KTSA	San Antonio, Tex.	1290	WTIC	Hartford, Conn.	1060

Milton Brown King of the Hillbilly Band

Milton Brown has had many names on the radio and has been introduced under different titles for the past four years, but the best of all and one that really is the one that is fitting for him is the "King of the Hillbilly Bands."

Milton started singing in this cowboy, Texas style, several years ago and has been with several different fiddle and until the right 'me came along and he now has one of the most popular bands of its kind on the air.

When the Southwest Broadcasting Company took the air on its official opening the ninth day of last February, Milton Brown and his Musical Brownies were a part of the celebration and has been a regular feature of the network up until the last thirty days when their commercial left the air and Milton received a vacation. He has possibly more radio hours to his credit than any other individual in the Southwest, participating not only his thirty minute regular noon spot over KTAT but the regular barn dance from Crystal Springs where he is heard and been almost every night in the week and then when he goes "barnstorming" over the state, he is always invited to play a program, either on WRR in Dallas, WACO in Waco or other stations, depending on the town he is in.

When the NRA was first introduced to the Southwest by our President Roosevelt, Milton introduced a tune which he wrote and dedicated to the NRA. He called it "Fall in Line With the NRA" and his thousands of friends and listeners fell in line and wrote for copies of the song. It was published and distributed to these thousands by the Lucas Funeral Home of Ft. Worth.

Milton and the Brownies are heard each noon over KTAT at twelve o'clock, except Sunday.

Around the Texas And KTAT

Ed Lalley and his orchestra, the band that has been entertaining and playing in the beautiful Colonial dining room of the Hotel Texas and heard over KTAT and the Southwest network since the fifteenth of September has been replaced by Mack Rogers and his band from San Antonio. The band features eleven musicians, trio and ensemble-singing, plus Ann Neeley, torch singer. All reports so far are to the good and the band looks like it might stay a while.

* * * * *

The *Fort Worth Radio News*, a supplement to the *Fort Worth Press*, celebrated Milton Brown's popularity in Texas with this profile on October 6, 1933. The term "western swing" would not be coined for another decade, hence the Brownies are labeled a "hillbilly band." Courtesy Preston and Wanda Hook.

"We took an intermission that night and Milton said, 'How about playing with us regularly?' Well, I had a good job as a fountain manager at a soda fountain downtown. Made pretty good money for the Depression. So I wasn't sure about it right then."

ROY LEE BROWN: "Fred worked at the soda fountain in the Rexall Drugstore at the bottom of the Trinity Life Building at Main and Seventh streets. KTAT was upstairs. At that time, many people went to fountains at drugstores for ice-cream sodas, root beer, cold drinks . . . that was all the go then. That was a treat. If you had a nickel that you could spare, you'd go in and get an ice-cream cone. If you had a dime or fifteen cents you could get a fudge sundae.

"Fred made twenty to twenty-five dollars a week working there at the fountain. As jobs went, Fred's paid pretty well. Common laborers were drawing ten to twelve dollars a week. Butchers got more, maybe twenty-five, after they had been on the job for a long time."

FRED "PAPA" CALHOUN: "So Milton said, 'Well, why don't you just play this Saturday night with us?' He said, 'I'll give you ten dollars.' Well, I could do that and still hold my job, so I played that Saturday at Crystal Springs. And I played Saturday nights with them three or four times. Then they got a job out at the Crazy Hotel in Mineral Wells. After that he got this job out in Whitney and he wanted me to go down there. That was a little rough 'cause I opened up the fountain at 6:30 in the morning and couldn't stay out too late.

"Finally, he got us a big job in Dallas at an automobile building in Fair Park on Harwood Street. They had a program scheduled there from 6:30 to 7:00 in the evening. I met them down near there [probably the parking garage in downtown Fort Worth], got in their bus next to Milton and we drove on in to Dallas.[7] When we got inside the Dallas city limits there were four motorcycle cops sitting there waiting. They were put there to escort us to Fair Park. Milton looked a little worried and said 'What's going on here?' We didn't know what was happening, we couldn't figure it out. When we got to the fairgrounds with this escort, there were cars parked as far as you could see. People were standing around in lines, all lined up. Milton said, 'Oh gosh, we're sunk now, they must be having a wrestling match or something.' So we pulled up to the place and started unloading the instruments and do you know, these people had all come to the dance? Every one of 'em.

"Milton paid a hundred dollars for use of the hall, this automobile building, and we had to rent these special big speakers to put inside the place so everybody could hear the band. Then he had to pay six off-duty cops to patrol and keep order. They charged 75 cents to get in and 10 cents for ladies. There were so many people there that when we finally got through with all those expenses we still made $103 apiece!"[8]

"On the way back to Fort Worth I again sat next to Milton on the bus. And he said, 'Fred, why don't you quit that drugstore job and go to work for me?' I looked at the hundred and three dollars I had just made for one night's work and said, 'Milton, you just hired yourself a piano player [laughs]!'

"I got the name 'Papa' because I enjoyed Earl Hines so much, you know. Well, I finally met him at a colored hotel called the Gem in Fort Worth. They had a five- or six-piece jazz band down there at the hotel and had a big chicken dinner fixed especially for Hines. This woman was the emcee and she said, 'Folks, we're gonna try to get Fatha Hines to play some for us.' I wouldn't have blamed him if he didn't because they had a little old upright there that was out of tune. She said, 'It looks like he doesn't play this type of piano.' I've played on some dogs myself, you know. Very seldom would I find a real good piano to play on. They had grands in the recording studios, though. I play fast, and a lot of pianos won't respond to too much speed. You'd hit it and they [the keys] won't come back fast enough. But grands, those kind of pianos, I can do that on them."

It was Milton Brown who gave Fred Calhoun his nickname "Papa." With the addition of Calhoun, the Brownies' rhythm section was complete. The band now numbered five instruments plus Milton. Calhoun provided the Brownies with a wealth of new songs to perform, all jazz and dance band standards. Milton, always eager to learn new material, picked up these tunes easily. Jesse Ashlock, still the only instrumentalist who played melody, adapted as well, with Ocie Stockard, Derwood Brown, Wanna Coffman, and Calhoun providing the rhythm. Now, with Calhoun supporting the bottom end of the sound with his pounding left hand, Derwood was able to abandon the rhythm at certain times and experiment on take-off choruses of his own. The Brownies' sound began to change almost the moment Fred Calhoun joined them.

JIMMY THOMASON: "When you come down to it, Milton was a jazz man. The Light Crust Doughboys had a good beat, but no, no, nothing like that Brown beat. Let me tell you something. In my day, there were very few beats like that. A lot of them imitated it and some of them had good beats, I'm not saying they didn't. Beautiful rhythm. What I'm talking about is this particular rhythm that this particular band had. I attribute it to Ocie Stockard. Now, Wanna, Fred, and Derwood were there too, but Ocie was the key. I can't explain it, but there is a difference with the way Ocie played from everybody else. When those guys were playing their rhythm, they enjoyed it. It's not as if they were sitting there, HAVING to do this rhythm, see? They enjoyed it. And boy, that Brownie beat, you couldn't budge it! Nobody could touch that beat."

FRED "PAPA" CALHOUN: "I'll tell you what it was. We had four guys that had the same idea about rhythm. And we never had any problem whatever. You could check a chorus by the second hand on your watch. We never rushed or dragged in our whole lives. The backbone of the rhythm of the Brownie band was Ocie. He set the beat. I played with him, Wanna played with him, and Derwood played with him. When I started playing with the Brownies, I used to get all enthused and I'd tend to rush. And then I'd feel Ocie holding me back.

"I liked the Brownies' beat right off because it was the same 2/4 Dixieland beat that I had been playing. Milton's band was the only fiddle band playing that beat. See, we had a fiddle band but we weren't playing strictly fiddle band music. We also played the same music that the Dixieland bands were playing, except we were using tenor banjo, guitar, bass, fiddle, and piano and we were playing that 2/4 beat. It's a dance beat. Actually, it's the best beat you can use for dancing. That's because it's accented and you can step with it. But you go hittin' 4/4 and tearing it up like they do now and you just don't feel it. Milton wouldn't let his band play anything but 2/4. And it took all of us to do it. Ocie had a fine 2/4 beat. His tenor banjo sounded like drums. With him on banjo, Wanna booming out the bass, Derwood beatin' that guitar, and me on piano, why, we had as strong a 2/4 beat as you could get.

"I never got over the fact that Milton stood up and sang as much as he did. Don't see how he could do it. He sang nearly every tune, except when Derwood would sing one once in a while. And instrumentals, of course. But, night after night, travelin', breathing that dust off the dance floor, he sang through all of that and it never did bother him. He just kept the same voice. He had a wonderful voice and a wonderful range. And it never seemed to be any strain for him, he just sang easy."

After their initial broadcast in September 1932, the Musical

Brownies developed rapidly, almost as if Milton had an agenda planned during his final weeks with the Light Crust Doughboys. Like all good businessmen, Milton Brown always thought several steps ahead, a wise strategy during the Depression. Milton surmised that if his band was going to be a success, it would have to expand its performing radius. Although the Brownies' radio program was extremely popular, Milton knew from the very beginning that the major purpose his radio program served was to promote his dances. The radio station best suited to publicize the Musical Brownies was obviously WBAP, with its 50,000-watt transmitter. However, WBAP did not make a habit of airing unsponsored programs, which is why Burrus Mill and Elevator (Light Crust Doughboys) and Aladdin Lamps (Aladdin Laddies) were able to obtain airtime. KTAT, however, was still a struggling radio station in 1932, eager to accept untested, unsponsored musical groups like the Brownies or the Southern Melody Boys.

ROY LEE BROWN: "At WBAP, the audiences weren't allowed in the studio with the performers as they were at KTAT. I think it was the same way at KFJZ. The audience had to sit in an outer room and watch the broadcast through a plate glass window. After KTAT moved to the Texas Hotel at Eighth and Main [now the Sheraton], the audience was allowed right in the studio. The studio was located just off the mezzanine floor and, when it filled up, as it did most of the time the Brownies played, they would move the audience out onto the mezzanine. You'd go up these stairs and there was a big balcony going all the way around. There would be people waiting, lined up clear on that balcony during that program, the noon program. The studio itself held about thirty-five or forty people. There was about eight seats to a row and about six rows. I've seen it so crowded that you couldn't get in and out the door. Thick carpet. And I believe they had two microphones, the announcer used one and Milton used the other. When Wanna did his steel number, they used one for him. Of course when they got Bob Dunn, he didn't need a microphone at all."

ELLEN BROWN: "There was no glass in this studio or anything. Before the show started, everyone would come flocking in. And Milton and the Brownies would come over and shake hands with a lot of people and of course the women were nearly fainting and pushing trying to get in. I remember what he called me the first time. He said, 'Hi there, honey chile!' [giggles] Thrilled me to death!"

FRED "PAPA" CALHOUN: "The piano at KTAT was an old upright. Upright goes better with a string band than a grand, see. So they got this special piano for me to play on. And we painted it white. Everybody that came by to see the program got to sign their name on this piano in ink. Let me tell you, that piano didn't have a spot on it that didn't have a name [laughs]!"

Although the daily radio program on KTAT became invaluable to Milton Brown, it was also something of a hindrance. Milton knew that in order to expand the group's popularity, he would have to book dances away from Fort Worth. But since he had to return to KTAT in time for the noon broadcast each day, there was a limit to how far the Brownies could travel in Papa Sam's bus. Occasionally the Brownies played a fifteen-minute or half-hour program on a radio station such as WACO in Waco or KGKO in Wichita Falls. But they always returned in time for their noon broadcast on KTAT in Fort Worth. This was the routine Milton Brown settled into for the next two and a half years.

By January 1933, Milton Brown was satisfied with his rhythm section. Now he put his next plan into operation: adding a second fiddle player. Jesse Ashlock was quickly learning the jazz Fred Calhoun helped introduce to the Brownies. But not being a trained musician and unable to read music, he was having trouble carrying the load by himself. Milton liked the sound of twin fiddles and knew that Jesse needed a tutor who knew the mechanics of the instrument, so he asked Ocie Stockard for a recommendation.

OCIE STOCKARD: "Actually I told Milton that he should hire Cecil Brower to replace Jesse. Cecil was a much better fiddle player but Milton kept them both. Cecil played harmony behind Jesse a lot of the time."

KENNETH PITTS: "In early 1933 Cecil left the Southern Melody Boys and joined Milton. Milton was making a lot of money already and the Southern Melody Boys were making nothin'. We were on KTAT like they were in a sort of regional network [the Southwest Broadcasting Company] and Milton was the main fiddle band thrust. We just didn't know how to organize our group to reach the people like Milton did. We just did what we wanted to do and what we thought was good. But Milton was a good promoter, that's the first thing. Also, he had a better savvy of what people wanted to hear. We were really trying to appeal to the quality line rather than what people really wanted.

Quality of tone and all that. I was the musical leader of the band and most of the time the business leader, too. But what we needed was a business manager like Milton Brown. We were really disorganized. People didn't think about careers during the Depression. You just went whichever way the wind pushed you. And few people had any ambition.

"I never made more than ten dollars a week with the Southern Melody Boys. I used to have to play a classical program four times a week on KTAT for Fishburn Cleaners in addition to that. The Southern Melody Boys played house dances mostly. We usually made about three to four dollars apiece. That's all. The biggest crowd we ever had was in a vacant car dealership on West Seventh Street. We had maybe five hundred people for that. We added a bass fiddle on that show. We never used piano. Fred Calhoun was the first piano man in a fiddle band.

"I remember when Roosevelt got nominated by the Democrats for president, we had a big party with lots of beer drinking and carrying on. Then we had a wild party and picnic on Labor Day in '32 with Bob Wren's family at Oakland Park. Bob played banjo with us.

"But after Cecil left, the whole thing just went to pieces. I quit music for a while and went to work as a janitor for a church. Then in 1934 I auditioned for the Light Crust Doughboys and I got the job. Played twin fiddles with Clifford Gross."

ROY LEE BROWN: "At first Milton put Cecil on commission. He didn't get a full share because he was sort of on probation. Derwood told me that the Brownies played the Mineral Plunge in Corsicana and Cecil was on a certain percentage, I forgot how much. Seemed like the band made fifty or sixty dollars apiece that night. And Cecil's part came to ten dollars and he was just tickled to death [laughs]! It wasn't long after that that Milton put Cecil on a regular percentage equal to everybody else."

JIMMY THOMASON: "When I started trying to play, there were no fiddle players around, really, in Waco at that time. The only ones around were the old-timers that played hoedowns. So I started trying to play fiddle. I wanted to play like Jesse Ashlock. Then when Cecil Brower came to the Brownies, that was it. That was the absolute end. He was the greatest I ever heard in my life! That was entirely different from the Wills type fiddle. A world of difference. And I appreciated what he was doing with his bowing. Wills had an 'extra bow' on everything you know. The difference between Brower and Wills and Jesse Ashlock was in the execution. Cecil's was perfect. Because he was classically trained, you know. When I got started playing, I picked up too many bad habits. Then I saw people like Cecil Brower and Thurman Neal over at WRR in Dallas, and that's who I wanted to play like."

The addition of Cecil Brower to the Brownies changed their sound almost immediately. As a schooled musician, Cecil was able to use his knowledge of chord progressions and musical structure to create more inventive take-offs. Attentive radio listener Red Varner recalled that sometimes the Brownies would close their program with an instrumental version of their theme song. Varner noted that the Brownies' theme, which is based on Milton's composition "Sunbonnet Sue," shared similar chord patterns with the popular song "Nola."

ROY LEE BROWN: "Cecil would hit the theme song at ninety miles an hour and play it all the way through. Then Milton and Derwood would sing the first part of the theme in harmony all the way through and then stop and start the first number on the program. At the end of the program Cecil would hit the theme real fast as in the beginning. Milton and Derwood would sing the closing part of the theme. Then, if there was some time left, Cecil would play 'Nola.' Sometimes if they were running out of time the station would fade them out, but if they didn't, Cecil would always have 'Nola' ready."

By early 1933, Milton Brown and the Musical Brownies' influence began to be felt not only in Fort Worth but in neighboring Texas towns as well.

DAVE STOGNER: "I listened to Milton Brown and the Musical Brownies on the radio, then one day I got to see them. I was just walking around in Gainesville and I saw their bus pull up and stop at the Barnes and Wooten Café. They got off the bus wearing their suits, white shirts, and ties. They looked like a million dollars! They went into the café to eat. I just went in and took a vacant stool by the cash register. As they paid, Milton stopped, patted me on the head, and said he bet I was going to be a musician. I said I was working on it. He said, 'Really, are you? You'll be all right. Stay with it!' I don't think I washed my head for two or three weeks after that! You have to admire a man for making it as big as he did when times were so hard."[9]

In addition to fans such as Stogner, the Brownies' broadcasts influenced other Texas musicians. Some were encouraged enough to start their own string bands, which they modeled after the Brownies. Others adjusted their styles to match the swing of the Brownies. KFJZ's High Fliers, which had been playing mainly country waltzes and breakdowns since their inception in 1929, began playing jazz tunes learned from Brownies' broadcasts.

In Dallas, a band called the Rhythm Aces formed late in 1932 which performed in the style of the Musical Brownies. It consisted of Thurman Neal and Art Davis on fiddles, Thurman's younger brother Buddy on guitar, Walker Kirkes on tenor banjo, and Jim Boyd on bass. According to Boyd, the Rhythm Aces played mostly jazz and very little hillbilly music. Songs such as "Dinah," "Avalon," "Milenburg Joys," and "Sweet Sue—Just You" dominated their repertoire. Thurman Neal provided the arrangements by adapting clarinet lead on jazz recordings to the fiddle. Neal, an admirer of jazz violinist Joe Venuti, soon became one of Texas's best hot fiddlers. The Rhythm Aces had a regular radio program on Dallas's WRR until they broke up in 1933.

It was then that Jim Boyd's older brother Bill formed the Cowboy Ramblers, a four-man group consisting of the Boyd brothers and former Rhythm Aces Art Davis and Walker Kirkes. Although initially specializing in western numbers, the Cowboy Ramblers eventually modeled its sound after the Musical Brownies. Jim Boyd and the other Dallas musicians had listened to the Brownies' broadcasts, but did not see them perform in person until 1933.

JIM BOYD: "I'll never forget the first time I saw Milton Brown. It was about the time the Rhythm Aces disbanded. Milton and the boys were playing at the old Labor Temple in downtown Dallas. I went up the stairs to where they were playing and I saw all those boys: Cecil Brower, Derwood Brown, Wanna Coffman, Ocie Stockard, and Papa Calhoun. And that Milton Brown was a goooood-lookin' rascal too! They had on brown suits with reversible vests. And I stood up there and looked at those boys and I thought they looked like a bunch of Greek gods! That was the finest-looking aggregation I had ever seen! I was really enthralled."

Roy Newman was one of many other musicians whose life changed after hearing the Musical Brownies. Since the mid-1920s, Newman had been staff guitarist and half of a WRR duo known as the Mystery Singers with station program director John Thorwald. Known as Prince Alexis and Grand Duke Sergius, Thorwald and Newman were "compelled by their friends to go masked against efforts against them by Russian guerillas. The duo can yodle [*sic*] with the most royal blood in the land, and can play the guitar and piano and sing with any dictators living today."[10] In 1931 Newman formed a trio called the Wanderers, consisting of himself on guitar, Dick Reinhart on mandolin, and Bert Dodson on bass. After hearing the Brownies in 1933, Newman expanded his band, hiring Jim Boyd to play take-off guitar (Boyd did double duty with Newman and Bill Boyd's Cowboy Ramblers), and the Neal brothers, who had been playing with the Rhythm Aces. Fred Calhoun was very helpful to Newman and taught him the rudiments of the Earl Hines stride piano style, and Newman's Wanderers soon began emulating the Musical Brownies' style and repertoire. The Wanderers were taken over by Jonah Dodson, Bert's father, and established a style similar to that of the Brownies, although, like the Southern Melody Boys, the Wanderers suffered from disorganization and musical combativeness. The Brownies held together by learning to operate as a team, with Milton Brown as its quarterback.

On May 17, 1933, President Roosevelt proposed what would become the National Industry Recovery Act, a sweeping conception that sought to regulate cutthroat competition within industry and commerce and guaranteed workers the right to organize labor unions. It also administered a vast program of public works designed to turn the unemployed into a productive working force. As part of Roosevelt's "New Deal," the National Recovery Administration initially was met with wariness by business leaders, who were hesitant about putting business under government regulation. However, Milton Brown, head of a commonwealth band that was actually a microcosm of Roosevelt's plan, wrote a song celebrating the NRA and presented it on the Brownies' regular radio program on KTAT. The audience response was so great that the Lucas Funeral Home of Fort Worth printed the lyrics to the song on a four-page flyer and distributed thousands of free copies to Brownie fans.

Fall in Line with the NRA

Verse 1
When Franklin Roosevelt walked into the White House,
The country turned into a land of smiles,
    It had been a land of frown,
    Because depression had been down,
But we are going to sing this chorus
    For miles and miles around.
CHORUS: Fall in line with the NRA

For our President has shown the way;
    Men and women, old and young,
    Put depression on the run,
Put Roosevelt's Blue Eagle on display;
    Now we know you don't want to be a slacker,
So we are going to stand together, up and say,
    In this dear old land of ours,
    Make more money, work less hours,
Fall in Line With the NRA.

Verse 2
You may run the peanut stand down on the corner,
Or a filling station, drug store or cafe,
    You may manufacture clothes.
    Sell bank stocks or radios,
You can do your part, stand up and shout,
    Come on now boys, let's go.[11]

CHORUS

The Musical Brownies' fame spread throughout Texas. In October 1933, the *Fort Worth Radio News,* a Friday publication published for the benefit of radio fans, noted in a featured article that "Milton Brown has had many names on the radio and has been introduced under different titles for the past four years, but the best of all and one that really is the one that is fitting for him is the 'King of the Hillbilly Bands.'" Milton had been well known in the Fort Worth/ Dallas area as being a good drawing card and effective salesman, taking advantage of the Brownies' popularity to assist local businesses in advertising their products. Not being tied down to one sponsor, as were the Light Crust Doughboys, Milton Brown and his Musical Brownies promoted many products, with Milton adroitly adapting the band's name to accommodate each one. The Southwest Broadcasting Company's string of radio stations had also spread the Brownies' music throughout Texas since its inception on February 9, 1933, and many local radio stations in surrounding areas eagerly looked forward to Milton's guest appearances during the Brownies' barnstorming tours.

On other frequencies of the radio dial, the Brownies' success inspired more and more string bands and country performers to make their debuts on the three Fort Worth radio stations. The early morning hours featured Cecil Gill, the Yodeling Country Boy, on WBAP, while on KFJZ, steel guitarist Andy Schroder, soon to be a member of the High Fliers, played a one-hour program of Hawaiian tunes with his brother. A popular all-male western vocal group, the Chuck Wagon Gang, also made its debut in 1933, sponsored first by Kernel Wheat and later by Bewley's Flour. This was not the famous sacred quartet consisting of D. P. "Dad" Carter and his three children. The Carters did, however, assume the name Chuck Wagon Gang after the former group left WBAP in 1936.

Meanwhile, the Light Crust Doughboys were experiencing more changes. In August 1933, W. Lee O'Daniel fired Bob Wills and replaced him with former High Flier breakdown fiddler Clifford Gross. Gross was replaced in the High Fliers by Pat Trotter, a hot fiddler capable of playing take-off choruses. With this change, the High Fliers began their transformation from string band to swing band.

Bob Wills subsequently left Fort Worth and started his own band in Waco. Business was not good for Wills there. Milton Brown kept in close contact with his former partner, assisting him by bringing the Brownies down for a "double-band dance" on October 2. Jimmy Thomason was Bob Wills's "band boy" in Waco, a teenager who usually set up the public address equipment, changed strings, and helped carry instruments.

JIMMY THOMASON: "Wills came to Waco and went to work for WACO radio. Their program was sponsored by Jones Fine Bread Company. He had the two Whalin boys, June and Kermit, Tommy Duncan, and Bob's brother Johnnie Lee. That was it. They were good, but it wasn't any Milton Brown sound. Milton came down to Waco and booked double-band deals with Wills all through that area to help things along. Things were rough, man. It cost forty cents to go see Milton Brown. Milton would book a round robin, circuit-type deal. See, he was hot all over, but he was especially hot in Waco. Wills didn't have that kind of power yet because WACO didn't get out very far. Fifty or sixty miles was all. So Milton would come down maybe once a month. The first time he played with Bob was at the Green Terrace at Lake Waco.[12] That was a huge place. We went out to see them that night, and the traffic across that lake was so bad we never did get in. Then there was another place out there at the lake called Shadowland where Milton played, and he also played uptown at the Woodmen Hall.

"What they would do in Waco was come and play a radio program before the dance. The station in Waco would tie in with the theater and the Brownies would do their show from the stage of this theater. Seven to seven-thirty, something like that. Then they'd go play the dance. See, they didn't care about radio except to plug their dance.

"Later on, I got acquainted with all of them. Heck, every time they came to town, I was the first one there. I never will forget one time when . . . oh, man they were griping that night, Calhoun, Ocie Stockard. What they were so discouraged about was that the place was too small. They couldn't get a place large enough to hold all the people.

"I was a freshman in high school when I was Bob Wills's band boy. I used to hang around the radio station. Me and Tommy Dunlap and Alfred Scott were doing shows over at WACO and that's how we got acquainted. The radio station was about three blocks from my house and I'd go up there on my lunch hour. Wills used the same theme song the Doughboys used: [sings to the tune of "Eagle Riding Papa"] 'Listen everybody from near and far, if you want to know who we are, Bob Wills's Playboys, W-A-C-O.' Same tune as the Doughboys theme song."

Red Varner was one of many Waco residents who remembered Milton Brown and the Musical Brownies playing dances at the various local clubs and dance halls.

RED VARNER: "My friend Roy Armitage and I heard Milton Brown and his Musical Brownies at Green's Terrace on a summer's night in 1933. We sat outside and listened. Air conditioning then was still just a dream so every window in the building was open. Those open windows made it possible for us to hear as well or better than anyone inside. We missed seeing the band in action but decided we could live with that one flaw in our outside listening.

"Fred Calhoun was a recent addition to the band, bringing the sideman total to five. Still, a very small band to be playing a dance at Green's Terrace, but you would never know it to hear that crowd. No one was having any trouble hearing the band. In words of a later time, 'the joint was really jumping.' And a good part of that jump was due to the work of the new piano player. Fred Calhoun was a real driving force in that band.

"When Wills got started down there, well, he had to have a piano player too. So he hired a guy named Don Ivey to play piano and sometimes guitar. He was what they used to call an 'F-sharp piano player.' What this usually meant was that such a player was limited to the key of F-sharp. In Don's case, he was able to function in other keys but had to avoid all of the conventional keys such as C, F, G, etc. It also meant that everybody else had to tune a half-step higher than regular tuning to accommodate Ivey's handicap at the piano and to be anywhere near comfortable in their own playing. The pickings were pretty slim for Bob and the Playboys in Waco. They were barely making ends meet and there didn't seem to be any chance of things improving."

As dim as prospects were for Bob Wills and his Playboys, they were that much brighter for Milton Brown and his Musical Brownies. Their radio program on KTAT was getting more and more popular, and word was traveling around the Texas countryside about this hot new dance band that played Saturday nights at Crystal Springs. As 1933 turned into 1934, Milton Brown found his the most popular fiddle band in the state. Although they had been together as a group for more than a year, no recordings had yet been made by the Brownies. In 1934 that would change, as Milton Brown found himself making records for the brand new Bluebird record label. Other changes would occur in Milton's professional, as well as personal, life during the next year, and he eagerly looked forward to even greater success for his developing musical sound.

SEVEN

Taking Off
(1934)

In the city of Fort Worth, Texas, there were not many businessmen who could claim to be successful in 1934. One who was hardly
on Easy Street yet was far from suffering either was Papa Sam Cunningham, who commemorated the new year by distributing complimentary 1934 calendars to Crystal Springs customers. The calendars
proclaimed "Season's Greetings from Milton Brown and the Musical
Brownies" and sported a photograph of the smiling dance hall owner, his son Henry, and their star attractions. Beneath the photograph
was a miniature twelve-page calendar and a brief poem:

> If you would Dance away your troubles;
> Live and Laugh as ne'er before,
> See us at Crystal Springs . . . more often,
> Throughout Nineteen-Thirty-Four.

Shortly after the new year began, Jesse Ashlock left the band. The
circumstances surrounding Ashlock's exit will probably never be
known, but it was apparent from the very beginning that Jesse's personality clashed with those of the other Brownies.

WANNA COFFMAN: "I would say that Jesse quit by request [laughs]! I
went to school with Jesse and knew him pretty well. I don't think
he and Derwood got along together too well. They had some trouble
there for a while. Jesse was a good musician but he couldn't play the
popular tunes like Cecil could. Then Cecil went to Milton and said,
'I can't play with him' and eventually, Jesse just quit. He thought he
was going to get fired anyway because he had been trying to tell everybody how to play, and was always tellin' everybody how to run
the business. Later on, he went to work for Bob Wills and Bob fired
him I don't know how many times. So Jesse would come back here

wanting to go back to work for Milton. He was just hard to get along with."

RED VARNER: "I remember playing a job with Jesse Ashlock in Fort Worth in the fall of 1934. Jesse was anything but a moron but on the Brown radio program he used one of the most moronic laughs I've ever heard. At times during the broadcast, he would let fly with one of those laughs. At other times he would confine it to the sign-off theme at the end of the program. The rest of the band seemed to enjoy this part of the Ashlock personality."

With Jesse Ashlock gone, Cecil Brower remained as the Brownies' sole fiddle player. Milton wanted to hire a replacement for Jesse, but by April he still had not found anyone capable enough to complement the quickly improving Brower.

On April 4, 1934, Milton Brown and the Musical Brownies drove down to San Antonio to attend their first recording session. Will Ed Kemble of Kemble Brothers Furniture Company of Fort Worth had approached a talent scout for Victor records and convinced him that the Brownies were Fort Worth's most popular band and had a repertoire of songs ready to record.

FRED "PAPA" CALHOUN: "We recorded upstairs in an old building across the street from the Gunter Hotel in San Antonio [the Texas Hotel]. We just played tunes that we were playing at dances. Eli Oberstein was the director at that session. They had a grand piano down there at that hotel, but they had the treble strings strung up too tight, where they would ring. So for that session I stayed down in the bass notes. I'd get up there and it'd sound ringy, you know. So on that session for Bluebird, I played from middle-F on down."

The Victor field unit had arrived in San Antonio late in March, prepared for a large number of recordings by a wide variety of talent, mostly country and blues artists. The sessions began on Monday, March 26, and continued every day except Sunday, April 1, through Wednesday, April 4. The Brownies and a Mexican jazz band led by Emilio Caceres recorded on the final day.[1]

The recording artists who attended the spring sessions comprised an impressive list, a veritable Hall of Fame of prewar rural talent. Blues artists included the Mississippi Sheiks, the popular black fiddle band from Mississippi, and Sheiks member Bo Chatmon, who recorded under the name Bo Carter. The legendary Georgia string band Gid

Tanner and his Skillet Lickers were reunited for this, their only session for Victor. Smooth-singing Riley Puckett, famous for his lyrical vocal style and innovative guitar work, recorded with his partner, mandolinist Ted Hawkins.[2]

Also making an appearance before the Victor microphones was Jesse Rodgers, cousin to the late "Mississippi Blue Yodeler" Jimmie Rodgers and groomed by Victor to be Jimmie's successor. Rodgers was the first person to cover Stuart Hamblen's "My Mary," a song with which Milton Brown would become closely associated.[3]

On April 4, the Brownies assembled before one lone microphone and recorded eight tunes. They began with two instrumentals featuring Cecil Brower, "Brownie's Stomp" and "Joe Turner Blues." The remaining six selections featured vocal performances by Milton with Derwood Brown and Ocie Stockard singing second and third harmony parts.

"Brownie's Stomp" showcased the virtuosity of Cecil Brower, who composed the instrumental with the help of Ocie Stockard. Although he played strictly tenor banjo with the Brownies, Stockard used his experience as a breakdown fiddle player in his hometown of Crafton to expand Brower's repertoire. As Milton Brown hollered encouragement, the Brownies showed Oberstein and the Victor company that they had come prepared. Brower began the tune by playing four-bar phrases, each ending with a "break," during which one of the other musicians provided four beats of fill. Stockard took the first break, strumming wildly on all four strings of his tenor banjo. Brower then repeated the melody with Derwood picking out single notes during his one-bar break. Two more repetitions of the melody followed, with the remaining musicians, Fred Calhoun (playing a simple descending scale) and Wanna Coffman (slapping his bass crisply), continuing the pattern of one-bar fills. Having completed this metaphorical introduction of all the Brownies, Cecil took off, playing a melodic variation on the main theme as the tempo quickened. Derwood, Ocie, and Fred then each took extended take-offs before returning the lead to Cecil, who finished the tune with a variation on the jazz standard "Milenburg Joys." Although basically a simple instrumental with alternating take-offs, "Brownie's Stomp" was not an easy piece to play. It required each musician to stop and start cleanly at various points during the tune while breaks were executed. It was the first time a string band featured such interplay in which all the musicians played both rhythm and jazz. All the elements now common to western swing were in place: the dance beat, the 2/4 Dixieland rhythm, improvised jazz solos, and fiddle lead.

The always smiling Milton Brown, as he is best remembered by his fans, c. 1934. Courtesy Roy Lee and Ellen Brown.

Derwood Brown, in a studio portrait taken sometime in the mid-1930s. Milton depended on his younger brother to lead the band when he was not on the bandstand. In addition, Derwood provided a solid beat with his guitar and sang harmony. Courtesy Roy Lee and Ellen Brown.

Milton Brown and his Musical Brownies, in the only known photograph taken of them performing during a radio broadcast, KTAT, Fort Worth, 1934. The neon sign was most likely superimposed at a later date. From left: Wanna Coffman (bass), Cecil Brower (fiddle), Fred Calhoun (piano), Milton Brown (vocals), Ocie Stockard (banjo), Derwood Brown (guitar, vocals). This is the group that recorded for Bluebird in April 1934. Courtesy A. B. and Helen Gilbert.

An Art Deco postcard of the town of Mineral Wells, Texas, the home of Crazy Water Crystals, Texas's legendary "miracle healer." The Musical Brownies played their first out-of-town engagement in Mineral Wells's Crazy Hotel, named for its most famous product. In the foreground is Woodward's Music Store, where Milton Brown purchased Bob Dunn's first amplifier, in late 1934. Courtesy Cary Ginell.

The second tune, "Joe Turner Blues," was another instrumental featuring Cecil Brower, a medium tempo dance blues highlighted by Ocie Stockard playing cakewalking triplets behind him, which were echoed by Fred Calhoun during his take-off.

Of the remaining six titles, four were credited to one "Dan Parker," most likely a pseudonym, for those tunes were either traditional or had been already recorded by other groups. On the third tune, a fast-paced novelty entitled "Oh! You Pretty Woman!" Milton Brown finally sang for the first time at the session. He had made a few exclamatory aaaah-ha's during "Brownie's Stomp" but remained silent during "Joe Turner Blues," allowing the spotlight to stay on Cecil.

The number that proved to be one of the most popular of all the Brownies' recordings was a sentimental tribute Milton wrote for Derwood's first son, Milton Thomas Brown, then a winsome six-month-old with curly blonde hair. Derwood's boy became commonly known as "Sonny Boy," and Milton's recording of "My Precious Sonny Boy," with his affecting Ted Lewis–inspired recitation became one of the Brownies' most requested songs.[4]

The fifth and sixth selections, "Swinging on the Garden Gate," a Milton Brown composition, and "Do the Hula Lou," went off without a hitch, but on the seventh song, a reworking of the Washboard Rhythm Kings' "Call of the Freaks," Milton made one of his rare mistakes. The Brownies' version of the tune, entitled "Garbage Man Blues," began with Milton rapping on Derwood's guitar and saying in black dialect: "Lady, get out your can, here comes the garbage man!" Ocie Stockard responded in falsetto: "Git away from here, man, I ain't got no garbage!"

FRED "PAPA" CALHOUN: "Then I introduced the number. I hit ninth chords, see, and I guess it threw Milton off a little. It was supposed to be in F and he got in G. So when he finally came in, he sang the whole first chorus in the wrong key! Well, Cecil took a chorus, and then Milton came in again in the right key and we finished the song. Oberstein had told us to keep going, no matter what happened, so we did. We all thought that they were going to turn it down and redo it but they never did."

ROY LEE BROWN: "Milton got real upset by that. He came home saying that he tried to get them to let him record 'Garbage Man Blues' over but they wouldn't let him."[5]

On the final song of the session, the Jimmie Noone classic "Four or Five Times," Ocie Stockard switched to tenor guitar as Milton sang the song in his best Cab Calloway "hi-de-ho" style.

The Musical Brownies' initial recording session was typical for early western swing bands. Hustled in and out of makeshift studios in one-day sessions, groups such as the Brownies recorded songs that they had been playing regularly on radio or at dances. Songs were rarely recorded twice and mistakes, sonic imbalances, and other imperfections were ignored. However, this general indifference to quality by A&R men such as Eli Oberstein was only partially due to condescension for "hillbillies." In addition, the assembly-line nature of the process and the primitiveness of the session mechanics contributed to the often unsatisfactory performances. Marvin Montgomery, then a member of the Dallas-based string band the Wanderers, talked about his experiences in the Victor studios with Oberstein the following January.

MARVIN MONTGOMERY: "In those early sessions they used wax discs to make records. I think they were made out of this soft beeswax-type material and they were about 1/4 to 1/2 inch thick. Anyway, when you recorded a song, they'd pack each disc in dry ice, so the grooves wouldn't melt together in the heat, and send it back to New York for processing. If you made a mistake in recording, then they'd have to shave off the old record and start a new one. The shaving and shipping turned out to be such a waste of time to them that they encouraged first-take only performances. This explains all the mistakes you hear on those old records. Oberstein asked each group to play as many tunes as possible. And they wouldn't play any of them back because the discs had to be processed first. The bands were at the mercy of the A&R men. They didn't even use electricity to run the recording equipment. Instead, they had hand-operated generators and cranks powered by weights. If an elevator in the hotel started moving, it would change the current and we'd have to start over! They would raise this crank and when they lowered it, the turntable would start to move. We did a lot of Brownies tunes but when we went to record, Oberstein wouldn't let us do things like 'Four or Five Times' because the Brownies had already done them."

The Brownies returned to Fort Worth after their first recording session without realizing the significance of what they had just accomplished. They were not the first Fort Worth string band to make records, but they were the first to employ jazz choruses and piano. Those phonograph records, however, were not as important to musicians in the thirties as they are to today's historians. It is fortunate that the Musical Brownies did participate in five recording sessions during their brief five years together (four sessions with Milton and one after Milton's death with Derwood as leader). But the Brownies never made much money from their Bluebird recordings. They were paid a flat fee of $50 per side for the performances, and Milton received a microscopic royalty of $.00225 per side for "Brownie's Stomp," and "Swinging on the Garden Gate," which he had copyrighted himself. The percentage was even smaller on "Joe Turner Blues," which Milton split with Cecil Brower ($.001125 per side for each). Six royalty statements covering the period from 1934 through 1936 saved by the Brown family indicate a total sales of 5,380 copies of the three tunes with Milton receiving a grand total of $14.73 in royalties. It is no wonder recording artists downplayed the importance of records made during this bleak period.[6]

Milton Brown's social life was also undergoing some changes.

ROY LEE BROWN: "Milton went with a number of girls. He met a lot of women at his dances while the Brownies were playing. At times, I would go to Crystal Springs and he'd drop me off at home after the dance. I'd usually ride the bus out there and then he'd take me home in his car. Sometimes he had a girl in the car with him when he dropped me off and would then head out somewhere with her. Then I would go to bed as soon as I got in. I don't know how late he came in or whether or not he came in at all. He had a good social life. But the business he was in kept him busy all the time and there simply was no time for a serious relationship. Occasionally they had a night off but they were playing somewhere just about every night."

Pretty, dark-haired Sally Beard was one young woman who dated the popular bandleader. After their relationship ended, Sally married guitarist Sleepy Johnson.

SALLY BEARD JOHNSON: "I first met Milton out at Crystal Springs. My sister had a date with him once and for some reason, she couldn't go. He was playing a program at the radio station in the afternoon. I would usually catch the bus downtown to go to Crystal Springs. This was during a time when Sleepy and I had broke up. So I told my sister that I'd tell Milton that there was no use coming by the house to pick her up if she wasn't going to be able to go. So I went up to the program there and Margaret Ashlock and a whole bunch of us were there. So after the program I went over to talk to Milton. And he said,

'Are you going to go out to the dance?' And I said, 'Yes, I'm fixing to go catch the bus.' He said, 'I'll take you out there if you want to ride with me.' So I agreed and that's how I met him. After that night he said that since my sister couldn't go, he'd rather go with me anyway [laughs]. I went with Milton for about six months. It must have been during 1933 because Sleepy and I got back together after Christmas, early in 1934. We were together a lot, most times at dances. But I was so madly in love with Sleepy that I couldn't really see anybody else. However, if Sleepy hadn't been in the picture I guess I might have married Milton. He asked me to marry him but I told him no, that I didn't really love him and that he deserved better than that. Milton was a real sweet person and I thought an awful lot of him."

Ellen Brown, Roy Lee Brown's wife, is in the unique position of having been both family and fan to Milton. Although she did not marry Roy Lee until Christmas 1937, Ellen O'Malley got to know Milton Brown by regularly attending Brownies' dances, where she met her future husband.

ELLEN BROWN: "In the thirties, mention Milton Brown to a woman, just about any woman, and watch her expression change to that of someone who had just stepped into a 'Wonderland with Prince Charming.' All the women, young, old, or in-between, were vying for his attentions. I used to go up to him and say 'Hello, Milton.' He'd respond 'Hello, sweetie-pie' or 'honey-child.' I'd almost collapse with pride and delight! All of us thought he was fascinating. His charm was more an inner magnetism that they could sense rather than see. His physical features, however, were nothing to complain about, not by a long shot. As with Clark Gable and Bing Crosby, Milton had rather prominent ears. But like Gable and Crosby, this did not detract from his overall good looks. Women would practically swoon when Milton would smile and crinkle the corners of his eyes at them. Very sexy eyes! He just had that knack of making a woman feel she was someone special when he talked with her. After he was dead and unable to defend his reputation, there were countless numbers of women who tried to convince others that they had dated Milton. One even claimed Milton wrote 'My Mary' for her. Milton made the tune popular, but it was written by Stuart Hamblen and not by Milton for any Mary he might have known, even Mary Helen, his wife. Milton could not have possibly found that much time to have romanced as many women as has been claimed.

"Milton also gave men the feeling that he welcomed their friendship. They were only too happy to be able to boast, 'Milton Brown and I are good friends!' Naturally, this boosted Milton's popularity. Most men never attain the position of being adored by all the women and still be considered 'a man's man.' But Milton Brown did."

Sometime after he broke up with Sally, Milton met Mary Helen Hames, who eventually became his only wife. She was born to William and Mary Frances Hames on September 17, 1916, in Pilot Point, Texas, close to Denton. The Hameses, like the Browns, were a close-knit family. At the time Mary Helen met Milton, Bill Hames was in the process of expanding an empire, the famous Hames Carnival. Bill Hames had started his carnival in Denton when he borrowed money from a bank to buy a merry-go-round. In the mid-1920s, the Hameses moved to Fort Worth. Mary Helen was the youngest of four children (she had one sister and two brothers). In Pilot Point, Mary Helen attended school, but because the Hameses were always on the road, she took correspondence courses after relocating to Fort Worth. An aunt encouraged Mary Helen to become a singer, and for brief periods she sang at local events and informal gatherings. Her father established the Bill Hames Shows in Fort Worth's Forest Park and soon began taking the carnival out on tour to the surrounding countryside.[7]

Mary Helen met Milton when she was out for an evening with a friend of the family. The friend talked Mary Helen into coming with him to a place called Crystal Springs, where he would introduce her to his friend Milton Brown. Mary Helen was reluctant, but went along and met Milton that night. She had been used to dancing at swanky ballrooms such as the one at Lake Casino, but never was able to understand "this western music." Upon arriving at Crystal Springs, she had a Coke and watched the dancers while her friend talked to Milton.

After the dance, Milton invited them both out for a bite to eat downtown. After establishing that Mary Helen's friend was simply a platonic companion, Milton asked Mary Helen out for a date. Several days later he picked her up and took her to a drive-in for barbecue sandwiches and Cokes. For the first time in years, Milton was thinking of dating somebody seriously. The attractive socialite daughter of the carnival manager was unaware of the bandleader's regional fame, but was instead enamored by his charm and gentlemanly manners, which were atypical of others in his profession. She too began to fall in love.

Things were finally going well for Milton Brown. During that summer of 1934, when he began dating Mary Helen Hames, he started thinking of settling down. However, the Musical Brownies were doing anything but settling. In addition to their regular Saturday night dances at Crystal Springs, the Brownies were now playing out-of-town engagements. Milton had established a regular circuit for the band, playing monthly dances in Waco, Corsicana, Weatherford, Mineral Wells, and other towns surrounding Fort Worth.

Sometime that summer, Milton hired a second fiddle player to complement Cecil Brower. Theodore Grantham was compatible with Cecil because he too was classically trained, with a particular fondness for jazz violinist Joe Venuti. Waco musician Red Varner knew Grantham and was impressed by him when the Brownies made one of their regular stops in Waco to appear on radio station WACO and play a dance at the Cotton Palace Grounds.

RED VARNER: "Theodore Grantham was known as either Ted Grantham or Ted Grant when I knew him. He was one of the first violinists to use a bowing which somebody started calling 'rockin' the bow.'[8] I probably should say that Ted was the first violinist that Texas fiddlers had ever seen using it. I believe Ted was from one of the northern states—which one, I can't say. But when Ted roared into Texas and started rockin' the bow, everybody who played the fiddle felt that he had to learn how to do it. Whether they all learned it directly from Ted or just picked it up from someone who had, I would guess that every fiddler in Texas was rockin' the bow within the next four or five months. A year at the most. Where had Ted himself learned how to rock the bow? He never said, but a good guess would be Joe Venuti. Venuti used it in one form or another on many of his recordings, but his Victor recording of 'Wild Cat' offers some good examples of bow rockin'. In the thirties, 'Wild Cat' and 'Doin' Things' were on a Victor record by Venuti and [it] was one of the most readily available of Venuti's recordings. I remember seeing Cecil Brower beaming his approval of Ted tearing the house down with one of his rockin' the bow choruses at the Cotton Palace Grounds dance."[9]

The Cotton Palace Grounds was one of several places where the Brownies played for dances during their frequent trips to Waco. Located ninety miles south of Fort Worth, Waco was, next to Dallas, the closest large town, and a good starting-off point for many of the Brownies' tours. Local fans such as Varner looked forward to the Brownies' monthly visits to play for dances and to do a broadcast on

WACO. Bob Wills's Playboys had not done well in Waco and had departed for Oklahoma by the spring of 1934, so Milton Brown was welcomed with open arms by the proprietors of the dance halls and the enthusiastic fans. One dance at the Cotton Palace left an indelible image on Red Varner's memory.

RED VARNER: "Local and out-of-town big bands often played for dancing at the Cotton Palace Grounds Dance Hall. The Brown unit of five men and leader drew, as usual, a record-breaking crowd. Never was the old and time-worn phrase 'and a grand time was had by all' more appropriate. For me, there was a memorable moment provided by Cecil Brower.

"Somewhere in the first or second hour, things were getting pretty well warmed up. There was real, if inaudible and invisible, communication between musicians and audience. The time came for a jazz solo by Cecil. I don't have any idea what the tune was but it doesn't matter. At some point in the solo, Cecil played a passage that affected everyone on the dance floor. I think everyone responded in his or her own way to that fleeting sound that was not likely to be heard again. But one old boy out there on that floor could not contain himself. His roar of complete, absolute, uncompromising, and joyous approval and appreciation completed the frosting on the cake, but must have deafened his dancing partner. I would bet that they heard that shout ten blocks away.

"And that great moment was brought about by a quiet, studious, totally unassuming, and amiable kind of man who was so busy doing what he was doing that he himself probably didn't even notice. How often are we affected by the song of a bird? Does the bird know that his song was heard and noticed? If Cecil did notice, he was too modest to have taken credit, even to himself.

"I didn't ever get to tell Cecil about that moment and how unforgettable it was. The longest visit we ever had together was a telephone conversation I had with him up in Oklahoma.

"Ted Grant [Grantham] had some good moments that night, too. The guys in the band were getting their kicks from what he was playing and the dancers noticed and applauded his rockin'-the-bow choruses.

"Derwood Brown had one of his record nights for breaking strings. He always carried two guitars along and had someone out behind the stage or bandstand to change strings for him. The helper was always ready with a fully strung guitar to hand to Derwood the very second he broke one or two strings. That night, I saw him turn around at least three times and hand a guitar to the helper with his right hand and take the fully strung instrument with his left."

Varner was also present at one of the Musical Brownies' radio guest appearances on local station WACO. At dances, Varner was unable to pay strict attention to the visual impact the Brownies had on the crowd, since he came to dance like everyone else. But at the radio station, Red was equally impressed by the Brownies' physical presence.

RED VARNER: "They put on a good show there at WACO. It was geared for radio broadcast, but would have also made a good stage presentation. Each member of the band looked like he had just stepped out of a band box; immaculate attire. White shirts, four-in-hand uniform ties, shoes shined to a mirror brightness, and trousers creased like you wouldn't believe on such a hot day. It was too hot for jackets in that studio or anywhere else inside in Texas in those pre–air conditioned days.

"The band looked good and sounded good. There was a rich body to their ensemble sound that, I'm afraid, did not get out on the air. And the recordings of the day never really captured it. It may have been there somewhere in those 78 rpm grooves, but the record players of that time were a long way from the live, right-in-the-room standards of the present."

In August 1934, Victor's field trip unit, headed by artists and repertoire director Eli Oberstein, traveled again to San Antonio to record Texas musicians. This time the trip was shorter, consuming only four days and recording four groups. The first two, on August 7 and August 8, respectively, were devoted to Bill Boyd and his Cowboy Ramblers and Milton Brown and his Musical Brownies. The recordings of the Cowboy Ramblers inaugurated a flurry of recording activity by similar bands in Texas inspired by the Brownies that continued until World War II. By the end of September, Roy Newman had begun recording for Vocalion, also in a style taken directly from the Musical Brownies.

The Brownies' session, their second and final one for Victor, took place on August 8, 1934. The band numbered six musicians plus Milton Brown. The Victor files list only one fiddle player but aural evidence indicates a second. It has been confirmed by Fred Calhoun, Wanna Coffman, Ocie Stockard, and Roy Lee Brown that the second fiddler was Ted Grantham. Cecil Brower also revealed this fact to

Bob Pinson in the 1960s. Ten tunes were recorded that day, with no composer credits being listed for any of the songs. Milton sang an old vaudeville-era waltz ballad at the session, "Loveland and You" ("I'd Love to Live in Loveland"), which featured another poignant recitation in the style of "My Precious Sonny Boy."

The remaining selections included an instrumental called "Trinity Waltz," based on a combination of the traditional fiddle tunes "Kelly Waltz" and "Wednesday Night Waltz" but renamed to honor Tarrant County's Trinity River. The Brownies began the session with five blues, which all showed the influence of the Mississippi Sheiks, the black string band that recorded during the Brownies' previous visit to San Antonio in April. Two of the songs became long-lasting standards in western swing bands' repertoire: "Where You Been So Long, Corrine?" (Oberstein's bastardized title for "Corrine Corrina") and "Just Sitting on Top of the World" ("Sittin' on Top of the World"). "Take It Slow and Easy" was a variant of a series of songs typified by "Bring It On Down to My House, Honey," in which humorous couplets are interspersed with a common two-line refrain, the couplets sung while the band members play "stop breaks." The W. C. Handy standard "Careless Love," the last tune recorded that day, was cut as "Loveless Love."

The second Bluebird session was not as dynamic as the first one in April, and was most likely done hurriedly, although second takes were attempted on three songs: "Talking about You," "This Morning, This Evening, So Soon," and "Girl of My Dreams." The Brownies were not happy with this second session, mainly because of Eli Oberstein's brusque attitude and impatience to get through the session. Fred Calhoun carelessly added a final note of frustration to "Loveless Love" after the rest of the band finished playing (which one can hear on the recording), and Milton and the Brownies piled back into Sam Cunningham's bus and returned to Fort Worth.

At the end of August Milton took note of a new record company being organized. Within a few months, he arranged for the Brownies to record for Decca in Chicago in the near future.[10]

Milton's personal life took a dramatic upswing as well in the late summer of 1934. He had fallen in love with the beautiful Mary Helen Hames and asked for her hand in marriage. Mary Helen readily accepted Milton's proposal, and the wedding date was set for September 17, Mary Helen's eighteenth birthday. Milton respected Mary Helen's parents, but knew that they would object to their daughter marrying a thirty-one-year-old bandleader. So the two agreed to keep their engagement a secret. They were married in Marietta, Oklahoma, and returned to Fort Worth late that night. Milton had to go back on the air the next day so the newlyweds did not even have time for a honeymoon. After living with Mary Helen's mother for a brief period, the two moved into a duplex at 913 West Peter Smith.

The late fall of 1934 saw two more personnel changes in the Musical Brownies. First came the departure of Ted Grantham to New York City, where the talented violinist played radio programs on the NBC network.[11] With Grantham gone, Milton decided against hiring another fiddle player straightaway and instead began searching for another method to bolster the volume of his band. The dance crowds were getting bigger. Rarely did fewer than one hundred couples show up for a Brownies dance now, and Milton was beginning to book engagements weeks and sometimes months in advance. Still, the Brownies' only amplification was the public address system utilized mostly for Milton's vocals and for Cecil Brower's solos. Fred Calhoun's piano and Ocie Stockard's banjo were powerful enough to cut through just about any crowd noise, but Milton wanted another take-off instrument to spell Cecil without removing the other musicians from their duties as rhythm keepers. As had happened two years before with Fred Calhoun, the answer to Milton's problem materialized. His name was Bob Dunn.

Robert Lee Dunn was born near the town of Braggs, Oklahoma, on February 5, 1908. His father, Silas Dunn, performed traditional country hoedowns, but the first solid musical influence on young Bob came in 1917, when he witnessed a stage show in Kusa, Oklahoma, featuring Hawaiian entertainers and became interested in the steel guitar.[12] Through correspondence with a well-known Hawaiian steel guitarist named Walter Kolomoku, Dunn took lessons on the instrument.[13] In 1927 he joined a professional touring unit called the Panhandle Cowboys and Indians, which traveled from the Midwest down to border stations such as XEPN in Piedras Negras.[14]

A critical point in the history of country music occurred when Bob Dunn somehow got the idea to amplify his steel guitar. Fiddler Jimmy Thomason came to know Bob Dunn and his wife, Avis, intimately, beginning in 1937 when Dunn was a member of Cliff Bruner's Texas Wanderers in Beaumont, Texas. At that time Thomason was Bruner's band boy, having moved to Beaumont from Waco. During his tenure with Bruner and later with the Shelton Brothers in Shreveport, Louisiana, Dunn told Thomason about how the amplification of his steel originated.

JIMMY THOMASON: "It happened when Dunn was working the Boardwalk at Coney Island in New York. Bob was up there just playing steel guitar, standard guitar, and trombone, he was a real good trombone player. Jazz. Not many people know that. Anyway, these were just little old pickup deals. And while he was doing this, he ran into this black guy who was playing a steel guitar with a homemade pickup attached to it. He had this thing hooked up through an old radio or something and was playing these blues licks. Well, this just knocked Bob out and he got this guy to show him how he was doing it. Just as they were getting acquainted, this guy up and ran off. And Bob followed him all the way to New Orleans before he found him again. I never knew this black musician's name but both Bob and Avis talked to me about him often. I stayed in the same boarding house with them in Shreveport when we played with Bob and Joe Shelton. I was real close to them, they were wonderful people. So anyway, this was right before Bob joined the Brownies. He was on tour in Oklahoma and Texas and somehow they ended up in Fort Worth and by that time, Bob had that steel guitar deal already perfected."

WANNA COFFMAN: "I played mostly bass for the Brownies, but I'd usually take out my steel guitar and play one Hawaiian tune on the program like 'Song of the Islands' or 'Hilo March,' stuff like that. Well, one day we were up at KTAT at the Texas Hotel getting ready for the program. We always made our programs out, that's up there where they had a mezzanine and they let the public in to watch the show. Sometimes we were on two hours a day. We went on out to the balcony to have a smoke after we had finished rehearsing. I don't even remember what I was going to play that day. I had my guitar in the studio and it was all set up and ready to play. Directly Milton came out and got Derwood because there was this guy in the studio who was going to try out and play with us. So he wanted Derwood to go over this tune with this guy. I looked in there and there was this great big guy wearing this ragged old suit. Well, it was ole Bob Dunn of course. And he started fooling with my steel guitar. I had one of those Nationals. I'd give anything in the world if I'd kept it. And I remember thinking, 'Good God, that guy's gonna get my guitar all out of tune!' Well, I went on in and Derwood was standing there with him with his guitar. I was just about to ask him, 'What the devil are you doing fooling around with my guitar?' when he and Derwood started off playing 'Over Moonlit Waters.' When Bob took off on that thing, why, my body felt like it was going to wilt!"

FRED "PAPA" CALHOUN: "That son-of-a-gun . . . I was watching him too now, you know. And I was used to Wanna playing steel real nice and pretty, and then there he goes with that fast stuff and I looked at Ocie, and Ocie looked at me and we said, 'What the HELL is he doing?!' That guy played the dangedest steel you ever heard!"

WANNA COFFMAN: "Well, the program finally started and the first song Bob played with us was '"Ida," Sweet as Apple Cider.' He played my steel guitar on that, unamplified. The amplifier came later. They had to lower the microphone so he could be heard on the air. And then he played 'Old Watermill,' ['There's an Old Water Mill by a Waterfall'] and 'Taking Off,' one of his own tunes. Three tunes he played that day. He didn't even know the words to 'Old Watermill,' so Milton sang it with him. After all that, why, I couldn't play that bass or nothing! Listening to him knocked me out. Bob was on a tour and he was playing a show over in Arlington that night. So after the broadcast, he asked to borrow my guitar. He had an old wooden thing with the strings raised up.[15] I didn't know whether to let him have my guitar or not. Then Derwood said, 'Aww, go on and let him use it, Wanna. He's going to come out to the dance after his show is over and sit in with us.' And I thought, 'I'm goin' to just kiss this thing goodbye.'

"Well, sure enough, about 10:00 that night, here comes ole Bob with my guitar. And he got up on that bandstand and when the people heard him play, they started to gather around wondering what that thing was. And Milton hired him on the spot. After that night, I never picked up a steel guitar again."

RED VARNER: "I first saw Bob Dunn play that steel guitar at a dance at the Shady Rest in Waco. It was our first time to see Bob Dunn in person and to hear the first electrically amplified guitar we had heard or seen that close up. We had heard the story of how that guitar had come to be amplified. When Bob auditioned for Milton Brown, everyone recognized the Dunn genius and they all wanted him on the band but there was one problem; how could he be heard on dance jobs?

"The public address system had been on the market and in use for several years. For Milton himself, it was an indispensable part of the band's equipment. How else could his vocals be heard over the roar of a crowded dance hall?

"Whoever it was that handled the Brown P.A. equipment came up with the idea of a magnetic microphone to be placed under the strings and over the sound hole of the guitar. The mike, equipped with a patch cable, would be plugged into an amplifier and speaker independent of and separate from the P.A. system. As we all know, it worked and with the problem of being heard solved, Bob was hired immediately.

"Was that the first 'electric guitar'? I don't know, but I've known people who think so. It almost had to be the first one in Texas. If it was not *the* first 'electric' guitar, it was among the first."

After Bob Dunn's debut with the Brownies on KTAT and at his first dance at Crystal Springs, Milton decided to invest in an amplifier for Bob's steel guitar. He could see by the reaction of the Crystal Springs regulars that Dunn had something special, not only an entirely new way of playing steel guitar but a totally new sound. Dunn was able to play Hawaiian tunes and did on occasion, contributing wonderful chime effects to complement the other musicians. But his main purpose in the Brownies was to play rip-snorting, fire-breathing jazz. During his days with the Brownies, Bob Dunn was a hard-playing, hard-drinking dynamo. Dunn's drinking exploits became almost as famous as his revolutionary steel guitar playing. After World War II, Dunn quit drinking, returned to school, and received a degree in music. Waco musician Red Varner knew Dunn well and the two often conversed about their mutual interest in theories about playing jazz.

RED VARNER: "Bob Dunn was a soft-spoken, gentle soul of a man. High good humor was also a part of his personality which he maintained through good times and bad. As far as I know, his marriage was a happy one. His sense of humor was like that found among most musicians. He loved a good laugh and enjoyed hearing and telling the jokes and/or stories that go with them. I don't ever remember his being down. If he had troubles or maybe didn't feel well, we didn't hear about it. He was rarely, if ever, cynical, but I do remember our talking about clergymen of one faith or another and his comment that 'Everybody has to have a racket.' It wasn't spoken with malice. In fact, I remember a distinct twinkle in his eye when he said it which removed any doubts we may have had as to having a cynic in our midst.

"I once asked him how he got started playing jazz on the steel guitar. His reply ran something like this. Note please that these are not Bob's exact words. Some of the words are his. All of the thoughts are his as I remember them. Here's how he described it to me: 'The "A" tuning of the Hawaiian guitar produces triads all up and down the neck of the instrument. [Roy Lee Brown recalls Dunn using the "E" tuning during his years with the Brownies.] I remember accidentally playing something that I had heard three saxophones play. That was a start. I began experimenting with simple triad passages patterned after three saxophones or three of most anything, trombones for instance. And it just sort of went from there to occasional single note passages to more single note passages to a kind of combination of one, two, and three voices. It didn't take a great deal of this kind of experimentation to convince me that jazz could be played on steel guitar as well as on other instruments. What's more, the steel guitar would add an entirely different color to jazz, just as the violin did in the hands of a Joe Venuti, Emilio Caceres, or Cecil Brower. It adds its marvelous voice and color to Jazz with a capital "J."'

"Bob played excellent Spanish guitar as well as trombone. He was a great admirer of Jack Teagarden and modeled his steel guitar improvisations on the trombone approach to jazz. When you come right down to it, the slide trombone is kin to the steel guitar in that sliding from position to position is common to both. With his background in trombone Bob must have realized this relationship between the two instruments and made good use of it in his early efforts to probe the mysteries of the steel guitar. I don't remember ever hearing him discuss this possible aspect of his studies but there would have been no reason for him to do so because nine string players out of ten at that time would not have understood what he was talking about. I have no idea of how far his study of the trombone had taken him but even the most limited or elementary knowledge of the instrument would have stood him in good stead in his study of the steel guitar.

"I'm sure that Bob would have been very pleased to know of the interest in him and his work, but his native modesty and humility would make it necessary to ask 'Who would want to read about me?' He would never quite be able to accept the fact that he is a legend and has been since the question was asked for the first time: 'Have you heard that new steel guitar player with Milton Brown?'"

Red Varner's analysis of Bob Dunn's adaptation of jazz trombone technique to steel guitar would no doubt have been lost on most Texas musicians in the 1930s. However, the impact Dunn had on the music world was tremendous. In addition to his inventing and popularizing an entirely new way of playing the steel guitar, Bob Dunn also had the distinction of being the first musician to play an amplified instrument on a phonograph record, when he recorded with Milton Brown for Decca in January 1935. Milton Brown and his Musical Brownies were already a phenomenon in Texas when Bob Dunn joined the band. With the addition of Dunn, there was no stopping the Brownies.

EIGHT

Why, the Springs Are Clear as Crystal!

"Dance Night"

Now when it comes to poetry
I'll admit I'm not so good.
But here is one for you,
And I did the best I could.

So when you feel like dancing
And things turn out all right,
Just go to Crystal Springs, on
Sunday or any night.

The Brownies make the music
And if that isn't all right,
Why call on Sam or Henry
Say they'll make things look bright.

They are both quiet, plump and heavy
And I guess you always knew,
Any time you need a friend
Either one will favor you.

—HOMER G. ROACH
411 ST. LOUIS AVE.[1]

For many fans and historians, western swing was born in a weather-beaten wooden dance hall called the Crystal Springs Dancing Pavilion. Few musical genres can trace their origins to one particular building, much less one particular town or city, but the ramshackle "resort" located four miles west of town at 5336 White Settlement Road and run by the Cunningham family was the testing ground for Milton Brown's experiments with his fiddle band. The crowds that danced to the Musical Brownies' music idolized the dapper young bandleader, an idolization that bordered on worship. Playing there nearly every Saturday night from 1930 until his death in 1936, Milton Brown reigned over a small entertainment empire, whose subjects, for several hours each Saturday night, were oblivious to the outside world and the gnawing effects of the Depression.

Born in 1883, Samuel C. Cunningham made his living operating two sand and gravel pits, one in Riverside on the eastern side of town, the other on White Settlement Road. During World War I, Papa Sam supplied many loads of sand and gravel to build the Camp Bowie training facility in Arlington Heights. According to legend, it was Hattie Cunningham, Papa Sam's wife, who first noticed the underground springs that were revealed after Papa Sam began excavation for the army training facility in 1918. Papa Sam was surprised to find that the deep holes from the excavation were filled with water. When he tried to drain them they simply filled up again. So he dug a ditch that led to the Trinity River, hoping the water would drain into it. But the water kept rising to the surface and soon a small lake formed. Deciding to make the best of the situation, Papa Sam built a small private recreation facility around the lake.

After the war, Papa Sam enjoyed entertaining friends with outdoor barbecues and live music. Joining him in his sand and gravel business was his only son, Henry, who became known as Babe. Even larger than his father, Henry Cunningham worshiped Papa Sam and, during the years when Crystal Springs' dance hall was in operation, worked as his father's business partner, bus driver, and security guard. Henry's widow, Mary, recalled the beginnings of Crystal Springs:

MARY CUNNINGHAM: "When Pop bought the property, the springs were already there. It wasn't artificial. It just came up through the ground; even when Pop had the swimming pool built, with cement and everything. Why, those springs were so powerful, the water just came up through the cement. His wife Hattie named it. He didn't know what to name it. She said, 'Why, the springs are clear as crystal! Why not call it Crystal Springs?' And she was right. The springs that came up out of the ground were just like crystal. They were just as clear and cool as they could be. Pop built a swimming pool above the lake which filled up with the spring water. And when they'd drain that swimming pool, they'd just open up those pipes and drain it into the Trinity River. Then, when they'd put that plug in to cap it, those springs would start filling it up again! It didn't take too long to fill that swimming pool up. They never put no chlorine or anything in that pool ever. It was pure spring water. And when you swam in that water, your body felt so good and healthy!

"He had a bunch of benches down there, picnic tables and such, and he'd barbecue a goat for his friends. What eventually became Crystal Springs was once a store for the soldiers, and when Pop took it over, it was just an empty building. Well, Pop built kind of a dance floor out there in the open because his friends used to come out there and bring their fiddles and play out on the picnic ground. Finally, some of them said, 'Pop, why don't you fix that old building up so we could have a place to play?' So he did. He fixed it up and put a roof over that outdoor dance floor and called it the Crystal Springs Dancing Pavilion."

The outdoor dance floor was situated under a big oak tree in front of Papa Sam's home, which was adjacent to the facility. Papa Sam often hired black musicians from lower Main Street in Fort Worth, where many blacks played at the Hippodrome Shine Parlor. Passersby on White Settlement Road became curious about the happenings under the old oak tree and stopped to watch. The picnics drew so many people that Papa Sam finally decided to become a professional dance hall owner. He put a roof over the dance floor and had a large sign built that read "Crystal Springs—Dancing and Swimming." On March 25, 1925, Crystal Springs officially opened to the public.[2] It struggled through the 1920s and did not become popular until Milton Brown and the musicians who played at the Eagles Hall began playing for dances there in 1930.

ROY LEE BROWN: "I don't know how Milton found out about Crystal Springs. When the Light Crust Doughboys left the Eagles Hall and began playing out there at Crystal Springs for dances, they got crowds immediately. One way they got crowds was because Papa Sam had a bus. See, back then they had streetcars. And he would send that bus into town to the courthouse. The bus met the streetcars when they came by the courthouse. He charged ten cents to ride the bus out to Crystal Springs and his son Henry was the driver.

"After the dance, the bus would leave Crystal Springs in order to meet the 12:00 streetcar and the 1:00 streetcar. The last one ran at 2:00. I rode the bus many times, but I usually rode out there with Milton or Derwood in their cars. The Brownies played till 2:00 in the morning sometimes, but Mama and Dad made me come home early. I'd catch the 11:30 bus from Crystal Springs and get home by midnight. The bus would hold maybe thirty people if you crowded it. I've seen it where people would be sitting on each other.

"Crystal Springs was a big dance hall. It could hold maybe eight or nine hundred people if you got them in just right. As dance halls

Crystal Springs, shortly after its opening, c. 1925. Hattie (Mrs. Sam) Cunningham stands in the doorway. This was most likely a summertime photograph, as the sides and ceiling panels of the building have been opened up. Courtesy Hank and Donna Cunningham.

The Musical Brownies smile from Crystal Springs' shuttle bus, in a photograph taken shortly after their formation in September 1932. Milton Brown also used this bus for his early barnstorming tours. Standing in front of the bus: Papa Sam Cunningham. Inside, from left: Henry Cunningham (driver), Ocie Stockard, Milton Brown, Derwood Brown, Wanna Coffman, Jesse Ashlock. Courtesy Hank and Donna Cunningham.

A rare photograph of the interior of Crystal Springs, probably taken during World War II (note the serviceman in the foreground). A band can be seen on the bandstand in the rear of the photograph. The guitarist in front is possibly Derwood Brown. Courtesy Hank and Donna Cunningham.

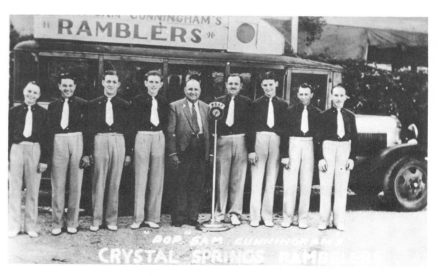

Papa Sam Cunningham's Crystal Springs Ramblers in 1935. From left: Buck Buchanan (fiddle), Morris Deason (banjo, vocals), possibly Kokomo Crocker (piano), Earl Driver (alto saxophone), Sam Cunningham (manager), Henry "Babe" Cunningham (driver), Jimmy McAdoo (bass), unknown guitarist, Jerry Byler (fiddle). Courtesy Roy Lee and Ellen Brown.

go it wasn't really all that big, but to me, a little bitty kid, it looked tremendous."

MARY CUNNINGHAM: "It had ceiling fans and those big old pot-bellied stoves which burned coal. It was always cold in the wintertime, but in the summer it was nice and cool on account of the swimming pool. We put in chicken wire to keep people from jumping in off the balcony. Then we had it beautifully landscaped with grapevines all along the fence and some of the most beautiful roses you ever did see all along the swimming pool."

FRED "PAPA" CALHOUN: "I remember it had wooden posts you had to dance around. In the summertime they had a big pavilion on the outside in back that they could open up and make it twice as big. When it was open we never had less than eight hundred to a thousand every Saturday night. Down the side of the dance hall they had built-in wooden picnic tables lined up that went all the way around the back. Nobody ever sat down, though. They just stood up and danced."

WANNA COFFMAN: "One night, we had so many people there that the floor fell in. That's no lie, either! It was a Halloween dance, which was one of our biggest nights. We were all dressed up like Brownies. Some woman there made us Brownie suits so we wore them that night. We had to wear long underwear underneath because it was cold as the devil! And there were so many people there that right in front of the bandstand that floor fell through a good foot. It's a good thing they had some extra braces or we might have gone into the swimming pool [laughs]!"

In its first few years, Crystal Springs remained unknown to most of the populace of Fort Worth, partly due to the "disreputable" music that was featured there. Fiddle bands and hillbilly music were frowned upon, especially in a city that was desperately trying to catch up to its sophisticated sister city, Dallas. It was the kind of music you listened to with your doors shut. Teenagers sneaked off to Crystal Springs behind their parents' backs, arriving home at some late hour with fabricated stories about "the movie running late" or "we saw an accident on the road and had to stop." Ellen O'Malley, who later became Mrs. Roy Lee Brown, was one of those teenagers.

ELLEN BROWN: "One night, a friend of mine told me, 'We can get the neighbor lady across the street to teach us the right way to dance.

Then we can slip off and go to Crystal Springs Dance Pavilion.' She was sixteen, I was fifteen. We had four friends about the same age as us and we went out to Crystal Springs on the sly, because our parents would never hear of our going to a public dance hall.

"During his radio show, Milton usually announced that he had a private bus that made two runs, at certain hours, from the courthouse to Crystal Springs for their dances. We had our own transportation, but we had to concoct a story as to where we were going and what we'd be doing on that Halloween night in 1935. A young neighbor lady let us say that we were having a party at her house, but I chickened out and told my mother the truth. She was afraid my dad would find out, but she agreed to keep it our secret. I think she too was excited about it and perhaps wished she could join us. 'Be careful!' she warned, 'but have a good time!' 'Oh, I will!' I assured her.

"My girlfriends and I had been going regularly to see and hear the Brownies' broadcast at KTAT where they did their show. Looking back, I know this must have been one of the most exciting periods of my life! In our area, Milton Brown and his Musical Brownies were virtually household words. During the Depression, having free entertainment was a blessing. The fact that Milton and his band were all so fantastic made you feel you were dead and in Heaven for a short while each day. It got so that I just lived for the Saturday night dances. For sure, the band really gave you your money's worth. There were only a few tables and chairs for seating, but no matter, most of us were on the dance floor constantly anyway!"

GLENNA MCBRIDE: "I must have gone to a million dances! I used to take my little baby along and put her on a table and then I'd go dance. We used to go out there all the time! That was just about the only place there was to go. We had an old car. And if it wasn't running we'd get in somebody else's car. We hardly ever went out there by ourselves."

Milton Brown and his Musical Brownies became such a local sensation that, in time, Crystal Springs became *the* place to dance for the rich as well as the poor. People showed up in every kind of vehicle imaginable, from Cadillacs to bicycles. Many walked several miles from the suburbs and farms to the dance hall.

ELLEN BROWN: "In the beginning there were some people who came to Milton's dances just to see who'd be there. They wondered why the place was so jam-packed, and the air crackled with excitement.

Some of the so-called upper-crust folks came to look down their noses, as a lark, and to sneer at the 'country hicks.' One man came up to Milton during the dance to complain, 'I expected some good orchestra music here, but this is pure corn!' Milton smiled disarmingly and replied good-naturedly, 'Yep, and I'm sure selling it!' The man didn't stay, but they did shake hands before he and his party left."

ROY LEE BROWN: "The bulk of the people came out there like Ellen did. She used to run around with several girlfriends, and one guy and his girlfriend used to pick up four or five others and they'd drive out there together in one car. A lot of the boys were within walking distance so they came that way. They lived out in Castlebury, Roberts Cut-Off, or White Settlement, areas near Crystal Springs.

"I remember the first time I went out there. I asked Dad, 'Can I go down to Crystal Springs tonight and watch Milton and Derwood?' And Dad said, 'Oh no, you can't go out *there!*' But Milton spoke up, 'Don't worry, Dad. Derwood and I will keep an eye on Roy Lee.' So Dad said OK. Milton's word was law around the house. He never crossed Dad or anything, but whatever he said, went."

Milton used his radio program on KTAT (and later, WBAP) to advertise the dances. When the band began playing out of town shortly after forming in September 1932, Milton spread the word about Crystal Springs to the surrounding countryside, and it eventually became a mecca for fans of fiddle band music. To youngsters in Texas during the Depression, Crystal Springs' dusty dance hall was a glittering palace, with Milton Brown its anointed king. Musician Sock Underwood was one fan who idolized the Brownies.

O. G. "SOCK" UNDERWOOD: "Me and Dickie McBride grew up together.[3] We were real good friends. And we used to sit around under the barn on rainy days and talk about how we was going to be Musical Brownies when we got big. That was the dream then. We never got to see Milton at Crystal Springs while he was living but we saw him when they were on the road. We finally got out there in the summer of 1936 when the centennial was still trying to limp down the road."

Crystal Springs also became the Saturday night home for many of the nefarious criminals and notorious characters of the Depression era.

J. B. BRINKLEY: "Back in the 1930s there were a lot of people who made the headline news: Machine Gun Kelly, Pretty Boy Floyd, Raymond Hamilton, Bonnie and Clyde, that type. At Crystal Springs the Brownies sometimes broadcast from there, maybe once a week. This was when Bonnie and Clyde were running from the law. Clyde Barrow had an old Ford which had a radio in it and they *always* listened to Milton's broadcast when they were in town. Clyde's favorite tune was 'My Mary' and he'd call Crystal Springs and get Papa Sam on the phone and say, 'Hey, Pop! Tell ol' Milton to play "My Mary" and dedicate it to "you-know-who!"' He'd never say who he was but Pop knew his voice. And Milton would go on the air and say, 'OK, here is "My Mary" and we want to dedicate it to "you-know-who"' [laughs]."

FRED "PAPA" CALHOUN: "I never will forget this as long as I live. You know how they used to have these big motometer wings that you'd put on your car hood? Well I had one of those, and I parked my car out in front of Papa Sam's house. Papa Sam lived right next to the dance hall. We were playing the dance one Sunday night and at intermission I went out to my car to get a drink and saw that the motometer was gone. Clyde Barrow and that bunch were all over there; that S.O.B. was stealing tires and hubcaps, stuff like that. So Clyde was out there dancing and I called him over and said, 'Clyde, did you take the motometer off my car?' He looked at me for a second and said, 'Where was your car parked [laughs]?' I said, 'I was parked right over by Papa Sam's house.' Ol' Clyde looked thoughtful for a moment, then he took off. Along about 11:00 here comes Clyde again. I'm back on the bandstand with my back to the crowd and I hear, 'Hey, Papa!!' I turned around and he's got something wrapped up in a white handkerchief. He says, 'Here, catch!' And he pitched it up to me. I caught it. It was my motometer [laughs]."

J. B. BRINKLEY: "We didn't have a car, but my daddy knew that all he had to do was walk down to the corner of University and Seventh Street and stand there and before long, somebody would drive by that he knew and say, 'Hey, Blackie! You going to Crystal Springs? Well, get in!' Well, one time, here comes Bonnie and Clyde. She was driving and he was on the passenger's side with a machine gun on his lap. They were going real fast but they stopped when they saw my dad. They knew each other, see. So Bonnie slams on the brakes. SCREEEE! She leans out and says, 'Hey, Blackie! You going to Crystal Springs?' He said, 'Yeah.' She says, 'Well, we're a little hot right now but you're welcome to ride with us if you want to.' Daddy looked in there, saw that machine gun, and just waved them on: 'No, I think I'll wait for somebody else. Thanks just the same, you go ahead [laughs].'"

Blackie Brinkley was one of several people Papa Sam Cunningham hired as bouncers at Crystal Springs. The dance hall developed a reputation as being a rough place, especially when word got out that Bonnie and Clyde were regular dancers. There was always an abundance of fistfights at Crystal Springs, but never a report of a killing.

ROY LEE BROWN: "The Brownies played for five hours solid each Saturday night. They'd rarely get an intermission because as soon as the music stopped, fights would start up. I've seen four or five different fights going on at the same time. Nobody ever got killed, but once in a while somebody pulled a knife. People like Bonnie Parker, Clyde Barrow, Raymond Hamilton, they were killers all right, but they never caused any trouble when they came out there. They just wanted to dance like everyone else. One reason there was never any real violence at Crystal Springs was Henry Cunningham, Papa Sam's son. Papa Sam had Henry act as bouncer, and if a fight started, he'd jump right in. They had as many as four or five bouncers working there at one time. Henry wore a big .45 caliber pistol. He got a permit as a special deputy sheriff from the Tarrant County sheriff's department and was allowed to carry a gun.[4] He wore it on the outside of his trousers. It wasn't concealed or anything. I never saw him pull it, but I'll tell you one thing for sure: it was loaded.

"Henry was called 'Baby Henry' or just 'Babe.' He was about six feet one or two and must have weighed about 250 pounds. And he was fat. A real big man. Papa Sam was big and fat, too, but he wasn't as tall as Henry. Henry also never cracked a smile. He was always ready to do battle."

Mary Cunningham often assisted her husband, Henry, taking in money at the door and helping to keep order.

MARY CUNNINGHAM: "My husband had the right to pick you up, put you in his car, and take you right to jail. I've seen him pick many a woman up just like she was a sack of flour, put her over his shoulder, walk on out and throw her, screamin' and kickin', in that car. And he'd take her right to the jailhouse and then come right back to get somebody else. Pop and Henry tried to keep order out there. And they wouldn't have none of this vulgarity or any of that stuff either.

If I was working the door and Henry was taking somebody away or throwing them out, he'd stop and say to me, 'Mary, take a good look at this one. I don't want this party in here no more!' So when they'd come back again and want in, I'd say, 'Sorry, my husband said no. You can't come back in here.' We could have used their money, but we didn't want no trouble. There were a lot of stories anyway, people warning people not to go out there because they might get killed or stabbed.

"My father-in-law was against drinking. He hated that drinking. But he had a bottle in his dresser drawer. And if he had a cold or anything, he'd turn it up and take himself a drink. But he hated drinking, oh MAN, he hated it! He hated it with a purple passion, but he sold that beer. He had to at the dance hall. That's the reason he got my husband the right to lock up drunks. They'd start drinking and then they'd start fights."

ROY LEE BROWN: "I've seen the bouncers use blackjacks on guys all the time. If the bouncer couldn't separate fighters, he'd knock one of them over the head with a blackjack.

"Milton knew almost everyone there and was liked by most people. At the Brownie Tavern, when a fight started, he would tell the band to keep playing, and he would get out on the dance floor and stop fights himself. I've seen Milton break up many a fight, and he'd get blood all over his shirt, none of it his. He didn't have to do that at Crystal Springs because Papa Sam always had four or five bouncers. Blackie Brinkley, J. B.'s father, was one of the bouncers. Also A. C. Coker, who was a part-time barkeeper. There was also a little guy named Sailor Baret who wore a gun. Nobody ever fooled with Sailor. He was a wrestler.

"During Prohibition, bootleggers were everywhere. The bootleggers paid protection by keeping the policemen stocked up on whiskey. If you drank back then, you either had to drink home-brew beer, gin, or bootlegged whiskey. One of the regular dancers was a guy named Ed Coplin. Ed ran a service station and the bootleggers would give Ed whiskey for gas or service, so Ed always had whiskey."

ED COPLIN: "I used to take whiskey out there in half-pint or pint bottles. Well, one particular night we didn't have no bottles so we went to the restroom and just drank out of the jug. Ol' Baby Henry Cunningham came into the restroom and caught us. Now, everybody else was drinking out of bottles in there but he was going to take the whiskey away from us for drinking out of the jug. We had a little tussle and finally Papa Sam barred me. He wouldn't let me come to the dance for a long time. One time there was a gal in there that I wanted to go out with, so I waited until Papa Sam left the door to go to the restroom and slipped in. I was dancing with that gal for about thirty minutes when Papa Sam finally saw me and tried to make me leave.

"I said, 'Papa Sam, I've been here thirty minutes already. How about letting me stay the rest of the night?' He said, 'Why should I? You brought in whiskey. You know that's against the rules!' I said, 'I won't do it no more, Papa Sam!' He thought for a bit and said, 'Well, all right [laughs].'"

ROY LEE BROWN: "That's what Papa Sam would do. He'd bar somebody but then they'd beg him to let them come back and they'd promise not to do it anymore. And he always said, 'OK, go on back in.' That's the way he was."

FRED "PAPA" CALHOUN: "I remember one thing that happened to Wanna out there. See, we took an intermission every night except on Saturday nights. Well, one time, we took an intermission and Wanna wanted to go out to a liquor store and get him a pint of whiskey. While he was in there, three or four guys walked in wearing black coats. And they had machine guns. And they went in and held the place up. Well, ol' Wanna came back and he was just white as a sheet. He said those guys were just about the meanest looking men he had seen in his life! They had sawed-off machine guns. And they took Wanna's pocketbook and I don't remember if he ever got his whiskey or not [laughs]!"

J. B. BRINKLEY: "One time, a guy came out there to Crystal Springs with a new Ford that he had just bought. He was so proud of that car. And he came in and yelled, 'Hey, Papa Sam! I want you and all the boys to come out with me and see my new car!' Papa Sam said, 'All right, we'll be out there in a minute and see it.' It must have been about three hours before anybody got a chance to go out there and see this guy's new Ford. When they finally got out there, somebody had already stolen all the wheels off of it and set it up on cordwood!"

FRED "PAPA" CALHOUN: "I'll tell you one of the funniest things that happened out there. My brother Paul was working the door, taking tickets one Saturday night. Blackie Brinkley was working the floor. Some guy got smart with Papa Sam or something, and Blackie hit him.

There used to be a big penny scale sitting there on the other side of the door, where you could weigh yourself if you wanted to. Well, when Blackie hit this guy, he knocked him cold and he fell across that scale. Paul handed Blackie a penny and said, 'Weigh him [laughs].'"

WANNA COFFMAN: "Boy, that was a rough joint! There were three or four guys that came out there, mostly on Saturdays, just to cause trouble. One of them was named Blackie Lawson. We used to call him 'the Bully of the Town.' He'd just as soon fight as eat. And all the time he was fightin' he'd be laughin'. Papa Sam would let Blackie in and he wouldn't be there ten minutes before he'd have one going. He'd been in jail many times. I don't know how he'd get out but he always did. Directly, somebody would say, 'There's that jailbird again,' and soon they'd wish they hadn't of said that. I saw Blackie Lawson whup four guys out in front of Crystal Springs one night. One of them had a car crank. But he licked 'em all. Blackie had scars all over his head. He'd killed three or four people. I don't know how he ever got out of the pen. Blackie just loved the Brownies and he would come and tip us twenty dollars to let him sing 'Wabash Cannon Ball.' He couldn't sing worth a lick but we'd take the twenty and let him try [laughs]."

FRED "PAPA" CALHOUN: "One night we played at the Black and White Club in Stanford. We stopped at a café to eat before the dance. Milton looked out the window into the parking lot and said, 'Oh, Lord, here comes Blackie Lawson, we're going to have trouble.' Blackie came in and sat down there with me and Cecil, and we ate our supper. Then Blackie said, 'Say, Fred, how about you and Cecil riding out with me to the club. I don't know where it is, maybe you could direct me?' We said, 'Sure, if you drive slow.' Blackie was a fast driver. So Cecil and I got in the car with him and we were off. It was a coupe, as I remember it. We drove on out there and we always pulled on out behind the club and parked, you know. We got out and Blackie said, 'Listen, fellas, I'd like to show you something.' He raised up the tail end of the car, and he had two machine guns and two pistols and everything else in there. And I said, 'Blackie, what have you been doing?' 'Oh, I've been doing a little hijacking on the side [laughs]!' He said, 'Say, Papa, you gonna ride back with me?' I said, 'Nooo, no! I'm not getting back in *that* car [laughs]!'"

The relationship between local tough Blackie Lawson and the

Brownies was strange but symbiotic. Although he was well known around Fort Worth as a troublemaker and small-time criminal, Lawson was one of the Brownies' biggest fans. He even traveled with the band on occasion when they went on the road.

FRED "PAPA" CALHOUN: "When we went out of town, we'd park our cars down at Glover's Garage. Well, ol' Blackie knew where we parked, so one day, we were fixing to go somewhere, and he came down there to see us off. It was real cold out and we all had on overcoats. I had on a pair of pigskin gloves. Blackie got to looking at my gloves and he said, 'Man, I'd give anything in the world to have gloves like those.' I had an extra pair in my overcoat, so I handed the pair I had on to him and said, 'OK, Blackie. Take 'em. They're yours.' His eyes opened real wide and he said, 'Oh, Papa! Thank you! Thank you!' The next time we went down there, Blackie met us again. He had a 24-karat gold belt buckle about four or five inches across and he said, 'Papa, I brought this for you. Here.' I've still got it somewhere. He probably hijacked it [laughs]."

WANNA COFFMAN: "Blackie Lawson was a pool hustler. He'd always go out to Crystal Springs and he never was broke. He always had a wad of money on him. And he never worked a day in his life, I don't guess. But it seemed like he'd do anything in the world for the Brownies. He'd fight for us or anything."

SOCK UNDERWOOD: "Now there was a guy who loved Milton like he was a brother. He just thought there was nobody in this world like Milton Brown. Blackie Lawson was their protector. If anybody ever jumped on Milton, they'd have to fight Blackie first. But you see, nobody ever wanted to fight Milton. He wasn't the kind of guy you'd get on, man! Not even if you were drunk. They didn't want to fight him, they wanted to LOVE him! I never heard ANYBODY say a harsh word about him. Everybody wanted to love him. He was just a lovable person. Too bad we didn't get all that love [laughs]!"

OCIE STOCKARD: "Ol' Blackie Lawson would play poker a lot. And it didn't matter whether or not he won because after the game, if he lost, he'd rob you anyway [laughs]!"

J. B. BRINKLEY: "My dad was named Blackie, too, and he and Blackie Lawson got into some trouble once when I was just a little bitty boy. So Blackie Lawson told somebody, 'I know how to get back at Blackie Brinkley: I'll just go run over his boy and kill him.' He shouldn't have said that, because there was a guy in Fort Worth named Cash Stevens. Cash had pock marks all over his face. He never smiled, and when he told you something, he meant it. This guy once poured gasoline over a guy down at Lake Worth and set him on fire. Well, when Cash heard what Blackie Lawson said, he got into a cab and went home and got his double-barreled shotgun. He knew the pool hall where Blackie hung out down on Main Street, so he went there and waited. After a while, Blackie walked outside and Cash stepped out of the cab and said, real polite: 'Mr. Lawson! I hear you had an idea that you were going to run over Blackie Brinkley's boy!' Blackie jumped backward, put his hands out in front of him and said, 'Oh, no, no, you heard it wrong, Cash!' Cash said, 'No, I don't think so.' And he cocked that hammer and Blackie raised his hands up and ducked behind this tall fireplug and pleaded, 'Oh, Cash, please don't kill me! Please don't kill me!' Cash put the gun down and pointed at Blackie, 'I'm telling you, if you ever harm a hair on that kid's head, I'll come and get you!' Man, there was some mean people back there in Fort Worth then.

"Now this next story never got in the papers, but it happened. Blackie Lawson got into a fight with some guy over at a joint on the north side of Fort Worth. They got into it pretty bad and somebody went and called the police. When the paddy wagon came, they arrested this other guy and put him in the back, but they forgot to lock the door. So they were trying to find out who started the fight when Blackie came outside. This guy thought he was locked safely in the paddy wagon and he was looking out these bars in the back calling Lawson all kinds of names: 'If I could just get out of here, I'd finish you off right now, you so-and-so!' Blackie walked up to that wagon and found out that that door was unlocked, and he dragged that guy out, knocked his neck up against a brick wall, broke his neck, and killed him. But the police couldn't do anything about it legally because this guy was officially under arrest and was under their protection. Nothing was ever said about it."

*   *   *

In the beginning, the Brownies played at Crystal Springs several nights a week. After they started booking dances out of town, the Crystal Springs dances were limited to Saturday nights.

ROY LEE BROWN: "Sometimes they had prizes for the best dancers if they were trying to build up a weekday dance like on Tuesday, for instance. The rest of the week, Milton was out of town. A Tuesday night at Crystal Springs might not draw too big a crowd, but say if the Brownies were going to play in Abilene, and Milton announced it on his program, there would be a packed house in Abilene, guaranteed. They didn't have dances there as much as they did in Fort Worth, in these smaller towns. So whenever they went out of town, they always had a full house. Not too many people came to Crystal Springs in the middle of the week. Fort Worth has always been a Saturday night town. Always has been and always will be. Saturdays and holidays were the big nights, although the Brownies sometimes played Thursdays and Sundays also. But on Saturday night, you couldn't even get in the place.

"The Brownies would get there about 8:00. Most of the people got there by 8:30 and the dances started right at 9:00. When I was traveling with them they started off the dance with 'About a Quarter to Nine.'[5] On Saturday nights they hired at least two men to park cars outside, so they would remain orderly. It was all gravel out in front of the place and they also parked cars behind the dance hall back by the swimming pool. There were two guys with flashlights out there all the time so people could get out if they wanted to.

"During the day, Crystal Springs was more or less open. A fellow by the name of Blackie Williams, who had a crippled leg, tended bar and lived in one of the cabins they had there. He stayed most of the time, swept up during the day, and also ran the bar. If Milton wouldn't have anything to do, he'd go down there and play dominoes.

"Eventually, they built an outdoor area over the swimming pool. In the summertime you could dance out there or dance inside. In the wintertime they covered it with a big tarpaulin and a big coal stove kept it warm. People used to dive off that dance pavilion into the swimming pool below. I did it myself.

"Directly underneath the dance floor were dressing rooms where folks could change into their bathing suits if they wanted to go swimming in the swimming pool. Crystal Springs was built on a bluff. There was a slope that went down to the springs. The swimming pool was down there and the lake was behind it. Up underneath where it slopes down they had the dressing rooms. On one side they had the ladies and the other side had the men. In between they had a place where they'd rent suits and towels. That all belonged to Papa Sam. He'd charge fifteen or twenty cents to swim but I didn't pay anything. I figured that since my brothers Milton and Derwood played there, I could do anything I wanted to. All the kids knew who

I was, so they'd call me over to the screen wire out front and ask me to get them in. I'd then walk outside and walk back in with them coming back in with me. Papa Sam never said anything, but I could see he didn't like that. I shouldn't have been passing kids in without them paying but you know how kids are! Papa Sam could be one of the nicest persons you'd ever want to meet, but he also was kind of cantankerous. He was just changeable that way."

FRED "PAPA" CALHOUN: "They had eleven natural springs there. Kept that water clear and pretty too. There was also a bathhouse under the dance hall. About half of the springs was covered and half was open. We used to go swimming after the dance on hot summer nights. Go right out back and dive in. Cecil Brower and I used to fish down there too."

MARY CUNNINGHAM: "Beyond the swimming pool was the catfish pond that Papa Sam kept stocked. His wife liked to fish and he would buy truckloads of old bread from Mrs. Baird's bakery and throw it all out there to the fish."

ROY LEE BROWN: "Papa Sam stocked catfish and crappie in that lake. He'd buy day-old bread that the bakers couldn't sell and keep it in a little house out there. Then he fed those fish every day. He charged fifty cents a hook to fish in the lake and the people got to keep all they caught.

"Papa Sam had one great big catfish in that lake on which he painted a big '50.' He let everybody know that whoever caught that fish with the '50' on it would get fifty dollars. Not to mention the fish. A. C. Coker lived right next to Crystal Springs and also worked for Papa Sam as a bouncer. Blackie Williams worked as a bartender. Well one day, one of A. C.'s brothers and Blackie Williams's boy Fritz went down there fishing unbeknownst to Papa Sam and caught the catfish with the '50' on it. Fritz told his daddy about it and Blackie Williams had a fit. Then after Blackie cooled off, he went and told Papa Sam, and Papa Sam had a fit and made them throw the fish back. Papa Sam wanted to make sure a customer caught that fish."

The fishing, swimming, dancing, and other activities made Crystal Springs a popular Fort Worth night spot. But despite all these attractions, it was Milton Brown himself who drew carloads of happy customers to the dance hall on White Settlement Road. The crowd that jammed Crystal Springs to the rafters was a regular crowd, appearing like clockwork each Saturday night to enjoy an evening of dancing. In time, the Brownies got to know many of the regulars. Milton was as congenial as ever during the dances, using his salesmanship and announcing abilities to emcee the evening's festivities. Realizing that public relations was a full-time job, Milton spent his days keeping in touch with his constituency when the Brownies were not playing out of town.

ROY LEE BROWN: "Milton was a mixer and he made the rounds. You might say that he'd go around town and 'politick.' This is not meant to indicate that he acted like a politician wanting to get votes. Far from it. He just genuinely liked people. He would drive down Darcy Avenue and stop and talk with the neighbors, even those that he knew just didn't like dancing and would never go out to Crystal Springs. The Brownies had two audiences: those who went to the dances and those who listened on the radio.

"When we lived on Roberts Cut-Off, I'd ride into town with Milton. He'd ask me if I wanted to sing a song on his program on KTAT so I'd go with him. Sometimes we'd go downtown in his car and go to a picture show. We lived maybe four or five miles from town then. Milton would take me downtown to the radio broadcast, park his car, and when we walked down the street, I guarantee you he'd speak to four or five people in each block who knew him."

SOCK UNDERWOOD: "Milton was just one happy guy from the word go. Always smiling, flashing those teeth, just as happy as he could be. EVVVVerybody loved that man.

"And that band of his, I'm telling you . . . Papa Calhoun was always an inspiration to me. I watched him like a hawk. It got to the point where I played piano so much like him that at a dance one time, some blind man turned to me and said, 'That sure was fine, Freddy [laughs]!' Milton was always coming on with new songs but Fred just wanted to relax and play the old barrelhouse-style piano, you know. Boy, I loved those guys, loved 'em dearly.

"Derwood was one of the damndest guitar players you ever heard. He'd just haul off and slam the hell out of that guitar. I mean, he could knock fire from the thing and not half try! He never learned none of those beautiful strokes you learn in school, he just learned by gouging it out. But I guarantee you, every lick he hit was right on time."

ROY LEE BROWN: "Derwood was Milton's right-hand man. When Milton got off the bandstand, he'd leave Derwood in charge to keep things going. Derwood was the unsung hero of the band. He not only played guitar but he sang a lot of songs and then he sang harmony behind Milton. The only one that Milton would let sing in the band besides himself was Derwood. Cecil would sing a specialty number now and then but that was it. Ocie would have liked to sing, but Milton never called on him for a solo, just harmony."

The regular Saturday night dances at Crystal Springs enabled the Brownies to experiment with their sound, become familiar with each other's musical habits and idiosyncracies, and expand their repertoire. The crowds certainly had their favorite numbers, such as "My Mary" and "St. Louis Blues," but Milton, always wanting to forge ahead, stayed on the alert for new tunes.

ROY LEE BROWN: "Milton listened to the radio for most of his songs. Most of the music that was played on radio back then was pop tunes. There wasn't a 'best sellers' list that I know of at that time. If there was, he didn't see it. Also, Milton bought very little sheet music. The western bands at that time weren't coming out with anything new anyway. They played the old tunes that had been around for generations. Even songs like 'About a Quarter to Nine,' which was featured in a movie, Milton first heard on the radio.

"I remember one night I was out at Crystal Springs, and before the dance started, Milton called Derwood, Ocie, and Cecil in the storeroom that was behind the bandstand and told them to bring their instruments with them. I heard him tell them this so I went with them. The tune 'The Music Goes Round and 'Round' had just come out. Milton had heard it on the radio and learned all the words and the melody. Milton had a good ear and memory for tunes. So he sang the song to the boys and they picked up on it immediately. They went over it twice and then when the dance started they played it that night.[6]

"Later Milton added extra verses to it. This is the way it went as best that I can remember:

> The Brownies play and sing
> And the music goes down and around
> Wo ho ho ho ho ho
> And it comes out here.
>
> Derwood picks the guitar strings
> And the music just rings and rings

Wo ho ho ho ho ho
And it comes out here.

Cecil brings the fiddle bow down
And the music goes down and around
Below, below weedie hey, hey ho
Listen to the jazz come out.

Now Fred brings both hands down
And the piano goes down and around
Wo ho ho ho ho ho
And it comes out here.

"Another song that Milton put extra words to was 'What's the Reason (I'm Not Pleasin' You).'"

Every time that I come in,
You say I've been drinking gin, tell me
What's the reason
I'm not pleasin' you?

If I fall into a chair
You say go out and get some air, tell me
What's the reason
I'm not pleasing you?

You say my breath smells like wine
When I've been drinking beer, I tell you
All the time
But you don't seem to hear.

If I bump into the wall
You blame it all on the alcohol, tell me
What's the reason
I'm not pleasing you?

One of the Brownies' most popular numbers at Crystal Springs was W. C. Handy's "St. Louis Blues." Their performance consisted of Cecil Brower's playing the melody in a slow-drag tempo, followed by Milton's vocal. At a given moment toward the end of the piece, Fred Calhoun would increase the tempo to presto and Milton and Derwood would sing the final choruses together. The crowds loved the arrangement and eagerly anticipated the change in tempo. When requests began pouring in for the song, Milton made sure the Brownies performed "St. Louis Blues" twice each Saturday night. He also milked the crowd's anticipation of the tempo change by drawing out the slow-drag portion, often consuming ten or fifteen minutes. By the time Calhoun signaled the change, the dancers were in a frenzied state, wondering just when it would come. At their first recording session for Decca in January 1935, Milton Brown and the Musical Brownies recorded a condensed three-minute rendition of that arrangement (Decca 5070). It became one of the Brownies' top-sellers on Decca, reissued on the label's postwar 46000 series and included on the ten-inch "Dance-O-Rama" LP issued in 1954.

Because of the threat of instantaneous brawls on the dance floor, the Brownies were forced to restrict their intermissions at Crystal Springs to no more than were absolutely necessary. During the brief breaks that did occur, Milton sometimes took Ocie Stockard, Cecil Brower, and Derwood to the storeroom behind the bandstand to teach them a new song. Stockard marveled at Milton's ability to listen to a song on the radio once and know all the chord changes and lyrics. Behind the bandstand, Milton would sing the melody for Cecil, who usually kicked off the songs. Derwood and Ocie would then go over the chord progressions and pass them along to Dunn, Calhoun, and Coffman. Derwood would also learn the lyrics in case he was needed to sing harmony. Through this process, the Brownies padded their repertoire until they were able to play nearly any popular song the crowd would ask for. With the dances lasting up to five hours each night, the audiences generally went home having had all of their song requests filled. This example was set at Crystal Springs and carried out at the other locations around the state where the Brownies played.

WANNA COFFMAN: "Jimmie Davis would come out to Crystal Springs every once in a while. He and Milton got acquainted pretty good there for a while. Jimmie used to carry a half a pint of whiskey with him all the time with rock candy in it. And every time he sang, he'd take him a tablespoon full of it. He said that would open his voice up. The funniest thing was when we made records with him in 1937, he brought a guy with him just to direct him. Jimmie didn't have a real good sense of rhythm. He'd break time like Bob Wills used to. So this guy would be there just to point at Jimmie when it was time to come in and sing. Then he'd also have to tell him when to quit [laughs]!"[7]

Not all the Brownies' guest vocalists were professionals. Occasionally they allowed ordinary fans to participate, a habit that endeared the band to many of their customers.

J. B. BRINKLEY: "One thing I'll never forget out at Crystal Springs. This was while I was playing with Papa Sam's band, the Crystal Springs Ramblers. Everything was going real good and here comes this big tall guy on the bandstand. He had his hands behind him and he stood there till we got through. We thought maybe Papa Sam had sent him there. Papa hadn't. This guy came up on his own. He had on a long-billed cap, real sharp shoes, big old watch fob. So we asked him what he wanted. He said, 'I'd like to come up and yodel one with y'all.' We asked him if he had any particular song in mind and he drawled, 'Wayallll, I'll tell you . . . I'm the onliest human being what can yodel with his lips closed.' And he done it too. He clamped his lips shut like ol' Cousin Jody used to do on the Opry and yodeled. So we're standing there watching this, and directly we caught Henry Cunningham's eye and called him over and said, 'Will you get this guy off of the bandstand [laughs]?'"

FRED "PAPA" CALHOUN: "There was one feller that always stood out right in front of the bandstand, shook his head and yelled, 'Mercy!' One time after the dance, we were fixing to leave and we saw him standing there. My brother Paul was working the door and he walked over to this guy and said, 'Tell me, where'd you get that inferiority complex [laughs]?'"

ROY LEE BROWN: "The guy who yelled 'Mercy' was named John, but I can't remember his surname. He was at Crystal Springs every Saturday night, without fail. He'd always yell something at the band like, 'Mercy! Where'd you get that pretty thing?' He'd yell at Wanna, 'Mercy, Wanna! Where'd you get that haircut?' He'd yell to the other guys, too, but he'd always use the exclamation 'Mercy!' first."

HARRY FOWLER: "One night we got real tickled when an old boy got pretty tight and staggered up to the bandstand where Milton was singing and he said, 'Hey, Milton! Play something slick and slimy [laughs]!' I never will forget that. Milton got quite a kick out of that old boy. Slick and slimy [laughs]!

"We were there just about every night they were open. We saw a lot of fights out there, but nobody ever tried to jump on Milton. If anybody had ever tried, why that would be his undoing. First, he'd have to deal with ol' Henry Cunningham. And also everybody else on the dance floor. You see, Milton Brown never knew a stranger. If you got to be known as a 'regular' out there, nobody'd better mess with you. It was like a family affair. Derwood never was as friendly as Milton was."

ELLEN BROWN: "Milton kept the band playing one tune right after the other so the only time we rested was by standing ganged up around the bandstand, watching the musicians. Lots of people standing around the bandstand just had to tell Milton or Derwood something. I think this was mostly a ruse to get to put their heads close together with Milton or Derwood. Surely they were often exasperated with the fans, but they never ever showed it. They were always receptive.

"One night, Milton and Derwood's younger brother Roy Lee was at the dance. He was sitting on the bandstand, helping Derwood keep an extra guitar fully strung. Derwood broke so many strings, he used two guitars. I thought Roy Lee was really cute, so I edged up to him and started talking to him. He was nice and friendly, so I did the unpardonable thing, those days, by *asking him* to dance. That's when and where I met my future husband, and how I happened to become Milton and Derwood's sister-in-law. We were not married until after Milton's death, however, so he never knew me as a member of his family."

Like most performing bands, the Brownies had prepared arrangements for their standard tunes, theme songs for opening and closing dances, specialty numbers for birthdays, special occasions, and seasonal events, and a well-paced presentation. Milton was supreme at sizing up a crowd, determining whether they were worn out from fast numbers, in which case he would call for a waltz or a ballad, and then signaling for an up-tempo two-step or a round dance. Crystal Springs made a good portion of its money from drinks, and the Brownies' sold a lot of liquid refreshments for Papa Sam by working up the dancers' thirsts. After Prohibition was lifted, Papa Sam's in-house bar did land-office business.

The Brownies' physical configuration was as regimented as their performances.

FRED "PAPA" CALHOUN: "I was always up against the back wall. Wanna was on what we called the 'bass end' or the left. Derwood and Milton were up in front on mike with Cecil. When (Bob) Dunn joined, he played up in front of Wanna on the left-hand side. Ocie stood up and played banjo on the right. There was a railing on the bandstand about chest high, so Dunn, who was the only other one besides me who sat down, put his chair up close to the front so he could be seen.

"I used to carry a towel with me all the time to wipe the sweat off the piano keys. After an hour in that place, we'd all be just wringing with sweat. Milton would announce the tune and the fiddle player would take off. It got so we'd know the tunes so well, we'd know what tune he was going to call off. As soon as the fiddle hit, we fell right in, we knew that intro so well.

"Sometimes we'd play a tune, stop, and then play it again. That got started because every encore was a tag dance."

ROY LEE BROWN: "The only other times they'd stop playing on a Saturday night would be when an announcement would have to be made. One time there was a car parked in front of Crystal Springs in the spot where the bus usually parked, and someone came in and told Derwood to announce over the mike that the car needed to be moved so the bus could unload people at the door. Cecil was standing directly behind Derwood as he made the announcement."

ED COPLIN: "And Derwood yelled, 'Will somebody move a 1928 Chevrolet coupe? It's blocking the bus!' Ol' Cecil goosed him and whispered, 'It's on fire.' And Derwood yelled, 'IT'S ON FIRE [laughs]!!' Well soon there wasn't but three people left in there! Derwood would fall for that every time [laughs]!"

Admission to Crystal Springs to dance to Milton Brown and the Musical Brownies was generally forty cents for men and ten cents for women. After the dance was over, Papa Sam gave Milton his share and then Milton would split up the money with the rest of the band.

MARY CUNNINGHAM: "You'd come in the entrance and pass the pay telephone booth in a little hallway there. Then you'd walk a little bit further and off to the right is where Papa Sam sat in that chair and took the money in. And when people came in he'd say, 'Sam's my name. Come on in!' Pop had a personality.

"Sometimes Mrs. Cunningham took in the money, too. She was a smart woman. And like Pop, she was real big and fat. I've seen her sit down and eat a pound of butter."

ROY LEE BROWN: "Papa Sam wasn't the only one who took the money at the door. He'd start things off and then Mama Cunningham would take over. After Mama stayed there a while, Baby Henry would work the door. Then Bowie or one of the bouncers would take over. Sometimes A. C. Coker, who worked for Papa Sam, would take the money. When people came in to Crystal Springs they would either get their hand stamped or whoever was on the door would just try to remember if they had paid or not. Usually if someone wished to go outside and come back in they would tell whoever was on the door that they would be coming back in a little while. Milton felt that this was a poor business practice. He would have preferred having tickets printed in order to make sure he'd get an accurate count.

"Milton figured that if Papa Sam wasn't willing to have tickets printed, then the best thing for him and the Brownies to do would be to find another place to play their Fort Worth dances. However, they couldn't do this until he got his own bus."

When Milton saved up enough money to buy his own bus, he and the Brownies left Crystal Springs. With the Brownies gone, Papa Sam decided to start his own band, which he called the Crystal Springs Ramblers. J. B. Brinkley was an original member.

J. B. BRINKLEY: "We were more or less the house band for Papa Sam after Milton left. Buck Buchanan and Jerry Byler were the two original fiddle players. Earl Driver played alto saxophone. Kokomo Crocker was on piano. Morris Deason on banjo. Jimmy McAdoo on bass, and I played rhythm guitar and sang. There was a boy from Oklahoma City named Ebb Gray who was the original guitar player, but he left after a short while."

The Crystal Springs Ramblers probably played their first dance on Monday, March 18, 1935, at Crystal Springs. The next two nights they played in Waco and Kaufman, followed by four consecutive nights at Crystal Springs.[8]

ROY LEE BROWN: "For about a month, Milton booked out of town on the nights they normally played Crystal Springs. He had bought his own bus and hired a guy named Peach McAdams to drive it. Everybody called him 'Mac,' but his real name was Fred.

"A short while after he quit Papa Sam, Milton came across a guy named Barrow who I think was Clyde Barrow's cousin. Barrow had a proposition for Milton. They would open up the old Peacock Garden on the Jacksboro Highway and start their own club. This was an old place about a mile and a half past the Lake Worth bridge that had been closed down. So they rented the building and started playing there on Saturday nights and occasionally on Sunday nights. They renamed it the Brownie Tavern. Barrow ran the bar, and Milton and the Brownies played there and just took a percentage of the gate like they did at Crystal Springs. In no time at all they had people hanging from the rafters out there. The place was smaller than Crystal

Springs and didn't have electricity, so they bought a Delco system with a generator. Several times every Saturday night the lights would go out. Sometimes they would be out for fifteen or twenty minutes. Of course that stopped the dance because when the electricity went out, so did Milton's P.A. equipment.

"Crystal Springs had pretty good crowds until Milton opened the Brownie Tavern. After that, nobody went to Crystal Springs. I remember I spent a Saturday night with G. W. Burns, who lived on White Settlement Road at that time. We decided to walk over to Crystal Springs, which was about a mile from his house. When we got there, Papa Sam passed us in free and the Crystal Springs Ramblers were playing and there were three couples dancing on the floor and not many more sitting around at the tables."

Papa Sam had underestimated Milton Brown's drawing power. To have his bread-and-butter leave Crystal Springs in the middle of the Depression had disastrous effects. Even with the Crystal Springs Ramblers playing dances as much as four and five nights a week, the dance hall crowds quickly diminished, most of them riding up the road to the Brownie Tavern. The Ramblers were a good band, as evidenced by the three discs they made for Vocalion in 1937. Many of the top instrumentalists in western swing's early history played with the Crystal Springs Ramblers. But the crowds were drawn to Milton Brown, and like the Pied Piper of Hamelin, wherever Milton went, the people followed.

ELLEN BROWN: "They say there are, generally, two types of people: the wheat and the emeralds. Now and then, you find the rare person who is a combination of both. This would describe Milton Brown. He had the quality of the creative, innovative artist. On the other hand, he had a down-to-earth, comfortable personality. He could get across to everyone that he genuinely liked people. This, I think, was one of his primary ingredients in his winning so many friends and followers."

ED COPLIN: "Milton had a voice that I don't think anybody else could duplicate. He just had a pleasant, easy-going style and a salesman's delivery. He could sell it, let me tell you. I don't know, when he'd get up in front of that microphone, why he was kind of like a snake charmer. He knew how to talk and get the best out of people.

"I remember when he quit playing out at Crystal Springs and started playing out at what we called the Peacock Garden. Some people called it the Lake Worth Country Club. He hurt Papa Sam's business at Crystal Springs, so Papa Sam had people come up to Peacock Garden and give complimentary tickets out so they would come back to his dance. Ol' Milton found out and got up in front of the microphone and said, 'I understand some of our competitors are giving complimentary tickets out here to go to their dance. Well, if y'all want to go to that dance, we want you to go to it. And we want you to have a good time. But you won't find none of our representatives out there giving complimentary tickets to come to our dance. Because when you come to a Brownies dance, we're going to give you your money's worth. So I'll tell you what I'll do. I'll just buy every one of those tickets from you for a dime apiece.' Well, I don't know how many tickets he bought, but he had a STACK of 'em about that tall!"

Business was so bad at Crystal Springs after Milton Brown left that Papa Sam decided to swallow his pride and get the Brownies back, at any cost. Milton had made his position clear: issue tickets, let him put his own man on the door, and he would return. Finally, Papa Sam agreed. On Thursday, September 26, 1935, after a six-month estrangement, Milton Brown and Papa Sam Cunningham were reunited.[9]

ROY LEE BROWN: "There are a number of reasons why Milton went back to Crystal Springs. The main reason I think was that Papa Sam was in bad shape financially and was pleading with Milton to come back. Milton had switched to WBAP by that time and Papa Sam would come down to the radio station and beg him to reconsider.[10] He even sent his daughter-in-law Pauline (Henry's first wife) out to the Brownie Tavern to beg Milton to come back. Papa told Milton that if he would only come back to Crystal Springs that he could have any percentage of the door that he wanted and that he would agree to tickets and let Milton put his own man on the door.

"Another reason Milton came back was because of the lighting system at the Brownie Tavern. You couldn't depend on the lights. Brownie Tavern was so far from town and it wasn't as large as Crystal Springs. So he was glad to get back on his own terms.

"The way they had it worked out when Milton returned was that they would issue two types of tickets, each with a different color. Men bought one color ticket and women bought another. This was because of the different prices for men and women. Milton hired Fred Calhoun's brother Paul to work the door for him. Paul would take the numbers of the first tickets and write them down on a piece of paper. At the end of the dance, he would get the last number and figure how many tickets were sold of each kind. Then, after multiplying by the price, he would have an accurate total.

"They stapled the tickets to the men's shirt collars and to the women's belt or collar. This was simply good business, and Milton was a good businessman. They never had any trouble after that."

With the addition of fiddler Cliff Bruner late in 1935, the Musical Brownies were complete. Milton was happy to return to Crystal Springs, now that things were being conducted in a more business-like manner. In addition, the switch to powerful WBAP in July helped spread the Brownies' music farther than KTAT ever had.

The Brownies' loyal fans were only too glad not to have to drive all the way out to Lake Worth to the Brownie Tavern and be subjected to frequent power failures and infrequent security. In gratitude, one loving fan composed the following treatise for her beloved Brownies. It speaks for all the hundreds of Depression-weary Texans who looked forward to Saturday night when a young man and his girl would drive up to the tumble-down wooden structure at 5336 White Settlement Road, walk in through the front door and be greeted by a fat, bald, jovial man with a half-chewed cigar in his mouth and shirtsleeves rolled up. "My name's Sam, what's yours?" he asks pleasantly. In they would walk and, along with several hundred other happy couples, embrace each other and begin to dance.

Dedicated to the "BROWNIES"
Written by Dorothy Ann Hogle.

If to a "Brownies" dance you go—
First you'll see Paul at the door you know.
He looks at you with a charming smile;
Then you'll go in and stay awhile.
As you look at his hair and tender eyes—
You feel as if you're looking in Paradice.

There's Milton Brown singing loud and clear—
You want to move closer, but not to hear;
He has a wonderful voice 'tis true,
And he sings his own compositions too—
He is nice and sweet to every one—
So you stay on, and enjoy the fun.

There's Cecil Brier who writes songs too—
Those songs will always remain so new;
He can play that Violen like few can do,

And he can almost make it talk some, too.
I think he can sing so very well
What he will do next, you can't ever tell.

Here's little dark-haired Clifton Bruner—
I've heard him sing and he is a good crooner;
He plays his Violen—it sounds just right,
You wouldn't mind hearing it the rest of the night.
His charming complexion is slightly dark—
With him, many girls would like to park.

There's Durwood Brown with his guitar—
His singing and playin' goes very far;
His winning ways and curley hair;
Makes Many girls stop and stare;
His "ever-ready" smile and sweet voice—
Makes him many peoples choice.

There's Harold Hart a boy so sweet—
Each time you see him, he looks so neat;
He has nice hair and lovely eyes,
And always sits there looking wise.
He always speaks and acts the same—
He fixes Durwood's guitar strings.

Bob Dunn with a steel guitar and a smile on his face—
Makes you—as you watch him—not feel out of place.
He composed "Taking Off" a beautiful number—
After hearing him play—you're not left in wonder;
He will speak to you with a big smile,
And remain friendly all the while.

And Ocie Stockard who is smiling ever—
But missing a note on his Banjo—never;
He's not so very tall—
But for him, girls do fall.
I've heard him sing on the radio—
He could make anything a go.

Now you hear the piano real soon—
No one can play it like Fred Calhoun;
He doesn't face the music all time he is playing
If you watch you'll see his eyes straying,
Fasnating and handsome is this man—
And you will watch him as long as you can.

There's Wanna Caufman with a nice smile and dimples—
But to know him isn't so simple;
He stands so straight, but isn't so bold,
But there's many girls after him—I'm told.

He can master his music easy enough with his hands
And he plays a base violen with the rest of the band.

There's Mack who takes the Brownies live's in hand—
But a very good driver in air or land;
He drives far into the nights,
But they don't mind because he drives right;
He's lovable, joyful and kind—
And hands all the girls a different line.

They are everybodys' friends you know—
To all their dances you will like to go;
When you hear the theme song that closes the dance—
You'll go next time you get the chance.
A nicer bunch of boys you never have seen—
Hear them each day at one-fifteen.[11]

NINE

On the Road

Aside from their regular Saturday night dances at the Crystal Springs Dancing Pavilion, Milton Brown and the Musical Brownies spent most of their time on the road. As popular as the Brownies were in Fort Worth, and as large as their repertoire was, Milton knew that there existed the danger of overexposure. He recognized the show business axiom "always leave 'em wanting more," and he eventually restricted the Brownies' Fort Worth appearances to Saturday nights at Crystal Springs. In doing so, he guaranteed Papa Sam Cunningham a full house on Saturdays every week.

The Brownies also went on the road for financial reasons. Although they would fill up Crystal Springs every Saturday night, the rest of the week was different. Good-sized crowds showed up, but never as huge as those appearing on Saturdays. Milton discovered that when the Brownies played out of town, they attracted audiences as large, enthusiastic, and receptive as those in Fort Worth, and on any day of the week. Thus, the band made better use of its time by traveling on weekdays.

By playing towns and cities away from Fort Worth, Milton Brown learned the benefits of free enterprise: selling one's services to the highest bidder. When word arrived at a small town that the Musical Brownies would be stopping by during a tour, dance hall owners engaged in wild bidding to get the band to play their establishment. Milton made it clear to the owners that he granted exclusivity to a hall during each visit; only one place would be graced by the Brownies' presence on that particular trip. Realizing the drawing power the Brownies possessed, the club owners agreed to pay Milton gate percentages as high as 75/25.[1]

Milton made sure to get confirmation from his clients that their facility was big enough to accommodate at least one hundred to two hundred couples. In a letter to a man in Crowell, Texas (located two hundred miles northwest of Fort Worth; population 1,946), Milton requested 75 percent of the gross receipts and suggested the then unheard-of admission price of one dollar per couple and ten cents for extra women and children. He got it.

Shortly after forming his band in September 1932, Milton began booking engagements out of town, saving Saturday nights and, in the beginning, occasional weeknights for Crystal Springs. As the Brownies' reputation spread, he was able to abandon the weeknight dances at Crystal Springs entirely, but still had to return to Fort Worth each day for the group's regular radio program on KTAT and later WBAP.

Milton found the radio programs essential as an inexpensive and effective means of advertising his dances and so refused to allow single sponsors to underwrite his program.[2] He wanted to be free to plug the band's appearances whenever and as often as possible. He also had a good knowledge of where radio stations in Texas were and the power of their transmitters. He knew that when he appeared on a local radio station (usually fifteen-minute programs), he could give advance notice to local residents about the Brownies' upcoming engagements in the area. Using radio as a "traveling billboard," Milton and the Brownies hopscotched their way across the state, spreading their music throughout Texas.[3] Upon joining the ranks of WBAP in July 1935, the Brownies no longer found it necessary to agree to perform on local radio stations. WBAP's 50,000-watt signal traversed the entire breadth of the state, crossing into Oklahoma, Louisiana, and Arkansas. Before long, the Brownies were in demand to play dances in those states also, although Milton knew it was impossible to travel such long distances in the brief eight-hour period between the time his radio program on WBAP ended and the usual starting time of a dance, around nine o'clock in the evening.

Thus began for the Brownies the endless, exhausting, monotonous road trips that have become associated with traveling entertainers to this day, in all fields of show business. From his very early days as a salesman, Milton Brown recognized the value of advertising, and he used every resource possible to establish the name of his band and spread it throughout the state. The Musical Brownies was one of the first organizations in country music to travel in a bus marked with their name on its side.[4] Shortly after organizing his band, Milton began taking Papa Sam's bus out of town. He had "Milton Brown and his Musical Brownies" emblazoned along its side and installed a sign that read "Brownie Special" in the destination window above the bus's front windshield. As the band traveled across the countryside, the bus became a traveling advertisement in itself, drawing curious stares even as it passed through towns where the Brownies would not be playing.

The moment their radio program concluded, the Brownies would walk to a garage nearby where the bus was parked, load their instruments on top, and take off. They would return the following day, sometimes shortly before their broadcast, dashing breathlessly into the studio just before one-fifteen. (After Milton bought his own bus, their program sometimes began one hour later, to allow for such situations.)

ROY LEE BROWN: "The garage where the Brownies' bus was parked was about a block from the Blackstone Hotel, where they played the radio program on WBAP. They also parked their cars there. Lots of times they'd have to go straight from the radio program and get on the bus and leave because it took that long to go wherever they had to go. When they played in Waco, they didn't have to leave until 5 P.M. because Waco was only ninety miles away. The bus stayed at the garage when the band was in town, unless Peach McAdams, their bus driver, took it home. So, after the bus came back to Fort Worth, the guys would get in their cars and go home."

ED COPLIN: "I don't think anybody else could have driven that bus but Peach. It had a little bitty short gear shift. I tried to drive it back there one time and park it and I could never get the thing in the right gear."

FRED "PAPA" CALHOUN: "We got just outside of Alvarado on the way back one night, and it was just an old country road, you know. Real narrow, two-lane highway. We come over a hill and were driving pretty fast, and the lights went out on the bus. You couldn't see your hand in front of your face. Ol' Mac was driving the bus and he sat there gripping that wheel, and directly he went and stopped. In the middle of the road. I leaned over to him and said, 'Mac, how'd you do that without being able to see the road?' He said, 'Well, just before the lights went out I memorized what I saw in front of me. When I got to that point, I stopped [laughs]!'"

ROY LEE BROWN: "The Brownies made tremendous money back then, but they spent it as fast as they could make it. Every member of the band had a brand new automobile. And I mean every member. Even Derwood had a Model A Ford when he was just a kid. Milton drove a Whippet and then later he got a 1933 Rockney, which was made by

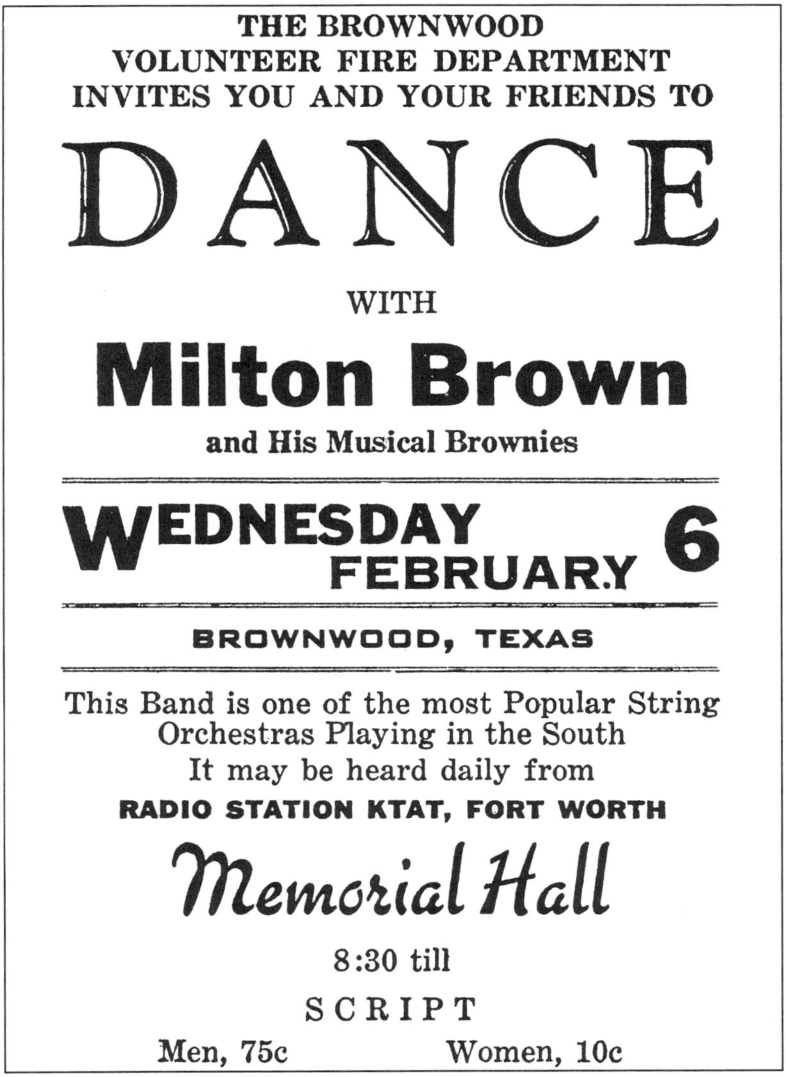

THE BROWNWOOD
VOLUNTEER FIRE DEPARTMENT
INVITES YOU AND YOUR FRIENDS TO

DANCE

WITH

Milton Brown

and His Musical Brownies

WEDNESDAY 6
FEBRUARY

BROWNWOOD, TEXAS

This Band is one of the most Popular String
Orchestras Playing in the South
It may be heard daily from
RADIO STATION KTAT, FORT WORTH

Memorial Hall

8:30 till

SCRIPT

Men, 75c   Women, 10c

A typical promotional card advertising a dance by the Musical Brownies, 1935. Note that the band is labeled a "string orchestra." Brownwood is located about 150 miles southwest of Fort Worth. Courtesy Cary Ginell.

The Brownies' driver, Fred "Peach" McAdams, poses on the running board of the band's bus in 1935. The bus was custom-designed for Milton Brown, built from a Packard body and LaSalle chassis with a Chevrolet motor. Courtesy Roy Lee and Ellen Brown.

Studebaker for that year only. Then he got a 1934 Studebaker. When he and Mary Helen got married they sold the Studebaker and Milton drove her car, which was an Oldsmobile. After they separated, Mary Helen kept the Oldsmobile and Milton drove Peach McAdams's Chevrolet coupe. I remember Milton was real disgusted with it because it wasn't brand new. I'd go up to the radio station with him in it and I thought, 'Man, if I had this car, I'd be in hog heaven!' But he was used to driving a new car all the time.

"In early 1936 he bought a green 1936 Pontiac four-door sedan. That's the one he had his accident in. Cecil had a six-cylinder Pontiac coupe. Grey. Fred had the same thing, they looked just alike. Ocie had a brand new Plymouth. Derwood had a brand new 1936 Ford. I don't know what Wanna had, but it was new.

"I traveled with the Brownies in the summer of 1935 and again in 1936 when I was out of school. I went as Derwood's string fixer. They used Papa Sam's bus until they left Crystal Springs in 1935 and played on the road Saturday nights. After that, they opened the Brownie Tavern. Then Milton bought a school bus which they used for a while. After that he bought a stretch job, which was like a jitney or a long limousine. It had a long body on it, I don't know how many seats there were, but it had a Chevrolet motor and a La Salle chassis.

"One time they played Palestine, Texas, and coming back from there they had carburetor trouble. 'Course this was nighttime and the whole band was asleep. I woke up and got out, and ol' Mac had the hood up and the carburetor out and he was working on it. And here we were way out in the country somewhere in the middle of the night. We all got out of the bus and I remember listening 'way off in the distance we could hear a colored preacher rehearsing a sermon. It just made the hair stand up on your head."

FRED "PAPA" CALHOUN: "Mac was an expert mechanic. Anything'd go wrong with the bus, he could fix it. Well, one time we were coming back from Childress and we broke an axle out the other side of Springtown. We were scheduled to play Childress again the next night, but we had to get back to Fort Worth first to play the radio program at twelve, see. So Milton said, 'Fred, you and Ocie try and get a ride back to town. Then get two cars, come on back and pick us up so we can all get back in time to do the program.' So Ocie and I got out on the highway and directly here comes a big Cadillac. They saw our sign on the bus: 'Milton Brown and the Musical Brownies,' and they stopped. There were two girls in the back seat and they had a chauffeur driving. They were coming from Wichita Falls. One of the girls said, 'What's the trouble, fellas?' I said, 'Well, we broke an axle and we're trying to get a ride into Fort Worth so we can do our radio program.' She says, 'Well, come on, get in!' So we started to get in the front seat and she said, 'No, come on back with *us,* you're the Brownies, aren't you?' And they took us right into town to the garage where our cars were parked. People would do anything for the Brownies. McAdams stayed with the bus. His brother had a garage in Springtown, so Mac got an axle, put it in, and brought the bus on in. We made it back in time to do the program."

The Brownies were idolized everywhere they traveled. Milton Brown's fans viewed him as a celebrity, not with the kind of frenzied hysteria associated with later performers like Frank Sinatra and Elvis Presley but with a more restrained, awe-inspired respect. On more than one occasion, Milton and the boys were invited to spend an evening with a local family, enjoying a home-cooked meal and Texas hospitality. Milton graciously accepted whenever he could.

ROY LEE BROWN: "Sometimes the Brownies played Denison. Well, near Denison was a town called Pottsboro, and the Scott family would invite the Brownies to come have dinner with them before they played the dance. So they'd drive out to Pottsboro a little early, have a big dinner, and go play the dance.
"In Penelope, there was a Czech family named Swoboda who would invite the Brownies out to their house for a chicken dinner. Around the house, Mr. Swoboda was showing the band his cotton fields, and evidently the cotton was ready to pick. So Milton picked a handful of it and gave it to Mrs. Swoboda. She really treasured that bunch of cotton. It was a great souvenir for her, picked by the great Milton Brown himself, even though it was her own cotton [laughs]! The Swobodas would come up to Crystal Springs every chance they got."

FRED "PAPA" CALHOUN: "We were invited out a lot of times. The man who was putting on the dance in these country towns would invite us in and we'd have country ham, chicken, anything we wanted."

Invitations from fans came as a pleasant distraction from the monotony of the constant touring. Roy Lee Brown recalled some of the more lengthy road trips that took them to the farthest reaches of the state.

ROY LEE BROWN: "They rarely, if ever, played outside of Texas. They got as far east as Kilgore, Longview, and Gladewater. They never did go to Marshall, but they might have played Tyler. Never Louisiana.

"South, they may have been down on a tour to Houston but I'm not sure. They were in San Angelo once and they also played Stanford. They went to places like Rising Star, Jacksboro, Comanche, Dublin, and Stephenville. Those last three are right in a row. Even though some of the towns were right in a row, they'd sometimes play San Angelo one night, come on back to Fort Worth, and play Longview the next night. But except for one time when I was with them, they always came back to Fort Worth. That was when they played Childress in August of 1935. We were to spend the night there and drive back to Vernon for a dance the next night. Blackie Lawson went with us on the bus. When we got into Childress, we checked into the Childress Hotel and got three rooms. Each room had two full-sized beds, so Milton, Fred, Cecil and I stayed in one room, two to a bed, Wanna, Bob Dunn, Derwood, and Blackie Lawson shared another, and Ocie and Peach McAdams shared the third. The Brownies played the dance in Childress in a hall upstairs somewhere, probably a lodge hall. During the dance, I noticed Blackie pacing back and forth in front of the bandstand. I asked Derwood why Blackie was doing this and Derwood told me that someone had said that they were going to jump on one or more of the band members that night. So Blackie sort of patrolled for us [laughs]. Everything went smooth that night and there was no trouble. I think this was probably a figment of Blackie's imagination.

"After the dance was over, the band was invited out to the lake for a party. Everybody went except me. Milton told me that I would have to go to bed at the hotel, so I went on up to the room and went to sleep. It was many hours later before Milton and the boys came in.

"The next morning, Milton and I went to a café to eat breakfast. Milton picked up a newspaper and there on the front page were Will Rogers's and Wiley Post's pictures. They had been killed in a plane crash.[5]

"About noon that day, we checked out of the hotel and headed for Vernon. That night we played a dance at the Log Cabin. As usual, there was a big crowd and everything went smoothly. After the dance was over, the wife of the guy who owned the Log Cabin cooked a bunch of fried chicken with all the trimmings and we really had a big meal, right there where we had played the dance. After we ate all we could hold, we got on the bus and headed back to Fort

Worth. Fifty-some-odd years later, I was telling my friend Ken Lasater about playing at the Log Cabin in Vernon, and Ken said that he was outside that night listening to the Brownies play. He was just a kid when he lived in Vernon and was too young to come inside. Small world, huh?"

WANNA COFFMAN: "The farthest away we played I believe was Muskogee, Oklahoma. That was Bob Dunn's hometown. And oh gosh, we had a crowd! A north wind blew in that night and it was COLD! I had to load and unload the bus all the time and as usual, I didn't want anybody messin' with my bass. One time I had a neck broke off of it.

"Some of Bob's brothers and sisters were there and so was his mama. At intermission, they took Bob out and must've got him oiled up pretty good because after intermission, he didn't come back in. They must have had some whiskey in a fruit jar. That'll knock you out quicker than anything. We guessed he'd inhaled the fumes and passed out. What happened was, Bob had gone to a bootlegger and never got back. The dance ended and still no Bob. Finally we found him walking from a filling station about a mile up the road. He just about froze to death.

"It got so cold that night that the oil pump in the bus wouldn't pump the oil. We got about twenty-five miles down the road and finally, the bearings in the bus burned up. We had to wake an old guy up who had a garage in an old tin barn. He burned waste oil in one of them old drums. Then Bob Dunn decided that he wanted something to eat. We had passed this little old café, up there about a half mile from where we had to stop. Me, Milton, and Derwood got out and started to walk back to this café and we couldn't get more than a hundred yards before we turned around and came back. Milton called WBAP from the garage and canceled the program for the next day. When he got back, Bob was gone again. We stayed the night, and the next day we went up to that café to find Bob. The guy there said, 'Yeah, that man was in here. He beat up two deputies because they wanted to take his whiskey away from him. He was sitting up here at the counter last night with it.' Bob got locked up and his wife had to come to bail him out. We ended up spending two days up there [laughs]!"

FRED "PAPA" CALHOUN: "I'm telling you, we played just about everywhere. One time we played out on an oil field near Wichita Falls. It was on a dirt road, and when we got there it started to rain. I think we made fifty cents apiece on that trip [laughs].

"We played Clifton one night and it was three degrees above zero. Well, it didn't matter to Milton, he wouldn't cancel for anything if he could help it. We thought he'd cancel because the roads were bad. But he said, 'No, I don't EVER cancel.' So we went down there and the road was icy. When we got to this place, it was a skating rink, and there were six couples there. Piano was sitting there at the back and the skating rink was cold, of course. They had a big old stove up at the front. So we rolled that piano up there by the stove and I played the whole dance with my overcoat and my gloves on."

WANNA COFFMAN: "I remember one place we played in Penelope, I think. This guy had a dance floor way out in the middle of a field. I believe it was used as a skating rink. So they put ropes around it and we had the dance right there. When we got there, the place was empty, we didn't think anybody would come all the way out there in the middle of the country. But by the time we got set up, there was a row of cars."

DAVE STOGNER: "There was a little radio station in the hotel in Gainesville, Texas, that our band played on. The station's broadcast area didn't cover anywhere outside of town. In fact, it didn't even cover all of Gainesville. One way people could hear us was out of the window if they were driving by! We played there for six months. We weren't paid money, but we could advertise our dances and it gave us experience. We were doing pretty good making two or three dollars apiece, sometimes five. It wasn't big money, but it was good money. We didn't know how far we could go. We thought maybe that was all that was possible. Bob Wills was playing in our backyard. We never knew what nights he was going to be there. Then, we had someone even more popular within traveling distance down in Fort Worth: Milton Brown. He could knock your props off if he came into your neighborhood. You'd just cancel what you were doing and go to his dance. He and the Musical Brownies played Thursday and Saturday nights at the Crystal Springs Ballroom. He had big crowds right off the bat. He couldn't miss. We got knocked down a time or two listening to other bands who were better than us, but we kept going.

"In 1935, Milton Brown and the Musical Brownies were voted the number one Texas string band. There were no other bandleaders that could match what he could do. He was the only bandleader that I ever knew who was respected and spoken highly of not only by his own musicians but by musicians who didn't even work for him. He created, with his musicians, a style of music which became known as Texas swing, which in the late 1930s was renamed western swing. He knew what he was looking for with his band and worked until he got it. They played the kind of music that I liked to play. Two of my most favorite songs that they recorded are 'Wabash Blues' and 'When I Take My Sugar to Tea.' I was very fortunate to be acquainted with Milton and to have had an opportunity to work around him."

As manager, treasurer, master of ceremonies, and booking agent for the Musical Brownies, Milton Brown had to utilize all of his experience, schooling, and intelligence to keep the band alive. As manager, he treated his musicians fairly and was close to all of them. Even though his brothers Derwood and Roy Lee traveled with the band, they were given no special treatment. Derwood received a share equal to those of the other Brownies, and Roy Lee was given the usual allotment one would earn as Derwood's string fixer: a dollar and a half per dance. There were few personnel changes during the Brownies' existence with Milton at the helm. They were the highest paid string band in Texas and were well rewarded for their efforts.

As treasurer, Milton negotiated with the dance hall owners, collected the money owed to the band, distributed it to the Brownies, and paid bills such as bus upkeep, uniforms, and placards for distribution in small towns. The members of the band paid for their meals out of their own pockets.

Modes of communication with dance hall proprietors varied. Telephone and wire services were faster than mail. However, telephones were not as pervasive during the Depression in Texas. As a result, Milton conducted most of his transactions by mail. Not only was this less expensive but securing terms on paper protected him against the occasional welsher.[6] Milton made sure he asked the town's distance from Fort Worth, the size of the dance hall, and the price of admission that would be charged. He preferred to keep the price down to a level most people could afford. Still, seventy-five cents (the usual "road" admission for men) was a steep price for the Depression. Ladies were admitted for ten cents.

He then quoted the Brownies' terms: they would supply the public address system and play the dance for either a 70/30 or 75/25 percentage of the gross receipts, depending on the situation. Usually, if the Brownies had to travel a great distance (over two hundred miles), Milton would ask for 75/25. For towns closer to Fort Worth, he might require only a 70/30 or 65/35 distribution.

FRED "PAPA" CALHOUN: "A lot of places would call Milton and give him a guarantee if he'd come out. Salary. Milton knew better than that. He'd just laugh at 'em. He knew how many we drew and how much more we made by playing for a percentage."

Milton always allotted time for advertising, as he often booked the Brownies weeks in advance. Local dance hall owners could then print and distribute placards and handbills, make announcements on local radio stations, and purchase ad space in local newspapers (Milton allowed the owners to deduct five dollars off the gross for the printing of placards). By the time the Brownies hit town in their bus, the region was in a frenzy, plied and promoted by the best salesman in the dance band business. Occasionally, local radio stations invited Milton to play a brief program and advertise his dance. Milton's price for playing a one-time-only radio program thirty to forty-five minutes long was $25.

In some cases, Milton refused outright to play in certain towns. Plainview, Texas, located over three hundred miles from Fort Worth in the central part of the Texas Panhandle, was one location too distant for the Brownies to travel in one day. Responding to a request to play a dance there, he politely refused, but kept his options open by proposing a possible tour of that part of the state in the future, at which time he would arrange a four- or five-city succession of dances.

Milton also made sure that there was a piano on the premises.

ROY LEE BROWN: "And they ran into a lot of trouble with the pianos. Most of them were out of tune, and sometimes Fred had to fix the piano while the dance was going on."

FRED "PAPA" CALHOUN: "One time that happened at a woman's club we were playing in Cameron. When we went in to set up the instruments, I hit a note on the piano and the key wouldn't go down. It was froze solid like I was hitting a brick. Apparently the bar had fallen down and locked all the keys. I remember one time Wanna broke the tail plate on his bass. That can knock a hole in a small band like the Brownies when you don't have a bass.

"Milton was disgusted when he found out the piano was broken and he said, 'Well, Fred, can't you do something?' So the woman there let me go to work on it. Pretty nice piano too. Nine o'clock came and Milton had to start the dance without me. He didn't like that. So I took the top and the bottom off of the piano and got to work. We played until ten and then Milton called an intermission. I still didn't have the piano fixed. I finally fixed it during the intermission.

"The Wanderers played with us over at Groves Bank, and they had the sorriest piano you ever saw. Half the notes were gone. I knew the Wanderers were going to play there two weeks after we did. Their piano player then was Jack Norwood, and Jack had pulled off half the keys so the owners might notice that it was broken. We came back there in a month and, dadgum, they still hadn't fixed it. I had to play two-note chords all night. Another time, the piano was tuned too low for Milton to sing to. So I had to transpose. When they played in A, I played in B-flat. That was hard to do: transpose half a tone up all night!

"I've played when the electricity went off. We didn't have amplifiers anyhow. Dunn did but not before him. We had speakers and a microphone. We played at the Crazy Hotel in Mineral Wells once. That's when I first started playing with Milton. We had a big dance over there in the ballroom and it was packed with people. The lights went out. There were no windows there so it was pitch dark. Milton started yelling, 'Keep playing! Keep playing!' And that's when I found out I could play without lookin' at the keys [laughs]! After that I could play and look around at the people."

By January 1936, the Brownies' popularity was so pervasive that Milton enjoyed the luxury of turning down dance dates at a time when most musical organizations in the area were accepting any engagements on any terms. He knew that whatever type, style, size, or configuration of building it was, he could fill it. Barring natural disasters like seasonal floods and thunderstorms, there was rarely any difficulty in attracting customers. Milton Brown and his Musical Brownies was a magical name in the mid-thirties, guaranteed to raise the rafters of any lodge hall, barn, or athletic club.

As booking agent, Milton designed a touring schedule for the band, structured to cover the territories equally without overexposing the band into any one area. Naturally, nearby cities such as Dallas and Waco played host to the Brownies more often than more distant locales like Amarillo and San Angelo, which he would play only if he could arrange a tour of towns between there and Fort Worth.

One of the more frequently visited cities was Waco, which had, in 1930, a population of 52,848. Its residents eagerly looked forward to the arrival of the Brownies every three or four weeks.

RED VARNER: "They called it Shady Rest and it was a place to dance.

The dance floor was three or four feet off the ground with unpainted two-by-four protective railings on all sides. There were enough oak and hackberry trees around to justify the 'Shady,' but why 'Rest'? Everybody seemed to think it had been named by an undertaker."

FRED "PAPA" CALHOUN: "Kokomo Crocker once came down to Waco and wanted to sit in with us on piano. So Kokomo sat down and I reached over and got Derwood's extra guitar. Now, you've got to realize I can't play a lick on the guitar. There was a big crowd around the bandstand, like always. And I got down on one knee and just beat the fire out of that guitar, runnin' my hand up and down the neck and beating that rhythm. Broke the band up completely. There was this great big tall old country guy who had been standing there all night, watching us. This guy looked like the American Gothic farmer. When I got through, he slapped his knee and said, 'DAMN, that's the hottest feller I ever did see!!' And I wasn't hitting ANY of the right notes! Couldn't play at all [laughs]!"

Other Waco halls at which the Brownies played included Shadowland and the White Oak Dancing Pavilion, located on the main highway (now Interstate Highway 35) between Fort Worth and Waco. To preserve the integrity of the dance hall's name, the oak trees surrounding the facility and its parking lot were whitewashed regularly, giving them an eery glow after dark.

A regular dancer at the White Oak was a breakdown fiddle player named Jeff Knight. Knight got to know Cecil Brower during the Brownies' visits to Waco and taught Cecil traditional fiddle tunes like "Fisher's Hornpipe," "Devil's Dream," "Sally Gooden," and "Arkansas Traveler." The two became good friends and Cecil was welcomed as an unofficial member of the Knight family. Eventually, Cecil met and married Knight's daughter Sybil.

SYBIL BROWER BOHM: "I was a senior in high school when I met Cecil. My dad was a big Brownie fan and he would take me to dances at the White Oak Dance Hall. We lived in Meridian, Texas, but we went to dances all over the area. I first met Cecil at the Woodmen of the World lodge in Waco. He saw me down there and wanted to dance with me. Of course, he asked Milton's permission first to leave the bandstand, and then we were allowed to dance. Well, after that first time, he traced me down and came to our home looking for me. My mother and father chaperoned us for a while. Cecil was persistent but at first I wasn't much interested in him. I sure liked his fiddle playing, though. He could play anything: waltzes, two-steps, you name it.

"I didn't think too much of musicians, you know. They all had girls chasing after them all the time. You could never count on having a good marriage to a musician, especially one with the popularity the Brownies had. So, anyway, at one of the Brownies' dances, Cecil came down after intermission and asked me if I'd like to go outside with him. I was real suspicious so I asked him, 'Well, whatever for?' He said, 'Let's go outside and have a drink. What would you like?' I said, 'All right. I'll have an orange soda pop.' I thought that would discourage him. Most musicians drank alcohol, but the Brownies never did on the bandstand.

"Cecil went over to the bar and got TWO orange soda pops. And we went outside and drank them. I remember I had to stand on the running board of a car that was parked out there because Cecil was so much taller than me. That was the first time I was alone with him. We dated for about a year and then got married in Cleburne on March 21, 1937. Cecil was with Roy Newman by that time and Ray Lackland, an announcer at WRR in Dallas, was our best man."[7]

Milton Brown also was responsible for a publicity gimmick that became a tradition in southwestern dances: the battle dance. Sometimes known as "double-band dances," battle dances were attractions similar to baseball's doubleheaders, in which customers were entertained by two bands for the price of one. There was no formal contest or competition, as implied in the term "battle dance." Rather, each band took its turn performing a set and tried its best to outplay the other.[8] In some cases, Milton booked double-band dances to help out other struggling organizations. The earliest battle dance the Brownies played was at Green Terrace in Waco in October 1933. Bob Wills and his Playboys had just formed and were having difficulty drawing crowds. Milton Brown offered his support and brought the Brownies to Waco for the dance.

It was only natural for the Brownies and their chief "rivals" in Dallas, the Wanderers, to schedule a double-band dance. Milton booked the occasion, as usual, but decided to throw in a surprise for the crowd.

FRED "PAPA" CALHOUN: "This must have been early in 1934. It was our first battle dance in Dallas and Milton wanted to do something special. On our radio show we sometimes used funny names. So Milton decided that, all right, this is our first big battle dance in Dallas, let's play our parts for the crowd. So we went out there in costume and the house went wild! I had on a silk hat and a frock coat and they called me 'Doctor Zilch.'"

ROY LEE BROWN: "Fred always carried a briefcase wherever he went. It had all of his sheet music in it. So, naturally, we made it sound like he was a doctor."

FRED "PAPA" CALHOUN: "Ocie had a pillow in his stomach to make him look fat, and he put something over his head to make him look bald-headed."

OCIE STOCKARD: "I also put on big ol' shoes that didn't fit. I was 'Rattlesnake.'"

WANNA COFFMAN: "I was real skinny back then, I must have weighed about 128 pounds, and I was six feet tall. I was supposed to be a long-haired Hawaiian, so I put on a long-haired wig and a grass skirt over my underwear. I looked terrible [laughs]! They called Derwood 'Chubby,' and he was dressed like a little ol' fat boy. Jesse dressed up like a little boy with knee pants on. Milton came as a parson. We called him 'Parson Brown.'⁹ So we got up there and Milton told us, 'Now I want to tell you, that before we go on I want to see you boys take one drink.' This was to pep us up, you know. I usually drank more than that but he never knew it. I could drink a half a pint before I went on the bandstand and nobody would ever know. Not even Milton. Well, we got up there and started playing all dressed up like that and boy, did that make the Wanderers mad. They didn't know we were going to do all this and show them up. Ol' Dick Reinhart and Jesse got in it and started a phony fight. They tore each other's clothes off while I played a little tune and did a little dance to it. Ol' Dick was playing mandolin that day we saw them out there and boy, that guy could play. He played good guitar, too."¹⁰

Although they were chiefly a dance band, the Brownies occasionally played stage shows. For these, Milton put on a program similar to the medicine shows he saw while growing up in Stephenville.

FRED "PAPA" CALHOUN: "We went to Lawton, Oklahoma, once and played the matinee program at the Rialto theater up there. We also played an early show in the evening and then our regular dance that night after the show. We took a fan dancer with us and two blackface comedians, Honeyboy and Sassafrass.[11] When the show started, the place was packed with people. The curtain was raised, and there we were playing our theme song. Then Milton introduced all the band members. He introduced Ocie, and then Cecil, and while he was doing that, I got up and went around and hid behind the piano. Just then, Milton turned around and said, 'Now here's the piano player, Papa CAL . . .' And his voice trailed away: ' . . . houn' [laughs]. He saw an empty piano. Then I came out from behind it and the whole house went crazy. Milton saw that, and after the show he said to me, 'That was good, Fred. Why don't you do that on the next show?' And we did, too. Went over big with the crowd."

WANNA COFFMAN: "One night we played a dance in Lubbock for a fireman's ball. 'Course, they did all the advertising, and let me tell you, firemen came from everywhere: Abilene and all up in there. They had so many people that night that they had to turn away a whole lot of 'em. When Milton divvied up our percentage after the dance it came to two pennies under a hundred dollars per man. That's about the most we ever made. A hundred dollars. I wish I could have held on to some of that. But I was young and if everybody in the band bought a new car, I would too. Cecil, Fred, and Ocie were always buying new cars, and hell, I couldn't stand to be left out!"

Greenville teenager Buck Spurlock was typical of many youngsters in Texas who aspired to be musicians like the Musical Brownies. They listened faithfully to Brownies' broadcasts and looked forward to the band's personal appearances in their home towns.

BUCK SPURLOCK: "I had heard Milton when he was with the Light Crust Doughboys. We didn't own a radio, but I would go to the neighbors' house and hear Milton Brown sing. Every chance I'd get I'd go over to the neighbors' house and listen to their radio.

"In 1932, Milton brought that big bus out here to play a dance at Fair Park. We'd just ooh and aah over that deal! A year or so later, I was playing on the radio with my little band and Milton, Derwood, Cecil Brower, the whole gang came in and sat in with us. They was all wearing double-breasted brown suits. All alike. Wanna Coffman played bass with us. And every song we knew, they knew better than we did! So after the broadcast, Milton said to the guys, 'Now you fellas come on out to the dance tonight and we'll pass you in.' Well, he could get twenty-five or thirty cents per person at those dances, and we didn't have that much in our pockets, so that was a nice thing for him to do. Times were hard. You'd better believe they were hard. So we went out there, and sure enough, they passed us in. The dance started about 8:30. By 9:00 the floor was full. And it was always full. Milton was a real businessman in those days. He knew how to work a crowd. After about thirty or forty minutes on these dances, he'd get down on the floor and dance with the girls. Then Derwood would do the vocals, but Derwood had a different style. His was more blues.

"Boy, that Milton knew what he was doing. After a while, he came up to us, he'd remembered us up at the radio station, and he said, 'Would you guys like to play a number with us?' And we said, 'Hell, yes!!' So we got up there and I stood right in front of Derwood 'cause I couldn't pick the guitar like Derwood could. We played one number and let me tell you, for a long while, we were the most popular kids in Greenville! Milton was considerate of lesser-known musicians and was never afraid that someone would take away a little popularity from the Brownies. They were sure no one could outshine them! I must have been only seventeen or eighteen years old, but I'll never forget that night as long as I live."

Spurlock described what a Brownies' dance in Greenville was like:

BUCK SPURLOCK: "Listen, I'll tell you they had more people come to those dances. . . . They had farmers come in their overalls. Back in those days, they didn't have tables, they had benches around the hall where people'd sit. People carried their whiskey in their hip pockets. When they'd want a drink, they'd just go over in a corner and take one; there wasn't any chaser, no water or nothing, they'd just drink it right out of the bottle. Now this was CORN whiskey. And Milton partook of it too, occasionally, to be sociable."

ROY LEE BROWN: "Milton told Mama and Dad in my presence that many times when people offered him a drink, he would turn the bottle up but block the whiskey from coming out of the bottle with his tongue. That way, he didn't hurt anyone's feelings by refusing to drink with them.

"I stood by the bandstand at Crystal Springs many times when people would offer Milton a drink out of their bottle. If Milton took every drink that was offered to him, well, he wouldn't be able to walk."

BUCK SPURLOCK: "Milton was a real promoter. He always had that big smile on his face. Even when he was singing. And the women just went wild over him. Now in small towns like Greenville, they had a lot of gals that walked the streets on Saturday. They call them prostitutes now. The local people wouldn't fool with them but I tell you, Milton would dance with every damn one of 'em! And every time Milton played a dance, every damn one of 'em was *there!* Well, that made the dance, because the more ladies you had at a dance, the more men came. And those farmers would come to town only once a week, on Saturdays, but they'd be there with their twenty-five or thirty cents.

"Right across the street from the dance hall was a little old sandwich shop called Queen Anne's. Back in those days, when you'd go to a dance, you wouldn't get any ticket or anything, they'd just stamp you on the inside of your thumb. Well this ol' boy that run that sandwich shop copied that stamp. And the next time the Brownies came into town, I think Fred Calhoun's brother was on the door, and I never seen so many people in one place in all my life! At intermission, Milton came down to see how much money they had and Fred's brother said, 'Gosh, Milton, we don't have but twenty-five dollars in the till.' This sandwich shop guy was selling those stamps for fifteen cents apiece. He'd stamp their hands, take their money and they'd get in for fifteen cents. When Milton found out what had happened, it was a long time before he ever came back to Greenville!"

FRED "PAPA" CALHOUN: "About the second time I went out of town with them, we went down to Whitney. They had a big feed store there and they moved out all the feed on one side and held the dance on the other side. It was a big place and it was summertime. There was, of course, no air conditioning, but they did have a few fans. On one side of the place there was a big double door where the railroad cars would unload. The owners put chicken wire across there to keep anybody from coming in. The band played in the back. During the dance I kept hearing voices and clapping going on outside the building. We played 'St. Louis Blues,' and when I got through with a fast chorus, a whole bunch of voices hollered 'Play it out, Papa!!' I couldn't imagine what it was. Sounded like a hundred people out there. So we took an intermission and I went around there behind the building to see who it was. I bet there was five hundred colored folks sittin' out there on a railroad dump. When they saw me, they yelled, 'Hey! There's old Papa now!' They couldn't come in but they had to listen."

ELLEN BROWN: "Blacks weren't allowed inside the dance pavilions back then. Milton had no objections whatsoever and probably would have invited them in if he could. Milton had a healthy respect for all humanity: black or white. This was his nature.

"I remember one person in particular who became very special to the Brownies and the Brown family. She was a sweet, elderly lady named Ida Smith. On Saturday nights, Ida would come and sit outside Crystal Springs during the dances and would listen for hours. This was during the summer when the pavilion was open, so she not only got to hear the music, but she could watch the band and the dancers through the opened-up sides of the dance hall. The Brownies got to know Ida and would miss her if she wasn't there. Derwood would usually tease her a bit, which she loved!

"Frequently during the course of the evening, Milton or Derwood would dedicate the song '"Ida," Sweet as Apple Cider' to her. She later told me proudly how they used to do the tune for her. As she would say, 'It sho' happied this ole woman's heart for Mista Milton or Mista Darewood to sing a song 'specially fo' me! They's mighty fine boys!' Ida was truly enchanted by the Brownies.

"After a while, Ida began coming to the Browns' home to help with some of the chores. When Dad Brown had to have surgery and was hospitalized for a week or so, Ida came and took over the household duties. This enabled Mama Brown to stay at the hospital with Dad. Roy Lee was just about thirteen then, and she tended to him and his needs too: cooking for him, keeping his clothes clean, getting him off to school, etc. They developed a real fondness for each other.

"After Roy Lee and I got married, Ida appeared at our door one day at about mid-morning. Mama Brown was surprised to see her and greeted her, 'Well, Ida! Hello! How did you get here? Did your son bring you?' 'No'm,' she answered, 'I walked.' Now, from her house near the river, and about a city block from Crystal Springs, the distance to the Browns' home was about a three-mile trip. This isn't such a great distance, especially for people who were more used to walking than riding during the Depression. But Ida was a woman well up in years and was handicapped by deformed feet. We were amazed and deeply touched that she had hobbled all that way just to be with us. My heart went out to her. Being accepted by the Browns obviously meant a great deal to her. Bless her. She *was* 'sweet as apple cider.'"

FRED "PAPA" CALHOUN: "There weren't too many colored bands in Fort

Worth then, but there was a few guys who were part of an eight-piece Dixie band. These fellows were barbers and they barbered white people in this barber shop across from the Texas Hotel. Matter of fact, they cut my hair all the time. Good barbers. Anyway, a guy from Marshall called me after the radio program one day. He wanted to get any kind of a band for New Year's Eve. He said, 'Man, we had a band cancel out on us and went to Oklahoma City, and here we had fifteen hundred tickets sold and no band. Can you rustle up any kind of a band at all? Anything! We'll pay plenty if they'll come up here.' 'Course that was the Depression and anybody making $20 on a dance was doing pretty good. I said, 'I know a band that'll come, but they're colored.' He said, 'Well, I don't give a durn what color they are if they'll come.' He said, 'We'll pay their expenses and $100 apiece if they'll come out.' So after the program I went down to the barber shop and talked to these barbers. I said, 'Say, you guys booked for New Year's Eve?' They said, 'No.' I said, 'Well I got a job for you if you want it.' They said, 'Where?' I said, 'Marshall.' They said, 'Oh, that's too far.' I said, 'Well, it pays a hundred dollars a man.' They said, 'That ain't too far [laughs].' So I told them where it was and they went out there. A couple of days later, the guy from Marshall called me, or came out to the dance and said, 'You know, that was one of the best bands I ever heard.' No colored bands did anything but book around. None of them had regular places. In fact, the only regular dance halls in town were Crystal Springs, Lake Casino, Cinderella Roof over on Jennings, and the Texas Hotel."

The visual image the Brownies projected on their tours was often as striking as the audio effect. Milton demanded that they always look sharp, refrain from drinking on the bandstand, and remain alert. This show of respect for audiences, no matter how small, was appreciated by the crowds.

FRED "PAPA" CALHOUN: "Oh, yeah, we dressed. We all had suits, ties, coats, nice shoes. . . . 'Course in hot jobs we'd take our coats off, but we all dressed and dressed alike. We ordered our suits tailor-made and had them all sewn from the same material so we'd match. Seven-piece band, that was a pretty good order for seven suits for some guy. We had white suits that we wore in the summer and we had gray, brown, and black ones, too. But we all dressed alike, ties and all."

ROY LEE BROWN: "I remember Mama used to wash those white pants, she washed them on a rub-board. We didn't have a washing machine then. She'd stand out there and break her back washing Derwood and Milton's white pants. Every day when we lived out there on Roberts Cut-Off, she'd wash those uniforms. Evidently they had more than one because she washed those pants and spot cleaned them and pressed them. She wanted to keep her boys in the music business."

ELLEN BROWN: "Those white suits, I think they were linen. And they were just terrible to iron! There was one suit they wore that had a checkered vest. It was a three-piece thing and they had a vest with small checks that went with it."

BUCK SPURLOCK: "But when those guys got to the dance, they took them coats off and got down to business! They'd play two songs in a row and then Milton would talk. They'd have maybe one short intermission during the whole dance. And they'd stand there sweatin' and a-playin' until 12:00 or even 1:00, depending on whether or not there was a curfew."

ROY LEE BROWN: "Perspiration was a fact of life then. It was not beneath anyone's dignity to be seen in damp clothing. Women carried pretty fans to ease the burden of the heat. Some women would even fan their escorts, too."

WANNA COFFMAN: "Milton was always real conscious about our appearance and how we acted. He'd always lay down the law to anybody that'd get drunk out on the bandstand. If they did that, they wouldn't get paid. Fred wasn't very much of a drinker anyway. Ocie drank some, but not too much. Milton wouldn't drink at all. Maybe he'd take one at intermission but that's it."

The Crystal Springs Ramblers followed a touring circuit similar to the Brownies', although they did not book nearly as many dances. Still, the two bands found themselves frequenting the same dance halls around the countryside. However, the crowds were not always receptive.

J. B. BRINKLEY: "Papa Sam booked us once at the Bluebird Dance Pavilion in Longview. It was between Longview and Gladewater. The Brownies had played there, and he decided to book the Ramblers there, too. Times were hard then and we were looking for anything. We walked in that joint and stopped and said, 'What in the world is this?' They had put the bandstand right in the middle of the dance floor and surrounded it with this double layer of chicken wire about three feet away. It went all the way up to the ceiling. There was a gate with a lock on it, and in order to get to the bandstand, they'd have to unlock that door and let you in with your instrument. We thought, 'What kind of a deal is this, anyway? We never played no place like this before.' So they let us in there and they locked the door behind us. We got out our instruments, cranked up, and then, all those roughnecks came in out of the oil fields. They had on their old work clothes, and they were drinking bourbon and Coke, beer, and whatever. But it didn't take us long to find out why that chicken wire was around the bandstand. Directly here comes a half a bottle of beer: 'HEY, BAND!!!' Wham! That old beer bottle just bounced off that chicken wire. Oh, mercy! When we left that night, all our instruments and clothes smelled like a brewery. Hard times or not, that was the last time we ever played *there!*"

FRED "PAPA" CALHOUN: "Back when we used Papa Sam's bus, Henry Cunningham was our driver, and he and Papa Sam sometimes went along with us when we went out on the road. One night we played a women's club over in Denton. Some young fella got real loud and hollered a lot, so Papa Sam asked him to quiet down. The guy not only refused but he hit Papa Sam in the nose. Henry was about 6'2" and weighed about 240, and he reached over his shoulder and knocked this boy down on the ground. Knocked him out. After the dance was over, we found out that Henry had knocked out the mayor's son. We took the speaker down and was getting ready to leave when a mob came on in. Growling mob. They had come to get Henry. And they kind of circled around him. Henry said to us, 'Fellas, I'm just goin' to walk on out of here. Somebody walk behind me.' I reached into his pocket and got his blackjack and followed him out. That crowd just kind of parted and we walked through there, put the stuff in the bus, and got in. There was about five or six motorcycle policemen there that didn't do a thing about that mob because it was the mayor's son. One of the policemen came up to Henry and told him he'd have to go down to City Hall. So we went down there, posted bond, and we went on home. Driving down the highway we noticed about twenty or thirty cars driving right behind us. They still weren't satisfied. Boy, I'll tell you one thing, I was scared.

"The roughest crowd we ever played for was in Mineola, Texas. It got to 12:00 and we were fixing to finish up, and these oil workers came in and said, 'This place ain't closing up, you're going to keep playing!' They got off work at midnight, see, so we had to play an extra thirty or forty minutes just for them. Those guys were tough, too. So we did it."

The days and nights Milton Brown and the Musical Brownies spent on the road were some of the most exhilarating as well as the most exhausting times of any musicians' lives. In a very short time, the Brownies knew nearly every building within a 200-mile radius of Fort Worth. The Brownies were a well-disciplined, professional organization, but the pressures of the road took their toll on the band. Pressure releases came in the form of alcohol and practical jokes.

WANNA COFFMAN: "Everytime we went to Longview, when we got through playing, me, Cliff, Derwood, and Bob Dunn would go get us a bottle. By the time we got home, the bottle was empty and we'd go to sleep or just pass out. When Johnny Borowski was with us, he could take two drinks and he was gone, just like that. One night, me and Cecil took these whiskey bottles that had corks in them and saved the corks. Johnny went to sleep one night after having a few, so we went to work. We burned that cork and blacked out his face, put a moustache on him, and stuck two cigarettes in his ears and two more up his nose. Johnny breathed through his mouth when he slept. We were always finding lipstick on the dance floor, so we put that on his mouth. Then Cecil tied his shoestrings to the bottom of the seat. When we got to the parking lot down at Fifth and Main where we parked our cars, we jumped out and yelled at the top of our lungs: 'THE BUS IS ON FIRE!! THE BUS IS ON FIRE [laughs]!!' Johnny got up, fell down, pulled his shoes off, ran out of the bus with the lipstick on his face, burnt cork on his eyes and cigarettes in his nose, and when he got out of there, there was his wife standing there waiting for him [laughs]!"

Crystal Springs may have helped make Milton Brown the king of Fort Worth, but it was the touring, the nightly trek to the small hamlets, sleepy towns, and occasional big cities that secured the Musical Brownies' place in Texas's musical history. An additional by-product of the Brownies' success with the public was their influence on countless other organizations bent on duplicating their fame. Although none approached the Brownies' overall popularity during Milton's lifetime, many groups used the Musical Brownies as a model, copying their style, repertoire, wardrobe, and instrumentation. In Waco, it was Doug Bine and his Dixie Ramblers. In Houston, it was Leon "Pappy" Selph's Blue Ridge Playboys.

LEON "PAPPY" SELPH: "Everybody in the whole state fashioned their band after Milton. They tried to get somebody who could play steel guitar like Bob Dunn, somebody who could play fiddle like Cecil Brower, somebody to play piano like Papa Calhoun. I fashioned my band after Milton, too. He was everybody's ideal in the music business, everybody's pattern. Everybody tried to make their band like Milton's.

"At that time, Milton's rhythm was new, like rock and roll was later on. The secret was that it was good sock rhythm. It was a good tempo: mm-pah-mm-pah, a 2/4 rhythm. The thing that Milton said was this, 'If I pattern my music and make a good polka tempo out of the songs I play, and play the polka tempo just a little bit harder, I think I'll have a good band.' And he did have, too. So his songs, and his melodies, and his rhythms, when you boil it down, was a good, simple, polka beat."

In San Antonio, Adolph Hofner began the longest active career of any Texas bandleader by imitating the Brownies. Beginning in the late 1930s, Hofner's various groups have lasted into the 1990s, an unbroken string of over a half-century.

ADOLPH HOFNER: "Although I never had the pleasure of knowing Milton, he and his band were my big inspiration. They played jazz then, the same as New Orleans jazz, but without the horns. They did it with strings. When Milton created the Texas swing sound with his string band, he was all the rage around here. He had the perfect band for it. Fort Worth was the heart of where it began, and Milton was the lifeline who opened the roads for other bands to play western swing. The High Fliers, Tune Wranglers, Texas Wanderers, etc.

"I started my band in 1938: Adolph Hofner and All the Boys. It was hard to sell our type of music because of the competition from the big bands. Milton sold, but with us it was a matter of wanting to do it and enjoying it. There was no money to be made then. There were times when we would have baloney for breakfast, lunch, and dinner along with a little bread and soda water. We were on the road, doing a lot of traveling. In fact, sometimes there was no time even to do the laundry. Once one of the guys had ring-around-the-collar so bad that he put white shoe polish on it!"[12]

By 1935 the constant touring began to pay off for the Musical Brownies. Their fame was spreading, and they began to reap the benefits of their hard work and long hours. That year also saw more personnel changes in the Brownies, as Milton experimented with further augmentations in his band. The group changed radio stations as well as record companies, and traveled to far-off Chicago for their third recording session.

It was also the year Milton Brown began to think seriously about leaving Fort Worth to move on to other territories and other challenges. He had a beautiful new bride, and by the end of the year, a new baby boy. In just a little more than two years, Milton had created a musical form that was having an effect on Texas similar to that of the seasonal tornadoes, blowing into town with his Musical Brownies like a cyclone, uprooting everything in sight, disrupting normal day-to-day schedules, and moving hundreds and even thousands of people to wherever he was going to be. All he had to do was get on the radio and say a few simple words: "Ladies and gentlemen, this is Milton Brown. I'd like to invite everybody to my next big dance."

TEN

The Biggest Little Band in the World

(1935–36)

During 1935, Milton Brown became increasingly restless. By January, he had become a successful bandleader. He managed his own affairs, supported his family, and was loved and respected by his public. He had recently married a beautiful socialite, and within the year his first child would be on the way. Other musicians would have been ecstatic to be in his shoes during that trying period in American history. But the ambition that motivated him to establish his mini-empire also drove him to look beyond Texas to bigger, more lucrative goals. He kept most of these ideas to himself, divulging them only to his parents or his brothers.

Milton Brown was never one to dream. His objectives and methods to reach those objectives were all carefully reasoned out. He weighed, considered, and reconsidered all possible alternatives. Even though he was sure he could put together a strong musical organization that would be prosperous and self-sufficient, Milton waited nearly two years to leave the Light Crust Doughboys. After forming his band in September 1932, he made few changes other than those over which he had no control. After adding Fred Calhoun, the only adjustments he made in the next two years were to add or subtract fiddlers.

The daring move of hiring Bob Dunn to play amplified steel guitar late in 1934 was the first in a series of steps Milton Brown took to broaden his base and extend his popularity. In the next sixteen months, the last months of his life, his actions became bolder. The first thing he did after hiring Bob Dunn was to find another record company for the Musical Brownies. The two sessions for Bluebird in 1934 resulted in little more than regional impact, which Milton knew he already had attained. What he needed was to find a company that would establish his name and his music throughout the country, thereby enabling him to move beyond Texas and the Southwest with the Musical Brownies.

ROY LEE BROWN: "Milton was dissatisfied with Victor and Eli Oberstein and was looking for another company to record for. Dave Kapp contacted Milton and that is why he went with Decca Records."

The American Decca Company was incorporated in the summer of 1934 by Jack Kapp, a former talent scout and sales promoter for the Brunswick record company. Kapp's father, Meyer, operated a record store in Chicago in the 1920s which dealt in mail-order race records in addition to having a successful walk-in business. The three Kapp brothers, Jack, Dave, and Paul, all became involved in the record business at an early age. Dave Kapp's son Michael recalled that daily sales on Paramount and other race labels were chalked on the sidewalks around the Kapp Imperial Talking Machine Shop in Chicago. Utilizing the same principle that later made Burma Shave famous, the ads attracted the attention of passersby, who would follow them directly to the record shop's front door.[1]

Jack Kapp's first personal triumph with Brunswick came as a result of a hunch he played in getting entertainer Al Jolson to record a song called "Sonny Boy," then featured in Jolson's second talking picture, *The Singing Fool.* Jolson's recording sold an estimated two million copies. Legend has it that Kapp instructed Jolson to abandon his mugging and elaborate gestures and instead concentrate on his delivery by singing distinctly into the microphone.

After taking a course in business administration, Jack Kapp sold the rights to press Brunswick records overseas to Edward R. Lewis, the owner of a British record company called Decca.[2] After the Depression all but destroyed the record industry in the early 1930s, Kapp dreamed of marketing a 78 rpm record that would sell for thirty-five cents, undercutting Victor, Columbia, and Brunswick's usual seventy-five cents to one dollar selling price and thus more affordable to the money-strapped public. Kapp's proposal to his Brunswick superiors was refused. He promptly resigned and with Lewis's financial backing started his own record company, American Decca. It was in the summer of 1934 that Kapp called on his younger brother Dave for assistance.

Born in Chicago on August 7, 1904, Dave Kapp was working as a personal agent for hillbilly acts such as Mac and Bob, stars of WLS's "National Barn Dance,"[3] when his brother called.

DAVE KAPP: "At the end of July I was sitting in my office when the phone rang. I knew that Jack had left Brunswick, the American Record Company. He called up. I remember the conversation so well. He said, 'How are you?' I said, 'Fine.' He said, 'When can you go away?' I asked, 'Go away where?' He said, 'Well, I want you to make a trip.'

"Up to that time I had been doing extra work in Chicago when Jack was with Brunswick. In those days they didn't have a man in Chicago. So when there were recording dates to be done, they would assign a recording date; and then they would hire me to handle the date in the studio. I used to get $25 for that.

"Jack at that time was recording manager for Brunswick. So I thought that this was an assignment which they were going to give me. He said, 'I want you to go to Indianapolis. There is a hillbilly artist there.[4] Then I want you to go to Minneapolis and talk to Whoopee John Wilfahrt. And I want you to go here, and I want you to go there.'

"I said, 'Well, I don't know whether I can go.' So he said, 'Why not?' I said, 'Because I got business here.' I was just beginning to get going again, handling artists. He said, 'Well, you don't sound very enthusiastic.' I said, 'What is there to be enthusiastic about?' He said, 'Don't you understand? We got a new record company, and you are with us.' So, all of a sudden I am now with Decca Records.

"He said, 'How much money are you making?' I said, 'Well, I made ninety bucks last week. I am getting along.' He said, 'How much do you average?' I said, 'About seventy-five a week.' He said, 'We can't pay you that much. We can start you for $50.' This happened just before I turned thirty.

"So, the next thing I knew was that I moved over to the Decca studios, which were in the Furniture Mart in Chicago, and I was working for Decca. My job was to build a hillbilly catalog. That is the thing for which I was hired. When Decca was organized, they made a deal with Warner Brothers. Warner Brothers bought out the Brunswick Record department from Brunswick-Balke-Collender. They paid eight million and some dollars for it, and they formed the Brunswick Radio Corporation. That was about 1929 or early 1930, because it was right after that that they brought Jack to New York. Then along came 1931 and 1932 when the record business just went to nothing. The record business went from 100,000,000 records in 1929 to 6,000,000 records in 1932. That is national. That was the number of records that were sold. Radio did it. I don't remember the date, but just about that time, Warners sold the record department to the American Record Company, which was operated by Herb Yates. Warners retained what they called the Brunswick Radio Corporation. This was the company which made radio combinations, and what is pertinent to this story is that they were in the radio transcription business. So they maintained studios in New York and Chicago. They had a factory on Fifty-fourth Street where they pressed the records. And the deal for the start of Decca was that Warner Brothers got a minority interest of 10 or 20 per cent. I forget exactly how much. So they turned over all the facilities to Decca. Overnight, Decca was in business with studios, factory, and everything. We began recording on August 1, 1934.

"Things were pretty rough in the beginning. As a matter of fact, I got a call from Jack after about five or six months. He wanted to cut my salary to $40 a week.

"I then started to build a Decca hillbilly catalog. That meant going all through the South. We went hunting music. We knew we had to go where these people lived, because they had a tradition there, and many of these people never left that part of the country, so the only way we could get this music was to go down after it. I remember the first trip I made was in January of 1935. I went to St. Louis, where I held auditions of colored talent and sat in a room about as big as this with about forty colored people. From there I went to Jackson, Mississippi. I went to New Orleans, Birmingham, Atlanta, and I signed up the first talent.

"In those days we had a very small budget. The musicians' scale was $20 a man for three hours. I used to have to turn out six sides in three hours. There were no arrangement costs. We used to get the best musicians in New York, and all we would do is put up piano copies, go in the studio, and say, 'All right, the first chorus you play the lead. You play this in back. And then in the middle you take a solo here. And then the vocal comes in, and you do this. All right. Let's make it.' And zoom.

"We made a deal with a hillbilly band by the name of Milton Brown and his Brownies. This band was the start of hillbilly bands. When I say 'hillbilly bands,' I differentiate between hillbilly bands and the old-time fiddling bands, because these hillbilly bands played popular music. They played them in dance tempo, so that the average person could dance to them. What happened in the South is that these people had a band to which they could dance. It was a band that played all the old standards. They played very few new things, but they would play 'Melancholy Baby' and the old 'Wabash Blues,' and they were in dance tempo. So much so, as a matter of fact, that to this day they stand as examples of dance records."[5]

ROY LEE BROWN: "Milton's contract with RCA Victor ran out at the end of 1934. Decca wanted them as soon as possible, so they asked the

Brownies to come to Chicago to make some records. The terms that
Decca made was to pay the band's expenses when they went to
record and so much for each record sold. Milton wrote a letter to
Dave Kapp scolding him about not paying royalties and expense
money once.[6]

"The way I remember it, Dave Kapp came to Fort Worth and contacted Milton at the radio station, and Milton signed a contract with
Decca after Dave went back to Chicago. I remember Milton telling
Mama and Dad that Dave had a little trouble convincing Jack Kapp
to record the Brownies. Dave told Milton that he told his brother that
he had never heard anything like the Brownies and that Jack would
not be sorry for recording them because they were the best he had
ever heard. I think Milton found out they were going to Chicago for
a session about two or three weeks before it happened."

Before the Brownies left for their first out-of-state recording session, they began playing a regular Friday night dance at the top of
the Texas Hotel, the home of KTAT. The dance was called the "Southwest Barn Dance" and was designed to promote acts that played over
the Southwest Broadcasting System (actually the Southwest Broadcasting Company). The Brownies and Hoppe, the Singing Ranger,
were the featured attractions, along with "other Southwest Broadcasting stars." The dances took place every Friday night from 9 P.M.
until midnight, beginning January 4, 1935. The seven-station SBC
network, including local outlet KTAT, carried the dance live from 10
P.M. until midnight. A weekly ad ran in the *Fort Worth Press* regularly during the early weeks of 1935, beginning with a large quarter-
page premiere announcement of the broadcast—quite an expense,
considering it was to promote "hillbilly music." Readers were encouraged to "Wear your overalls and ginghams." If the music was not
sufficient enticement, the ad also announced: "We are serving Nickel Beer and Nickel Sandwiches. Plenty of seats and Dancing Space
for Everyone. Everybody Invited!"

Then Milton received word from Dave Kapp that a recording session had been scheduled for the Brownies at Decca's Chicago studios. Travel expenses for the band to travel by train to the Windy
City would be forwarded and recording would commence on Sunday, January 27.[7]

ROY LEE BROWN: "Milton was excited about going to Chicago, as were
the rest of the Brownies. Milton wasn't living at home at this time
because he and Mary Helen were married, so we weren't able to get

Publicity picture of Milton Brown taken in 1934. The photo was used in handouts such as the one featuring Milton's song "Fall in Line with the NRA." Milton inscribed this photo "Love, Milton" for his then steady, Sally Beard (later, Mrs. Sleepy Johnson). Courtesy Roy Lee and Ellen Brown.

Milton Brown and his Musical Brownies in the studios of WBAP, Fort Worth, 1935. From left: Ocie Stockard (banjo), Fred Calhoun (piano), Wanna Coffman (bass), Milton Brown (vocals), Cecil Brower (fiddle), Bob Dunn (steel guitar), Derwood Brown (guitar, vocals). This is the unit that recorded for Decca in Chicago, January 1935. Courtesy Roy Lee and Ellen Brown.

Milton Brown, "sitting on top of the world," c. 1935. Courtesy Ronnie Brown.

Milton Brown and his Musical Brownies at the height of their fame, in a photo taken at WBAP, Fort Worth, probably early 1936. From left: Wanna Coffman (bass), Cecil Brower (fiddle), Bob Dunn (steel guitar), Cliff Bruner (fiddle), Fred Calhoun (piano), Milton Brown (vocals), Ocie Stockard (banjo), Derwood Brown (guitar). This was the unit that recorded for Decca in New Orleans, March 1936. Courtesy Roy Lee and Ellen Brown.

the details of the goings-on that we did when Milton was at home. I'm not sure whether this was the first time the Brownies left Texas. It is possible that they had played in Oklahoma by this time. Milton wasn't nervous or anything, although he was looking forward to the session. He always took things in stride. He had goals and he pursued them with great enthusiasm."

WANNA COFFMAN: "We went up to Chicago by train. We always carried a piece of cardboard with us when we traveled. On the train, we put it in the aisle between the seats and played dominoes all the way up there. On the way back there was another band that had gone in to record. An orchestra, actually. Anyhow, they got a jam session going and ol' Dunn laid 'em out good! He wasn't drunk, he'd just had enough to make him play real good. I got my bass out. There wasn't enough room in there to set up drums, but I think they did set up a snare drum."

OCIE STOCKARD: "I remember that when we left Fort Worth, it was seventy degrees outside. By the time we got to Chicago, it was about ten or twenty below zero!"

FRED "PAPA" CALHOUN: "They had a special train car just for us. When we pulled in there, Milton said, 'Now boys, we're going to record as soon as we get to the studio. They're in a hurry and want to get the records out. I don't want any drinking. Nobody take a drink.' So we said okay and nobody took a drink. There were two big limousines there at the station to pick us up and carry us over to the studio. We loaded our stuff in and went up on Lake Michigan to the Warner Brothers studios. That's where Decca was recording. We got in at about three in the afternoon and sure enough, we went right on in to record. Jack Kapp, the president of the company, recorded us himself."

OCIE STOCKARD: "We started to record and it didn't sound quite right. We played one or two tunes and Jack Kapp said, 'Boy, that don't sound like you at all.' Everybody was kind of nervous, you know."

DAVE KAPP: "On certain occasions we brought [artists] to New York or Chicago. They weren't the same thing. It seems they were in an atmosphere in which they were not familiar, and they sang as if they were expected to sing differently because they were in the city."

FRED "PAPA" CALHOUN: "So Jack said, 'Tell you what. Let's all go into this office here and talk a minute.' We all went in the office. He reached into a desk drawer and pulled out a fifth of whiskey and said, 'Now I want you boys to take a little drink and relax [laughs].'"8

WANNA COFFMAN: "I never will forget how Milton looked when he saw him take out that bottle. He just turned all colors [laughs]!"

OCIE STOCKARD: "Bob Dunn went out and bought the ice [laughs]!"

FRED "PAPA" CALHOUN: "So we sat there and talked awhile and then he passed the bottle around again. Then we went back in there and started cutting records. And we went right through them. One after the other. I don't think we ever had to make one over. 'Course, we were playing tunes we played all the time. However, they had a restriction of two-and-a-half to three minutes on those records so we had to time them out. We timed the choruses and knew how many choruses we had to play. The thing that bothered us more than anything was the way they had us separated. They only used one microphone. The piano was over here and the tenor banjo was way over there, twenty-thirty feet away. The sound was so perfect in there, you could hit a note on the banjo in the corner and it would sound like it was right in front of you. The bass was all the way on the other side of the room. Steel guitar was settin' back on the other side. Derwood and his guitar were way back too, except when he sang harmony. Cecil worked up close to the microphone and Milton, of course, was singing. That's the way they had to balance it out. We were used to being a tight group sittin' around playing. It kind of bothered us being so far apart, but it came out good."

WANNA COFFMAN: "I remember I had to put a mute on my bass, it was so loud. We recorded straight through the night and then recorded the rest the next day. Jack Kapp wanted Milton to sing 'Beautiful Texas' and he had him call W. Lee O'Daniel to get permission to record it. When we finished the session, Kapp gave Milton $500 and said, 'I want you boys to stay over two extra nights and go to all these clubs in town.' I guess he was happy with the records.

"We went to see Wayne King play. Cecil wanted to meet some of the fiddle players. We went out there and got us a table and Cecil said, 'I'll buy the set-up and get us a tub of ice.' When he went to pay for it, it came to eight dollars [laughs]! Here in town, we could go out to Casino Park and get a tub of ice for fifty cents. Cecil didn't offer to pay for anything else that night [laughs]!"

FRED "PAPA" CALHOUN: "Then we heard Carroll Dickerson's band at the Grand Terrace where Earl Hines played.[9] Hines wasn't there at the time. Dickerson's group was a colored band and they were good. This band was taking Hines's place. They had about a fifteen-piece band with five tenor saxophones and three baritone saxes. And boy, they'd hit those chords! They had a singer named Arthur Lee Simkins who used to sing with Hines. We came in there and he saw we had on suits that were all alike. He came over to our table and said, 'You fellas are musicians, aren't you?' We said, 'Yeah.' He said, 'Well, I figured you were, you all dressed alike.' He sat down there and talked to us, real nice. They had floor shows and everything, you know. Then he said, 'Say, how would you like to meet Duke Ellington?' We said, 'We sure would!' He said, 'Well, he's sittin' at the table over there.' So he went over and said something to Duke and Duke came over and brought a fifth of whiskey with him [laughs]. We had a drink with him and talked for about an hour. We talked about tunes we played. He said, 'I always like to come to Texas. I enjoy Texans.' We had a big, long conversation."

The Brownies recorded thirty-six songs during the two-day session in Chicago, January 27–28, 1935. All but one, "When I'm Gone Don't You Grieve," were issued. (At their New Orleans session the following year, the Brownies rerecorded the tune.) The personnel included Milton Brown, vocals; Derwood Brown, guitar and harmony vocals; Cecil Brower, fiddle; Fred Calhoun, piano; Wanna Coffman, bass; Bob Dunn, amplified steel guitar; and Ocie Stockard, tenor banjo and third harmony vocals. The session was Bob Dunn's first and the first ever for an amplified stringed instrument.[10] Even the experienced recording engineers at Decca were perplexed by Dunn's contraption. They had recorded steel guitars before, but never one that was amplified. They finally sat Dunn and his amplifier in a corner of the studio where he blared away. Feedback from Dunn's guitar can be detected on many of the recordings, especially "Sweet Jennie Lee."

Milton handled all the lead vocals except for "You're Tired of Me," "Sweet Georgia Brown," and "Little Betty Brown," all featuring Derwood; and "In El Rancho Grande," in which Cecil Brower and Derwood sang the words in Spanish.[11]

The first of the records were not released until April 1935. Records made during Decca's first six months in existence are now vilified by collectors as having some of the worst, grittiest sound Decca ever produced. According to a feature on Jack Kapp and Decca by the *New Yorker*'s Howard Whitman in 1940:

Kapp had taken over an old factory in Orange, New Jersey, once used by Brunswick. The machinery proved to be in bad shape and incapable of top-speed production. At unpredictable intervals, the power and the presses failed. Moreover, the "hot biscuit," the compound from which records are made, was produced from an unreliable recipe. Nearly all the Decca records turned out in the first three months of production were returned to the factory, warped, poorly grooved, or with their holes off centre. At one time it seemed to the unhappy pioneers that more records were being returned than had been produced, as if some fiend in a secret lair were at work forging imperfect Decca records. Time, and Mr. Lewis, who loyally added an extra $400,000 to his original investment of $250,000, eventually straightened things out. At the end of 1935, Decca showed a tiny profit.[12]

Milton Brown wanted to make sure his most popular numbers were recorded at their first session for Decca. He was hoping that the new company would promote the Brownies' records and help establish an out-of-state reputation for the Fort Worth group. Accordingly, the Brownies waxed versions of "St. Louis Blues," Stuart Hamblen's "My Mary," "Some of These Days," "Who's Sorry Now," and "Sweet Georgia Brown," some of the most requested tunes at Brownies dances. They also recorded several instrumentals, including Ocie Stockard's sprightly "Crafton Blues" (played by Cecil Brower on the fiddle) and Bob Dunn's showcase tune, "Taking Off."

Returning to Fort Worth, the Brownies resumed their hectic schedule of broadcasts and dances and waited for Milton to make his next move. That move came sometime in the spring when Milton Brown decided to hire his first and, as it turned out, only horn player.

FRED "PAPA" CALHOUN: "We had a saxophone player there for a little while named Iris Harper. Tenor sax. He was a wild sax man, Iris was. Played kinda like Boots Randolph. Lot of execution, lot of notes. He had a different style on saxophone than anybody I ever heard. He played a lot of fast licks, not like Coleman Hawkins. Hawkins played a lot of pretty notes. Once in a while on a slow tune, Iris would play melody, but normally, he just played choruses.

"Anyway, Iris stayed with us the summer of '35. Milton used to augment our band once in a while on certain jobs. We had a big band at one time when we played the Cotton Club in Henderson. Had two trumpets, saxophone, clarinet, drums. They wanted a bigger band for that. Charlie Chase used to play drums with us. We had Snuffy Klaus and Harry Palmer on trumpet,[13] Earl Driver and maybe Bob Gibson on sax, and our regular band. They sounded big. Several times we played up at Olney and Milton would use Cody Sandifer on drums."

ELLEN BROWN: "In 1935 Milton tried adding a saxophone player named Iris Harper to the band, but the general public just was not ready for a horn in this type of a band. So, adding the saxophone was a mistake at that time. It must be stated, however, that Iris Harper was one of the best sax men around. Brass, reeds, and drums in a string band in 1935 was simply too premature. Milton had already put together a western swing band by adding twin fiddles and a piano, and he didn't feel he wanted an orchestra. This was too sophisticated for his type of patrons. Combining country-western and big band tunes was the secret of Milton's reaching so many people and their finding it so thrillingly addictive."

Iris Harper traveled with the Brownies through the summer of 1935, playing with them during their brief term at the Brownie Tavern on Lake Worth.

ROY LEE BROWN: "Milton figured Iris would fit in with the band, which he did. I think it was a mutual agreement for Iris to leave, because of a disagreement between Milton and Iris. The Brownies were making good money and Milton wasn't trying to have a big band. The fewer men to split the take with, the more money each made. Milton wanted a compact band that sounded full, like the Brownies always did. He only added musicians when he thought they would add a lot to the sound."

Another brief change occurred in early March when Cecil Brower received an offer to join a musical organization known as the Georgie Porgie Boys, who were playing over the CBS network in Columbus, Ohio. "Georgie Porgie" was a breakfast cereal manufactured by Kellogg's that sponsored many hillbilly groups in the Northeast, including Hugh Cross and his Radio Gang, which played on WWVA in Wheeling, West Virginia. Former Brownie fiddler Ted Grantham became a member of Cross's aggregation during this time, so it is possible he was the source of the offer to Brower.

While playing with the Georgie Porgie Boys, Cecil Brower entered a statewide fiddler's contest and was awarded a trophy as "National Champion Fiddler for 1935."[14]

While Cecil was in Ohio, Milton hired fiddler Johnny Borowski to replace him. A tall, large, gentle man from Yankton, South Dakota,

Borowski, like Brower, was a trained violinist. However, after a few weeks, Cecil Brower had had enough of Columbus, Ohio, and asked Milton if he would take him back. Milton readily agreed. Johnny Borowski then decided to return north, leaving the Brownies with one fiddler. Borowski replaced Cecil again the following year, when Derwood Brown led the band after Milton's death.

FRED "PAPA" CALHOUN: "Johnny Borowski knew Lawrence Welk up there in South Dakota. Johnny had played some with Bob Dunn, so when Cecil left, Bob told Milton about Johnny and he hired him. Johnny played good saxophone and clarinet, too. He also played them little tin whistles. He'd get two of them, one in F and one in C and play harmony, he'd play them both at the same time. And he'd play hot choruses on them.[15] He was sure a good musician. Lawrence Welk tried to hire him while he was with us, when we had that 'biggest little band in the world.' He wanted him because Johnny doubled on so many instruments, but he couldn't offer him as much money as Milton could. So Johnny didn't take it."

On July 4, 1935, Jack Gordon, columnist for the *Fort Worth Press,* reported that "Milton Browne [*sic*] and his Musical Brownies switch from KTAT Fort Worth to WFAA, Dallas after Saturday, but will keep on the job at the Brownie Tavern out by the lake." Actually, the Brownies had signed on with WBAP, Fort Worth, which shared the 800 kilocycle frequency with WFAA, its sister station in Dallas. The two stations used the same 50,000-watt transmitter (eclipsing KTAT's relatively puny 1,000 watts), trading programming during the day and nighttime hours. According to Roy Lee Brown, the switch-off was signaled by the ringing of a cowbell.

The first appearance of the Brownies on WBAP was on Monday, July 8, 1935. WFAA had been the radio home of the Brownies' friendly rivals, the Wanderers, since June 16, 1934. After the Brownies joined WBAP, the two groups shared a half-hour program broadcast from 10:15 to 10:45 A.M. on WBAP and WFAA Monday through Saturday. The program, entitled "The Round-Up," featured the Brownies and the Wanderers, each having fifteen-minute segments in which they played music and plugged their dances. The Brownies, led by "Maestro Brown," performed from WBAP's lavish studios at Fort Worth's Blackstone Hotel, while the Wanderers' portion, featuring King Rector, "the world's smallest xylophone player," emanated from WFAA's facilities at the Baker Hotel in Dallas. The Wanderers' lineup also included future Light Crust Doughboys Dick Reinhart, Marvin Montgomery, and Bert Dodson. "The Round-Up" program may have been established to capitalize on the increasingly popular battle dances the Brownies and the Wanderers had been playing together since early 1934. Since the Brownies were sharing the time slot, the Wanderers could occasionally turn over their share of the program to Milton Brown and join WFAA's traveling stage show, the "WFAA Radio Revue." This consisted of popular WFAA artists performing live on stage three times daily in conjunction with the screening of popular motion pictures such as *Orchids to You,* with John Boles and Jean Muir. While the Wanderers were away, listings in the *Dallas News* and the *Dallas Journal* made mention that the Musical Brownies would carry the Round-Up banner until the Wanderers, who were touring in Oklahoma, returned. According to Roy Lee Brown, "The Round-Up" program did not survive long. However, it did help broaden the base of the Musical Brownies' listenership.

According to a photograph that appeared in Dallas newspapers publicizing "The Round-Up" program, the Brownies' lineup included Milton and Derwood Brown, Ocie Stockard, Wanna Coffman, Fred Calhoun, Bob Dunn, Iris Harper, and Johnny Borowski. Calhoun, Coffman, and Sybil Brower Bohm all recalled that Cecil Brower had again left the Brownies, this time to join Ted Fio Rito's orchestra in New York City. As in the spring, when Brower played with the Georgie Porgie Boys in Ohio, Johnny Borowski took Cecil's place with the Brownies. After Cliff Bruner replaced Borowski that fall, Brower returned.

In addition to "The Round-Up" program, the Brownies were also featured in their own fifteen-minute broadcast, which aired Monday through Friday at 1:15 P.M. WBAP was affiliated with the Texas Quality Network, and now the Brownies could be heard on WOAI San Antonio, KPRC Houston, and WKY Oklahoma City. As a result, their music began to spread across the entire breadth of the Southwest, from far-off west Texas to Louisiana, Arkansas, Mississippi, and parts of Alabama. Almost instantly, the Brownies' income increased as more and more demands for personal appearances and broadcasts on local stations flooded in.[16]

In the fall of 1935, Milton Brown decided that the idea of a saxophone was not working out, a decision that resulted in the departure of Iris Harper. It had been Milton's desire all along to have two fiddles as the band's focus, but competent fiddle players were still scarce in Fort Worth. Johnny Borowski was a good musician, but not as schooled in jazz as Cecil Brower was. So Milton made another change, hiring twenty-year-old Cliff Bruner. Soon, Brower returned from New York and Milton once again had his twin fiddle sound.

Clifton Lafayette Bruner was born April 25, 1915, in Texas City,

Texas, located across the bay from Galveston. His musical education, like that of many other Texans, began when he was a small boy.

CLIFF BRUNER: "I was about four when I started playing. The fiddle was in the family. I found an old fiddle under the bed and started fooling with it. My daddy could tune one, so he tuned it up for me. I was actually the only musician in the family, even though Mother played the guitar and the French harp. I could play fiddle before I could talk plain. That's quite a few years ago! The first tune I ever learned was 'Old Coon Dog': [sings] 'Somebody stole my old coon dog / I wish he could bring him back / He'd chase the big hogs over the fence / And the little ones through the crack [laughs].' It was just an old breakdown.

"My daddy was a longshoreman down at the docks in Houston. Most of my family came from Arkansas. When I was three months old a big storm hit Texas City. Not too long after then, my folks moved back to Arkansas. We had seven in our family, five boys and two girls. I'm the youngest and the only one left.

"My dad would save a couple thousand dollars and then go back to the farm. He loved farming but he could never make any money at it. At this particular time when I started playing, we were in Arkansas. Back in those days it was hard times, boy, really hard times. I attended school in a little old one-room schoolhouse. They taught grades one through ten all in that one room. And I remember the teacher rode to school on a horse and he used to let me ride home behind him on his horse.

"When I was seven we moved back to Texas. Dad went back to work on the waterfront. That being the case, we did move around quite a bit, I guess that's where I got my gypsy blood. I always loved to move and travel. So we came back to Texas, moved out on the farm, and by this time, I was in junior high school and I started playing the fiddle for the little country shindigs they were having in different people's homes. They'd throw some corn meal on the floor and we'd have a dance. A friend of mine would play the guitar and I would play the fiddle, and we'd get on our horses, put the instruments in a flour sack, and we'd head for the blue yonder. Sometimes we'd make three or four dollars, five maybe. That was a lot of money then. People worked for a dollar a day back then. You'd start work when the sun came up and you wouldn't stop until the sun went down. Pickin' cotton and choppin' bermuda grass. In the summertime that could get to around fourteen, fifteen hours. For one dollar. And I thought there just had to be an easier way to make a living.

"As soon as I began to grow up I got a little more gypsy in me, and I'd catch me a freight train and I'd go seek my fortune. My daddy just could not keep me on the farm. He tried to. Any direction that freight train was goin' was all right with me as long as it was goin' to a big town: Fort Worth, Dallas, Waco, it didn't make any difference. I knew I'd make it as long as I had my fiddle.

"In those days, if there was enough talent, we'd get somebody to beat rhythm on the neck of the fiddle with two pencils or sticks or whatever they could get.[17] But mostly, I played square dances by myself.

"But then I started forming bands. My first band was called the Sun Dodgers. We played dances up in around Mexia and Groesbeck in central Texas. Oh, it was hard times!

"I never did like breakdowns much. I set myself a little style of my own. We didn't have radio or television so we didn't have anybody to listen to. We had to set our own styles. Mine was kind of jazzy. I'd deviate from the melody and improvise a little. Even as a young kid I did that. I started to beautify the tune and I still do that now. We played songs like 'Some of These Days,' 'Nobody's Sweetheart Now,' all those great tunes. We only needed to hear a tune one time and we could play it.

"The first radio I ever saw was a carbon set attached to a battery by a thin wire. This wire would bend over and touch this carbon. You found your station by moving this wire along that carbon. And you'd listen to it through earphones.

"One Saturday I went to town, and there was a medicine show coming through. It was run by a guy who called himself Doctor Scott. He heard me play and wanted me to join the medicine show. And I said, 'Just get me out of this cotton patch, I'm ready, let's go!' They had a band on this medicine show, and on this band was Leo Raley, who later on I hired when I organized my own band, and Cotton Thompson, who later went with Bob and Johnnie Lee Wills. Nobody could sing 'Milk Cow Blues' like Cotton. This was Doctor Scott's Medicine Show. What a doctor . . . We sold something called Liquidine. It was mostly colored water. He might have put a little alcohol in there for all I know. Probably did! Made folks feel a little different, anyway.

"There was also Doctor Tate, he had Tate-lax. These guys would mix the medicine up in the daytime and sell it at night. It was good for anything: lumbago, cramps, stomach trouble, ulcers, back pains, colds, you name it, it'd cure it.

"Anyway, we'd have a big parade downtown. Doctor Scott had this big long Pierce Arrow touring car, it was about a block long with lights in the front fenders. And all these country people would see this big long car coming downtown and they'd say, 'Boy, that is something!' And the big FREE medicine show was going to be held, so they'd come from miles around by the hundreds, sometimes by the thousands to see our show. We had a regular stage and they sold candy and they sold soap and they sold Liquidine. One of the funny things was old Doc Scott selling his soap. Before he'd go out on the stage he'd take this smoke-white soap, he'd buy it by the box. He'd get a bar of it and rub it in his hands real good, get a lot of it rubbed in his skin and then go out on the stage and he'd start talkin' 'bout his soap. Then he'd reach over and get a little glass of warm water and he'd throw a little dash of it on his arm and hit that soap one time and it'd just foam right up [laughs]! And evvvverybody'd buy that soap! And then the musicians would get that Liquidine, I'll never forget Leo Raley, bless his heart. I can just hear him, he'd say, 'Soooold out, Doctor, gimme some more of that good ol' Liquidine!!'[18] Doctor Scott would then bring me up there and he'd say, 'I'll give anybody $25 if they could beat this boy playin' fiddle!' It's a wonder nobody came and tore me up, I guess I was lucky.

"Milton Brown had a fiddle player with him that didn't play the style that Milton liked. He was a good musician, classically trained, but he knew that it wasn't exactly what Milton wanted. He said, 'Milton, I know that I'm not the one for this particular job but I know a kid that I heard down in Austin that will do the job for you.' He told Milton about me and at that time I was twenty. [The fiddle player was probably Johnny Borowski.]"

FRED "PAPA" CALHOUN: "We played in Austin one night at a women's club down there. And we got there in time to hear Cliff play on a radio program. Milton remembered how good he played so he called Cliff after the program and asked him if he wanted to go to work."

CLIFF BRUNER: "I was organizing another band at the time in Houston. We were still looking for the end of the rainbow, and I told the boys, 'Look, fellas, we're just getting started, I don't want to leave you.' Rip Ramsey was a dear friend of mine, and Rip said, 'Cliff, this time, you're going. I'll even take you up there myself!' So Rip took me up there and he went to work with Papa Sam Cunningham. When I arrived, there was Milton, Papa Calhoun, and all those great musicians, and me, this little ol' kid. . . . I was a little shaky!

"The first dance I played was up at the Brownie Tavern. I got there and Milton called me up on stage and said, 'Come on, Little Cliff, get your fiddle out!' And Bob Dunn liked to have scared me to death with the kind of steel guitar he was playing. Oh, my goodness! I never heard anything like it. Nobody else had either. All of the musicians were older than me, I was just a fuzzy-faced kid. Milton used to put everybody on a percentage when they started, I think about 10 per cent. But he took me off of it and put me on regular like everybody else after only a little while."

ROY LEE BROWN: "When Cliff came to Fort Worth and joined the Brownies, I was traveling with them. I don't remember if Cliff played the radio program that day, but I do remember when I first saw him. It was out at the parking garage when we started to leave to go out of town for a dance. I remember that Cliff's shirt was dirty and he didn't have a clean one, so one of the Brownies, I think it was Ocie, let him have one of his shirts to wear that night."

CLIFF BRUNER: "We were all just one family, the Brownies. My best buddy was Bob Dunn. He was my seat partner. Bob and I rode together night after night, side by side. We lived on that road. Fred and Cecil kind of paired off with each other. They were real close. We didn't have transcriptions then, you had to come all the way back to Fort Worth just to make the daily radio show. We played in Enid, Oklahoma, one night, drove all the way back to Fort Worth to make a broadcast. The next night we went in the other direction to Stamford.

"Milton had such a dynamic personality, he just walked out on the stage and that's all it took. People by the thousands, everywhere would come to see him."

It might have been while he was scouting for another fiddle player that Milton started thinking about leaving Fort Worth. The first Decca records had not set the world on fire, so Milton knew that the time was not right to make a major change. However, he was interested in relocating to another part of the Southwest. His first choice was Houston. Milton never discussed the possibility of moving to Houston with any of the Brownies. Bruner, Calhoun, Coffman, and Stockard knew nothing of Milton's plans in the fall of 1935. On October 11, 1935, Milton Brown wrote a letter to the station manager of KPRC radio in Houston, offering his services.

Dear Sir:

Having talked to several people from Houston, Texas, I find that my organization, known as Milton Brown and His Musical Brownies, are very popular in that territory. I am writing you in regard to same working on your station. I do not know how much of this type of entertainment you have in Houston, and you probably do not know of, or have not paid any particular attention to my band; so I am referring you to the firm of Amusco Incorporated, to whom I am sending some commercial photographs for advertising purposes, regarding my Decca Recordings, whom I wish you would get in touch with.

I am working, at this time, on Station WBAP, a daily program, except Sunday. I also have the privilege of announcing all of my personal appearances, these being mostly dances and some few theatre engagements. I would want you to check my popularity in that territory as nearly as possible and I also would want to come down and check the territory myself in regard to dances, etc. So I will appreciate a reply from you as soon as possible, if you are interested in my organization working on your station.

I do not think you would have any trouble selling my program to some advertiser.

Trusting to hear from you soon, I am

Respectfully,

MILTON BROWN

ROY LEE BROWN: "Milton talked to my family a lot about moving to Houston. We didn't want him to go because we didn't know what Milton might want us to do. He had a lot of things going at the time. He must have struck a deal with KPRC, because he told us he had a spot there and the station covered a large area. KPRC played a lot of the Brownies' records, and when 78s went out of style, KPRC gave Milton's records to Pappy Selph."

Mary Helen was pregnant during most of 1935, which contributed to the stress Milton must have been feeling. He was hiring new musicians, had tried operating his own club, and switched to a powerful radio station. Night after night, Milton had to juggle the band's finances, schedule dances, and worry about Mary Helen, all the while remaining his own smiling, energetic self on stage.

Shortly before he became a father, Milton wrote a song about his then-unborn child. Two sets of lyrics were prepared, one for a boy and one for a girl. On December 20, 1935, Milton and Mary Helen had a son, whom they named Buster Lee. The masculine version of the song now became part of the Brownies' repertoire. "Our Baby Boy" was similar to his previous composition about Derwood's son, "Precious Little Sonny Boy." Fort Worth was apprised of the new addition to the Brown family, and WBAP was bombarded with requests for the sentimental tune, delivered with Milton's usual heartfelt emotion.

On January 19, 1936, Milton wrote a brief letter to an Ira Martin in Chickasha, Oklahoma, apparently responding to a query as to whether the Brownies would be in Oklahoma in the near future. Milton answered, "I am not in a position just now to come to Chickasha but I am planning on Touring Okla. soon and I will contact you then." This was the first indication that the Brownies would be leaving Texas for any extended period of time. It was no doubt due to the Brownies' broadcasts on the Texas Quality Network, which extended into the Sooner State. Milton was anxious to set up an itinerary for his Oklahoma trip, but hesitated to commit himself because Decca wanted the Brownies for another recording session, this time somewhere in the South. Milton's letters during January indicate that the Brownies were booked ahead for the next month with no open dates for dances available.

By February, Milton had received a request from R. N. McCormick, manager of the Dallas, Atlanta, and New Orleans branches of Decca, for a list of tunes the Brownies would be prepared to record. It had been just over a year since their last session, so Milton had a stockpile of new selections that the Brownies had been playing on WBAP and at dances. On February 6 Milton sent a list of forty tune titles to McCormick in Dallas.[19] Knowing that Decca preferred original compositions, Milton highlighted the two numbers ("Our Baby Boy" and "Roseland Melody") he had written.[20]

H. M. Crow, Houston's Decca representative, wrote Milton on February 11 from the Blue Bonnet Hotel in San Antonio, informing him that the recording session would be held in New Orleans sometime in March. He also enclosed a copy of a record entitled "Too Long" for the Brownies to learn. Milton wrote back the following day acknowledging receipt of the record and assuring Crow the Brownies would get to work on it immediately.[21] Milton also requested the exact date of the recording session, explaining that he needed to arrange his dance engagements around it and to advise WBAP of his impending absence.

Milton was still considering his trip to Oklahoma and was now planning a joint tour with his old friend Bob Wills, whose Texas Playboys were gaining popularity on Tulsa's KVOO. On the same day he wrote to Decca, Milton drafted the following letter to Wills:

Dear Bob;

I am getting the pictures of which we were talking ready at present, but dont do any booking until you hear from me again as I have another recording coming up soon and I havent as yet found out just when and where it will be, but I will let you know when and where just as soon as the recording company let me know.

I assure you that I am still interested and the more I think of it the better I think we could do.

Give my regards to the boys and the best of luck to you all, I remain,

Yours Truly,

MILTON BROWN AND HIS
MUSICAL BROWNIES

Word arrived from Decca within the next few days that the Brownies' recording session would be held at the Roosevelt Hotel in New Orleans beginning Tuesday, March 3.[22] Relieved to know the recording session date and location, Milton proceeded to take care of the mail that had been stacking up at WBAP, requesting the Brownies' services. He wrote thirteen letters on February 15 to club owners from San Angelo, Texas, to Henrietta, Oklahoma. Milton wrote so many letters that day that he ran out of the Brownies' official WBAP stationery and had to draft six of the letters on out-of-date KTAT paper.

He also wrote to Eli Oberstein in New York City. Oberstein, director of artists and repertoire for RCA Victor, had written to Milton on January 29, inviting the Brownies to return to his label. Milton's answer hinted at dissatisfaction with his relationship with Decca, indicating a possible reconciliation with Victor. He also took the opportunity to scold Oberstein for holding back royalties from original numbers from his 1934 sessions:

Dear Sir,

I have your letter of the 29th.

Decca has taken up their option so you see I am tied up for the remainder of this year, however I am not giving them another option and I am just fulfilling my contract which is up January 1st, 1937.

My dealings with you have been very pleasant and I shall be glad to go into the matter later on. I am now getting two cents for ordinary recordings and three cents on original numbers.

Now Mr. Oberstein, something has gone wrong with my copywright [*sic*] royalties on the numbers "Swinging on the garden gate" "Joe Turner Blues" and "Precious Little Sonny Boy." I will appreciate it very much if you would get me some immediate action on this matter.

Trusting that I will hear from you soon I remain,

Yours Truly

MILTON BROWN

An indication of the Brownies' popularity during the last months of Milton's life comes in the form of a letter dated February 12 from Howard Davis of KMAC radio in San Antonio, inviting the Brownies to spend the entire summer of 1936 at his station. On February 23, Milton wrote Davis that he could not devote the entire summer but could possibly come for a week or so "if the proposition was interesting." He then said that Davis would have to match the Brownies' weekly income of $450 for it to be worthwhile. Milton turned down KMAC, probably because he had his eye on the forthcoming Texas centennial celebration. Davis did not accept Milton's offer of playing for a week.

Milton was now getting stress from all sides. He had an important recording session upcoming, which would necessitate a long journey to New Orleans. He was negotiating with Bob Wills for a series of equally important engagements in a new territory. Word was also buzzing around town about the Texas centennial, scheduled for that summer. Milton thought of the centennial as an ideal remedy for the Brownies' seemingly endless series of dance dates. If he could become a hit at the centennial, a major event that would attract millions of customers from all over the country, he knew that he would be able to get off the road for a while before returning to his dance circuit.

And then Mary Helen filed for divorce.

The hectic life Milton was leading with his band was apparently not compatible with Mary Helen's idea of domesticity. They now had a son who was a little more than two months old. Mary Helen wanted Buster Lee to have a father who would be around more than one day a week, and she tried to get Milton to quit the music business, get off the road, and settle down. She was also jealous of the young women who had become followers of the Brownies. Temptation was part of the business, but there was no evidence that Milton Brown was anything but faithful to his wife.

ROY LEE BROWN: "Mary Helen's father, Bill Hames, called Milton before the divorce was granted and asked him to come to Waco to talk with him. Mr. Hames tried to get Milton back with Mary Helen and join his carnival, probably to operate one of the rides or something. Later on, Buster Lee ran a booth for years for him. Milton told Mr. Hames, 'I've got a career with my band.' As much as he loved Mary Helen, Milton would not quit his band for her or for anybody."

On Sunday, March 1, the Brownies left Fort Worth by bus for New Orleans. Before leaving town, Milton called somebody he knew at Leonard Brothers' department store downtown. Although they were closed, they opened up just for the Brownies and Milton bought boots and a cowboy hat for each member of the band.[23] At their first stop, Milton wrote to Mary Helen's father at the winter headquarters of the Hames Carnival in Waco:

March 2nd 1936

W. H. Hames
Raleigh Hotel
Waco Texas

Dear Mr. Hames;

Referring to our conversation of Sat. 29th.

I called Mary Helen just before I left town yesterday and her Mother told me that she was out of town and would not be back until late in the afternoon, and I couldnt get much information out of Mrs. Hames.

I told Mrs. Hames to tell Mary Helen that I called and told her to tell her just what You told me to, however I dont know wheather she will or not and she dident like the idea of my having talked to you, of course I expected that.

I am expecting to be back in Fort Worth by friday and I will contact you then.

Trusting everything will come out for the best I remain,

MILTON BROWN

That day, the divorce was granted. It is unlikely that Milton knew that the divorce had been finalized before he returned to Fort Worth. In any case, an important recording session lay ahead, and he proceeded to New Orleans as scheduled.[24]

When the Brownies arrived in New Orleans, Milton sent a telegram to his mother:

New Orleans, LA.
Mar. 3rd, 1936

ANNIE BROWN
3419 Darcy St.
Fort Worth Texas

Dear Mother

Arrived OK and we are all feeling fine.

We are going to start recording this morning. Tell Dad and Roy Lee hello and dont worry about us.

We made the trip fine and expect to be in some time friday.

Love to all

MILTON

The Decca sessions in New Orleans produced Dave Kapp's first field recordings for the new label. Previously, the Brownies, along with other hillbilly and race artists, had been traveling to either Chicago, New York, or Los Angeles to record, but Kapp recognized that something was lost in removing the musicians from their natural milieu and decided to take an assistant and some portable recording gear, and make trips twice a year to the South to record.

DAVE KAPP: "We had no studios. So, the first trip and the subsequent trips were basically the same. We had no money. Jack [Dave's brother, Decca president Jack Kapp] knew Seymour Weiss at the Roosevelt Hotel in New Orleans. So Seymour Weiss gave us two rooms. The rooms were sample rooms, and they were at the end of a hall.[25] [Draws a diagram.] Here is the corridor. Here are your rooms. This was our recording room, the monitor room, and this was the studio. We would take drapes, monk's cloth. A guy would go in and hang the stuff up.[26]

"In those days we recorded with waxes, which were an inch and a half thick. You have to understand what a recording trip meant in those days when contrasted with today, where you can take a tape machine and an amplifier which is so [indicating with his hands] big. Our equipment amounted to about twenty trunks with all the amplifiers and speakers. There were special trunks made for these things, and because you could never depend on the current, we had a hand-wound recording machine."

CLIFF BRUNER: "We'd be in one room, just a hotel room. There were three lights up there: green, yellow, and red. The red one meant to be real quiet. Yellow meant to get ready. When they hit that green light, that meant 'start playin'.' And the recording people were in the next room. They had these old cords laid around from our room to theirs. We had one microphone. One big ol' microphone right in the middle of the room. All the musicians gathered around this one microphone, the piano, fiddles, the bass, everything."

DAVE KAPP: "Well, I could never see the people in the recording room when we recorded, because I had to be in here listening. You could never tell them anything. They were in a room which might have been twelve feet square. We set them up, and they would record; and I would run across the hall for the next one, and so on and so forth."

CLIFF BRUNER: "It was quite comical. They'd bring all their equipment out from New York. They had it packed in some big trunks made out of some kind of tough leather and they'd ship them down in a baggage car. When they got there, they'd have one hotel room stacked full of these big trunks. These trunks were all filled with waxes, which were about two feet across. And they were yellow, it looked like it was beeswax. They had some type of needle in there that they recorded with. If you made a mistake or the technician made a mistake, he'd look down a microscope at those lines, went through all that mess to see if the grooves were all right. When it wasn't, they'd have to take this wax off, throw it over in another trunk labeled 'discard,' and send it all the way to New York to get it shaved off where they could use it again. And they kept on using those things until they got so thin . . . [laughs]!

"Before we started recording, they'd all get in there and pick around and we'd play a tune and they'd say, 'Get a little closer, you're not comin' through good.'"

FRED "PAPA" CALHOUN: "The recordings came out real well. We never took anything over. We did it just like we were playing a dance. Mistakes and all."

CLIFF BRUNER: "'Long about the end of the first day, we were running out of numbers to record. Milton asked me if I knew anything we could do and I said, 'Do you all know "I've Got the Blues for Mammy"?' He said, 'No, sing it for me.' So I went through it once. Then he asked me to write the words down on a sheet of paper. We put it on record immediately. First take. Everything was perfect. I never worked with a more professional bunch of musicians."

DAVE KAPP: "We brought people in from as far as six hundred miles away, all converging on this hotel. We brought the Cajuns in from the bayou country of Louisiana. In fifteen days of recording we made 350 selections.[27] And we knocked them out! Speaking of knocking them out, Milton Brown recorded forty-nine sides in two and a half days. You get into a place like Dallas. What are you going to do? So you start recording in the morning; and you have lunch; and you record—because the whole idea was to get the things finished and get back. You couldn't try to arrange a schedule like they do in a studio here, where you do one date a day. We used to do five dates a day.

"There was a demand for those records, a demand which, of course, was relative. I will never forget the first time that the records started to break. I sent Jack a note very exultingly, and I said, 'I just got the figures, and we shipped 50,000 hillbilly records this month.'

Of course, you would have to know Jack. Jack, on my note, said, 'Tell me about it when it gets to a hundred.'"

Milton Brown and his Musical Brownies spent parts of three days recording for Decca. On March 3, they recorded sixteen sides; on March 4, twenty-two; and on March 5, they finished with a flourish, producing eleven more, concluding with a selection recommended by Dave Kapp, "The Old Grey Mare."

The records at the New Orleans session were looser than the ones cut in Chicago in 1935. There was more inventiveness on the part of Brower and Dunn, but there were also forgotten lyrics and a few mistimed cues. With the addition of Bruner, Cecil Brower played harmony and provided trick fills and nuances to some of the songs while Bruner played lead and hot choruses. Cecil also used his tremolo mute device on six tunes, including the Southern Melody Boys' old theme song, "La Golondrina." Milton sang all the songs, with Derwood and Ocie Stockard providing second and third harmonies. Derwood sang lead on the rousing "Stay on the Right Side Sister" and "Song of the Wanderer," and Cecil and Derwood sang the Mexican favorite "Cielito Lindo [Beautiful Heaven]." Fred Calhoun's piano was sharper and clearer than on the Chicago sessions, and for the first time his solos were introduced by Milton's effusive "Papa CAL-houn!" Wanna Coffman can be heard accentuating Calhoun's take-offs with his slapping bass. Upon hearing Bob Dunn's steel guitar solos, Cliff Bruner shook his head in wonder.

CLIFF BRUNER: "I'll tell you one thing: it's never been captured what Bob Dunn could really do. See, Bob didn't like to record. Oh, he hated to record. I don't know why. In those days, we did a lot of fast stuff, but it's never been captured what he could actually do. He just kind of froze up in front of that microphone."

Exhausted from the just-completed session, the Brownies decided to sightsee around New Orleans. Frankie Masters and his orchestra, a popular "sweet band," was the featured entertainment at the Roosevelt Hotel during the Brownies' stay, but the boys wanted to hear some jazz, so they ventured out into the French Quarter.

WANNA COFFMAN: "Cliff Bruner had been down there, so he knew where to go. So Cliff took us to a place that was open all night. We sat down there at the counter and ordered us a drink. A guy was sitting next to us, and he had a big ol' bowl of oysters. Then he had another big ol' chili bowl sittin' there next to it that had what looked like ketchup in it. I don't know what he was using to pry the oysters open, but he took them out of that shell and swallowed 'em without ever chewing. Boy, that just tore us up [laughs]! Oh, man, I had to get outta there, I couldn't stand it.

"Then we decided to ride one of those big pleasure boats up the Mississippi. One of them great big ol' rear paddlewheels. There was a colored band playing so, naturally, that's where me, Fred, Cecil, and Milton gravitated to. Back then, if there was any music going on, that's where you'd find me.

"Anyway, there had been warnings that there was a storm a-comin' in and they were a little late about leavin' the dock. Finally, Derwood and Cliff said, 'Aww, this thing ain't gonna leave, let's get off and go on back to town.' Well Derwood opened that gate and we had to grab him before he fell into the Mississippi, because the boat had left without us knowing it [laughs]! A wind then kicked up and we had to come back anyway."

The Brownies returned to Fort Worth late Friday, March 6. The next night, they continued their usual touring schedule, playing their regular Saturday night dance at Crystal Springs. On March 10, Milton resumed his letter writing, arranging his upcoming four-day tour of Oklahoma. He also wrote to an Irene Stowe in Frederick, Oklahoma.

> Dear Irene;
>
> I received your letter of the 27th and It was indeed a suprise and a pleasant one.
>
> We are playing in Electra Monday the 16th, and I wish you would be sure and be there because I really want to see you.
>
> I am going to tell you something that I dont think you know so here goes,—I am single Man again now already Divorced and every thing, so be sure and be in Electra next monday night
>
> Yours Truly
>
> MILTON BROWN

Although he was still in love with Mary Helen, Milton knew that their marriage was over, and had begun dating again.

On March 15, he wrote to Dave Kapp, who was still in New Orleans recording, tersely admonishing him for not delivering the Brownies' royalties for the last half of 1935. His dance dates were now booked until the end of April, and Milton had to turn down several prospective clients because of the distance the Brownies would have to travel. Thanks to their radio program on WBAP, the offers were now coming from farther and farther away, and the Brownies, after their long trip to Louisiana, desperately needed some time off. Milton's letters got briefer and increasingly vague. The following letter, dated March 17, had no heading and was not typed on Brownie stationery, unusual for the normally meticulous Milton.

Dear Bo;

I have your letter of the 16th.

It seems that I have so many dates ahead that I will not be able to reach you in the near future, but I will figure out something as soon as possible.

Trusting you can understand my position, I remain,

Yours Truly,

MILTON BROWN

The Oklahoma itinerary was scheduled as follows: the Brownies would play Crystal Springs on Saturday, April 4. They would depart the next morning for Oklahoma, playing Colgate on Monday, April 6. Following that would be dances on successive nights: April 7 in Henryetta, April 8 in Muskogee, and April 9 in Fort Smith, Arkansas. According to the surviving Brownies, the band never made the tour. No reason for the cancellation is evident.

On Saturday, April 11, the Brownies played their regular dance at Crystal Springs. It would be Milton's last. The following day was Easter Sunday, and he looked forward to a much-needed night off.

ELEVEN

Goodby Ma, Goodby Pa

(April 1936)

They called it "Thunder Road."

Through the years, Texas Highway 199 symbolized the rough-and-tumble frontier that helped earn Fort Worth the reputation of "the most Texan of Texas cities." Constructed in the 1920s, Highway 199 became a major artery between Fort Worth and routes to Wichita Falls, Amarillo, and points north. For sixty-five miles, with one end in Fort Worth and the other in the town of Jacksboro, the highway extended in a barren, high-speed strip of asphalt, dotted with run-down motels, sleazy bars, and greasy spoon cafés. To Fort Worthians, it was known as the Jacksboro Highway, a four-lane divided road that served as a fast, uncluttered route away from or toward town. Rarely a day went by when Milton Brown and the Musical Brownies would not come rattling up the highway in the Brownie Limited after making a quick getaway from their radio program on their way to a dance that night. The next day, they would roar back in the other direction, Peach McAdams at the wheel. At night, a single light illuminated the bus's interior, bright enough for insomniac Fred Calhoun to read a magazine.

WANNA COFFMAN: "Every trip we'd go on, Fred would find him a *Reader's Digest,* and he'd read that all the way over and all the way back. He never would go to sleep at night."

CLIFF BRUNER: "Mac was a real wild driver. He only knew how to drive one speed: wide open [laughs]!"

In later years, after World War II, the Jacksboro Highway became the venue for knifings, gunfights, holdups, prostitution, and assorted drunken brawls in its smoky taverns.[1] But in 1936 there were few harbingers of this future character. The Brownies were all familiar with the road. They traveled it confidently and regularly in their individual automobiles as well as on their bus.

The weather on Easter Sunday in Fort Worth was fair and hot. By mid-afternoon the temperature at Municipal Airport reached 95 degrees. The evening would be pleasant, dipping to a low of 62 shortly before dawn: a balmy spring evening in Texas during the Depression. Preparations for Fort Worth's role in the Texas centennial celebration were being announced in local papers daily. The famous entrepreneur and showman Billy Rose had been hired as managing director for the city's "Frontier Days" extravaganza, a job that involved being in charge of amusements, publicity, and concessions, and that paid him $1,000 a day for one hundred days. The celebration was to center around a specially constructed full-size replica of a typical frontier main street, complete from Judge Roy Bean's shanty office to a nineteenth-century graveyard. Contests were already being organized, and construction of museums, leather shops, a tonsorial parlor, and an elaborate set for a Wild West show was underway, in anticipation of a festive opening on July 1. The operation would consume 22.6 acres at the corner of West Lancaster Street and University Drive and contain eight major structures, the world's largest open-air café-theater, Casa Mañana, with seating for 3,800 (subsequently increased), and a 130-foot circular stage floating on water. In a full-page ad in *Billboard, New York Post* columnist John Mason Brown was quoted as saying, "Billy Rose has wrapped the voluminous cloak of P. T. Barnum around his shoulders."[2] Even noted burlesque artist Sally Rand was scheduled to bring her "Nude Ranch" (originally called the "Dude Ranch") to Fort Worth, in which she and her cadre of similarly well-endowed "hired hands" would pitch horseshoes, twirl ropes, and engage in other western-oriented activities in the altogether.[3]

On April 11, "The King of Jazz," Paul Whiteman, was signed to appear in the Frontier Follies with his orchestra. Over in Dallas, Cab Calloway and Duke Ellington were negotiating to perform at the centennial band shell in Fair Park. All announcements on WBAP concluded with the phrase "Fort Worth: The Frontier Days City." It was an exciting time for all Texans, and the thirty-two-year-old Milton Brown was looking forward to negotiating with Billy Rose to have the Brownies entertain at the Frontier Dance Hall, revamped to become the Pioneer Palace.

The excitement had been building throughout the spring as auditions were held, signings were announced, and construction began on the massive five-million-dollar project. That week, *Billboard* magazine raved about the plans:

> Frontier Days, the Rose production, which is to be Fort Worth's part of Texas' Centennial celebration, has surely got this thriving city all agog. Talk to a citizen of Fort Worth five minutes and four minutes of the conversation is about Frontier Days. Drunken sailors never spent money as Fort Worth is spending it to make Frontier Days the greatest event of its kind.
>
> 'Tis rumored that Rose is being paid $100,000 salary to stage the production. . . . Thirty years ago a cowtown, today a metropolitan city. If Billy could only pick up this whole thing and transport it to New York for the proposed World's Fair, what a sensation! Fort Worth Chamber of Commerce is using an entire floor in a large building. Thirty young women and a battery of telephones to take care of Frontier Days' business. It looks to me as tho Frontier Days is going to be a great show. To my mind, the only thing that will stop it is money giving out, but from where I sit the Bank of England is nearer broke than these Fort Worth enthusiasts."[4]

Sunday, April 12, was the Brownies' day off. At Crystal Springs, Papa Sam Cunningham's Crystal Springs Ramblers were to play a dance that night. Although the Brownies were on their own when they weren't performing, they generally saw one another in town on their day off.

ROY LEE BROWN: "Milton left home sometime in the afternoon. That night he showed up at Crystal Springs by himself."

WANNA COFFMAN: "Derwood and I went to a show first and then went out to Crystal Springs after it was over. This must have been around 10:30. On our way out there we stopped and picked up a half-pint. When we got there, Milton was already there. Derwood asked him out to the storeroom there behind the bandstand and offered him a drink. But Milton said, no, he wasn't drinking that night. He said that he had eaten something that day that made him sick and didn't want a drink."[5]

MAEBELLE FOWLER: "We were out at Crystal Springs that night. Milton was really upset, and I stood and talked to him for a long time. Harry and I and another couple was out there. Milton and his wife had just gotten divorced; they had made a bad go of it. And Milton said, 'I don't know, Sis, everything's a mess.' So I said, 'Milton, why don't you come go with Harry and me and Jo and Walter Lewis. We're gonna go eat somewhere.' He said, 'Oh no, thank you, I don't feel like eating. I'm gonna go someplace else.' He told me where, but I forgot. The dance ended at 11:30 or 12:00 and he had left by then."

ROY LEE BROWN: "From there, Milton went to the Oasis Nightclub, which was located off of White Settlement Road where Crestwood Addition is now, right before you go down what they call Dynamite Hill heading toward Crystal Springs. After a while, Fred Calhoun and his date Idell arrived with Idell's friend Katy."[6]

Sixteen-year-old Katherine Prehoditch was born on July 6, 1919, and attended the Russian Polish Baptist Church on Clinton Avenue in Fort Worth. According to her brother Paul, the Prehoditch family came to America from Russia in 1913 or 1914. They were a large family, consisting of Katy, her parents, two sisters, and three brothers. They were poor, uneducated, but very religious. Katy's father had been a laborer in a packing company, but had been laid off because of the Depression. Katy's parents, Mr. and Mrs. Dennis Prehoditch, were extremely proud of their pretty, dark-haired daughter, who had graduated from North Side High School in February. Katy's ambition, like that of many other young girls in America, was to become a singer. Paul Prehoditch recalled that his sister once had won an amateur contest as a vocalist. She was a big fan of Milton Brown and his Musical Brownies and frequently joined the small studio audience that witnessed Brownies' broadcasts at the WBAP studios in the Blackstone Hotel.

Like Ellen O'Malley (later Mrs. Roy Lee Brown), Katy Prehoditch was forbidden by her parents to go out to Crystal Springs, but she slipped out with two friends, Lillie and Idell Rotosky, who knew Katy from their church. That night, Katy, Idell, and Lillie caught the bus on Twenty-fifth Street on the North Side and headed out to Crystal Springs for the dance that night.

In the flowery, dramatic prose typical of the *Fort Worth Press* at that time, Katy was described as having "made her Easter dress with her own hands, of material given her by a neighbor at the girl's graduation from North Side High School. The frock was red, duller than crimson. There were white collar and cuffs and large white buttons up the back. Katherine finished the dress Saturday. She put it on for neighbors to see. With money saved from work as a practical nurse she bought white shoes, gloves and a white purse. Katherine had further cause to rejoice yesterday. Her father, Dennis Prehoditch, had learned he was to get a job, his first in two years."[7]

ROY LEE BROWN: "Idell met Fred at Crystal Springs, but since Katy didn't have a date, she went up to the Oasis with them. The Oasis was a place where many big band musicians went after they finished playing their gigs in Fort Worth. Jack Teagarden went there when he was in town. I have heard the musicians talk about this, especially Bob Dunn, who was a big Teagarden fan.[8]

"At the Oasis club, Fred, Idell, and Katy met Milton. Fred told Milton that his sister Jean's sorority was giving a dance down at the corner of University Drive and the Jacksboro Highway at a place called the Ringside Club. Big nightclub. He suggested they all go out there first and then he asked Milton if he could take Katy home. Milton said okay. So Milton took Katy in his car, Fred took Idell in his, and they drove on out to the Ringside. When they got there, it was so crowded that they decided to go up to the old Brownie Tavern and see if there was anything going on out there. When they got up there, the Brownie Tavern was closed. So they turned around and started coming back toward town. Fred and Idell were driving ahead of Milton and Katy."

It was now early Monday morning, April 13, 1936, just after midnight. Riding down the unlit Jacksboro Highway toward Fort Worth, Fred and Idell passed the Rockwood Motel. In front of the motel, sitting in his car parked on the right shoulder was twenty-one-year-old Weldon Massey.

WELDON MASSEY: "I was a night manager at the Rockwood Tourist Court. It was called the Rockwood Motel then. It's still in operation today. During the Depression, I guess any type of job you had was a profession. My uncle owned the motel. I had gone to work at seven o'clock Sunday night and things were quiet around our business so I went out to my car to listen to the radio.

"It was well after midnight. I was in the parking lot there by the office of the motel and I could see straight up the highway. If the road had gone for three miles, I could have seen that far, but it curves to the right about a half-mile to three-quarters of a mile up the road. Between this curve and the Rockwood Court there's a straight stretch of highway. At that time, there was nothing to impede my line of vision. Now, if the same thing happened, why, there's so many signs and businesses, you couldn't see that far.

"My car was pointing up the highway, on the south side of the road. I happened to be looking in the direction of this curve about where the Cowtown drive-in theater is now, and I saw the headlights

En route to New Orleans in March 1936, Milton Brown sports his Texas centennial cowboy hat, looking uncomfortable and forlorn. This is the last known photograph taken of Milton Brown. Courtesy Roy Lee and Ellen Brown.

A photograph printed in the *Fort Worth Press* of the wrecked 1936 Pontiac "Silver Streak" eight-cylinder touring sedan which Milton Brown was driving when he had his accident in the early morning hours of April 13, 1936. Sixteen-year-old Katherine Prehoditch, who was sitting in the passenger seat, was killed instantly by the impact. Milton's injuries were mostly likely incurred when he was ejected from the vehicle. Courtesy Roy Lee and Ellen Brown.

Milton Brown died on Saturday morning, April 18, 1936, too late to cancel the printing of this broadside advertising the Brownies' forthcoming engagement in Denison, Texas, the following Tuesday. The Brownies honored their leader's dying wish by playing the date without him. Courtesy Roy Lee and Ellen Brown.

Attention Everybody

Get Ready 'Cause Here We Come! Don't Hesitate!

Milton Brown
and His Musical Brownies

Will again stage a big night

-AT-

OAK VIEW INN
DENISON, TEXAS

Tuesday, April 21

Come on everyone let's Dance

Bids 75c, Tax Included   All Ladies 10c

Time 9 till 1

The Brown family plot, located in Smith Springs Cemetery, outside of Stephenville, Texas. The large headstone to the right of the tree marks the final resting place of Milton Brown. Courtesy Cary Ginell.

of a car coming down the road toward the city of Fort Worth. It was more or less traveling southeast. Well, the headlights started quivering, like it had left the highway and hit the rough shoulder. Then it rose a little and seemed like it flipped over to the right. In my mind, it looked like it hit a guy wire, took 'em off the ground, and then flipped over.

"I started my car and drove to the all-night service station next door and picked up Clifford Proffit, who was operating the station at that time. I told him, 'There's been an accident, come and go with me.' So he got in my car and we took off.

"It couldn't have been more than three or four minutes after the accident that Clifford and I got there. There might have been one or two cars that stopped before we got there, but there were very few people there when we arrived.

"When we got there we saw a wrecked automobile. I don't recall where the victims were, whether they were thrown from the car, were inside, or what. I don't remember that. But we did see a man and a woman and they were both unconscious. I had taken first aid courses before that time and they tell you not to move people who have internal injuries, so we didn't move them. It seemed like someone said, 'This girl is dead, but we'd better get him to the hospital.' I don't know who it was that said that.

"After about fifteen or twenty minutes a taxicab came by, and the driver put the man in it and took him to the hospital.[9]

"I knew who Fred Calhoun was. I didn't know him personally, but I had a friend that dated his sister. While we were waiting for the taxicab, Fred and another woman arrived from the same direction. I didn't talk to him or anything, I just saw him there and recognized him. It was obvious that Milton was still alive, but they were not sure whether the girl was or not, so they took him away first. Later on, an ambulance came and took her away."

Nobody knows where Fred, Idell, Milton, and Katy were going after they stopped at the Brownie Tavern. Milton said in the hospital that he was taking Katy home when the accident occurred. Fred and Idell were far enough ahead of the other car that they had no idea what had happened. They arrived in town and waited for Milton and Katy to show up. After fifteen minutes, they drove back up the Jacksboro Highway looking for them and came upon the wreck about three miles from town. Since the Jacksboro Highway (identified in local newspapers as the Northwest Highway) was divided, they had to go past the scene of the accident, find a turnaround, and come back in the other direction. This explains why Weldon Massey saw Fred's car arriving from the northwest.

Milton Brown was taken in the taxicab to the Methodist Hospital near downtown Fort Worth and put in a private room on the third floor. He was conscious and in pain. The initial diagnosis indicated probable internal injuries, a back injury, several broken ribs, face and knee lacerations, and a right shoulder blade fracture. Katy Prehoditch was pronounced dead upon arrival at Methodist Hospital at 3:45 A.M., the cause of death a massive skull fracture. She had also sustained a fractured right wrist and a fractured jaw. Monday's edition of the *Fort Worth Press* featured the accident prominently on its front page, including Katy's high school graduation picture. Milton Brown, physicians reported, would survive.

ROY LEE BROWN: "Mama had the flu that night and Dad was sleeping in the back room. I was in the bedroom with Mama when the phone rang. I remember it very well. She answered it, and it was this cab driver, and he said that Milton had been in an accident. He said he had taken Milton to Methodist Hospital, which is Harris now. Then he said, 'Do you want me to come and get you?' Mama said yes and the cab came and picked up me, Mama, and Dad, and we went down to the hospital. When we went into the room where Milton was, he was conscious. He was in pain, but not in what we could see was extreme pain. I don't remember how long we stayed there that morning, but when we left, Dad, Derwood, and I went out to the scene of the wreck.

"When we got there, I saw skid marks on the shoulder of the road where the car had been. Then Dad found Milton's watch lying about fifteen feet or so from this utility pole that the car had turned over into. Milton's watch was still running. Dad also talked to the manager of the Avalon Motel, which was right across the highway from where Milton had the wreck. The manager said he heard the crash and was the first one at the scene. He told Dad that the headlights of the car were shining through the front window of the motel.

"Then we went over to where they'd towed the car, over on the North Side at a garage at Clinton and Twenty-first St. The wrecker still had the back end of the car lifted up. Evidently, the impact threw Milton and Katy from the car. The man that ran the motel across the road said that when he got over there, they were both lying beside the car. The car evidently fell over against the pole and then fell back. The pole crushed the top of the car on Katy's side so that's probably how she died."

The firsthand testimony from Weldon Massey and the secondhand testimony from Roy Lee Brown can help us reconstruct what occurred on the Jacksboro Highway that morning. Milton's automobile, a 1936 green Pontiac eight-cylinder four-door sedan, was traveling down the highway at an unspecified speed. The Jacksboro Highway was a good road with a speed limit comparable to that of a freeway today, probably 50 MPH. The *Fort Worth Press* reported that the speedometer of the auto had locked at ninety-six miles an hour. However, investigators said the impact of the crash may have caused the indicator to jump to that position. Milton Brown was a careful driver and was not likely to have been going that fast. The Pontiac Eight was a large, heavy automobile, which retailed for $730, advertised as the lowest priced eight-cylinder car built by General Motors. Renowned for its durability, it was not unusual for this model to surpass 200,000 miles, averaging twenty-two miles per gallon of gas.[10]

The car was traveling down a slight incline in the road when it approached the curve. Beyond the bend in the curve and past the shoulder was a utility pole, anchored to the ground by a guy wire. At some point, the Pontiac left the road and hit the shoulder. Milton apparently slammed on the brakes as the auto veered to the left (either by the action of the brakes or by Milton's turning the wheel to the left). The car then hit the guy wire on the passenger's side, between the front and rear wheels, the right rear tire punctured. After hitting the guy wire, the car rose up, following the wire to the pole, into which it crashed. The pole splintered and the car fell back to the ground, ejecting its two occupants and landing in an upright position.[11] Although speculation about the accident has endured for a half-century, Fred Calhoun and Wanna Coffman were certain about what caused it.

FRED "PAPA" CALHOUN: "I know what happened to him as well as anything in the world. He went to sleep. A lot of times, we'd take our cars on dances. We'd get tired of the bus and we'd drive our own cars up to Denton or Gainesville or somewhere. He'd always want me to drive him in his car, because he couldn't stay awake. He'd start out driving, and we wouldn't get two or three miles. We'd be talking about the band or something, and he'd say, 'Fred, I'm getting so sleepy, you'll have to drive.' Well, I'd get over and drive and ask him a question. He wouldn't answer, so I'd look over at him, and he'd be sound asleep. I know that's what happened to him. I don't think he was drinking at all, 'cause he was sick to his stomach that night. I just think he went to sleep. Milton wasn't a very good driver anyhow.

One time he went off the hill going home from the radio program. In the middle of the day. He'd be driving and he'd doze off, and as soon as he hit the shoulder, it'd wake him up. He just couldn't drive without going to sleep."

WANNA COFFMAN: "One time we were going to Wichita Falls and Milton was driving. Just before we got to Bowie, why if I hadn't been sitting there beside him, he'd have took the ditch. He'd go to sleep in a second, so I figured that's what happened. Besides, he never knew what caused it, he never told us in the hospital. But I think he went to sleep. I always will."

Calhoun and Coffman's descriptions indicate that Milton may have suffered from a disorder called narcolepsy.[12] Ocie Stockard, Cliff Bruner, and Roy Lee Brown all corroborated Milton's tendency to fall asleep without warning. If Milton had indeed fallen asleep that night, it is entirely possible that this could have contributed to the accident. Up the road from the curve where the pole was situated, the Jacksboro Highway is straight. If he had fallen asleep, Milton could have been awakened by the car leaving the road and hitting the rough shoulder (as Weldon Massey indicated when he noticed the car's headlights "quivering"), slamming on the brakes as the car skidded sideways up the guy wire and into the utility pole. The rear tire blowout has been blamed as the cause of the accident. However, it is also quite possible that the burst tire was not related to the car's inability to maneuver, but merely resulted from the impact with the metal spike that anchored the guy wire to the ground.[13]

Milton Brown rested easily through most of Monday. By evening, he was reported as "improved," although still in serious condition. Of Milton's injuries, the six broken ribs on his right side were the most serious. One had punctured his right lung, which became infected when efforts were not made to treat it. This quickly developed into pneumonia, and on Tuesday, the doctors placed Milton, who was having difficulty breathing, in an oxygen tent.[14]

ROY LEE BROWN: "We first thought he was going to be all right until this pneumonia developed. The first inkling we had that he might die was when the doctor ordered an oxygen tent for him. Back then, when someone got pneumonia, they rarely ever got over it. When they got that oxygen tent out I heard Dad say, 'Ohh, I sure hate to see that thing.' That was always one of the last things they do and it was never successful.

"Milton insisted on bringing in the family doctor, Dr. Dan Matheson. Matheson wasn't anything but an old family doctor and he wasn't up on what was current in medicine. At least I don't think he was. He suggested they bring in a bone specialist. So the specialist X-rayed Milton and found that all of his ribs were broken on one side except one. One rib had punctured his lung, but they didn't do anything about it. Why, I don't know. This doctor charged Dad $50 to come in and read the X-rays. And Dad told Dr. Matheson: 'Look, I'll pay you what you want and you can give that other doctor something, but I'm not paying him a red cent 'cause he didn't do anything.'

"I stayed up there with Milton one day during the week he was in the hospital. He was conscious, and I just sat there and waited on him. I don't think we talked much at all. When I went up there, Mama went home and rested. She was just worn out. She got there the first night with me and Dad after Milton got hurt. Then I went on back home and she stayed. She only went home to clean up and change clothes. I had to help Milton use the bathroom because he couldn't move his right arm; his shoulder had been broken."

WELDON MASSEY: "On Monday, I went to the hospital with an attack of appendicitis. I was operated on that evening. I guess a couple of days after my operation I was informed that Milton was on the same floor at the Methodist Hospital that I was on. I don't know how the word got to his father, but he and one of his brothers came in to talk to me. Evidently someone had told them that I was at the scene, and they wanted to see if I knew anything about what happened. But really, when you're one-half to three-quarters of a mile away and you see lights flipping over, you don't see much else."

On Tuesday morning, April 14, funeral services were held for sixteen-year-old Katherine Prehoditch at Shannon's Funeral Home on North Main Street. Barty Brown attended, along with Derwood and Roy Lee. Katy was buried in Greenwood Cemetery.[15]

FRED "PAPA" CALHOUN: "Katy was a real nice girl. She was just out at the dance and Milton got acquainted with her out there. My wife knew her real well from their church. She wasn't any one-nighter or nothing like that. She was a real nice person. Milton told me later before he died, 'That sure was a nice little girl.' He just hated to hear that she died."

On Wednesday, the *Fort Worth Press* reported: "Physicians still had hopes today that Milton Brown, fiddle band leader, would survive pneumonia, which developed yesterday complicating critical injuries received in an auto crash early Monday morning. Methodist Hospital switchboard operators say they are literally besieged with telephone calls asking about the popular musician. He has not been told that his 16-year-old companion, Katherine Prehoditch, was killed when his car turned over on the Jacksboro Highway."[16]

By Thursday, Milton again showed signs of improving,[17] although by now it was clear even to him that his injuries would prove to be fatal. During the long vigil, he was paid regular visits by his family, friends, and the Brownies.

WANNA COFFMAN: "He knew he was going to die because he told me and Derwood in the hospital, 'You boys hang on.' I never will forget that."

CLIFF BRUNER: "Milton was always right on top of all the latest tunes, you know. And right before he had his wreck we had learned the song 'I'm Putting All My Eggs in One Basket.' He sat up in bed and we sang it together in the hospital."[18]

FRED "PAPA" CALHOUN: "We were up there nearly every day before we went out on the road. We kept playing. Milton told us to keep all of our dance dates so we did. Then Derwood let the cat out of the bag about the girl being dead. Milton didn't know it. We weren't going to tell him until he got well. Somebody asked Derwood where he'd been and he said, 'I've been down to the funeral home.' Milton said, 'What funeral home?' and 'Why?' And he had to tell him about Katy [long pause]. It was a sad thing."

ROY LEE BROWN: "I think he knew that Katy had been killed, because he said, 'I'll never drive again.' Then he told Derwood, 'You carry on with the band just like I was there. You can do it.' Then he called Mary Helen in and talked to her and told her that he'd always love her. He wanted her to take Buster Lee to see Mama after he died. He told her she didn't have to worry because he had made his peace with God."

Attendants at Methodist Hospital reported that Milton Brown had a "fair day" on Friday, April 17, although his condition remained practically unchanged.[19] That afternoon, however, he began sinking gradually, feverishly calling the names of towns where the Brownies had played.

When Dr. Matheson came into Milton's room Friday afternoon, Milton said, "How about a cigarette, doc?" Matheson jokingly replied, "Why, you'll burn my oxygen tent up, Milton. Later, perhaps."

In his delirium, he sang a few lines from an old hymn, "Goodby Ma, Goodby Pa," which his nurse, Neva Nell Stringer, heard him mumble early Saturday.[20] With his mother and father by his side, Milton began to slip away.

ROY LEE BROWN: "On Saturday morning, Mama called to tell me to come down to the hospital. Dad and Derwood were already there. She said, 'You'd better get over here somehow, get somebody to take you over here.' Then she said, 'Wait a minute.' Somebody then said something to her and she hung up. She didn't say goodbye or anything. I went across the street and got Jack Cone to take me to the hospital. When I got there, Mama was crying and I knew then that Milton was gone."

Milton Brown died at 9:10 A.M., Saturday, April 18, 1936, at the age of thirty-two. The cause of death was listed as "pneumonia, traumatic," incurred April 15 as a result of an auto accident on the Jacksboro Highway on April 13.

HARRY FOWLER: "Glenna heard it announced on the radio that Milton had passed away and she called us. I thought the world would end when I heard that Milton had died."

ROY LEE BROWN: "Some of the radio stations in town announced it. They had one minute's silence for Milton that day."

On the Texas Quality Network, Milton's last employer, W. Lee O'Daniel, gave a heartfelt eulogy (as only he could do). O'Daniel dedicated two songs to Milton: "That Silver-Haired Mother of Mine" and "Our Baby Boy," the tune Milton had written for his infant son, Buster. They were played by O'Daniel's band, the Hillbilly Boys, featuring vocalist Leon Huff. On that broadcast, O'Daniel said, "I can remember only one time that I saw tears in Milton's eyes. That was when he was singing for me and I asked him to dedicate a song to his mother."[21]

Milton Brown's last request was for his body to be laid to rest among the hills of his boyhood days. The funeral services were scheduled for Sunday, April 19, at 2 P.M. at the Lucas South Side Funeral Home in Fort Worth, with the Reverend Ike T. Sidebottom officiating.[22]

ROY LEE BROWN: "When Milton died, he didn't have any money. The marriage and divorce had taken it all. Mama and Dad had to bear the expense of Milton's funeral, plus the hospital and doctor bills. Bob Lucas of Lucas Funeral Homes charged $500 for Milton's funeral, and that was a lot of money back then. Milton was put in a steel vault which cost more.

"Milton had a $1,000 insurance policy with my mother as beneficiary. This money from the policy was used to bury Milton and pay his debts. My dad wasn't working at the time and they were unable to help Mary Helen and Buster.

"Milton also had a $1,500 insurance policy with Mary Helen as the beneficiary. But when the divorce became final, he made Buster the beneficiary and put it in a trust fund until Buster turned twenty-one. The policy was double indemnity, so Buster was left $3,000 plus interest for twenty-one years."

The Lucas Funeral Home had seats for about three hundred mourners. Early on Sunday those seats were filled, and before long a line stretched out the building and down the street. Local newspapers estimated the crowd at as many as thirty-five hundred people.[23]

FRED "PAPA" CALHOUN: "You never saw a funeral like that in your life. Over three thousand people went by the casket. The Brownies were pallbearers, and we sat there for two hours while everybody filed by to see Milton one last time. There were people lined up for four, five blocks, waiting to come in. When they stopped them, they almost had a riot out there. They wanted to come in and see him. Boy, they griped out there, but it was getting to late afternoon and they had to drive clear to Stephenville where he was going to be buried."

WANNA COFFMAN: "It was, I believe, the saddest funeral I ever saw. I was sick that day and I was taking pain pills, but I went anyway. And you couldn't find a place to park for ten blocks. They had people standing up in there, and on the outside, out in the street. Nobody could get in. When they took his body out and put him in the hearse, we all got in the family car and there was a row of cars . . . we never could find the end of it. All the way to Stephenville."

GLENNA MCBRIDE: "Roy and I drove Mary Helen to Milton's funeral. It was one of the biggest funerals I ever saw. That procession must have been a mile long. We had a Chevrolet, but Mary Helen didn't drive to the funeral, she was too upset. She had money, though. The Hameses were what we called rich people then. So we took her and brought her back. I don't even know why we took her to Milton's funeral. We knew her pretty well at that time. We all went over to her house after he died."

At the services, the Chuck Wagon Gang, then appearing on WBAP, sang "As the Life of a Flower," "God Shall Wipe All Tears Away," and "We Shall Meet (beyond the River)."[24]

The Musical Brownies—Fred Calhoun, Cecil Brower, Ocie Stockard, Wanna Coffman, Cliff Bruner, and Bob Dunn—were listed in the funeral program as pallbearers. Derwood Brown received a telegram of condolences from Bob Wills in Tulsa. Wills and a few members of his band attended the services in Fort Worth. Many of Milton's friends, business associates, and fans sent floral offerings. They included Kemble Brothers Furniture Company and its employees, Pearl Barton Cox (Milton's high school sweetheart), employees of the Bain Peanut Company, Decca Records in Dallas, Iris Harper, Hy Myer (Milton's clothier), the Bar-X Cowboys in Houston, the Crystal Springs Ramblers, the Light Crust Doughboys, Bob Wills and his Texas Playboys, KTAT announcer Marshall Pope, customers of Crystal Springs, the Hames family, and Dr. and Mrs. Dan Matheson.

Milton Brown was buried in the little country cemetery in Smith Springs next to his sister Era. An impressive tribute came from a woman who anonymously donated a three-foot-high, solid granite tombstone. Roy Lee Brown said that it cost $300.

ROY LEE BROWN: "The woman who was responsible for Milton's tombstone was named Margaret Nash. She designed and paid for it. She got acquainted with Mama and Dad after Milton passed away. She came to the house one day and told us that she would like to put a tombstone at Milton's grave. She asked if we had any objections, and Mama and Dad said no. They didn't have enough money to buy a tombstone anyway. So she bought the tombstone out on North Main Street and they delivered it to the cemetery. She told us that she had never dated Milton and that he never even knew who she was, but she was a great admirer of his and wanted to do this in his memory. It's a beautiful monument and it's still there today."

The tombstone bore a depiction of a microphone with the call letters WMB (for William Milton Brown) emblazoned on it, flanked by two radio transmitter towers. The name Brown was bordered by two large hearts in each upper corner of the marker, and his first two names, William Milton, were suspended between the towers. His birth and death dates (September 8, 1903, and April 18, 1936) were chiseled beside each tower.

Dave Stogner summed up the feelings of many of the musicians in the Southwest.

DAVE STOGNER: "I was in Gainesville when I heard about Milton's death on the radio. It hit me hard. It was as if I'd lost my last friend in the music business. All at once the person I had patterned my life after wasn't there any more. That made me more determined than ever to try to carry on his unique style of music. I didn't want to let it die too. I had lost the person who had inspired my music playing, but I hadn't lost his sounds. They were the sounds that would stick in my mind and give me the direction that my dream would follow."

Of all the obituaries that appeared in local newspapers, one of the most moving appeared in the *Sulphur Springs News-Telegram*'s story on the wreck and Milton's funeral. It put into words what his friends and fans were unable to express, the tremendous impact he had had on their lives: "Milton was a great lover of people, and furnished many hours of entertainment in their behalf. He was loved by all who knew him, and the tone of his silvernoted voice, of this great friend to all who really knew him, will be remembered by his many friends throughout time immemorial."[25]

As a final tribute, Milton's mother wrote her son a poem.

Since You Went Away
by Mrs. B. L. Brown

There is sadness in our household
Since you went away
We miss you more my darling son
Then words could ever say

There is sadness in our household
With joy you filled our home
But to heaven you have journeyed
To the angels in the dawn

There is sadness in our home son
Oh, how we miss your face
Our hearts can find no comfort
No one can take your place

There is sadness in our household
Every night and day
Our hearts are sad and breaking
Since you went away

Your body now lies sleeping
Beneath the silent clay
But soon we're going to join you
In the land of endless day

TWELVE

There'll Be Some Changes Made

(1936–37)

His songs have thrilled a nation
His death has shocked the same
In every eye there's tear drops
On every lip his name.

It seems my heart is breaking
As they place him far from sound
And the entire world will miss
The "golden voice" of Milton Brown.

—BY NELLY (MCDONNELL) CAVER[1]

The suddenness of Milton Brown's death left the Musical Brownies stunned. To them, Milton was more than just their singer and leader. As manager, treasurer, promoter, and booking agent, Milton executed the jobs of five or six men. In addition, the Brownies felt Milton's death even more keenly because he was their friend, counselor, and father figure.

The one who felt the impact of Milton's death most was Derwood Brown, who was now in charge of the Musical Brownies. Only twenty when his brother died, Derwood did not have the advantage of Milton's years of schooling, nor did he possess the sales experience and business savvy Milton developed when working for the Henry Lowe Cigar Company. Milton had labored for seven years after his graduation from high school before forming the Musical Brownies. Derwood, who started following Milton around when he was twelve, knew only the life of a musician and had never held any regular position. Milton made all decisions, arranged dance dates, and looked out for his musicians. After Milton's death, all of these responsibilities were thrust upon Derwood. As if running the Musical Brownies was not enough, Derwood also had a wife and child to provide for, in addition to his mother, father, and younger brother Roy

Lee. Barty Brown was ill most of the time and was unable to work, so Derwood now became the breadwinner.

ROY LEE BROWN: "Times were very hard for my family then. Dad wasn't able to work much, and I was still trying to finish school. We had a milk cow and Mama would sell milk and butter to help with the living. Later on, while I was still in school, I worked on an ice truck in the summertime delivering ice for $1.25 a day."

Barty and Annie Brown never recovered from their son's tragic death. They had lost a daughter eighteen years before, an event that was the deciding factor in their move to Fort Worth. However, Era was now just a distant memory. Milton had been the lifeblood of the Brown family, just as he was for the Brownies. Now the horrors of the Depression loomed like a black cloud as the Browns looked more and more to their second son for salvation. Valiantly and with a heavy heart, Derwood set about the task of satisfying his brother's deathbed wish, to carry on with the band just as if Milton himself were still there.

ROY LEE BROWN: "Derwood had to keep Milton's bookings during the week Milton was in the hospital. They missed one show, the Monday after the accident. WBAP wouldn't let the Brownies go on the air that day. On Saturday, the day Milton died, the Brownies were supposed to play Crystal Springs. They skipped that night and the Crystal Springs Ramblers took their place.[2]

"After Milton died, Derwood took control of the band and carried on as before. They had no problem getting dance dates. They were still in demand and they still played their radio show on WBAP. They were still a top band even after some key members left. Milton hadn't discussed his future plans with the rest of the band, and when Derwood took over he was in the dark as to what Milton had in mind. Derwood was young and inexperienced in the business end of the band and it made it very difficult for him. That is one reason Paul Calhoun was made business manager. Derwood also had Paul do the bookings. He had worked the door for the Brownies at Crystal Springs after the band came back from the Brownie Tavern. He also worked the door when they went out of town."

All of the deals Milton had been working on at the time of his death were now null and void. He had only recently negotiated with Republic Pictures for the Brownies to appear in Gene Autry's upcoming western, *Oh, Susanna!* After Milton's death, Republic hired the Light Crust Doughboys.

GENE AUTRY: "With *Oh, Susanna!* we began what was to become a policy for most of the movies I did at Republic: employing various country music groups, usually regional, with at least some radio fame. The Light Crust Doughboys were first, out of Fort Worth."[3]

Milton was also working on featuring the Brownies in a series of short subject films, similar to today's videos, with the Brownies performing several songs. The films were to be sandwiched between full-length features in theaters along with cartoons and newsreels.[4]

With Milton's death, the Brownies' proposed move to Houston and radio station KPRC was also canceled. According to Roy Lee Brown, negotiations with KPRC were still pending and Milton was anxious to make a change. He had an additional reason for moving to a new territory: the haunting pain of his divorce. Mary Helen had been so much a part of his life that nearly everything in Fort Worth reminded him of her. He also realized how attractive she was and did not want to remain where he would always know what she was doing and whom she was seeing.

Not long after Milton passed away, the Brownies were given the opportunity to satisfy one of his wishes: to entertain at Fort Worth's Frontier Follies celebration and get off the road.

FRED "PAPA" CALHOUN: "Billy Rose came down from New York and went to WBAP and told them that he wanted to hire the best fiddle band in the business to play the Pioneer Palace. So he was told, 'Well, the best one's right here in Fort Worth: Milton Brown and his Musical Brownies.' After Milton got killed, Rose came up to the program. The next day he wanted us to audition for him and some other people. Derwood and my brother Paul wanted to strike a deal and get us off the road a while. We was gonna kill ourselves if we kept it up much longer.

"Billy was impressed with the band and offered Derwood $30 a week per man to play six nights a week. Derwood turned him down. Then Rose's secretary called and offered $40 a week. Derwood still wasn't interested. A day or two later it was 50. That *still* wasn't anywhere near what we was making. Finally it got up to $75 a week a man. And when Derwood turned him down again Rose said, 'Well I don't think *any* fiddle band is making that much money.' Derwood said, 'This one is,' and told him to quit calling. I think if they had offered us $100 Derwood might have taken it."

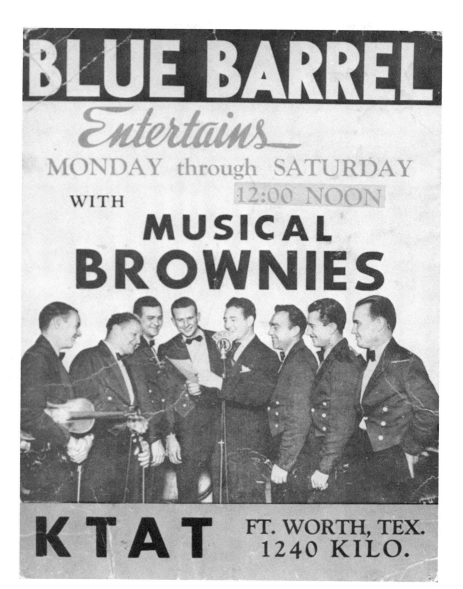

A placard advertising the Musical Brownies, under the direction of Derwood Brown. The group had returned to KTAT in February 1937. From left: Buck Buchanan (fiddle), Derwood Brown (guitar, vocals), Lefty Perkins (steel guitar), Wanna Coffman (bass), Mike Gallagher (announcer), Johnny Borowski (fiddle), Fred Calhoun (piano), Ocie Stockard (banjo). Courtesy Roy Lee and Ellen Brown.

Roy Lee Brown, sixteen, and Ellen O'Malley, seventeen, in their engagement picture. They were married on Christmas Day, 1937. Courtesy Roy Lee and Ellen Brown.

Derwood Brown's Musical Brownies, KTAT, Fort Worth, 1937. This was the unit that recorded for Decca in February 1937. From left: Lefty Perkins (steel guitar), Mike Gallagher (announcer), Derwood Brown (guitar, vocals), Wanna Coffman (bass), Buck Buchanan (fiddle), Johnny Borowski (fiddle), Fred Calhoun (piano), Ocie Stockard (banjo, vocals). Courtesy Roy Lee and Ellen Brown.

Even with the flood of money and influx of powerful, experienced, and eager entrepreneurs, there was not enough money in the budget to pay the Musical Brownies what they were already earning playing country dance halls. Billy Rose had underestimated the popularity of fiddle bands in the Southwest in 1936 and considered it a waste of time to haggle with these particular "hillbillies." His intention was to provide a colorful musical backdrop for his western-flavored exposition. The band he was looking to hire would perform in the Pioneer Palace, entertain patrons as they purchased their tickets at the front entrance, and generally serve as roving minstrels, wandering throughout the grounds, singing and playing for visitors.

After Derwood and Paul Calhoun's negotiations with Billy Rose broke down, another local fiddle band, Blackie Simmons and his Blue Jackets, was hired to entertain at the Frontier Days celebration in Fort Worth in place of the Brownies. Simmons was a fiddler in his forties who had just begun broadcasting a daily program at 6:45 A.M. on WBAP.[5] After Derwood rejected Rose's final offer of $75 per week for each band member, the Blue Jackets eagerly accepted Rose's first offer to them of $25 per week per man. Roscoe Pierce and banjoist Sam Graves were members of the Blue Jackets.

SAM GRAVES: "We were playing dances with Blackie Simmons before the centennial came along. Making a living as a musician was a tough go back then. The Blue Jackets had a great piano player named Knocky Parker then. He was a great showman and a fantastic musician.[6] We were hired to play at the Pioneer Palace between shows. Billy Rose interviewed us, listened to us play, and hired us. Milton's band auditioned the same time we did. They got the job first but Billy Rose didn't have enough money to pay them. They were making big money playing dances back then. So Rose hired us instead. I think we were supposed to get $35 a week but Blackie cut his wife in so that reduced our share to $25 [laughs]. That was still pretty good money for the Depression. In fact, it was DAMN good!

"Paul Whiteman played the centennial and he had a great banjoist named Mike Pingitore who I liked to listen to but he was a hunchback, was crippled, and wasn't too sociable. But Paul Whiteman was sociable. He was a friendly guy. He'd talk to you and carry on a conversation with you."

ROSCOE PIERCE: "In the afternoon we played out on the front porch of the town hall. For publicity, he came out there and stood up on a chair, and he had his baton with him, and he directed us. It made a pretty nice publicity picture."

SAM GRAVES: "We tried to get Sally Rand to play in our band, too, but we weren't successful. Sally had a side show there called the 'Nude Ranch,' and the barker would say to the crowd, 'Come on in and see what Sally's got [laughs]!' What she had in there was a bunch of girls [laughs]."

The ambitious progress of the Brownies during 1935 and 1936 ceased abruptly with Milton's death, and under Derwood's leadership the band resumed its local dance-date circuit. After only a few months, disillusioned and worn out, the Brownies began to disintegrate. Although there was no noticeable decrease in their popularity, it was clear that the magic was gone, and despite Derwood's efforts to keep the band together, key personnel began to leave.

Cliff Bruner was the first. The youngest member of the Brownies had learned a lot about running a musical organization from Milton, something he was unable to do when leading his ragtag groups in south Texas. But Cliff soon proved to be a born bandleader and left the Brownies to form the Texas Wanderers in Houston that summer.[7] To replace Bruner, Derwood brought back Johnny Borowski, who had replaced Cecil Brower during Cecil's brief stint with the Georgie Porgie Boys in Columbus, Ohio.

The next to defect were Brower and Bob Dunn. Although probably the Brownies' most accomplished musicians, both men needed the strong guidance Milton Brown had provided to keep them in line. Dunn and Brower began nomadic existences, playing and recording with many Texas and Oklahoma bands.

To replace Bob Dunn, Derwood hired a portly nineteen-year-old left-handed guitarist named Robert Wilson Perkins. Known as Lefty, for obvious reasons, Perkins was born on September 3, 1917, in the town of Clarksville, located in the extreme northeastern sector of Texas. He spent his early years learning guitar, until the Musical Brownies, in particular Bob Dunn, changed his direction.

WILSON "LEFTY" PERKINS: "I started playing when I was big enough to pick the guitar off the floor. I liked Jimmie Rodgers back then. Everybody liked Jimmie Rodgers. I also liked Vernon Dalhart, and Gid Tanner and his Skillet Lickers.

"I studied for a while there in Clarksville. A man come through town teaching so he taught me how to read music. I lived in Denison when I was a little ol' bitty kid and later moved on up to Oklahoma City. That's where I met Charlie Christian. He was on the same radio station I was on up there.[8] This was about 1934. The first band

I was with was called the Texans there in Oklahoma City. We had a hot sax player named Don Williams, and my brother Walter was also in that band playing bass. There was about three or four of us boys from Denison up there, just a little old stomp band. We'd heard of Milton Brown by that time, and when I heard Bob Dunn play on the radio, I decided to go down and see them in Fort Worth. Milton had a real unique style, kind of like a cross between Cab Calloway and Jimmie Rodgers.

"One time when I came down from Denison, I stopped in at the Brownie Tavern to see the Brownies. Well, Bob Dunn was there, and he was playing guitar with this damn Volu-Tone amplifier. I watched him a while and then we talked a little. Then he said, 'Get up here, kid, and play some for me, man!' I sat in for a while, and he went outside to get gassed or something. After that, every time I went out there he'd say, 'Come on, sit in for me!' When I first saw Bob, I was already playing steel guitar. But I was playing all that Hawaiian, Kanaka stuff. I loved Sol Hoopii doing that 'Farewell Blues.' But Bob Dunn changed all of that.

"I joined W. Lee O'Daniel in 1936 when he had his flour company. That was before he became governor.[9] We hung around in Fort Worth for two or three weeks, and then we went to Mexico to play on XEPN. When I came back, that's when I joined the Brownies. Fred Calhoun sent me a wire to come out when Bob Dunn went to Abilene."

Lefty Perkins was one of the best of Bob Dunn's disciples. Although nobody ever was able to duplicate Dunn's trombone-influenced style, Perkins was the most accomplished, playing on the high strings and using more chords in his take-offs than Dunn.

Cecil Brower's replacement was Robert "Buck" Buchanan, a talented violinist who, like Cecil, was a former student of Fort Worth teacher Wylbert Brown. The pairing of Buchanan and Borowski was a natural, and the two redefined the Brownies' sound, utilizing a tightly constructed twin fiddle lead. Unlike the rurally trained Bruner, who attacked take-offs like a wild mustang, Buchanan and Borowski played more as a team, each capable of playing harmony behind the other.

LEFTY PERKINS: "Buck was one hell of a harmony man. He could double-stop that fiddle and make it sound like three or four fiddles. Johnny would play lead and Buck would play both second and third harmony behind him. It was the damndest thing you ever did see [laughs]!"

The third Brown brother, Roy Lee, was, at fifteen, already a veteran of the dance band business, having traveled with his brothers during his three-month hiatus from high school during the summer of 1935. After Milton's death, Roy Lee again went with the Brownies, now led by Derwood. Roy Lee's role was the same as before, repairing broken strings for Derwood. By this time, some people urged him to start his own band.

ROY LEE BROWN: "I never thought much about having a band of my own, because at that time the Brownies were still popular. People would come to me and ask me why I didn't get a band of my own. I would tell them that the Brownies were still going and they were a hard act to follow!

"But the idea seemed to be a good one, and I decided to organize a band of my own and call them the Junior Brownies. I didn't realize the pitfalls that lay ahead. I was young and inexperienced, but I believed that the people would support me in my endeavors.

"After we got started, I asked Papa Sam if I could bring my band to Crystal Springs for a dance, and he agreed and said I could have a Thursday night. The Saturday before we were to play, I went out to Crystal Springs and talked to many people that I knew and asked them to come next Thursday to my dance. Everyone I talked to assured me that they would be there.

"Thursday night came and my band and I were ready to go. When we got to Crystal Springs, we found out that there was no P.A. system. The Crystal Springs Ramblers had taken it on the road. I didn't know where to get another P.A. system at that late date, so we decided to play without one. The fact that we had no P.A. system was discouraging enough, but on top of that, I don't think a one of the people that promised me they'd be there showed up. We didn't have very many people there at all.

"We started playing and did the best we could under the circumstances, but the singing and the fiddle just couldn't be heard. The only instrument that people could hear was the steel guitar, which was amplified. We were playing our hearts out trying to be heard, when all of a sudden someone put a nickel in the juke box and a record started playing so loud that it drowned out the band completely. We then gathered up our instruments and left. It was a real bad water haul.

"But the fiasco at Crystal Springs didn't stop the Junior Brownies. We played gigs wherever we could, but finally we disbanded.

"Later, I got a chance to play a radio program over KTAT from the

New Isis Theatre, located on North Main Street at the Fort Worth
Stockyards. Bob Chancellor and Kenneth Cobb, two members of my
original band, played the program with me. We had a thirty-minute
program Monday through Friday. We got some money from spot announcements on the program and played elsewhere whenever we
could. This lasted a few months and then we quit playing. By this
time it was 1937."

Meanwhile, the revamped Musical Brownies, led by Derwood
Brown, did well in Fort Worth during the remainder of 1936. In
March 1937, they returned to their original station, KTAT. With announcer Mike Gallagher, the Brownies' broadcasts aired weekdays
from noon until 12:30 P.M.

In October 1936, a settlement between Decca Records, Inc., and
Bart Brown, administrator of Milton's estate, was reached in the
amount of $2,000. Although Milton had not intended to renew his
contract with Decca, Derwood did, and the band was scheduled for
a recording session in Dallas's Adolphus Hotel on Friday, February
19, 1937.

Derwood Brown's Musical Brownies' only session yielded fourteen titles, all showing evidence of the band's still potent talents and
versatility. Lefty Perkins proved to be an able replacement for the
departed Dunn. He played a wonderfully crazed, Dunn-inspired take-
off on "Everybody Loves My Marguerite." Buck Buchanan's twin
fiddle arrangements with Johnny Borowski brought to mind the
smooth sounds of the old Southern Melody Boys.

The Brownies were joined at their Dallas session by vocalist Jimmie Davis, who sang two songs, "High Geared Daddy" and "Honky
Tonk Blues," the latter a variation on the Shelton Brothers' "Deep
Elem Blues." One of the first songs to feature the new term "honky-
tonk," "Honky Tonk Blues" signaled a new era in entertainment, in
which the coin-operated record-playing machine, or "jukebox," began supplanting live bands in dance halls on a widespread level.

The remaining vocals were shared by Derwood Brown and Ocie
Stockard. Although not as effective as Milton, Derwood was a capable singer, showing his affinity with jazz entertainer Fats Waller on
songs such as "Cross Patch." Ocie Stockard's high-pitched, effusive
voice, more amenable to blues than to pop songs, was put to good
use on "I Just Want Your Stingaree."[10]

Derwood's name was left off the record labels (which read
"Brown's Musical Brownies"), as Decca hoped to cash in on whatever marketability remained of the Brownies' name.[11]

But despite the new recordings and the group's continued popularity, everyone knew that Milton's death had taken the soul out of the Musical Brownies. They played their last dance at a lodge hall in Breckinridge early in the spring of 1937. Shortly afterward, a brief notice in the *Fort Worth Press* marked the end of an era.

> FLASH: The Musical Brownies, Fort Worth's most famous fiddle band since 1932, has gone to pieces. Five members have organized the "Wanderers," a new band. Fred Calhoun, pianist, has taken to the road as a traveling salesman.
> Milton Brown, leader and organizer, died in an auto wreck a year ago.

With that simple announcement, the explosive, cyclonic career of the Musical Brownies ended with a whimper. Five of the Brownies, Ocie Stockard, Wanna Coffman, Lefty Perkins, Buck Buchanan, and Johnny Borowski, formed another band with Stockard as leader, called Ocie Stockard and the Wanderers.

FRED "PAPA" CALHOUN: "Derwood just couldn't make it a go, I guess. I quit, then Ocie quit about a week later, then Wanna. Then Ocie organized his own band. But when you lose a guy like Milton . . . [heavy sigh]. When he's gone, the band's gone.

"After I quit, I went on the road, a-sellin'. I was a salesman. Traveled out through west Texas. My brother-in-law put in a potato chip plant up at Lubbock and wanted me to go there and work with him. So I moved to Lubbock. I was delivering potato chips. Then I went to Amarillo to work for the government. I was in security. Then I started to play the Rainbow Garden, where the Sons of the West played. After that I joined Ted Daffan and made records with Cliff down in San Antonio while I was with Ted."

ROY LEE BROWN: "There wasn't any one reason why the Brownies disbanded. There were a number of things. Even though Derwood's band was a good one, it just wasn't the same. Cliff wanted a band of his own and wanted to go back to south Texas. Cecil was a fine musician, and he didn't stay very long with any band except with Milton. He could get a job with another band any time he wanted. Bob Dunn was about like Cecil and wanted to explore new areas also. Wanna Coffman was different. Fort Worth was Wanna's home for so long that he didn't care about leaving. When I traveled the last summer with the Brownies, Ocie talked often about getting his own band and calling it the Wanderers."

OCIE STOCKARD: "When I started my band, I called Jonah Dodson over in Dallas and got his permission to use the name 'Wanderers.' We had one session for Bluebird that fall, and I used Harry Palmer on trumpet because Lefty had gone over to work with Roy Newman on WRR."

Ocie Stockard and his Wanderers was the last group directly related to the Musical Brownies. With only Stockard and Wanna Coffman remaining from the original 1932 band, the Wanderers made one stellar session for Bluebird on September 14, 1937, using George Bell on piano to replace the departed Fred Calhoun. As a last-minute substitution, Stockard called on Fort Worth grocer Harry Palmer to play trumpet. Buck Buchanan and Johnny Borowski reprised their twin fiddle arrangements from the Musical Brownies' Decca recordings in February. Derwood was replaced by Buster Ferguson, a guitarist and songwriter who had changed strings for Derwood when the Brownies were still together.[12]

Even Roy Lee Brown tried to keep the memory of his brother alive. In 1937 Decca's Dave Kapp called Roy Lee and his Junior Brownies in for an audition in Dallas. Roy Lee's band included his boyhood friend G. W. Burns on rhythm guitar; Kenneth Cobb, bass; J. D. Kaylor, tenor banjo; Bob Chancellor, fiddle; Jimmy Everett, guitar; and Katy Brown (no relation to the Brown family) on steel guitar. Roy Lee sang two songs at the audition. One was "An Old Watermill by a Waterfall," which Milton had sung often at dances. However, Kapp was looking for original material and rejected the Junior Brownies.

ROY LEE BROWN: "After Milton passed away and I started my band, I would book a playing job and make a little money that helped the family out some. Ellen and I had been going together about a year now, and on Christmas Day, 1937, we got married in Hobart, Oklahoma. Clifford Wheeler, a good friend of Milton's, was dating a girl named Loma Hankins. So the four of us went up to Hobart to visit Clifford's mother. While we were there, we had a double wedding ceremony. Ellen and I decided to keep our marriage a secret because we were both still in high school."

For all intents and purposes, the Musical Brownies' era was finished. At the time of his death, Milton himself knew that changes were imminent and that the routine of dances and radio programs the Brownies had become locked into would be changed by increasingly sophisticated technology, the slow obliteration of regional barriers, and new tastes in popular music as America approached World War II.

Electrical transcriptions became more and more prevalent in the late thirties, and bands were able to tour more extensively, spending days and even weeks away from their home bases. The introduction of ornate, multicolored jukeboxes in the mid-thirties enabled tight-fisted dance hall owners to dispense with house bands.

Western swing was now moving into its second stage of development. The first stage included the contributions of Milton Brown, who established the repertoire and instrumentation of the genre. Once that was solidified, formally trained musicians like Buck Buchanan and the Texas Playboys' Eldon Shamblin began structuring arrangements. Derwood Brown's Musical Brownies was one of the pioneers of this new maturation process.

The next step would be the influx of more original compositions, helped along by the new cowboy/western fashion fad of the late thirties, triggered in part by the success of Fort Worth's Frontier Days celebration, and the increased popularity of western vocal groups like the Sons of the Pioneers. With Texas swing musicians Hugh and Karl Farr, the Pioneers combined western imagery with the Musical Brownies' rhythm and Milton Brown's smooth vocals, creating the familiar western swing image of today. Almost immediately, this image was embraced by Bob Wills in Tulsa, who became the new leader of the western swing movement.

As B-westerns became more popular, Bob Wills, the Sons of the Pioneers, Ray Whitley, and others helped spread this new western-flavored image of string band music. Wills moved to California to become a supporting player in movies opposite Saturday shoot-em-up idols like Tex Ritter, Russell Hayden, and Charles Starrett. Remakes of the old Tin Pan Alley standards and jazz tunes disappeared as Cindy Walker, Fred Rose, and other songwriters began composing western-oriented songs for Wills and other groups.

The Musical Brownies went on with their lives, some continuing their musical careers, others moving on to other endeavors. But every once in a while, Fred Calhoun or Ocie Stockard would look back at an old photograph or wipe the dust off a scratchy 78 and reminisce about the days when the Musical Brownies ruled the Southwest—an innocent, thrilling era in Texas history, when Milton Brown was king.

Epilogue

Although Milton Brown is the central figure in this book, his career and accomplishments would not have been possible without the support of his family, his association with the many talented musicians he worked with, and the encouragement of his fans and friends. Since this book is about them as well, this chapter traces briefly their lives in the ensuing years since Milton Brown's death. Roy Lee Brown tells what happened to his brother Derwood.

ROY LEE BROWN: "About the time the Brownies broke up, a guy named Floyd Sykes made Derwood an offer to take a new Brownie band to south Texas. Houston was the place they would make their headquarters. So Derwood hired Link Davis on fiddle, Ace Lockwood on banjo, Crock Vincent on bass, Jack Henson on piano, and a steel guitar player who I can't remember.

"The new Brownies operated out of Houston for six or eight months, when Floyd decided he wanted to leave and go somewhere else. I don't know where he went. Derwood stayed in Houston and then took his band to Tyler, Texas. The Brownies had a regular daily radio program on the Tyler radio station and operated out of there, playing dances mostly in east Texas.

"In 1938, Ellen, my mother, and I drove to Tyler to visit Derwood and his family. It was on a Saturday and the Brownies were booked in Corsicana for a dance that night. I went to the dance with the band on their bus and Opal, Ellen, and Mama came later by car. After the dance we came back to Fort Worth. Derwood stayed in Tyler several more months and then disbanded the Brownies and came home.

"He hadn't been back very long before Bill Boyd asked him to come to Dallas and work for him on WRR. Derwood did a lot of radio work with Bill and some personal appearances for quite a while. He also was on the radio with a guy named Marvin Williams, who had a show on WRR also. Finally, Derwood quit and came back to Fort Worth to join Ocie in another band called the Musical Brownies. Wanna Coffman was in this group, too, and they played a daily program on KGKO in Fort Worth. They also booked dances on weeknights out of town and played Saturday nights at the old Winter Garden, which had been changed to Danceland.

"Ocie never made big money with his band. He just didn't have the personality Milton had. Derwood played with Ocie a while and then quit and got a job working at Texas Steel Mill in Fort Worth. While Derwood and Ocie were playing at Danceland I worked the door for them. Bruce Pierce was playing with them at the time, if memory serves me. Later on, after Ocie's band broke up, he and Derwood started playing at the Bohemian Club on Roberts Cut-Off on Saturday nights and I took tickets at the door.

"By 1939 Derwood and Ocie were playing together as the Brownies and were traveling quite a bit. My wife, Ellen, was expecting a baby in February, and Derwood's wife, Opal, was expecting one in June. Well, on February 15 our oldest boy, Danny, was born, and I was at the hospital for the big event. When June rolled around Derwood was out of town playing a dance with Ocie, so I took Opal to the hospital. As luck would have it, it was the same hospital Danny was born in, and the nurses looked at me kind of funny. They were probably wondering why I was back so soon with another woman named Brown who was having a baby [laughs]! When I told them Opal was my sister-in-law we had a good laugh over it. Opal and Derwood had a boy, whom they named Ronald Derwood Brown.

"When World War II broke out Derwood went to work in the construction of army camps. He took his family to Brownwood and then went to Mineral Wells to help build Camp Wolters. When he came back to Fort Worth he worked for Texas Steel Company and played Saturday nights at Crystal Springs for Papa Sam.

"I went into the Navy in 1944, and when I got out two years later I joined Derwood in a new band. He and Blackie Luttrell had started it, and they were playing out at Stella's night club five nights a week. I played banjo with them, and the band played a radio program on KDNT in Denton every Saturday morning.

"But after a few months, that band broke up, too, and Derwood moved his family to Colorado to work in the oil fields. Stella's was the last place Derwood played with a band regularly."

Derwood's first wife, Opal, died of a heart attack when she was forty-two. Derwood subsequently remarried. He died on Christmas

Eve, 1978, at the age of sixty-three. His second wife, Marie, passed away on August 18, 1991. Derwood is the only member of the immediate Brown family who is not buried in the Smith Springs cemetery outside of Stephenville. He rests in Fort Worth's Mount Olivet cemetery.

BARTY AND ANNIE BROWN lived at the house at 3419 Darcy Avenue for the remainder of their lives. On July 13, 1938, when W. Lee O'Daniel was running for governor of Texas, Barty got word that O'Daniel was using Milton's name in campaign speeches. That day Barty had dozens of flyers printed up, with a vehement defense of Milton's memory. He distributed these throughout Milton's home town of Stephenville.

> To the People of Stephenville and Erath County:
>
> Sometime ago W. Lee O'Daniel spoke in Stephenville in the interest of his campaign for Governor. He mentioned the name of my deceased son, Milton Brown, in an attempt, I presume, to get votes.
>
> If Milton were here today I know he would not support O'Daniel, because when Milton was the head of his band he worked him for starvation wages and Milton was forced to quit. Milton always said that W. Lee O'Daniel was insincere. None of my son's relatives are supporting O'Daniel.
>
> I make this statement in justice to the memory of my deceased son, and also that my former friends and neighbors at Smith Spring [*sic*] and in Erath County, may know the facts.
>
> Sincerely yours,
>
> B. L. Brown

Barty Brown's efforts were no match for O'Daniel's charismatic abilities in vote-getting, and the former Light Crust Flour general manager was elected governor later that year.

Martha Annie Brown died on January 9, 1949, at the age of sixty-five. Barty later married the former Ethel Smith. His health continued to fail, and he eventually passed away on October 5, 1958, at the age of seventy-seven. Ethel Smith Brown lived until January 13, 1985, when she died at ninety-four.

BUSTER LEE BROWN contracted polio at the age of four and was paralyzed from the waist down. However, even this debilitating disease did not deter Milton Brown's only son from furthering his own ambitions. Buster worked for his grandfather, Bill Hames, and eventually became head of the Hames carnival. He built the Texas Star, at 212 1/2 feet the world's tallest Ferris wheel. In later years, Buster was president of BLB Panorama, Inc. In an ironic twist, Buster met a similar fate as did his father, dying as the result of an automobile accident, in Wyoming, on August 4, 1990. He was fifty-four.

MILTON THOMAS "SONNY BOY" BROWN works for the Veteran's Administration in Dallas making dentures for veterans. Derwood's oldest son, he of the "chubby hands and big brown eyes," lives in Arlington, between Dallas and Fort Worth.

RONALD DERWOOD BROWN, Derwood's second son, was born in 1939. He works as a salesman for a printing company in Fort Worth.

MARY HELEN BROWN was married a number of times in the years following the death of her first husband, Milton. Tarrant County records show that she had a brief marriage to the Brownies' piano player, Fred Calhoun. She was also twice married and divorced to Bob Wills. As of this writing, Mary Helen lives in Fort Worth where she continues using the surname Brown.

JESSE ASHLOCK, the Musical Brownies' first fiddler, played with Roy Newman, Bill Boyd, Blackie Simmons's Blue Jackets, Bob Wills and his Texas Playboys, Ray Whitley, Jimmy Wakely, Foy Willing, and a number of other western bands. He recorded under his own name for Columbia in 1947. Jesse died in 1976.

JOHNNY BOROWSKI, who replaced Cecil Brower twice in the Brownies, played with Ocie Stockard and with Bob Dunn, Lefty Perkins, Buster Ferguson, and other musicians on border station XEPN for Major Kord. He then returned to South Dakota. Little is known about Borowski's later years. He is believed to be deceased.

CECIL BROWER joined the staff of WRR, Dallas, where he worked for $14 a week. He played dances with Roy Newman's band after leaving the Brownies in 1936. That October, Cecil attended a recording session in San Antonio with Bill Boyd and his Cowboy Ramblers. Boyd occasionally appropriated WRR staff musicians when called upon by Victor to make records. Of the eighteen tunes recorded, ten were cover versions of songs the Musical Brownies had recorded for Decca. The following June, along with buddy Bob Dunn, Cecil recorded with Roy Newman. The same week, he was also an unpaid nonmember of Bob Wills's Texas Playboys when that group recorded. According to Leon McAuliffe, Cecil questioned Bob Wills's "liberties" with meter and never played for Wills again. Shortly thereafter, he joined Ted Fio Rito's orchestra in New York City. He toured with Fio Rito from 1937 until 1939, when he returned to Fort Worth to join the Light Crust Doughboys, where he was reunited with former Southern Melody Boy Kenneth Pitts. From 1942 to 1946 Cecil served with the Coast Guard. After World War II he worked for Leon McAuliffe in Tulsa (1949–51) and for Al Dexter (1951–52). He moved to Springfield, Missouri, to play with Red Foley on Foley's "Jubilee USA" television program (1954). Cecil then accompanied Foley to Nashville, where he was in demand as a session musician. He remained there until singer Jimmy Dean called from New York and invited him to join his band. On November 21, 1965, Jimmy Dean brought his show to Carnegie Hall. After the concert, the cast celebrated with a party at the Waldorf Hotel prior to moving to Los Angeles. Without warning, Cecil fell over, dead from a perforated ulcer, fiddle still in his hand. He would have turned fifty-one one week later.

CLIFF BRUNER returned to Houston, where he formed his own band called the Texas Wanderers. Bruner became almost as successful in Houston and later in Beaumont as Milton Brown was in Fort Worth. He made many recordings over the years and became master of ceremonies at the annual Old Fiddler's Reunion held on Memorial Day weekend in Athens, Texas. Today, in his seventies, Bruner is a retired Houston insurance salesman. He still performs weekends with local musicians and amazes fiddlers half his age with his stamina and virtuosity.

BUCK BUCHANAN played fiddle with the Light Crust Doughboys and the Sons of the West, becoming one of western swing's first accomplished arrangers, adapting big band recordings by Benny Goodman and Glenn Miller for the Sons of the West in Amarillo, Texas. Buck is deceased.

FRED "PAPA" CALHOUN became a traveling salesman and moved to Amarillo, Texas, where he played occasionally at the Rainbow Garden, home of the Sons of the West. In 1937 he recorded with Cliff Bruner before joining Ted Daffan's band in Houston. In 1945 Fred opened a small neighborhood grocery store on the north side of Fort Worth. He remained there, happily running his store, smoking cigars, and occasionally playing piano and vibraphone with friends until his death at eighty-two on July 4, 1987.

WANNA COFFMAN worked for E. L. White Office Supply until his retirement. He played bass part-time for a short while after leaving the Brownies, but as the years passed he quit altogether. Suffering from arthritis, Wanna spent his final days in a nursing home in Whitney, south of Fort Worth. He died there of pneumonia on Thanksgiving Day, November 28, 1991. The last surviving original Musical Brownie was eighty.

CRYSTAL SPRINGS was never the same after Milton Brown died, although World War II gave the dance hall a new lease on life as airmen from nearby Carswell Air Force Base became regular customers. After the war it continued as a popular night club through the 1950s (Jerry Lee Lewis, among others, played there). In August 1959, two children drowned in the swimming pool, which city health authorities then closed. The pavilion remained open only one night a week after that. Eventually, Henry Cunningham closed Crystal Springs. It lay dormant until 1965, when Henry leased it to a man named Ray Chaney, who installed a new western front made from redwood, a lower, modern ceiling, new vinyl tile around the dance floor, and central air conditioning and heat. Chaney renamed the dance hall the Stagecoach Inn. In December 1966, fire destroyed the building.

MARY CUNNINGHAM: "My husband was in the hospital after a heart attack. There was a policeman up on the bridge out there trying to settle a wreck or something. All of a sudden they looked up and saw flames shooting out of the top of the dance hall. They called the fire department right away. It didn't cause too much damage, but they said that the waitresses had picked up the tablecloths with all the ash trays still on them and threw them in the linen closet. And that's what started the first fire.

"Then, Henry had gotten out of the hospital and by that time, all the utilities in the place had been shut off. The place had been locked up. I had just come back from our mobile home park and was walking by the vacant building on my way home. Directly somebody passed by in a car and said, 'That building's on fire down there!' It was about 9:00 at night. I turned around and man, I saw that thing going up in flames again, and I went home and told Henry, but the fire wagons arrived too late. Henry and I stood there and watched it burn to the ground."

For years all that remained on the site that once reverberated from

–{ **COMING SOON** }–
MUSICAL BROWNIES
FAMOUS RECORDING
STRING BAND

Roy Lee Brown, Durwood Brown, Blackie Luttrell
Tommy Echols, Fred Lockwood
Frankie Boy, "Millilo"

▼ ▼

"Of Course You Want to Hear Us and Dance"
9 'til 12

EAGLE'S HALL	EAGLE'S HALL
EVERY TUESDAY	EVERY TUESDAY
MINGUS, TEXAS	MINGUS, TEXAS

Derwood Brown and his Musical Brownies, 1946. The advertisement features the band members inside the bus used by the Crystal Springs Ramblers in the 1930s. Personnel identifcations are incorrect as shown. Correct personnel from left: Derwood Brown, Blackie Luttrell, Tommy Echols, Tom Rutledge, Green (first name unknown), Pop Vance, unknown, Roy Lee Brown. Courtesy Roy Lee and Ellen Brown.

Roy Lee Brown and his Musical Brownies, at the Hill Billy Inn, Fort Worth, early 1950s. From left: Bill Brown (guitar), Johnny Molleda (guitar), Ross Peacock (guitar), Joe Smith (fiddle), Roy Lee Brown (vocals), E. N. Waits (club owner), David Brown (drums), Frankie Horner (piano). (Bill and David Brown are no relation to Roy Lee Brown.) Courtesy Roy Lee and Ellen Brown.

Roy Lee Brown (left) and Barty Brown (right), taken in 1957. Barty died the following year, at seventy-seven. Courtesy Roy Lee and Ellen Brown.

Former Musical Brownie Cecil Brower in the 1950s. Courtesy Sybil Brower Bohm.

Former Musical Brownie Cliff Bruner, performing at the Hitching Rail Lounge, north of Houston, June 1983. Courtesy Cary Ginell.

Derwood Brown (left) and his two sons, Ronny (center), and Milton Thomas ("Sonny Boy"). Photo taken in the 1960s. Courtesy Milton Thomas "Sonny Boy" Brown.

Former Musical Brownie "Lefty" Perkins entertains old friend Bruce "Roscoe" Pierce at Perkins's Fort Worth home, May 1984. Courtesy Cary Ginell.

the sounds of the Musical Brownies was a mobile home park. The lake was still intact, although its waters became green and murky, with heavy marshes growing around its banks. The cement wall that once bordered the swimming pool was crumbling beneath a barbed wire fence, and the gentle slope of the bluff on which the dance hall was built became overgrown with weeds and tall grass. Early in 1991, the terrain itself was eradicated as the springs were filled in and the banks leveled. All that remains of Crystal Springs today is a weatherworn neon road sign by the side of White Settlement Road. Its letters are faded and most of the glass is broken, but the words "Crystal Springs Trailer Park" can still be read.

"PAPA" SAM CUNNINGHAM continued to run Crystal Springs through World War II. After his wife, Hattie, died in 1945, Papa Sam's health began to decline. He suffered a back injury in a bathroom accident in 1952 and later suffered a stroke. A year after his stroke, in 1955, Papa Sam died. He was seventy-two.

HENRY CUNNINGHAM took over management of Crystal Springs after his father died in 1955. In addition, he and his wife, Mary, ran a mobile home park on the site (which still stands). Henry died at sixty-four in 1970.

BOB DUNN made records with many groups during the thirties and early forties, including Roy Newman, Cliff Bruner, Bill Mounce and the Sons of the South (including Sock Underwood), and Buddy Jones. The Decca recordings that bear Dunn's name (Bob Dunn's Vagabonds) were not made by Dunn's own group. This was simply another name given to Cliff Bruner's Texas Wanderers, which served as a studio session band during Decca's 1939 recording trips to Houston. Dunn served during World War II, received a degree in music, and opened a music store in Houston, which he ran until his death from cancer on May 27, 1971. Bob Dunn was sixty-three.

TED GRANTHAM returned to New York where he played on a variety of radio programs throughout the thirties and forties and also played club dates. In 1937, he returned to Fort Worth for a brief stint with the Crystal Springs Ramblers. According to Roy Horton of Southern Peer International, Grantham later became a superintendent in the New Jersey school system.

W. LEE O'DANIEL won his race for governor in 1938 and was reelected two years later. In 1941, Texas senator Morris Shepherd died and O'Daniel became embroiled in a race to fill his seat. Among those he ran against was an ambitious young congressman named Lyndon Baines Johnson. In one of the most implausible campaigns in American history, fraught with backbiting, ballot-stuffing, and vote-stealing, O'Daniel won. (The various misadventures of this often hilarious political battle are related in Robert A. Caro's monumental work *The Years of Lyndon Johnson: The Path to Power* [New York: Alfred A Knopf, 1983], pp. 675–741.) O'Daniel retired after an unproductive term in the Senate, came in a poor third in an attempted comeback in 1956, and died in 1969 at the age of seventy-nine.

LEFTY PERKINS made records with Bill Boyd's Cowboy Ramblers, W. Lee O'Daniel's Hillbilly Boys, and the Universal Cowboys in the late 1930s. After the Brownies broke up, he worked as a staff musician for Roy Newman on WRR in Dallas and later went to Piedras Negras, Mexico, in 1937, and made radio transcriptions for XEPN pitchman Major Kord. Joining Perkins were members of the Hi Flyers and former Brownies Bob Dunn and Johnny Borowski. On these programs, Perkins and Dunn played twin steel guitars. Upon returning to Fort Worth, Perkins barnstormed for W. Lee O'Daniel during the latter's successful 1938 campaign for governor of Texas. As governor, O'Daniel provided Perkins with a job as his statistician. Perkins also played in O'Daniel's senatorial campaign of 1942. After World War II, Perkins played with Marvin Montgomery, Carroll Hubbard, and Roscoe Pierce in the Flying X Ranch Boys, the first musical group to play on Texas television. The band began broadcasting on WBAP-TV in Fort Worth in September 1948. In later years, Perkins performed with various groups at a pizza parlor in West Fort Worth. He was also in the water-well-drilling business. Lefty died of cancer on September 18, 1984, at the age of sixty-seven.

OCIE STOCKARD led his own band, the Wanderers, until the late 1940s, when he moved to California to join Bob Wills. While there, he also played with Tommy Duncan's Western All-Stars at the 97th Street Corral in Los Angeles. Eventually, Ocie quit playing music, returned to Texas, and ran a bar in Fort Worth until his retirement. He died in a Fort Worth nursing home on April 23, 1988, at the age of seventy-eight.

BOB WILLS achieved national fame after his composition "New San Antonio Rose" was covered by Bing Crosby and other recording artists in the 1940s. He made hundreds of recordings in a long career fronting his Texas Playboys. Health problems curtailed his career in the 1960s and he was forced to perform only occasionally. At a reunion/recording session in Dallas in December 1973, Wills was able only to utter a few hoarse hollers. At the end of the first day of the session, he returned home and suffered a stroke. He died on May 13, 1975, at the age of seventy. Bob Wills's massive success in popularizing the genre created by Milton Brown cannot be overestimated.

ROY LEE BROWN tells his own story:

ROY LEE BROWN: "In June 1939, I graduated from high school and went to work for Mrs. Baird's Bakery. I needed some regular money coming in to support the family because I wasn't making much playing music. I was working on the night shift, and in the mornings when I got off from work, I would stop by Rockefeller's hamburger place before going home to bed. There I'd have breakfast. Ernest Tubb would come by and have a cup of coffee on his way to KGKO, where he had an early morning radio program. He walked to the station from wherever he was staying. I knew who he was but I never spoke to him. He was just another local singer then. I worked at the bakery for four years and three months and then quit to go to work for Crown Machine and Tool Company, making shells for the Navy. Ellen soon joined me, working on the same shift.

"In May 1944, I went into the Navy and served almost two years. When I got out, I went back to work for Crown but was laid off after three months. Derwood and Blackie Luttrell had formed a new Brownie band, and I worked with them for a while until Derwood quit to go to Colorado to work in the oil fields. When Derwood left the band, Blackie wanted me to play guitar and front the band, because he couldn't be at Stella's every night. I did this for a while and then decided to get a band and go on the road. This wasn't successful, so I started playing the small places around Fort Worth again.

"I had a radio program in 1947 on KCNC in Fort Worth and was playing at the Bomber Grill that boasted the longest bar in Texas. We broadcast from there every day from 12:00 to 12:30 P.M. In the meantime, I had passed a civil service exam and went to work for the Fort Worth fire department. In addition, my band played at the Hillbilly Inn seven nights a week. While I was playing at the Hillbilly Inn I took my band to McClister's Electronics Company and made two records. E. N. Waits ran the Hillbilly Inn and he arranged the recording session. We recorded four tunes: 'Don't Ever Tire of Me,'

'Wednesday Night Waltz,' 'Weeping Willow' [not the old Carter Family tune], and 'The Ice Man Song.' I sang three of the songs and Earl Milliorn sang 'Weeping Willow.' The Swing Record Company, based in Paris, Texas, pressed and distributed the records. The personnel were myself on vocals, Earl Milliorn on vocal and rhythm guitar, Weldon Pitman and Johnny Strawn on fiddles, Tommy Whatley on steel guitar, Johnny Molleda on bass, Leon Worley on lead guitar, and Cliff Kendrick on drums.

"Because of my job with the fire department, I couldn't be at the Hillbilly Inn every night, but my band played without me when I couldn't be there. I was getting fairly popular around Fort Worth, but it got to the point where I couldn't do either job justice. I decided that the fire department held more promise for me and my family than running a band, so I gave up the band. I worked for the fire department from June 16, 1947, until I retired in 1982.

"Ellen and I have two wonderful sons: Danny, who works for the post office in Fort Worth, and Tim, our youngest, who is a captain on the Arlington fire department. He lives at Eagle Mountain Lake.

"I think I made the right decision not to play music full-time, because I thought about all the musicians I had known who followed the music business all of their working lives who never made it big. Even the ones that did never had enough money when they passed on to pay for their own funerals. The band business is one of the hardest lives one can lead. If you are married, it is no life for your family.

"I also thought about all the musicians I knew that had gotten divorced. Some of them had been married and divorced a number of times. Many more of them wound up as alcoholics or dope addicts. I decided that this wasn't the life for me, so in the early 1950s I gave up my band altogether and stayed with the fire department. Ten years before I retired I attained the rank of district chief and was in charge of one-fourth of the fire departments in Fort Worth on the shift that I worked. I quit playing for thirty years, but music never gets out of your blood, and after I retired, I got with a group and started playing music again. I play now for my own pleasure and as a hobby. It is also a way to supplement my income.

"Some day I know I won't be able to play any more, but when that time comes, I will still love to listen to the music I was raised on: good old western swing."

Roy Lee and Ellen Brown still live in their comfortable country home in Aledo. In 1990, Roy Lee suffered a mild heart attack and underwent bypass surgery. He came through the ordeal with flying colors and was able to continue playing with his band, a new edition of the Musical Brownies. They participated in two recording sessions, from which two cassettes were issued, the most recent released in 1991 (see Discography for details).

Postscript

Aledo, 1985

June 9, 1985, was a blisteringly hot day in Fort Worth, Texas. I had arranged for three of the four surviving Musical Brownies—Fred Calhoun, Ocie Stockard, and Wanna Coffman—to participate in a round robin discussion of their years with Milton Brown. The interview was to be held at Roy Lee Brown's home in Aledo. (Cliff Bruner, who lived in Houston, was unable to attend.) I had volunteered to drive the Brownies and Roscoe Pierce to Roy Lee's for the big event, which would be videotaped. Ellen Brown had turned the occasion into a party and was cooking up a vat of Texas chili. I was staying with Roscoe that week, and as soon as Ocie Stockard, seventy-six, came shuffling through the back door, the three of us got in my rental car and drove up to the North Side to pick up Fred and Wanna. Fred Calhoun, eighty, was well prepared with a shirt pocket full of cigars, and his wife Idell waved us on as we left their home. Wanna Coffman, the youngest of the trio at seventy-three, was troubled by arthritic knees and walked with a cane. He laboriously squeezed into the back seat next to Ocie and Fred. With Roscoe in the front seat and the Brownies' rhythm section in the back, I drove through Fort Worth heading for the highway that would lead us west to Aledo.

As we approached White Settlement Road, I had a sudden impulse and asked the Brownies and Roscoe if they would mind stopping at the Crystal Springs site. They said no, and in less than ten minutes we were there. The sun was beating down as we pulled into the gravel parking lot. Fred Calhoun got out, wandered out through the tall weeds, and shook his head. "Ocie, this is where it all happened. . . . We sure had some times here, didn't we?" Ocie grunted in the affirmative as he tried to navigate around a mound of tin cans and assorted garbage.

A sign nailed to a telephone pole read: "Crystal Springs Mobile Home Park. 5MPH Speed Limit. No Dumpin', Fishin', Parkin'." We took some pictures around the decrepit sign—the only miserable monument that remained to mark the birthplace of western swing—got back in the car, turned on the air conditioner, and drove on.

From that point, the car resounded with anecdotes, most of them ribald, about Milton Brown and the Musical Brownies. By the time we pulled into Roy Lee's driveway, my passengers were having the time of their lives reliving past experiences. Their old friend J. B. Brinkley greeted us as we walked inside. So did Marvin Robinson and A. B. and Helen Gilbert, all longtime fans of the Brownies and friends of Roy Lee and Ellen Brown. The Brownies sat together on a couch, and the others gathered around on chairs. While the chili simmered, the stories flowed, each musician reminding the others of an incident that had occurred or a person they had known long ago. I remained glued to my video camera and listened, fascinated at the detail and recall of the assemblage. In fact, I barely had to ask any questions, for each story triggered another, and then another.

After the dishes were cleared, Fred Calhoun lit up a cigar, ambled over to the piano, and sat down, testing the action of the keys. J. B. Brinkley had brought his guitar and, seeing that Fred was in the mood to play, started to plug in his amplifier. Roy Lee Brown went into a back room and brought out his guitar and a tenor banjo for Roscoe. The impromptu jam session that resulted had everyone singing and laughing the rest of the afternoon. Wanna Coffman and Ocie Stockard, unable to play, stayed on the couch, watching and smiling. How they must have wished they could have been up there playing with their old friends just one more time. (Since 1986, Milton Brown Day has been celebrated at the A. B. Gilbert Ranch in Santo, on the Sunday closest to Memorial Day. Friends and relatives gather for an afternoon of home-style barbecue, western swing, dancing, and reminiscing about the days of the Musical Brownies. Coffman, Calhoun, and Stockard attended the first event.)

When the sun began to set, Fred put out his cigar, indicating it was time to return home. There were hugs all around and promises to do it all over again. But somehow, everyone knew that it would not happen. J. B. Brinkley died the following spring, and since then, Ocie Stockard, Fred Calhoun, and Wanna Coffman have also passed away. Watching the videotape again in my office, I saw the excitement in Ocie Stockard's eyes, watched as J. B. Brinkley slapped his knee after telling another Blackie Lawson story, and marveled at Roy Lee Brown's recall and attention to detail. It brought to mind Milton

Wanna Coffman (left) and Ocie Stockard (center) listen as Fred Calhoun talks about the "Brownie beat" at the Brownie Reunion, held at the home of Roy Lee and Ellen Brown, Aledo, Texas, June 9, 1985. Courtesy Cary Ginell.

Roy Lee and Ellen Brown celebrate their fiftieth wedding anniversary, Christmas 1987. Courtesy Roy Lee and Ellen Brown.

Brown's moving recitation on the Brownies' recording of "My Mary,"
which summed up the thoughts of everyone in that room that magical afternoon:

> Oh gee, wouldn't it be great
> to open the doors of the past
> and live again in yesterday?

Appendix 1

Crystal Springs Ramblers Dates
as listed in Sam Cunningham's booking diary

1935

Mon. March 18	Fort Worth
Tue. March 19	Waco
Wed. March 20	Kaufman
Thu. March 21	Crystal Springs (Fort Worth)
Fri. March 22	Crystal Springs
Sat. March 23	Crystal Springs
Sun. March 24	Crystal Springs
Mon. March 25	McGregor
Tue. March 26	Dallas
Wed. March 27	Dodd City
Thu. March 28	Crystal Springs
Fri. March 29	Fort Worth
Sat. March 30	Crystal Springs
Sun. March 31	Crystal Springs
Tue. April 2	Mexia
Wed. April 3	Clifton
Thu. April 4	Crystal Springs
Fri. April 5	Fort Worth
Sat. April 6	Crystal Springs
Sun. April 7*	Crystal Springs
Wed. April 10	Denison
Mon. April 15	Cisco
Tue. April 16	Stephenville
Wed. April 17	Corsicana
Mon. April 22	"Tours"
Tue. April 23	Waco

*After this point in his diary, Papa Sam, for the most part, stopped listings for the Ramblers' appearances at Crystal Springs. It can be assumed that they played there Thursday, Saturday, and Sunday nights until the Brownies returned in September.

Wed. April 24	Gladewater
Mon. April 29	Olney
Tue. April 30	Whitney
Fri. May 3	Bosque Downs, Waco
Sat. May 4	Waco
Mon. May 6	Penelope
Tue. May 7	Dodd City
Fri. May 10	Bosque Downs, Waco
Wed. May 15	Clifton
Wed. May 22	Corsicana
Tue. May 28	Dallas
Wed. May 29	Dodd City
Mon. June 3	Penelope
Wed. June 5	Corsicana
Wed. June 12	Dodd City
Wed. June 19	Corsicana
Wed. June 26	Corsicana
Wed. July 10	Corsicana
Mon. July 15	Penelope (percentage listed as 35/65)
Fri. July 19	Pete's Place, Mingus
Mon. July 22	Shadowland, Waco
Tue. July 23	unreadable
Wed. July 24	Corsicana
Fri. July 25	Confederate Hall, Dallas (double band dance)
Tue. July 30	Ennis
Wed. July 31	Bob Wills at Crystal Springs (unknown if this was a double band dance with the Ramblers)
Sun. Aug. 4	Dallas
Tue. Aug. 6	St. Joe
Fri. Aug. 9	Mingus
Mon. Aug. 12	Penelope
Wed. Aug. 14	Clifton
Wed. Aug. 21	Corsicana
Fri. Aug. 23	Mingus
Tue. Sep. 10	Stephenville
Wed. Sep. 11	Corsicana
Fri. Sep. 13	Mingus
Tue. Sep. 17	Midway, Midlothian (percentage listed as 75/25)
Mon. Sep. 23	Penelope
Tue. Sep. 24	Stephenville
Wed. Sep. 25	Corsicana
Thu. Sep. 26**	MILTON BROWN'S HOME COMING DANCE
Fri. Sep. 27	Mingus

**After the Brownies returned to Crystal Springs, the Ramblers played Sundays and occasionally Thursdays, but never on Saturday.

Tue. Oct. 1	Stephenville
Fri. Oct. 5	Cactus Club, Waco
Tue. Oct. 8	Denison
Wed. Oct. 9	Corsicana
Thu. Oct. 10	DeLeon (attendance listed as 54 men, 97 ladies)
Fri. Oct. 11	DeLeon
Sat. Oct. 12	DeLeon ("free-for-all")
Tue. Oct. 15	Denison
Wed. Oct. 16	Corsicana
Thu. Oct. 17	unknown location (attendance listed as 63 men, 78 ladies)
Fri. Oct. 18	Mingus
Sat. Oct. 19	Corsicana
Tue. Oct. 22	Stephenville
Thu. Oct. 24	Wolfe City
Fri. Oct. 25	Legion Hall, Rosebud
Sat. Oct. 26	Corsicana
Tue. Oct. 29	Eagles Hall Security Dance
Wed. Oct. 30	Rock Lake
Thu. Oct. 31	Corsicana (Halloween dance; the Brownies played Crystal Springs this night. This was the night the floor fell in.)
Fri. Nov. 1	Mingus
Sat. Nov. 2	Corsicana
Tue. Nov. 5	Denison
Thu. Nov. 7	Wolfe City
Fri. Nov. 8	Mingus
Sat. Nov. 9	Denison
Sun. Nov. 10	Crystal Springs
Mon. Nov. 11	Shadowland, Waco
Thu. Nov. 14	Bluebird Pavilion, Longview
Fri. Nov. 15	Wolfe City
Sat. Nov. 16	Wichita Falls
Tue. Nov. 19	Corsicana
Wed. Nov. 20	Vernon
Thu. Nov. 21	Olney (admission: 75 cents for men, 10 cents for ladies)
Fri. Nov. 22	Mingus
Sat. Nov. 23	Elks Club, Breckinridge
Mon. Nov. 25	Wichita Falls (percentage 70/30)
Tue. Nov. 26	Oak View Inn, Denison
Wed. Nov. 27	Confederate Hall, Dallas
Thu. Nov. 28	Wolfe City
Sat. Nov. 30	Brownwood
Sun. Dec. 1	Crystal Springs
Tue. Dec. 3	Ladies Auxiliary, Palestine (percentage 70/30)
Wed. Dec. 4	Cisco
Thu. Dec. 5	Corsicana
Fri. Dec. 6	Confederate Hall, Dallas

Sat. Dec. 7	DeLeon
Sun. Dec. 8	Crystal Springs
Mon. Dec. 9	Bouban
Tue. Dec. 10	Log Cabin, Corsicana
Wed. Dec. 11	Wolfe City
Fri. Dec. 13	Dallas
Sat. Dec. 14	Brownwood
Sun. Dec. 15	Fiddlers' contest, Crystal Springs
Mon. Dec. 16	Bouban
Tue. Dec. 17	Waco
Thu. Dec. 19	Dublin
Fri. Dec. 20	Wolfe City
Sat. Dec. 21	Breckinridge
Tue. Dec. 24	Denison
Wed. Dec. 25	Denison
Fri. Dec. 27	Palestine
Sat. Dec. 28	Elks Hall, Abilene
Mon. Dec. 30	Confederate Hall, Dallas
Tue. Dec. 31	Wolfe City

Appendix 2

Sybil Brower Bohm's Dance Itinerary

All dances featured the Musical Brownies unless otherwise indicated.

1935

July 30	Barney Swenson's Pavilion, near Meridian
September 18	Shadowland, Waco
September 30	Barney Swenson's Pavilion
October 21	Barney Swenson's Pavilion
November 4	Barney Swenson's Pavilion

1936

January 25	Stephenville City Park, Stephenville (Papa Sam Cunningham's Ramblers)
April 22	White Oak, Waco*
May 14	Clifton
May 20	Woodmen of the World, Waco
June 23	White Oak, Waco
June 28	Street dance, Grapevine
July 5	Woodmen of the World, Waco
July 23	White Oak, Waco
August 13	Woodmen of the World, Waco
August 20	Taylor
September 3	White Oak, Waco
September 16	Woodmen of the World, Waco
September 30	White Oak, Waco

*Milton Brown died on April 18, the previous Saturday. The dance at the White Oak Inn was the first dance the Brownies played without him, with Derwood Brown as their leader.

Appendix 3: Musical Brownies Time Line

Since membership in western swing bands is often transitory, a time line charting active performers within a band can be helpful. We have included such a chart for Milton Brown and the Musical Brownies during the years the band was run by Milton and Derwood Brown.

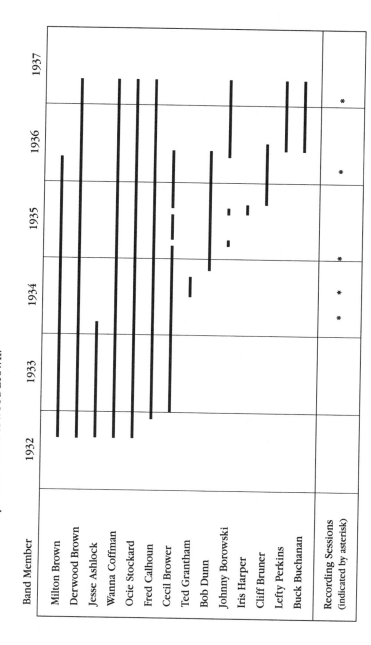

Notes

Chapter 1. Stephenville

1. Erath had previously surveyed the town of Waco in 1849, situated near the site of the old abandoned village of the Huaco Indians.

2. Up to that time, the area designated as Erath County was a subdivision of Bosque County with the town of Meridian as the county seat. According to the *Waco Tribune Herald*'s centennial edition in 1949, "George B. Erath had more to do with the actual settling of Central Texas than any other person."

3. The Fort Worth and Rio Grande railroad line closely followed the route of the Chidchester Overland Mail Route, established in 1877, one of the longest mail routes in the world at the time—1560 miles from Fort Worth, Texas, to Fort Yuma, Arizona. See also "History of Stephenville," Stephenville Public Library pamphlet, p. 19.

4. Succeeding generations in the Brown family—two of Barty's children, Roy Lee and Era Lee, Milton Brown's son Buster Lee, and one of Derwood Brown's grandsons, also named Lee— continued this naming tradition.

5. For a good description of cotton farming during this period, see "Growing Up in Rural Tarrant County Had Few Comforts 70 Years Ago," article by Smithfield resident Arthur Guy Meacham, eighty-two, reprinted in Mack Williams, *In Old Fort Worth* (a collection of articles published in the *Fort Worth News-Tribune* in 1976 and 1977) (Fort Worth: Williams and Williams, 1986), p. 86.

6. Milton Brown's early brush with death may have contributed to his fatal auto accident in 1936. It has been speculated that Milton suffered later in his life from narcolepsy, a disorder resulting in recurrent attacks of sleep. Members of Milton's band as well as his brother Roy Lee testified to Milton's sudden spells of falling asleep, sometimes while driving. The cause of narcolepsy is unknown. However, symptoms have been reported after acute infections, such as appendicitis.

7. All written references to Derwood Brown spelled his first name "Durwood." This includes newspaper articles from the 1930s as well as liner notes, articles, and transcribed interviews published later. It is the express wish of the Brown family that Derwood's name be spelled with the "e" in this book.

8. At its peak in 1906, the cotton industry in Erath County supported forty cotton gins, which yielded 55,000 bales. Each gin employed from six to a dozen men during the cotton season. The big money years for cotton ended in about 1930. See Arden Jean Schuetz and Wilma Jean Schuetz, *People-Events and Erath County, Texas,* rev. ed. (Stephenville: Ennis Favors, 1971–72), pp. 89–90.

Erath County farmers were urged to diversify their farming when the continuous cotton planting began to destroy their land. A 25 percent reduction in cotton was approved in a 1911 resolution. By 1920 cotton was no longer the principal crop in Erath County, supplanted by increased farming of berries, grapes, pecans, peanuts, watermelons, and sweet potatoes. See Vallie Eoff's master's thesis, "A History of Erath County, Texas," University of Texas at Austin, 1937.

Chapter 2. The Harmony Boy

1. The Camp Bowie army facility was built with the help of many local sand and gravel pit owners, including one Sam "Pop" Cunningham. Cunningham's gravel pit became a lucrative source of income for its owner. Unbeknownst to him, the digging of the pit revealed evidence of an underground spring. Eventually, this spring became the Crystal Springs resort, the central location for the development of western swing by Milton Brown in the 1930s.

2. An excellent source on the history of Fort Worth during this period is Janet L. Schmelzer, *Where the West Begins: A History of Fort Worth and Tarrant County* (Northridge: Windsor Publications, 1985), pp. 66–78.

3. Milton Brown's own dance hall, the Brownie Tavern, which operated during the summer of 1935, was located just northwest of the Lake Worth Casino on the Jacksboro Highway.

4. According to musician J. B. Brinkley, the initials KTAT stood for "Keep Talking about Texas." Of this informal rule for staff members and musicians, Brinkley noted, "They used to tell us, 'If you ever run out of things to say, remember that!'"

5. Bill Malone, *Country Music, U.S.A.,* rev. ed. (Austin: University of Texas Press, 1985), pp. 33–34.

Chapter 3. Peanuts, Cigars, and Aladdin Lamps

1. Keith Produce, a longtime institution in Fort Worth, still survives.

2. The entire sordid case of F. M. Snow can be found in Arden Jean Schuetz and Wilma Jean Schuetz, *People-Events and Erath County, Texas,* pp. 127–41. The murders were still being discussed as their fiftieth anniversary approached. See "Erath County's Most Famous Mass Murder Recalled," *Erath Observer,* Apr. 17, 1975, pp. 1, 8.

3. "Old Man Snow" was recorded by Ray Pack and Halfbreed in 1975 (Telephone, TSA-109). Pack is a cousin of the Brown family. My thanks to Roy Lee Brown for transcribing the lyrics. I have not discovered other variants of this tune or other songs celebrating the Snow murders. Ray Pack learned the song from his mother, a former resident of Erath County. Like "The Heartsick Blues," "Old Man Snow" was never copyrighted.

4. Roy Lee Brown recalled that Milton usually paid between $15 and $20 for his suits. Roy Lee remembered, "After Milton's death, Mama and Dad had two of his suits tailored to fit me. One of them had leather buttons on it and a split tail on the coat. They were the latest styles. Milton preferred dress slacks and shirt or a suit. The only time I ever saw him in overalls was when he played barn dances."

One of my cherished possessions is a check for $6.00 made out to Hy Myer on Apr. 14, 1930, and signed by Milton Brown. I am grateful to Roy Lee Brown for his generosity in presenting me with this gift.

5. "Three Programs to Be in Parks," *Fort Worth Press*, Sept. 26, 1927, p. 10. Arnold Park is a small park located behind the Fort Worth courthouse.

6. Light Crust Flour was milled by the Burrus Mill and Elevator Company. Their sponsorship of the group called the Light Crust Doughboys officially began sometime between the fall of 1930 and January 1931. The group survives to this day, led by longtime member Marvin "Smokey" Montgomery, who joined in 1935. The Doughboys in its early stages (1930–34) cannot be classified as a "western swing" band because of the absence of a bona fide take-off fiddler. Its first two fiddle players, Bob Wills and Clifford Gross, played strictly melodies and variations. The first Doughboy fiddler to play what was then known as "hokum" was Kenneth Pitts, who joined in 1934.

7. "Roll Up the Carpet," W. Lee O'Daniel and his Light Crust Doughboys, Vocalion 02842, recorded Oct. 11, 1933. The lyrics, sung by Leon Huff, celebrated the house dance tradition and urged dancers to "roll up your troubles, fold up your cares, just because you haven't got a dime; roll up the carpet, push back the chairs, you're bound to have a wonderful time."

8. Another performer of minstrelsy, Al Bernard, also sang in a manner similar to Wills's acknowledged idol Emmett Miller. On a 1928 recording of "St. Louis Blues" (Madison 1642) Bernard, using the pseudonym "John Bennett," performs the W. C. Handy classic as a monologue, accompanied by a small band (including a fiddle lead). In comparing this record with Bob Wills's own initial recording of the song (Vocalion 03076, recorded Sept. 23, 1935), one can easily conclude that Wills was aware of the Bernard record, copying its patter nearly word for word. The Wills recording features Tommy Duncan playing straight man to Wills. A transcript of the two versions follows:

Bernard: "Doggone it! Doggone that gal, too! She done left me F-L-A-T flat. But I ain't gwine to worry about her no more. 'Sides, I never did like her store-bought blonde hair. I'm a man that's crazy 'bout black hair on wimmins, I is [laughs], so St. Louis Blues, be on your way!"

Wills: Doggone it.
Duncan: What's the matter, boy?
Wills: Doggone that gal, too.
Duncan: What's she gone and done to you now, son?
Wills: Man, she done left me F-L-A-T flat.
Duncan: That spells flat, that's right.
Wills: But I don't care, though.
Duncan: You don't care?
Wills: Nozzir!
Duncan: How come you don't care, son?
Wills: I don't like this store-bought blonde hair.
Duncan: [unintelligible] What kind of hair *do* you like?
Wills: [laughs] Lord, man, I's crazy 'bout black hair.
Duncan: Tell me 'bout that black hair, son.
Wills: Well, St. Louis Blues be on your way.

Both versions then conclude with similar vocal passages beginning, "Lord, a black-headed woman make a freight train jump a track." This comparison strongly suggests that Bob Wills's knowledge of black dialect and city blues repertoire came from his minstrel show experience and not from his close contact with field hands on his father's farm as indicated in Charles R. Townsend's biography of Wills, *San Antonio Rose: The Life and Music of Bob Wills* (Urbana: University of Illinois Press, 1976).

9. Joseph Burnice "J. B." Brinkley was a singer and guitarist who played with the Crystal Springs Ramblers and later the Light Crust Doughboys, replacing Muryel "Zeke" Campbell as the Doughboys' lead guitarist. Brinkley's father, Blackie, was employed as a bouncer at Crystal Springs (see Chapter 8). Before his death in April 1986, J. B. provided me with a wealth of valuable anecdotes and information about his relationship with the Brown family and Fort Worth musicians (in accordance with J. B.'s wishes, the more ribald stories remain off the record).

10. I am indebted to Eugene Earle for lending me three rare Brunswick 78s by the Red Headed Fiddlers. These records confirm Steeley's reputation as a top-notch breakdown fiddler. The tunes included "Never Alone" b/w "Texas Quick-step" (Brunswick 285) (the latter can be heard on *Texas Farewell*, County 517, liner notes by Charles Faurot), "Rag-time Annie" b/w "Texas Waltz" (Brunswick 388), and "Fatal Wedding" b/w "St. Jobe's Waltz" (Brunswick 460). Additional titles can be heard on the LP reissues *Mountain Banjo Songs and Tunes* (County 515, liner notes by John Burke, featuring "Cheat 'em") and *Folk Music in America*, vol. 3 (Library of Congress, LBC-3, liner notes by Richard Spottswood, featuring "Far in the Mountain" ["Fire in the Mountain"]).

11. This would have to have occurred in 1925. Johnson's claim to being part of the first string band on Fort Worth radio is possible but unproven. Red Steeley and Red Graham also lived in Fort Worth and were popular radio entertainers in the mid- to late twenties. It is not known how many oth-

er fiddle/guitar duos played on WBAP since the first "barn dance" program in 1923.

12. Interview with Sleepy Johnson by Keith Titterington and Stephen F. Davis, published in *Old Time Music,* 7 (Winter 1972–73), pp. 8–11.

13. According to Ed Brice, "Mr. Answerman" for the *Fort Worth Star-Telegram,* Meadowmere was built by the Red Cross in 1917 as a recreation center for soldiers at Camp Bowie. It came to prominence in 1920 and was the most popular spot for the city's younger set. Later improvements were made for the 1936 Texas Centennial, but it closed shortly after the celebration. The first private owner was T. E. D. Hackney of Chicago, who later leased it to a group from Kansas City. The complex was razed in 1947 to make way for apartments. *Fort Worth Star-Telegram,* Mar. 15, 1988.

14. Milton Brown mistakenly assumed that the Famous Hokum Boys were from Tennessee because the lyrics to "Eagle Riding Papa" stated: "Listen everybody from near and far, if you want to know just who we are, Eagle Riding Papa, from Tennessee." The original 1930 recording of "Eagle Riding Papa" by the Famous Hokum Boys can be heard on *The Young Big Bill Broonzy,* Yazoo L-1011, liner notes by Stephen Calt, Nick Perls, and Michael Stewart. The word "eagle" in the original recording (released simultaneously on the ARC labels: Oriole, Perfect, Banner, Romeo, and Jewel) was changed to "easy" on the Brownies' recording of "Easy Ridin' Papa" (Decca 5325, recorded Mar. 3, 1936). Broonzy participated in another recording of the song on May 4, 1937, when blues singer Washboard Sam (Robert Brown) and his Washboard Band recorded "Easy Ridin' Mama" (Bluebird B-6970). My thanks to John Tippet for bringing this record to my attention.

Bob Pinson reports that Georgia Tom Dorsey had recorded "Eagle Riding Papa" and "Somebody's Been Usin' That Thing—No. 2" previously, for Gennett on July 8, 1929. Dorsey also recorded with Tampa Red (Hudson Whittaker) and Frankie "Half Pint" Jaxon, two blues musicians whose records influenced Milton Brown and other Texas bandleaders through their "race" recordings of the twenties and thirties. Milton never met any of these musicians but learned their tunes from records sold at Will Ed Kemble's furniture store in Fort Worth. Georgia Tom Dorsey later became famous as Thomas A. Dorsey, writing sacred songs such as "Peace in the Valley." It is to be emphasized that Milton Brown rarely, if ever, sang traditional country blues. Although artists such as Broonzy and Tampa Red did do these numbers, Milton only sang the up-tempo, happier tunes from their repertoire, which went better with the Tin Pan Alley songs he enjoyed so much.

15. William Ed and Walter S. Kemble, Jr., operated Kemble Brothers Furniture Company, located at 214 W. Weatherford, at the corner of Weatherford and Throckmorton streets. The Kembles sponsored an occasional radio program on KFJZ in 1930. The show, listed as "Kemble Bros. Record Program," aired from 7:00 to 7:30 in the morning and probably was used to advertise the store by playing phonograph records, which were sold there.

16. Until he met Milton Brown, Bob Wills's musical repertoire was limited to the traditional fiddle tunes he learned from his father and songs he

picked up while traveling with minstrel shows. Bob Wills learned many songs from Milton Brown during their nearly three years playing together, including such numbers as "Four or Five Times," "The Waltz You Saved for Me," "Right or Wrong," and "Fan It," all recorded first by the Musical Brownies and later by the Texas Playboys. During his years with his vocal group, Milton learned "I Ain't Got Nobody" from the June 1928 version by minstrel singer Emmett Miller. The song became a favorite of Wills's, and, according to legend, it was the song that Tommy Duncan sang when he auditioned to replace Milton in the Light Crust Doughboys. Both Brown and Wills were fans of Emmett Miller, blues songstress Bessie Smith, and the "father of the blues," W. C. Handy. It was Handy's "St. Louis Blues" that first brought them together and they remained great friends for the rest of Brown's life.

17. Stockard recorded "Crafton Blues" and "The Blue Bonnet Waltz" at his first recording session, with the Texas High Flyers [*sic*] for Brunswick on Nov. 28, 1930. The selections remain unissued.

18. One of the most successful songs of the twenties, "My Blue Heaven," was recorded by Gene Austin in September 1927. This would mean Stockard was eighteen when he began studying violin in Wichita Falls.

19. Stockard probably arrived in Fort Worth during the fall of 1928. The High Fliers started sometime during the latter part of 1929.

20. Born in Virginia, Zack Hurt was part of the duo Zack and Glenn that recorded for Okeh in 1928. Hurt's solo work consisted of "Gambler's Lament" (Okeh 45212, reissued on the LP *Gambler's Lament,* Country Turtle CT-6001, liner notes by Pat Conte and Frank Mare) and "The Old Tobacco Mill," a 1937 Vocalion recording by the Hi Flyers in which Hurt sang lead vocal. The latter can be heard on *The Hi Flyers,* Texas Rose TXR-2705, liner notes by Cary Ginell. The High Fliers changed the spelling of their group name to "Hi Flyers" when Elmer Scarborough took over leadership of the group in 1932.

21. Raymond (sometimes spelled Ramon, but pronounced "ʀᴀʏ-muhn") DeArman was born in Newark, Texas, on Apr. 5, 1911, and moved to Springtown in 1917. He and Roscoe Pierce moved to Fort Worth in 1929. DeArman joined the Light Crust Doughboys in 1935 and was with them until his death in an accidental car fire on Sept. 23, 1940. Nicknamed Snub by Doughboy announcer Eddie Dunn, DeArman played energetic bass and standard rhythm guitar, becoming popular with Doughboy audiences. See *History of Springtown-Parker County* (Parker County Historical Society, n.d.), pp. 218–19, which includes the tribute poem "Just Snub" by Light Crust Doughboy announcer Parker Willson.

22. Popular entertainers such as Ted Lewis and Rudy Vallee had been using the megaphone as a primitive vocal amplifier for years. Although Milton Brown was not the first singer to use it, he did recognize its necessity when performing at the noisy house dances and later at Crystal Springs.

23. For further details on Crystal Springs and its colorful founder, see Chapter 8.

24. Stricklin recalled in his autobiography that the other numbers played

during the audition were "Four or Five Times" and "The Crawdad Song." See Al Stricklin and Jon McConal, *My Years with Bob Wills* (San Antonio: Naylor, 1976), pp. 9–11.

Chapter 4. *We're the Light Crust Doughboys from the Burrus Mill*

1. C. L. Douglas and Francis Miller, *The Life Story of W. Lee O'Daniel* (Dallas: Regional Press, 1938).

2. Douglas and Miller, *Life Story of W. Lee O'Daniel,* p. 79.

3. See Townsend, *San Antonio Rose,* pp. 80–82. O'Daniel sued Bob Wills after Bob was fired from the Light Crust Doughboys in August 1933, and formed his own band in Waco, which he called Bob Wills and his Playboys. In promoting the new band, announcer Everett Stover said that the Playboys were "formerly the Light Crust Doughboys." O'Daniel also sued to stop Wills from using the theme song, which Wills had altered to proclaim: "We're the Playboys from WACO." According to Roy Lee Brown, Wills went to Milton Brown and told him that O'Daniel was about to ruin him and could he do something about it. What O'Daniel did not know was that Milton had copyrighted the Doughboys' theme song while he was still a member. Eventually, O'Daniel dropped the lawsuit. Wills's group in Waco did not fare well and the Playboys subsequently moved to Oklahoma. Milton gave Wills permission to use the music to the Doughboys' old theme song. By the time Milton formed the Musical Brownies in September 1932, he had already written a new theme song based on his composition "Sunbonnet Sue."

4. Milton could hardly have chosen a better song to start off the Light Crust Doughboys' career. "Twenty-one Years" became one of the most recorded songs of the 1930s. Popular with country audiences, the song (along with many others in the Doughboys' repertoire) was never recorded by Milton Brown. The instant and overwhelming success of "Twenty-one Years" led to a long line of of "answer songs," creating a veritable saga. These included "The Answer to Twenty-one Years," "Woman's Answer to Twenty-one Years," "Ninety-nine Years (Is Almost for Life)" (the Nashville equivalent, sung by the Vagabonds on the Grand Ole Opry), "Last of the Twenty-one Year Prisoner," "The Twenty-one Year Prisoner Is Dead," and others. See Dorothy Horstman, *Sing Your Heart Out, Country Boy* (Nashville: Country Music Foundation, 1986), pp. 291–92.

5. Douglas and Miller, *Life Story of W. Lee O'Daniel,* p. 81. Milton Brown sang many Rodgers songs while he was with the Doughboys because the songs of "the Singing Brakeman" were extremely popular in Texas. Rodgers himself lived in Kerrville, Texas, at the time, in the famed "Blue Yodeler's Paradise." When Milton formed his own band, adding musicians capable of playing jazz, many of the more country-oriented vocal tunes disappeared. Brown was never particularly fond of Jimmie Rodgers as a singer but liked some of his songs, such as "Roll Along Kentucky Moon" and "My Carolina Sunshine Girl."

6. Gene Fowler and Bill Crawford, *Border Radio* (Austin: Texas Monthly Press, 1987), chap. 5, "Please Pass the Tamales, Pappy," pp. 116–18.

7. Townsend, *San Antonio Rose,* p. 73. Remark made to Townsend by Sleepy Johnson.

8. Douglas and Miller, *Life Story of W. Lee O'Daniel,* p. 83.

9. I am indebted to Mary Cunningham and her son, Henry Cunningham, Jr. (Papa Sam's grandson), for lending me their copy of the Crystal Springs flyer.

10. Obituary for Wylbert Brown: "Musician Wylbert Brown, owner of 'Eyes of Texas,'" *Fort Worth Star-Telegram,* Feb. 5, 1987, p. A27.

11. Cecil Brower purchased his own "tremolo mute" at Sparks's Fiddle Shop in Fort Worth. He used it on several recordings with the Musical Brownies, including "The Sweetheart of Sigma Chi" and "I'll String Along with You" (Decca 5239), "The Yellow Rose of Texas" (Decca 5273), "The Roseland Melody" (Decca 5295), "La Golondrina" (Decca 5356), which was the Southern Melody Boys' theme song, and "Carry Me Back to the Lone Prairie" (Decca 5382). The late Mineral Wells fiddler Tommy Camfield learned to play the tremolo mute from listening to these records. He used it in a re-creation of the Brownies' "Roseland Melody" at several reunion recording sessions in Dallas's Sumet-Bernet Studios. Roy Lee Brown was the vocalist on the tune and the remarkable resemblance of his voice to his late brother's was one of the highlights of the sessions. Video and audio tapes of the sessions are in the author's possession.

12. Fort Worth's Southern Melody Boys are not to be confused with the group from east Tennessee (Odus Maggard and Woodrow Roberts) that recorded for Bluebird and Decca in 1937 and 1938. Unfortunately, the Fort Worth group of 1931–32 never made records.

13. "Sweet Georgia Brown" was written in 1925, but it was probably Bing Crosby's 1932 hit recording that Pitts was referring to.

14. "Business in F" was recorded by Gene Kardos for Victor on Dec. 18, 1931 (Victor 22899). He later recorded it again for Perfect (ARC) in the mid-thirties. It was possible for the Southern Melody Boys to have learned the song from Kardos's 1931 Victor version. The Light Crust Doughboys cut an unissued version of the song on Apr. 22, 1935. The Ross Rhythm Rascals, a Dallas fiddle band led by businessman Ross Aldridge, was another Texas group to record "Business in F" (released on Decca 5344, recorded Feb. 16, 1937). Pitts's reference to the song as "an old jazz tune" was from his present perspective.

15. Lamour, who would become famous as Bob Hope and Bing Crosby's love interest in the string of "Road" pictures in the 1940s and 1950s was, in the early 1930s, a young torch singer in Dallas. The bandleader mentioned was probably her first husband, Herbie Kaye.

16. Rodgers recorded eight songs between Feb. 2 and Feb. 6, accompanied by local musicians including WRR staff musician Bill Boyd, who was soon to form his famed Cowboy Ramblers, a group inspired by Milton Brown's Musical Brownies. For detailed information on Rodgers's part in the

Dallas session of February 1932, see Nolan Porterfield, *Jimmie Rodgers: The Life and Times of America's Blue Yodeler* (Urbana: University of Illinois Press, 1979), pp. 313–19.

17. Interview with Will Ed Kemble, transcribed by Fred Hoeptner, at Kemble Brothers Furniture, Fort Worth, Texas, July, 1959. Kemble realized that the people who liked the Doughboys' kind of music would purchase a lot from his stores. Kemble claimed to have sponsored the band on KFJZ, but this has not been confirmed.

18. See Brian Rust, *The Victor Master Book*, vol. 2 (Highland Park: Walter C. Allen, 1974), p. 424. "Nancy Jane" was actually taken from a recording by the same name by the Famous Hokum Boys, who recorded it on Apr. 9, 1930. My thanks to Mike Kieffer for lending me his copy of that record for study. The Famous Hokum Boys also recorded the prototype for the Dough-boys' theme song: "Eagle Riding Papa." Milton apparently was partial to the "good-time," risqué infectiousness of these selections, since he used two of the Hokum Boys' songs during these critical moments in his career. One was adapted for his new group's theme song, while the other was part of his first recording. Although Milton Brown did not write "Nancy Jane," he was as-tute enough to add two original verses and file a copyright on the song after he found out that neither Bill Broonzy nor Georgia Tom Dorsey had done so. See the song analysis that follows for details on the recordings.

19. Townsend, *San Antonio Rose*, p. 72.

20. U.S. copyright number 57395.

21. Wills's 1929 Brunswick duets with Herman Arnspiger of "Gulf Coast Blues" and "Wills Breakdown" were never released. The masters were ap-parently destroyed.

22. String band music in Texas functioned for entertainment, that is, dancing. Milton Brown changed the music with the addition of vocals and subsequent expansion of the repertoire to include contemporary pop tunes, adding to the usual array of traditional waltzes and breakdowns. Although string bands often used popular tunes in their repertoire, these were gener-ally songs from an earlier era, such as turn-of-the-century Victorian ballads—hence one derivation of the term used for country music of the 1920s and 1930s, "old-time." Transitional groups such as the East Texas Serenaders would add elements of ragtime to this base, which better suited Texans' growing fondness for dance steps such as the two-step and the fox trot.

23. Some of Wills's best hot fiddlers included Jesse Ashlock, Louis Tier-ney, Joe Holley, Bob White, and Johnny Gimble.

Chapter 5. *How Do You Do, We're Here to Sing to You*

1. According to Roy Lee Brown, Bob Wills and Sleepy Johnson were too poor to risk giving up a regular paycheck on a chance venture with Milton so they remained with O'Daniel. Johnson later regretted his decision.

2. A native of Honolulu, Joe Kaipo developed a reputation as an accom-

plished steel guitarist in Dallas, working at a swank west Dallas speakeasy known as the El Tivoli Club. Hearing of Kaipo's talents, Jimmie Rodgers caught his act in 1929 and used him on his recording sessions whenever he came to Dallas. See Porterfield, *Jimmie Rodgers,* pp. 206, 208–15. Kaipo's "hell-raising" incidents as session man for the legendary Singing Brakeman indicates that he would also have gotten along with the rambunctious Derwood Brown.

3. The "k" in "Musikal" was rarely used in promoting the band. According to Roy Lee Brown, Milton discovered that he would not have been able to copyright an English word such as "Musical" so he copyrighted it as "Musikal."

4. Roy Lee Brown's reference to "modern stuff" refers to popular tunes heard on radio or recordings by jazz bands. Milton wanted to keep abreast with whatever new tunes the public was listening to so that he could offer fiddle band versions of songs while they were still popular. Bob Wills could play the melodies of these songs, but his inability to keep pace with Milton's schedule of learning new tunes probably contributed to their mutual reluctance to team up. Although Jesse Ashlock's personality created problems, the younger fiddler could improvise and knew more pop songs than Wills, making him better suited for the Brownies.

5. The "slapping" technique was a way in which the bass player snapped the strings against the wood of the instrument, supplying a crisp, intense foundation to a dance band ensemble. In the 1920s, New Orleans jazz musicians such as George Murphy "Pops" Foster first popularized the technique, which created a more precise staccato pulse than the tuba. See Joachim Berendt, *The Jazz Book* (New York: Lawrence Hill, 1975), pp. 278–84. Also see the Pops Foster biography in Roger Kinkle, *The Complete Encyclopedia of Popular Music and Jazz* (New Rochelle: Arlington House, 1974), pp. 923–24. Record collectors and jazz historians John Fraser and Don Gray also name Steve Brown of Jean Goldkette's orchestra as a bass player who first used the slapping style in 1924.

It is not clear where Milton Brown got the idea to have Wanna Coffman slap his bass. Whether it was from phonograph records or from a live performance by a Dixieland band in Fort Worth, Coffman pioneered this use of the bass in country music.

6. See Ken Griffis, "The Jesse Ashlock Story," *JEMF Quarterly,* 27 (Autumn 1972), 121–27.

7. "New Manager at KTAT Here," *Fort Worth Press,* Sept. 9, 1932, p. 16.

8. "Program Director Is Named at KTAT," *Fort Worth Press,* Sept. 28, 1932, p. 7.

9. I use the term "prime time" anachronistically to illustrate a change occurring in Texas radio listening habits during the early 1930s. Today, "prime time" implies a part of the day in which premium commercial rates are charged for more popular radio programs. In 1932, there was no such thing as "day-part" advertising rates. All radio time on a station was equal. However, there was a noticeable shift in the time slots featuring fiddle bands beginning with the Light Crust Doughboys' move to WBAP in 1931. This coincided with the commencement of touring by the Doughboys. Although they

were not a dance band, the Light Crust Doughboys did play shows on location from their sound truck. W. Lee O'Daniel moved the time of their program to the noon hour so the group could return to Fort Worth in time to rest up for their show. The other bands eventually followed suit. The Musical Brownies began playing dances out of town almost immediately after their formation, and Milton also found it preferable to broadcast during the lunch hour as opposed to early morning. This still left enough time when the program ended for the band to get in their bus and travel to that evening's dance engagement. One must realize that since electrical transcriptions were not used in Texas at that time, all groups had to play their programs live. Eventually, the noon hour became the preferred time slot for fiddle bands in Texas and Oklahoma, even after transcriptions became prevalent.

10. Roy Lee Brown became Derwood's "string fixer" during the summer of 1935 and 1936 when he was on vacation from school. For details, see Chapter 9.

Chapter 6. *Take a Chorus, Mister Calhoun*

1. Calhoun was always careful to distinguish between "fiddle bands" and "horn bands." The difference between the two was determined by the instrument playing melody or lead. Trumpet, trombone, and sometimes clarinet usually would be the lead instruments in horn or jazz bands in the late teens and twenties. The Musical Brownies was the first "fiddle band" Fred Calhoun played in.

2. According to Roy Lee Brown: "Woodshedding is slang for practicing. Back on the farms, when someone was trying to learn to play a fiddle or such, it would drive the other people in the house up the wall. So if a person wanted to practice, they would go out to the woodshed so it would not bother anyone. People burned wood back then and they usually had a woodshed to store their wood and keep it dry."

3. The Three Jacks, including leader Jack Stone and Rodney Rogers, recorded three songs for Okeh on June 28, 1928, in Chicago. "Spanish Shawl" and "Chile Blues" were released on Okeh 41102. A third title, "Twelfth Street Rag," remains unissued. The records can be classified as "hot Hawaiian," incorporating steel guitar, ukulele, and standard guitar. I am indebted to Barry Hansen for lending me his pristine copy of this rare recording.

4. Fred Calhoun estimated the month he first played with the Brownies as December of 1932. This would have been a little over two months after the Brownies formed. Since Ocie Stockard claimed to have told Milton about Calhoun, it is possible Milton already was aware of Fred's ability. According to Stockard, Fred Calhoun played piano duets with another musician on KTAT. "They called them 'The Twin Pianists,' because that other guy had a mustache just like Fred. I went up there and watched them a while and then told Milton about them." Roscoe Pierce's understanding was that Milton already knew about Fred Calhoun and sent word for him to come out to Crystal Springs for the Thursday dance.

5. Papa Sam had installed a snack bar where a cook served hamburgers, hot dogs, and sandwiches in addition to coffee, cold drinks, etc. When Prohibition was officially repealed on Apr. 7, 1933, there was an instantaneous celebration at Crystal Springs and beer was added to the menu.

6. A "Paul Jones" is a popular Texas round dance in which the dancers form two circles in concentric formation, women in the middle and men on the outside. The men would initially dance with whatever woman they faced in the inner circle. At a given signal, usually a blown whistle, the men would leave their current partners and grab the nearest female.

7. Papa Sam Cunningham owned a school bus that he used to transport patrons from the courthouse in downtown Fort Worth to Crystal Springs. When Milton Brown began booking dances out of town, Papa Sam allowed him to use the bus, with Henry Cunningham driving. For more on the bus and the courthouse shuttle, see Chapter 8.

8. The Musical Brownies was a commonwealth band, meaning that all net profits from a dance were divided equally among its members. The shares were decided after money was taken off the top for promotion, equipment, expenses for the bus, and a small allowance for Derwood's string-fixer. Milton, as leader and manager, took no more money for himself than he gave to anyone else. In order for each band member to receive $103, we can estimate that there were between four and five hundred couples at the dance in Dallas that night.

9. Dave Stogner did indeed become a musician. With Milton Brown as his idol and inspiration, Stogner moved to central California, where he formed a popular western swing band in Fresno. Former Crystal Springs Rambler Joe Holley was one of the many talented musicians employed by Stogner, who made records for several California labels in the 1950s as well as one full-length LP for Decca in 1957. I am grateful to Stogner's biographer, Judy Pybrum Malmin, for providing me with the manuscript of her work and for allowing the inclusion of Stogner's thoughts on Milton Brown in this book.

10. *Dallas Morning News,* various articles and captioned photographs, 1926.

11. Roy Lee Brown, probably the only living person who still remembers the melody to "Fall in Line with the NRA," sang it for me on tape. Roy Lee remembered Milton singing the song with slightly different words than those given in the text. The differences are:

Line 4: "Because Depression had it down"

Chorus, line 7: "So we'll stand right up and say"

Chorus, line 8: "In this jolly land of ours."

12. The battle dance took place on Oct. 1, 1933.

Chapter 7. Taking Off

1. Also attending the session was Victor's southern field representative, Elmer Eades.

2. Some have compared Derwood Brown's guitar playing to that of Puckett. Derwood was the first Texan to play take-off choruses in a white string band. Like Puckett, Derwood was adept at providing heavy rhythm when needed, but adroitly combined this rhythm with intricate runs on the bass strings.

3. Hamblen recorded "My Mary" and "My Brown-Eyed Texas Rose" for Victor in Hollywood on Nov. 11, 1931 (Victor 23685). Jesse Rodgers covered both sides at the San Antonio session.

4. When Milton and the Brownies moved to WBAP in 1935, the lyrics to Milton's two "baby songs," "My Precious Sonny Boy" and "Our Baby Boy" (the latter dedicated to Milton's own son, Buster Lee), were printed up on Milton's special brown-tinted stationery and distributed to listeners. I am indebted to Harry and Maebelle Fowler for lending me their copy. Fifty years later, Roy Lee Brown was still receiving requests to perform "Sonny Boy." He delivered the tune with the same feeling his brother did when the song was new. The correct title of the song is "Precious Little Sonny Boy."

5. "Garbage Man Blues" was issued, mistake and all, on Bluebird B-5558. When the Bluebird label was redesigned in 1937, the song was mistakenly labeled "Garage Man Blues." The original jazz version of the tune was recorded by New Orleans bandleader Luis Russell and his Burning Eight as "The Call of the Freaks" (Okeh 8656, recorded Jan. 15, 1929). Russell remade the song with lyrics and called it "The New Call of the Freaks" (Okeh 8734, recorded Sept. 6, 1929). However, it was probably the Washboard Rhythm Kings' version that Milton Brown copied, because of the similarity in the spoken introduction, and because the flip side of the Rhythm Kings' record was "You Rascal You," which the Brownies also covered. See Discography and Song Analysis. My thanks to Mike Kieffer for bringing these records and others to my attention.

A white Tennesee string band called the Tennessee Ramblers also recorded a song called "Garbage Man Blues" for Brunswick in 1928. Although this is also a possible source of the Brownies' version, it is unlikely that Milton was aware of this record. The Brownies listened mainly to pop, jazz, and blues records. Rarely did they get inspiration from a hillbilly group.

6. The sales distribution of the first Bluebird sessions was as follows: "Swinging on the Garden Gate" (Bluebird B-5444): 2,126 copies; "Swinging on the Garden Gate" (Montgomery Ward M-4540): 884 copies; "Brownie's Stomp" and "Joe Turner Blues" (Bluebird B-5775): 2,370 copies. Curiously, sales figures for what was probably the Brownies' best-selling Bluebird record, "My Precious Sonny Boy," were never mentioned on the royalty statements in Roy Lee Brown's possession.

These are the only sales figures available for records made by Milton Brown for either Bluebird or Decca. At the Brownies' second and final session for Bluebird in August 1934, no composer credits were given and consequently, Milton received no royalties for them.

7. Today, the Hames Carnival has one of the world's largest Ferris wheels. The carnival was operated by Milton Brown's only son, Buster Lee, up until his death in 1990.

8. The "rockin' the bow" technique was a flashy method of showing off one's bowing skill, later used in such tunes as "Orange Blossom Special." It became widely used because it was not a difficult style to execute. Cliff Bruner told me that whenever he ran out of things to play, he'd just "rock the bow" and he'd get an ovation. Jesse Ashlock became extremely proficient at the style and used it frequently to great effect.

9. Varner's memory was correct. "Wild Cat" and "Doin' Things" was a best-selling Victor recording by Venuti and guitarist-partner Eddie Lang, accompanied by pianist Frank Signorelli. The selections were recorded in New York on June 21, 1928, and were available on Victor 21561. (Venuti and Lang had first recorded the songs for Okeh the previous year.) The record was popular throughout the thirties and alternate takes were later released on Bluebird B-10280.

10. English Decca was formed by Sir Edward Lewis in 1929. Its American counterpart, founded in 1934, was headed by a former Brunswick records salesman, Jack Kapp. With Kapp's brother Dave acting as talent scout and field-recording chief, Decca made remarkably good progress during the Depression as an upstart record company, recording many of the important country and blues artists in the South. In the mid-thirties, Decca sent field units to southern locales to seek out regional musical talent, instigating a new numerical series (5000) devoted solely to "Hill Billy" recordings. For more on Decca's 5000 series, see Cary Ginell, *Decca Hill Billy Discography: 1927–45* (Westport: Greenwood Press, 1989).

11. Cecil Brower told Bob Pinson that Grantham also played with Paul Whiteman's orchestra. As "Ted Grant," Grantham soon joined Hugh Cross and Shug Fisher's Radio Pals on WLW, Cincinnati. The group recorded sixteen titles for Decca in New York City on July 16, 1937. Those recordings give a clearer representation of Grantham's prowess than do the Brownies' records. For more information on this group, see Ken Griffis, "The Shug Fisher Story," *JEMF Quarterly,* 34 (Summer 1974), 55–61.

12. The history of the steel guitar has been well documented in many books and articles. The most useful source is George S. Kanahele, ed., *Hawaiian Music and Musicians* (Honolulu: University of Hawaii Press, 1979), pp. 365–78. Kanahele and Donald D. Kilolani Mitchell recognize Joseph Kekuku as the chief stylistic innovator of the steel guitar, beginning in 1885. After experimenting and teaching his technique to students in Hawaii, Kekuku arrived in the United States in 1904, as did many other Hawaiian musicians, to entertain. By World War I, touring Hawaiian units such as Kekuku's helped spread the steel guitar's popularity.

13. Details on Bob Dunn's early life are sketchy. He was interviewed by country music historian Bill Malone in Houston on July 17, 1966. Malone's findings are summarized in *Country Music, U.S.A.,* pp. 157–58.

14. After Milton Brown's death Dunn eventually returned to XEPN, where he worked as staff musician for a station pitchman known as "Major Kord" (Don McKord), joining members of the Flying-X Ranchboys and the Hi Flyers. See Fowler and Crawford, *Border Radio,* pp. 77–95.

15. The "old wooden thing" to which Coffman refers is now in posses-

sion of the Country Music Foundation. It had been found in the attic at Crystal Springs and wound up in the hands of drummer and former Texas Playboy Bill Mounce, who sent it to Bob Pinson for the CMF's collection. Mounce, Dunn, and Sock Underwood played together in the Sons of the South, a western swing band that recorded for Bluebird in 1941. The band featured Bob Dunn progressing into the boogie woogie vein on songs such as "What's Bob Done?" (Bluebird B-8976, recorded Oct. 9, 1941). These were Dunn's final recordings before joining the navy.

Chapter 8. Why, the Springs Are Clear as Crystal

1. This poem, written in pencil, was one of many tributes to Crystal Springs composed by loyal fans and sent to the Cunninghams. I am indebted to Henry Cunningham, Jr., for lending me his father's scrapbook containing the poem and other memorabilia.

2. See Jack Gordon's column "Old Chair at Crystal Springs Is Empty Today" (Sam Cunningham obituary), *Fort Worth Press,* Sept. 8, 1955.

3. McBride became vocalist for Cliff Bruner's Texas Wanderers and recorded many classic songs for Decca in the late thirties and forties, including "It Makes No Difference Now." He married Laura Lee Owens, Bob Wills's first female vocalist.

4. Henry Cunningham's 1932 permit was shown to me with pride by his widow Mary.

5. "About a Quarter to Nine" was made famous in 1935 by Al Jolson in the Busby Berkeley/Warner Brothers musical *Go into Your Dance,* which also starred Ruby Keeler. See Ted Sennett, *Warner Brothers Presents* (New York: Castle, 1971), p. 105; and Ted Sennett, *Hollywood Musicals* (New York: Harry N. Abrams, 1981), p. 83.

6. On Jan. 11, 1936, *Billboard* reported that "The Music Goes Round and 'Round" was a favorite sing-along hit for New Year's celebrants. Sheet music of the tune was selling at the rate of 16,000 copies a day, and radio stations throughout the country were being bombarded by requests for the song.

7. Jimmie Davis recorded two songs with the Brownies after Milton's death: "High Geared Daddy" (Decca 5349) and "Honky Tonk Blues" (Decca 5400). This was the only Brownies recording session led by Derwood Brown (Feb. 17, 1937, in Dallas). Coffman's observation of Davis's shortcomings in timing is borne out when one listens to these sides.

8. Of invaluable help in researching this period was a small datebook that belonged to Papa Sam Cunningham. In it, Papa Sam scribbled notes about and the addresses and phone numbers of prospective band members, bouncers, and various Texas club owners. The journal is blank until Mar. 18, when the first city entry was listed. I have assumed this to be the first engagement for the Crystal Springs Ramblers. The journal continues throughout the spring and summer of 1935 with the names of towns the Ramblers played. My sincere thanks to Henry Cunningham, Jr., for lending me this

valuable artifact as well as many other items from his father's scrapbook which document the history of the Crystal Springs Ramblers. For a listing of the towns played by the Ramblers, see Appendix 1.

Even after Milton Brown returned to Crystal Springs in September, Papa Sam kept the Ramblers going. They recorded ten titles for Vocalion in Dallas; three on June 9, 1937, and seven more on June 19, 1937. Three discs were issued: Vocalion 03646: "Swingin' to Glory"/"Fort Worth Stomp"; Vocalion 03707: "Tired of Me"/"Tell Me Pretty Mama"; and Vocalion 03856: "Down in Arkansas"/"Swingin' and Truckin'." Four titles remain unissued: "When Somebody Thinks You're Wonderful," "My Texas Home," "Mr. Deep Blue Sea," and "Springtown Shuffle" (Springtown is a town close to J. B. Brinkley's hometown of Weatherford, Texas, west of Fort Worth). Personnel on the Crystal Springs Ramblers' session include: J. B. Brinkley, rhythm guitar and vocals; Link Davis, fiddle and vocals; Morris Deason, guitar and vocals; Earl Driver, alto saxophone; Joe Holley, fiddle; Jimmy McAdoo, bass; and Loren Mitchell, piano. Left-handed hot fiddler Joe Holley, the last survivor of the original Crystal Springs Ramblers, passed away in 1987. He was also a longtime member of Bob Wills's Texas Playboys and saw service as well in Tommy Duncan's Western All-Stars, Luke Wills's Rhythm Busters, Dave Stogner's Western Swing Band, and numerous other groups.

9. The occasion was immortalized in Papa Sam's datebook. Under the date Sept. 26 is the boldly penciled inscription: "Milton Brown's Home Coming Dance."

10. The Brownies switched to WBAP in July 1935. For details, see Chapter 10.

11. The poem "Dedicated to the 'Brownies'" was typewritten on three sheets of unlined paper. It was kept by the Brown family with their other memorabilia. It is printed here exactly as it was written, with misspellings intact. It shows, more than any other document, the affection fans felt for Milton Brown and the Musical Brownies, and their familiarity with the separate personalities that made up the band. The author of the poem, Dorothy Ann Hogle, lived in Electra, Texas, a town west of Wichita Falls. The Brownies played there often. Although Fort Worth was a long journey for Dorothy Ann, her parents, and her two sisters, the family came to Crystal Springs whenever they could and always attended Brownies dances in Electra. One of the sisters later married fiddler Buck Buchanan, who was a Brownie after Milton's death.

Chapter 9. On the Road

1. Before Milton left Crystal Springs to open the Brownie Tavern, his split with Papa Sam Cunningham was 50/50. The agreement reached to lure Milton back to Crystal Springs gave Milton the heavy end of a 60/40 split. The Brownies usually drew a greater percentage on the road than in Fort Worth and made the bulk of their money away from their home base.

Only when it was impossible to obtain a percentage did Milton agree to a flat guaranteed salary for the band. On Feb. 25, 1936, the Brownies played a radio program and dance in Lubbock, Texas, for $175, each band member receiving roughly $20. Although this was a good week's work for the average Texan, it was decidedly under what the Brownies usually made.

2. It was also the reason why the Brownies could not get a program on WBAP immediately. WBAP rarely allowed unsponsored programs on their air schedule. Although Milton Brown plugged various products during his KTAT broadcasts and occasionally tailored his band's name to the products (Milton "Sal-o-Mint" Brown, the Globe-Trotters, etc.), these were not regular sponsors but spot announcements. The Brownies were never salaried spokesmen for individual products as were the Light Crust Doughboys. WBAP policy preferred the guaranteed income a sponsored program provided. When the Brownies moved to WBAP in 1935, their popularity eliminated any worries of attracting advertisers. By not tying himself to a particular product, Milton Brown was able to free himself to plug his dances.

3. According to the *Variety Radio Directory*'s first issue (1937–38), there were forty-five radio stations operating in Texas during that year, with an estimated 862,100 homes having radios. Tarrant County had 40,700 radio homes, or about one radio for every four households. Radio's heyday was still some years off. In better times, Milton Brown's fame would probably have spread faster with more radios in use.

4. The Brownies was not the first organization to "barnstorm" or to play successive dates around the country. However, an eight-man group necessitated a vehicle the size of a bus. Single acts, such as Jimmie Rodgers, sometimes traveled in a marked car or a stretched-out sedan, but the modern tradition of the country artist parking his or her bus outside an establishment where all could see it probably began with groups such as the Musical Brownies.

The Light Crust Doughboys toured in a specially marked sedan. It was used for the purpose of selling and advertising Light Crust Flour and not for promoting the Doughboys, who did not play dances, only stage shows in front of the car.

5. Humorist/cowboy philosopher Will Rogers and aviation ace Wiley Post crashed shortly after takeoff near Point Barrow, Alaska, on Aug. 15, 1935. Their deaths set off a shock wave throughout the world. Tributes to Rogers continued for years in his native state of Oklahoma and in Texas. Fort Worth named its main entertainment facility after Rogers. Will Rogers's death made an indelible imprint on many Americans' lives in 1935, much as the death of President John F. Kennedy did for a future generation.

6. Several dozen copies of Milton Brown's letters survive, preserved by his brother Roy Lee. Milton typed two copies of every letter, one to be sent, and one to be filed. The letters usually were written on KTAT or WBAP stationery. Their language was businesslike but cordial, with "Dear Sir" or "Dear Madam" as salutations. When confirming a dance engagement, Milton always made sure to include a promise for "a big dance." Nicknames

sometimes were used when Milton corresponded with friends who owned the facilities. Otherwise, the letters were strictly business. The letters show him to be in total control of the Musical Brownies' schedule and finances and completely aware and capable of dealing with the intricate politics and varied personalities prevalent in the music business. In the context of the Depression, the financial success of the Brownies was indeed phenomenal.

7. Sybil Knight was an avid fiddle band fan, favoring the Brownies but also attending dances by the Crystal Springs Ramblers and the Wanderers. Sybil took careful note of the dances she attended, writing down each one on pages of her family scrapbook. When the Brownies began issuing tickets to their dances (at Milton Brown's insistence), Sybil stapled each one to her scrapbook as well. See Appendix 2 for a listing of Brownies dances Sybil Knight Brower (later Sybil Brower Bohm) attended during 1935 and 1936. Although sketchy, Sybil's notations are valuable in indicating the frequency with which the Brownies played certain areas in Texas.

Although the Crystal Springs Ramblers were not as successful as the Brownies, and were unable to obtain as many bookings, they played many of the same locations. Sybil's list gives an accurate representation of the distribution of string bands' dance dates in the area surrounding Fort Worth.

8. The New Orleans equivalent of the Texas battle dance was known as a "carving contest," in which members of two rival jazz bands would try to blow each other down to attract the larger crowd. This occurred mainly with Dixieland groups in the 1920s.

9. Listen to "Pray for the Lights to Go Out" (Decca 5111), in which Ocie Stockard and Derwood Brown say "Sing it, brother Parson Brown!" Milton also calls "Play it, Rattlesnake, play it, boy!" to Ocie during Stockard's banjo take-off on "Down by the o-h-i-o" (Decca 5111).

10. One of the original Wanderers, Dick Reinhart was one of the first musicians associated with western swing bands to make records. He cut two cowboy songs for Brunswick, "Rambling Lover" and "Always Marry Your Lover," in 1929. Milton Brown's vocals had a dramatic impact on Reinhart's singing style. By the time he joined Roy Newman in the Wanderers, Reinhart had changed his own style from the stark sound of Texas's cowboy balladeers to the energetic pop vocals of Milton Brown. He would later become a member of the Light Crust Doughboys, playing electric guitar and singing blues and pop standards. Reinhart reportedly had learned some of his blues licks from legendary Dallas musician Blind Lemon Jefferson. After forming his own band called the Lone Star Boys, which recorded for Okeh, Reinhart joined the Jimmy Wakely Trio in 1940 and moved to California, appearing with Wakely and Johnny Bond on Gene Autry's "Melody Ranch" program. Reinhart died on Dec. 3, 1948.

11. Honeyboy and Sassafrass (Fields and Welsh) were popular radio personalities on Dallas and Fort Worth radio stations. Their act was similar to a myriad of local blackface dialecticians spurred by the national success of the team of Amos and Andy (Correll and Gosden).

12. Hofner's comments are included in the unpublished autobiography of California bandleader Dave Stogner, by Stogner and Judy Pybrum Malmin.

Chapter 10. The Biggest Little Band in the World

1. I interviewed Michael "Mickey" Kapp on Dec. 10, 1985, in his office at Warner Brothers studios in Burbank, California, where he works as president of Warner Special Products, a division of Warner Brothers Records. Michael Kapp worked for his father and participated in the nuts and bolts of the recording industry, operating lathes and cutting record lacquers in the 1940s and 1950s. Dave Kapp died Mar. 3, 1976, at the age of seventy-one.

2. The name "Decca" supposedly originated with the location of the material used in the formula for the shellac pressings: the Deccan plateau in India. An oft-mentioned yet apocryphal theory reasons that the letters "D-E-C-C-A" correspond to the beginning of a musical composition by classical composer Ludwig van Beethoven, of whom E. R. Lewis was particularly fond. This theory was prompted by the appearance of a bust of Beethoven on the English Decca record labels.

3. The famous blind hillbilly duo Mac and Bob (Lester McFarland and Robert Gardner) obtained a stripped radio program through Dave Kapp. Kapp told his son Michael that Mac and Bob "lived on Sterno." Although it was known to contribute to blindness, Sterno obviously had no adverse effects on Mac and Bob, who were already blind. Another of Dave Kapp's jobs was to help Mac and Bob climb stairs to get to their radio station and various stage performances.

4. According to music historian Donald Lee Nelson, the artist in Indianapolis was mountain singer Emry Arthur.

5. Dave Kapp's comments came from an interview with John Krimsky at Kapp's offices in New York City on July 27, 1951. I am indebted to Jonathan Kapp (Jack's son) for lending me a transcript of that interview. Jack Kapp passed away in 1949 of a cerebral hemorrhage.

6. The letter, dated Mar. 15, 1936, was sent to Dave Kapp at the Roosevelt Hotel in New Orleans, where the Brownies had recently completed their second recording session for Decca. As tactfully as possible, Milton displayed his dissatisfaction with Decca: "Dear Dave; Received your wire and am waiting on New York to furnish me a statement of royalties. Dave, I have not received my check for the last half of 1935 and it was due the fifteenth of the month. I dont want to be cranky but business is business and it is past due and I would like to have it. I will let you know about the information about the wire as soon as I get some results from the company but it seems to me that they are a bit neglectful about paying their artist. Trusting this will be taken in the same good will in which it is spoken I remain, Yours truly, Milton Brown."

Shortly after, Milton received a check for $269.09, which he immediately deposited in the First National Bank of Fort Worth. Milton had already written Eli Oberstein at RCA Victor on Feb. 15, informing him that he would not be recording for Decca after Jan. 1, 1937. It appears that Oberstein, too, was reticent in paying royalties, for Milton demanded those from him as well, for the tunes "Swinging on the Garden Gate," "Joe Turner Blues," and "Precious Little Sonny Boy."

7. A Sunday recording session was unusual for Decca, which normally began sessions on Mondays. Since the Brownies were booked for dances throughout the week, it is likely that Milton proposed using their day off, Sunday, as a travel day so he would not have to cancel too many dances.

8. Apparently this was standard operating procedure for Jack Kapp, who often used this ploy to loosen up recording artists playing away from their natural element. Willie Phelps of Norman Phelps's Virginia Rounders related a similar experience before the group's 1936 New York session for Decca. Les Paul, who worked as a sideman for various Chicago blues artists in the 1930s, recalled Kapp encouraging pianist Georgia White to imbibe before recording for Decca. Blues singer Furry Lewis remembered Kapp doing the same thing at his first recording session for Brunswick in 1927. Listen to Lewis's comments on "Furry Lewis" (Folkways FS-3823).

9. Violinist Carroll Dickerson was one of Chicago's best-known bandleaders of the twenties and early thirties, although his reputation never became national. His band, Carroll Dickerson's Sunset Orchestra, played at Chicago's Sunset Café during the 1920s. The mob-run Grand Terrace Café opened on Dec. 28, 1928, and became Earl Hines's headquarters. See Frank Driggs and Harris Lewine, *Black Beauty, White Heat: A Pictorial History of Classic Jazz* (New York: William Morrow, 1982), pp. 57, 63, 72.

10. There is at least one rumor that Bob Dunn had recorded once before. Shelly Lee Alley, a violinist and bandleader in the Houston area in the thirties, made many records with his band, the Alley Cats. He also recorded with Jimmie Rodgers in San Antonio in January 1931. According to Alley's son, Shelly Lee Alley, Jr., "I got to know Bob Dunn real well. We worked together in Dickie McBride's band. Bob taught trombone and guitar in his music store. I remember standing around a music store and somebody said they had read in a guitar magazine that some Hawaiian guy had played the first recorded jazz steel guitar in the thirties. Bob Dunn, who never bragged, just said, 'Well, I've got a mind to write those boys a letter about that. I cut a recording of "Sweet Georgia Brown" in 1927 on steel guitar.'" At this time, there is no evidence to support this secondhand claim by Bob Dunn, but it is certainly worth further investigation.

There have been many claims as to who was the first person to record using an amplified instrument, among them peripatetic musician/inventor Les Paul. Paul estimates that he began experimenting with amplification as early as 1929. However, Dunn's performances on the Brownies' 1935 Decca records mark the earliest commercial appearance of an amplified instrument.

11. See the Song Analysis devoted to the Brownies' recording sessions.

12. "Profiles: Pulse on the Public," *New Yorker,* Aug. 24, 1940, pp. 22–26.

13. Harry Palmer, a part-time trumpet player, part-time grocer, became one of the most admired musicians in Fort Worth. Possessing a full, rich tone, Palmer idolized Louis Armstrong. Even his voice sounded like that of the great "Satchelmouth." Fortunately, Palmer's genius was captured on disc. He made one recording session with Ocie Stockard's Wanderers on Sept. 12,

1937, for Bluebird. Former Brownie Wanna Coffman was also part of this group. The session has been reissued in its entirety by Origin Jazz Library (OJL-8103).

14. Sybil Brower Bohm still has the trophy and proudly displays it on her mantelpiece.

15. Borowski can be heard playing "hot penny whistle," sometimes known as a "potato whistle," on "Cross Patch," recorded with Derwood Brown's Musical Brownies (Decca 5413-B). The instrument was probably an ocarina.

16. In the fall, however, the Wanderers broke up. According to group member Marvin Montgomery, "We didn't have the leadership the Brownies had. We just had a bunch of guys who wanted to outplay each other. So some of us went with Roy Newman and some of us went with the Light Crust Doughboys."

W. Lee O'Daniel was fired by Burrus Mill in September 1935. Some say it was because he was devoting too much time to promoting W. Lee O'Daniel instead of Light Crust Flour. The new Doughboy manager and announcer, Eddie Dunn, hired Montgomery, Dick Reinhart, and Bert Dodson from the Wanderers, and began the "modern era" of the Light Crust Doughboys. At this writing, Marvin Montgomery is still an active member of the band.

17. This technique is sometimes known as "beating the straws." A pair of knitting needles could also be used for this purpose. For an example, listen to "Hunky Dory," played by Alva Greene, fiddle, and Francis Gillum, straws, heard on *That's My Rabbit, My Dog Caught It: Traditional Southern Instrumental Styles* (New World NW-226). According to that album's annotator, Mark Wilson, the practice gave rise to the expression "fiddlesticks."

18. Leo Raley, a talented musician, played the first amplified mandolin on record (actually a mandola) with Cliff Bruner's Texas Wanderers in February 1937.

19. The Brownies would record twenty of the forty tunes Milton listed in the Feb. 6 letter to Decca. See the Song Analysis for the omitted titles.

20. Actually, Cecil Brower wrote the music while Milton penned the words to "Roseland Melody." According to Fred Calhoun, Cecil had been trying to remember the melody to "The Naughty Waltz," when he stumbled on an entirely new tune. Milton then set words to it. "Roseland Melody" was one of the songs on which Cecil used his tremolo mute.

21. The Brownies failed to record any song by that title during the March 1936 Decca session. Most likely, the tune was a blues composition written by black artist Papa Charlie McCoy. The record Milton received in the mail may have been by one of two artists: the Mississippi Sheiks (Okeh 8953, recorded Oct. 24, 1931) or Papa Charlie McCoy with Georgia Tom Dorsey (Vocalion 1712, recorded Feb. 4, 1932). McCoy rerecorded it for Bluebird on Apr. 3, 1936. Blues singer Washboard Sam (Robert Brown) also recorded the tune as "You Waited Too Long" on Dec. 16, 1938 (Bluebird B-8018).

The first western swing band to record McCoy's "Too Long" was Bob Dunn's Vagabonds for Decca on Mar. 2, 1939 (Decca 5667), with vocal by

Moon Mullican. Dunn's group was a studio band consisting of members of Cliff Bruner's Texas Wanderers. Bruner was not present at that session. Johnnie Lee Wills and his Boys also recorded "Too Long" on Apr. 28, 1941 (Decca 5957), with vocal by Cotton Thompson.

22. Decca actually began recording with Alabama's Rex Griffin on Monday, Mar. 2. Other artists recording included Jimmie Davis, the fiddle-guitar duo of Charlie and Ira Stripling, Shreveport's answer to the Brownies, Leon (Chappelear)'s Lone Star Cowboys, and the Cajun acts Joseph and Cleoma Falcon, Leo Soileau's Four Aces, and the Louisiana Strollers. Cowboy singer Roy Shaffer and the Paradise Entertainers, a Hawaiian unit, also recorded two titles apiece during Dave Kapp's three-week stay.

23. The cowboy hat was one of many items marketed that featured the Texas centennial emblem. After the Brownies returned from New Orleans, Milton had his picture taken while wearing the cowboy hat. He looked uncomfortable and forlorn in that photograph, wearing the hat at a jaunty angle along with his three-piece suit. It proved to be the last picture ever taken of him.

24. On Feb. 28, Milton received a Western Union money order for $50 from R. N. McCormick in New Orleans for travel expenses. McCormick's instructions read: "Reservations Made Hotel Desota See You Tuesday Morning Latest Regards." The Brownies left Fort Worth two days later (1936 was a leap year) and played dances on the road Mar. 1 and 2. Wanna Coffman believed that the Brownies played either Tyler or Longview on Mar. 1 and Texarkana on Mar. 2 before driving down the western border of Louisiana to New Orleans.

25. Rooms 238 and 240 in the Roosevelt Hotel.

26. Dave Kapp's assistant on these field trips was Harold C. "Brad" Bradshaw. R. N. McCormick, manager of Decca's three southern branches, was also in attendance. H. M. Crowe, Houston's Decca representative, also visited the makeshift studios at the Roosevelt Hotel during the three-week long session. See "Making Phono Records," *Billboard,* Mar. 28, 1936, p. 74.

27. Kapp's estimate was incorrect. The New Orleans sessions began on Mar. 2, 1936, and continued until Mar. 21, yielding 247 sides.

Chapter 11. Goodby Ma, Goodby Pa

1. For a wonderfully descriptive essay on the history of the Jacksboro Highway, see Mark Seal, "Thunder Road: The Jacksboro Highway Deals with Its Violent Past," *Scene Magazine* (*Fort Worth Star-Telegram*), Feb. 1, 1981, beginning on p. 6.

2. *Billboard,* Mar. 14, 1936, p. 5.

3. Needless to say, Sally Rand's Nude Ranch proved to be one of the festival's most popular drawing cards, attracting 52,000 paid admissions during the first week alone. See *Billboard,* Aug. 8, 1936, p. 43 for a description of the show. Rand's "Nude Ranch" was a misnomer. Viewers explained that she would have revealed more wearing a trench coat.

4. "Fort Worth Rosebuds," *Billboard,* Apr. 18, 1936, p. 41.

5. Fred Calhoun, who saw Milton later that night, confirmed that Milton had complained to him of having a "sour stomach" and said that he was not going to drink. Wanna Coffman also recalled that "if Milton had been drinking, I would have smelled it on his breath." After the accident, many people assumed that Milton had been drinking.

6. Milton told Roy Lee and others what had occurred that night during his five-day ordeal in Methodist Hospital. He knew nothing, or said nothing, about the cause of the accident.

7. "Girl Singer Is Killed as Car Smashes Pole," *Fort Worth Press,* Apr. 13, 1936, pp. 1–2. Also see "Deaths of Girl, Jockey Raise Auto Toll to 20," *Fort Worth Star-Telegram,* Apr. 13, 1936, pp. 1, 4. Dennis Prehoditch was working as a night watchman in Fort Worth's Trinity Park when he heard of the accident. Katy's sister Vera remembered a police officer arriving at the Prehoditch home and shining a flashlight in the window the morning of the accident. Vera, then thirteen, and Katy had attended church together Sunday morning.

8. Idell Rotosky later married Fred Calhoun. She has been unable to recall details of the night of the accident.

9. The cab driver, Maurice B. "Skeet" Young, was returning from a call to Lake Worth when he saw the wreckage.

10. See advertisement for the 1936 Pontiac Eight in the *Literary Digest,* May 16, 1936, p. 21. Thanks to Mike Sandusky of Sandusky's Magazine Art in Tucson, Arizona, for finding the Pontiac ad for me.

11. The photograph that appeared in the *Fort Worth Press* the next day distinctly showed the impression caused by the car's impact with the pole, which probably crushed Katy Prehoditch's skull, yet because of the angle of impact, missed Milton. Milton's injuries were incurred after he was ejected from the vehicle.

12. Narcolepsy is defined as "a syndrome of recurrent attacks of sleep, sudden loss of muscle tone (cataplexy), hypnagogic hallucination, and sleep paralysis." It is rare, but four times more common in men than in women. Symptoms have been noted in patients who have suffered from head trauma, encephalitis, or other acute infections. If Milton Brown indeed suffered from narcolepsy, it may have been brought on by his near fatal bout with appendicitis when he was a teenager living in Stephenville. See *The Merck Manual,* 12th ed. (Rahway, N.J.: Merck Sharp & Dohme Research Laboratories, 1972), pp. 1289–91.

13. The inquiries I made into the cause of the automobile accident that resulted in Milton Brown's and Katy Prehoditch's deaths convinced me that, despite rumors to the contrary, there is no tangible evidence of drunkenness, excessive speeding, or vehicular recklessness, nor was it in Milton Brown's nature to be capable of such irresponsible actions.

14. Dr. Ron Shearer of Bakersfield, California, provided me with the medical information necessary to understand Milton's injuries. According to Dr. Shearer, Milton was suffering from what is commonly known as acute post-traumatic respiratory insufficiency, or "shock lung," caused by respiratory

difficulty resulting from massive trauma to the chest. If not treated with proper maintenance of adequate ventilation to all parts of the lung and prevention of fluid overload, the patient would generally get much worse during the 24- to 48-hour period following the accident. Dr. Shearer also suggested that ventilation of the lung could have been accomplished through "positive end-expiratory pressure" (PEEP). Because of the steady deterioration of the patient, a single X-ray upon admission revealing a pulmonary contusion could have been misleading. By the time Milton was placed in the oxygen tent on Tuesday, he was probably already suffering from acute pulmonary edema. Antibiotics, which did not exist in 1936, might have saved him, but it was apparent as early as Tuesday that he would not survive.

15. Sadly, Katy's family could not afford a decent funeral, and the girl was buried in a simple pine box costing $12.50. Either the Prehoditch family's Russian accent was too thick or their handwriting was poor, because the undertaker misinterpreted the spelling of Katy's name and she was buried beneath a tombstone that reads "Kacherine Puhoditch, 1920–1936." (The undertaker also got Katy's birth year wrong. She was born in May 1919.) Ironically, Katy was almost exactly the same age that Milton's beloved sister Era had been when she died.

16. "Milton Brown Battles Pneumonia," *Fort Worth Press,* Apr. 15, 1936, p. 9.

17. "Brown Rallies," *Fort Worth Press,* Apr. 17, 1936, p. 12.

18. The Irving Berlin tune was a major hit for Fred Astaire, who recorded it for Brunswick (Brunswick 7609) and sang it in the RKO musical *Follow the Fleet,* costarring Ginger Rogers.

19. "Brown Is No Better," *Fort Worth Star-Telegram,* Apr. 18, 1936, p. 2.

20. "Auto Injuries Take Life of Milton Brown," *Fort Worth Press,* Apr. 18, 1936, pp. 1, 3.

21. O'Daniel's emotional eulogies and tributes to Mother, God, and American patriotism were all delivered with the skill of a modern-day evangelist preacher, although there were many who doubted his sincerity.

22. Sidebottom was a friend of Milton's who met him at WBAP, where both broadcast.

23. See "3000 Attend Last Rites for Milton Brown," *Fort Worth Press,* Apr. 20, 1936, p. 14. The *Fort Worth Star-Telegram* estimated the crowd at 3,500, an extraordinarily large turnout for any entertainer, even by today's standards.

According to Roy Lee Brown: "There was also a huge crowd that attended Milton's funeral at Smith Springs Cemetery. The many friends, fans, and kinfolk from Erath County and other counties came as well as those who followed the procession from Fort Worth. The people who lived near the cemetery had to take down their pasture fences so that everybody would have places to park."

24. The popular quartet, composed of D. P. "Dad" Carter and his three children, Ernest, Rose, and Anna, were originally called the Carter Quartet on WBAP and were sponsored by Morton Salt. In 1936 they replaced a male

western band called the Chuck Wagon Gang and assumed their name, playing a popular fifteen-minute program sponsored by Bewley Mills, which aired just prior to the Brownies' program at 1:00 P.M. See Harold Timmons's liner notes to *Columbia Historic Edition* (Columbia FC-40152), a retrospective on the Chuck Wagon Gang's recordings from 1936 to 1957. Six days after Milton Brown's funeral, the Chuck Wagon Gang had their first recording session for Uncle Art Satherley and Vocalion Records. The funeral service booklet listed D. P., Ernest, Lola, and Effie Carter as the musicians. Later on, the family assumed their more familiar nicknames: Patriarch D. P. became "Dad," Ernest became "Jim," Lola became "Rose," and Effie Juanita became "Anna" (and would also marry Jimmie Davis). Also see Roy Carter and Bob Terrell, *The Chuck Wagon Gang* (Goodlettsville, Tenn., and Asheville, N.C.: privately published, 1990), pp. 29–31.

25. "Milton Brown Is Auto Wreck Victim," *Sulphur Springs News-Telegram,* Apr. 20, 1936.

Chapter 12. There'll Be Some Changes Made

1. Nelly Caver listened to the Brownies' broadcasts from her home in Oklahoma. She now lives in Fort Worth.

2. Milton had scheduled a dance at the Elks Hall in Abilene for Monday, Apr. 20. His death came too close to the date for the hall to cancel their advertisement in the *Abilene Reporter-News.*

3. Gene Autry, with Mickey Herskowitz, *Back in the Saddle Again* (Garden City, N.Y.: Doubleday, 1978), pp. 53, 211. The movie completed production on July 18, 1936. Reviews were generally sour although it was well received by Autry's public. "Song stuff is cowboy yodeling and hillbilly whining. Too much of it" (*New York Times,* Mar. 24, 1937). In a letter to me, Autry said, "I was very familiar with Milton Brown and the Brownies and thought he and his band were very talented. They were quite popular in the '30s. Unfortunately, I cannot recall the circumstances surrounding my use of the Light Crust Doughboys as opposed to the Brownies for 'Oh, Susanna!'" (May 8, 1988). Marvin "Smokey" Montgomery, who appeared in the movie, recalled, "Milton had already signed a contract with Gene Autry to do *Oh, Susanna!* Had Milton lived, the Brownies would have made the picture instead of the Doughboys."

Roy Lee Brown believes that the reason the Brownies did not appear in Autry's movie was probably financial. As with Billy Rose, Republic Pictures had no idea of the amount of money the Brownies were earning from their dances and were unable to match it. The Light Crust Doughboys, on the other hand, were on salary from Burrus Mill and could afford to travel to California. The Doughboys were not a dance band and earned their salary playing personal appearances. Their inclusion in *Oh, Susanna!* proved to be good exposure for Light Crust Flour.

4. Musical shorts have had a long history in the film industry, dating back

to the 1910s. For a representative listing from one of the most prolific producers of these shorts in the 1940s, see Maurice Terenzio, Scott McGillivray, and Ted Okuda, *The Soundies Distributing Corporation of America: A History and Filmography,* (Jefferson, N.C.: McFarland, 1991).

5. "Blue Jackets to Open Series," *Fort Worth Star-Telegram,* Apr. 19, 1936, p. 6. This article listed the band's instrumentation as two violins, guitar, piano, banjo, saxophone, and bass. By the time the centennial celebration began, the band had been reduced to six: Blackie Simmons and Jesse Ashlock, fiddles; Bruce Pierce, guitar; Sam Graves, tenor banjo; Knocky Parker, piano; and Albert Brant, bass. Brant was later replaced by Brownie Simmons, Blackie's brother.

The role the Blue Jackets played in the centennial was relatively minor when compared to the other featured attractions at the exposition, including Paul Whiteman, Sally Rand, and a version of Billy Rose's musicalized circus, *Jumbo,* which had just completed a successful engagement at New York's Hippodrome Theatre. For a detailed description of the Texas centennial celebration, see Kenneth B. Ragsdale, *The Year America Discovered Texas: Centennial '36* (College Station: Texas A & M University Press, 1987).

Despite the amount of detailed information in the above work, neither the Blue Jackets nor the Brownies were mentioned. The only references I found to the Blue Jackets' role in the centennial were a captioned photograph in the *Fort Worth Star-Telegram* and a brief mention in a lengthy article in *Billboard* magazine. The photograph in the *Telegram* showed the Blue Jackets performing and noted that the band "plays at the free dance pavilion in front of the Monkey Mountain at the Fort Worth Frontier Centennial and at various points on the grounds." *Billboard* noted that the Blue Jackets "is [the] official band for midway attractions and plays for square dances at [the] pavilion, in front of [the] 'Jumbo' building just before performances and at the Chuck Wagon and Pioneer buildings on Sunset Trail" (Aug. 29, 1936, pp. 60, 65).

6. John "Knocky" Parker later became a member of the Light Crust Doughboys and the Flying X Ranchboys before getting his Ph.D. in English. He taught college in Tampa, Florida, while playing in various Dixieland groups with former Doughboy partner Marvin "Smokey" Montgomery for many years. I had the pleasure of knowing Knocky when he retired to Los Angeles shortly before his death in 1986.

7. Cliff Bruner would never again stray far from the Houston area. His band, the Texas Wanderers, became Texas's successor to the Musical Brownies' fortune. For details on Bruner's remarkable post-Brownies career, see my liner notes to *Cliff Bruner's Texas Wanderers,* Texas Rose LP TXR-2710, which contains recordings Bruner made for Decca from 1937 to 1944.

8. Born in Dallas in 1919, Christian is recognized as being one of the fathers of the electric guitar. A member of the Benny Goodman Sextet, Christian was even then a revered figure in music, commanding both respect and awe by black and white musicians alike for his revolutionary prowess on the guitar. He had only recently begun his professional career in Oklahoma City

when Perkins met him. Charlie Christian died of tuberculosis in 1942 at the age of twenty-three.

9. O'Daniel had been fired from the Burrus Mill and Elevator Company in 1935. Undaunted, the founder of the Light Crust Doughboys formed his own band around former Doughboys lead vocalist Leon Huff. O'Daniel called his band the Hillbilly Boys and in 1936 went to Mexico to play on border station XEPN. Perkins was one of the members of the band that helped elect O'Daniel governor in 1938. See Fowler and Crawford, *Border Radio*, pp. 115–47. Also see my liner notes to *W. Lee O'Daniel and His Hillbilly Boys*, Texas Rose LP TXR-2702.

10. Ocie rerecorded the song as "Turn Your Lights Down Low" at his first session with his own band the following September.

11. Decca also shortened the band's name on releases made when Milton was still alive. All Decca recordings featuring Milton Brown, including many LP reissues into the 1980s, read "Milton Brown and his Brownies."

12. The 1937 Bluebird session by the Wanderers now has its own place in history. It proved to be Harry Palmer's only appearance on record. His Armstrong-inspired trumpet playing is now revered among jazz fans. The entire session has been reissued on *Ocie Stockard and His Wanderers: The Famous Fourteen*, Origin Jazz Library OJL-8103.

Discography

This discography includes all 78 rpm commercial recordings made by Milton, Derwood, and Roy Lee Brown and recordings made by Roy Lee Brown for issue on audiocassette. Except for the 1932 Victor session, all issues are first takes only. There is no evidence that alternate takes exist for any of the Browns' Decca recordings, nor is there any evidence of radio transcriptions of broadcasts or privately recorded transcriptions of either Milton or Derwood Brown.

The first Milton Brown discography was originally printed in *Country Directory* (Issue #4, 1963, compiled by Bob Pinson). Portions of this discography were compiled with the help of Pinson's original work.

Label abbreviations

AU Aurora (Canada)
BB Bluebird
BR Brunswick (England)
DE Decca
EL Electradisk
MI Minerva (England)
MW Montgomery Ward
RZ Regal Zonophone (Australia)
SR Sunrise
VI Victor

Instrumentation abbreviations

(v) vocal, (hv) harmony vocal, (bj) tenor banjo, (f) fiddle, (sb) string bass, (g) guitar, (tg) tenor guitar, (sg) amplified steel guitar, (p) piano, (dr) drums, (oc) ocarina, (eg) amplified guitar, (m) mandolin, (em) electric mandolin.

"I" indicates instrumental performance. For information about the numerous reissues of material on LP, consult Willie Smyth's *Country Music Recorded prior to 1943* (Los Angeles: John Edwards Memorial Forum, 1984).

Fort Worth Doughboys

Victor

Milton Brown (v), Derwood Brown (g, hv), Bob Wills (f, hv), Sleepy Johnson (tg)
Jefferson Hotel
Dallas, February 9, 1932

70670-2 Sunbonnet Sue	VI 23653, BB B-5257, EL 2137, SR S-3340, MW M-4416, 4757, AU 415
70671-2 Nancy Jane	———

Note: Montgomery Ward issue M-4757 gives artist credit to "Milton Brown and his Musical Brownies."

Milton Brown and His Musical Brownies

Bluebird

Milton Brown (v), except where indicated, Derwood Brown (g, hv), Cecil Brower (f), Fred "Papa" Calhoun (p), Wanna Coffman (sb), Ocie Stockard (bj), tenor guitar on 82802-1

Texas Hotel
San Antonio, April 4, 1934

82795-1 Brownie's Stomp (I)	BB B-5775
82796-1 Joe Turner Blues (I)	BB B-5775
82797-1 Oh! You Pretty Woman	BB B-5444
82798-1 My Precious Sonny Boy	BB B-5558, MW M-4759
82799-1 Swinging on the Garden Gate	BB B-5444
82800-1 Do the Hula Lou	BB B-5485, MW M-4756
82801-1 Garbage Man Blues	BB B-5558
82802-1 Four, Five or Six Times	BB B-5485, MW M-4756

Note: Bob Pinson reports that some issues of B-5444 were issued as Fort Worth Boys.

Texas Hotel
San Antonio, August 8, 1934
Add Ted Grantham (f)

83860-1 Where You Been So Long, Corrine?	BB B-5808, MW M-4755
83861-1 Talking about You	BB B-5808, MW M-4755
83862-1 Just Sitting on Top of the World	BB B-5715, MW M-4758
83863-1 Take It Slow and Easy	BB B-5654
83864-1 Get Along, Cindy	BB B-5654
83865-1 Trinity Waltz (I)	BB B-5690, RZ G22668
83866-1 Loveland and You	BB B-5610
83867-1 This Morning, This Evening, So Soon	BB B-5610

83868-1 Girl of My Dreams   BB B-5690, RZ G22668
83869-1 Loveless Love   BB B-5715, MW M-4758

Decca

The letters A, B, C, and D follow each master number in the wax of the original recordings of all Decca issues. In most cases, only one take of each song was recorded. No member of the Musical Brownies recalls having to repeat any number, although Bob Pinson reports aural evidence of alternate takes occurring for C-9697 ("A Good Man Is Hard to Find"). Alternate takes on other Chicago selections and in New Orleans are hinted at by session cards at the Country Music Foundation, but the existence of these takes has not been proven. The presence of the letter D after a master number indicates a dub, a remastering due to the wearing out of the original stamper. This can be seen on issues of "St. Louis Blues" (DE 5070) and "The Object of My Affection" (DE 5072). Others may exist, but they have not as yet come to my attention.

Furniture Mart Building (Warner Brothers Studios)
Chicago, January 27, 1935
Grantham out. Add Bob Dunn (sg)
All recordings listed as "Milton Brown and his Brownies."

C-9691 Put On Your Old Grey Bonnet	DE 5134
C-9692 Pray for the Lights to Go Out	DE 5111
C-9693 In El Rancho Grande (vocal	
by Cecil Brower and Derwood Brown)	DE 5071, 46000
C-9694 Down by the O-H-I-O	DE 5111
C-9695 I Love You (from "Little	
Jessie James")	DE 5091
C-9696 Sweet Jennie Lee	DE 5091
C-9697 A Good Man Is Hard to Find	DE 5070
C-9698 St. Louis Blues	DE 5070, 46001
C-9699 The Object of My Affection	DE 5072
C-9700 Love in Bloom (from "She	
Loves Me Not") (vocal by	
Derwood Brown)	DE 5072
C-9701 Chinatown, My Chinatown	DE 5166
C-9702 Copenhagen (I)	DE 5158
Baile en Mi Rancho	DE 10097*
C-9703 Brownie Special	DE 5174
C-9704 Some of These Days	DE 5134
C-9705 Wabash Blues	DE 5108

Chicago, January 28, 1935	
C-9716 Beautiful Texas	DE 5071, 46000
C-9717 Just a Dream	DE 5317
C-9718 Cheesy Breeze	DE 5166
C-9719 When I'm Gone Don't You	
Grieve	Unissued

C-9720 Who's Sorry Now	DE 5158
C-9721 One of Us Was Wrong	DE 5317
C-9722 The House at the End of the Lane	DE 5194
C-9723 My Mary	DE 5080, 46001
C-9724 You're Tired of Me (vocal by Derwood Brown)	DE 5080
C-9725 (recording by Trio Melodias Mexicanas)	
C-9726 I'll Be Glad When You're Dead You Rascal You	DE 5149, MI 15166
C-9727 Sweet Georgia Brown (vocal by Derwood Brown)	DE 5121
C-9728 Shine On, Harvest Moon	DE 5121
C-9729 You're Bound to Look like a Monkey When You Grow Old	DE 5108
C-9730 Wheezie Anna	DE 5342
C-9731 Taking Off (I)	DE 5149
C-9732 Darktown Strutters' Ball	DE 5179
C-9733 Crafton Blues (I)	DE 5179
C-9734 Black and White Rag (I)	DE 5129, MI 15166
Blanco Y Negro (I)	DE 10097*
C-9735 In the Shade of the Old Apple Tree	DE 5129
C-9736 Little Betty Brown (calls by Derwood Brown)	DE 5194
C-9737 Going up Brushy Fork (I)	DE 5174, MI 14167

*DE 10097 is in the Decca Mexican series. Artist credit is by "Meliton Y Sus Rancheros."

Roosevelt Hotel (Rooms 238 and 240)
New Orleans, March 3, 1936
Add Cliff Bruner (f)

60610 Somebody's Been Using That Thing	DE 5201
60611 The Sheik of Araby	DE 5303
60612 Beale Street Mama	DE 5295
60613 Mama Don't Allow It	DE 5281
60614 Our Baby Boy	DE 5199
60615 Mexicali Rose	DE 5200
60616 Stay on the Right Side Sister (vocal by Derwood Brown)	DE 5281
60617 If You Can't Get Five Take Two	DE 5211
60618 Cielito Lindo (Beautiful Heaven) (vocal by Cecil Brower and Derwood Brown)	DE 5303
60619 The Waltz You Saved for Me	DE 5233, BR SA-1140

60620 The Eyes of Texas	DE 5209, 46071*
60621 I Had Someone before I Had You (and I'll Have Someone after You're Gone)	DE 5429
60622 I've Got the Blues for Mammy	DE 5199
60623 Texas Hambone Blues	DE 5226, MI 14167
60624 Easy Ridin' Papa	DE 5325
60625 Am I Blue?	DE 5272

*On release DE 46071, title is given as "Texas University–The Eyes of Texas Are upon You." Writer credit is given to Wylbert Brown.

New Orleans, March 4, 1936

60626 The Wheel of the Wagon Is Broken	DE 5209
60627 Memphis Blues	DE 5382
60628 Somebody Stole My Gal	DE 5462
60629 Under the Double Eagle (I)	DE 5429
60630 Washington and Lee Swing (I)	DE 5266, 46071*
60631 When I'm Gone Don't You Grieve	DE 5273, MI 15153
60632 The Sweetheart of Sigma Chi	DE 5239, BR SA-1140
60633 An Old Water Mill by a Waterfall	DE 5233
60634 The Hesitation Blues	DE 5266
60635 Avalon	DE 5462
60636 Sadie Green (The Vamp of New Orleans)	DE 5311
60637 Show Me the Way to Go Home	DE 5211
60638 The Yellow Rose of Texas	DE 5273, BR SA-1202, MI 15153
60639 The Roseland Melody	DE 5295, BR SA-1202
60640 My Galveston Gal	DE 5356
60641 Yes Sir!	DE 5260
60642 La Golondrina (I)	DE 5356
60643 When I Take My Sugar to Tea	DE 5201
60644 Song of the Wanderer (vocal by Derwood Brown)	DE 5251
60645 Right or Wrong	DE 5342
60646 Chinese Honeymoon	DE 5244
60647 Alice Blue Gown	DE 5311

*On release DE 46071, title is given as "Washington and Lee University–Washington and Lee Swing."

New Orleans, March 5, 1936

60648 Fan It	DE 5244
60649 Tired of the Same Thing All the Time	DE 5226

60650 I'll String Along with You	DE 5239
60651 Goofus	DE 5200
60652 "Ida," Sweet as Apple Cider	DE 5325, 46002
60653 When It's Harvest Time, Sweet Angeline	DE 5272
60654 Carry Me Back to the Lone Prairie	DE 5382
60655 A Thousand Good Nights	DE 5255
60656 Keep A Knockin' (but You Can't Come In)	DE 5251
60657 Baby Keep Stealin'	DE 5255
60658 The Old Grey Mare	DE 5260

Derwood Brown and His Musical Brownies

Derwood Brown (g, v), except where indicated, Johnny Borowski (f, oc), Robert "Buck" Buchanan (f), Fred "Papa" Calhoun (p), Wanna Coffman (sb), Wilson "Lefty" Perkins (sg), Ocie Stockard (bj).

Decca
Adolphus Hotel
Dallas, February 19, 1937

61866 Confessin' (That I Love You) (vocal by Ocie Stockard)	DE 5349
61867 The One Rose (That's Left in My Heart)	DE 5346
61868 Bring It On Down to My House Honey (vocals by Derwood, Ocie, and Buck)	DE 5394, 46002
61869 Louise Louise Blues	DE 5371
61870 How Come You Do Me Like You (vocals by Derwood, Ocie, and Buck)	DE 5486
61871 High Geared Daddy (vocal by Jimmie Davis)	DE 5349
61872 Honky Tonk Blues (vocal by Jimmie Davis)	DE 5400, 46137
61873 =BY BUDDY JONES=	
61874 =BY BUDDY JONES=	
61875 Long Long Ago (vocal by Ocie Stockard)	DE 5346
61876 I Can't Give You Anything but Love (vocal by Ocie Stockard)	DE 5443
61877 There'll Be Some Changes Made	DE 5486
61878 Rose Room (I)	DE 5443
61879 Cross Patch	DE 5413
61880 Everybody Loves My Marguerite	DE 5394

61881 I Just Want Your Stingaree
  (vocal by Ocie Stockard)   DE 5371
Note: On release DE 46002, artist credit is given to "Milton Brown and His Brownies."

Roy Lee Brown and His Musical Brownies

McClister's Electronics Company
Fort Worth, 1947
Records pressed by Swing Record Company, Paris, Texas
Roy Lee Brown (v), Clifford Kendrick (dr), Johnny Molleda (sb), Earl Milliorn (g), vocal on "Weeping Willow," Weldon Pitman (f), Johnny Strawn (f), Tommy Whatley (sg), Leon Worley (eg)

Unk MX#'s	Ice Man Song	Cowtown 101, Swing 101
	Weeping Willow	Cowtown 101, Swing 101
	Don't Ever Tire of Me	Cowtown 102, Swing 102
	Wednesday Night Waltz	Cowtown 102, Swing 102

Pantego Sound Studios
Fort Worth, August 27, 1989
"Western Swing Heritage"—Issued on Priority Records (cassette only)—PTS-3001

Roy Lee Brown (v), Randy Elmore (f, em), Wes Westmoreland (f), Johnny Case (p), Tom Morrell (sg), Billy Luttrell (g), Leon Rausch (sb, v), Bob Venable (dr).

If You Can't Get Five	
Take Two	PTS-3001
Texas Hambone Blues	PTS-3001
Stealing*	PTS-3001
Right or Wrong	PTS-3001
House at the End of	
the Lane	PTS-3001
Four or Five Times	PTS-3001
Roseland Melody	PTS-3001
One of Us Was Wrong	PTS-3001
Don't Ever Tire of Me	PTS-3001
You're Tired of Me	PTS-3001
I Had Someone Else	PTS-3001
Old Watermill	PTS-3001
Chinatown	PTS-3001
My Mary	PTS-3001
Theme	PTS-3001

*Written by Ellen (Mrs. Roy Lee) Brown.

McGuire Sound Studios
Arlington, Texas, March 4, 1991
"Western Swing Heritage II"—Brownie Recording Company (cassette only)—
No catalog number

Roy Lee Brown (v), Johnny Case (p), Randy Elmore (f, m), Billy Luttrell (eg),
Tom Morrell (sg), Leon Rausch (sb, hv), Bob Venable (dr), Wes Westmoreland (f)

> Beale Street Mama
> I'll Be Here*
> Yes Sir
> If You're Happy
> Stay on That Right Side Sister
> La Golondrina
> Corine, Corina
> Sitting on Top of the World
> Oh! You Pretty Woman
> Precious Little Sonny Boy
> Garbage Man Blues
> Sweet Jenny Lee

*Written by Ellen (Mrs. Roy Lee) Brown.

In addition to the above commercially released recordings, there are also
many private jam sessions and local get-togethers featuring Roy Lee and/or
Derwood Brown. I also have video recordings of Roy Lee Brown performing on many occasions between 1983 and 1991.

Song Analysis

Inasmuch as Milton Brown and the Musical Brownies established the initial repertoire of western swing, it is important to know how these songs were chosen and where they came from. We know that the Brownies spent many hours listening to phonograph records on the mezzanine of Kemble Brothers Furniture Company, learning melodies, lyrics, and chord progressions. But when they were on the road six days a week, they did not have the luxury of sitting around listening to records. Instead, Milton Brown often tuned in to network radio broadcasts, picking out popular tunes and teaching them to his band. Milton's sharp ear was able to memorize melody and lyric quickly. In conversations with his constituents, he also became attuned to what his public wished to hear the band perform. The Brownies' versatility and musical proficiency allowed them to adapt almost any song to their style. The ability to present a program of the songs most desired by their audiences was one reason the Brownies became as popular as they were in the early thirties.

Since the Brownies performed four hours or more each night, it became necessary for them to amass a sizable repertoire, most likely consisting of hundreds of songs. Having no documentation of actual dances or radio broadcasts to draw from, we can reconstruct western swing's original body of songs only through the commercial recordings of the Brownies and other groups. In this appendix, I have endeavored to speculate, based on aural evidence, comparisons, and testimony from the surviving band members, as to the origins of the Brownies' chiefly derivative repertoire.

I have listed the songs in chronological order beginning with the Fort Worth Doughboys recordings and ending with Derwood Brown's 1937 Decca session. The term "take-off" indicates an improvised solo, which was sometimes called a "chorus." Take-offs are listed in the order they occur on the record. A statement of the melody is not considered a take-off. "Writer" indicates the composer(s) of the tune, if known. "Notes" includes an analysis of the Brownies' recording plus a list of contemporary releases Milton and the Brownies may have heard at Kemble Brothers Furniture Company or on the radio. In some cases I list several possible sources; in others, a representative recording. Except in a few instances where there is no doubt about the source ("My Mary," "Somebody's Been Using That Thing"), this is strictly guesswork, but it gives us a good idea of some of the musical genres the Brownies drew their material from in the 1930s.

I'd like especially to thank Roy Lee Brown and record collector/historian Mike Kieffer for assisting me in this section. My gratitude also goes to the following record collectors who shared their collections and cumulative knowledge with me on this project: the late Don Brown, Eugene Earle, John Fraser, Bill Givens, Don Gray, Barry Hansen, Michael Helwig, Donald Lee Nelson, Harvey Newland, Bob Pinson, Alan Roberts, and John Tippet.

Fort Worth Doughboys

1. Nancy Jane
Vocal: Milton Brown; harmony: Derwood Brown and Bob Wills
Take-offs: None
Writer: Probably Big Bill Broonzy but listed as by Milton Brown.
Notes: Adapted from the Famous Hokum Boys' version (Banner 0716, Oriole 8013, Perfect 155, Romeo 5013, Jewel 20013), recorded April 9, 1930, featuring Big Bill Broonzy, Georgia Tom (Dorsey), and Frank Brasswell. Milton used all five verses of the Hokum Boys' version but was able to copyright the song after adding two of his own. Here are Milton's verses:

> We tell you no stories
> We tell you no tales
> When she starts to do her stuff
> She makes a tadpole hug a whale

> She don't go auto riding
> She don't take no chance
> When you go out with that gal
> You got to wear asbestos pants.

In the Hokum Boys' third verse, Broonzy sings "My heart started bumping and it got so hot it burned a hole in my undershirt." Milton sings "My heart got to *jumping* and it got so hot. . . ." Broonzy cut another version of the song as Big Bill Johnson for Gennett on May 2, 1930. It is unissued.

Blues/minstrel Jim Jackson may have cut the first recording of the song on July 16, 1929, for Vocalion ("Crazy 'bout Nancy Jane"). However, this version remains unreleased as well.

2. Sunbonnet Sue
Vocal: Milton Brown
Take-offs: None
Writer: Milton Brown
Notes: The melody was later used as the Musical Brownies' theme song with new words ("How do you do . . .") written by Milton Brown (see Chapter 5). This song is different from another song by the same title that was written by Gus Edwards and Will D. Cobb in 1908.

Milton Brown and His Musical Brownies

3. Brownie's Stomp
Vocal: None
Take-offs: Cecil Brower, Derwood Brown, Ocie Stockard, Fred Calhoun, Cecil Brower.
Writer: Milton Brown
Notes: This instrumental was written by Cecil Brower, although the copyright is in Milton's name. Cecil plays the melody, which is punctuated by brief four-beat breaks by, respectively, Stockard, Derwood Brown, Calhoun, and Coffman, exhibiting a metaphorical introduction of each Brownie. After that, the take-offs begin. When Calhoun finishes his solo, Brower returns with the closing melody, a variation on "Milenburg Joys."

4. Joe Turner Blues
Vocal: None
Take-offs: Brower, Calhoun
Writers: H. Brown and Cecil Brown. The record label indicated H. Brown and Cecil Brown as the authors. This mistake may have resulted from an error interpreting Milton Brown and Cecil Brower's signatures on the copyright form.
Notes: The song bears no resemblance to the W. C. Handy classic of the same name. Western swing bands of the 1930s played this melody under a variety of titles. Roy Newman recorded it as "Drag Along Blues" (Vocalion 02864, September 30, 1934) with credit to Newman as songwriter. Bob Wills recorded it as "Bluin' the Blues" (Vocalion 03614, September 29, 1936), giving writer's credit to Original Dixieland Jass Band pianist Henry Ragas. The song bears no resemblance to that song either. The Hi Flyers covered the Brownies' version of "Joe Turner Blues" for Vocalion on June 13, 1937.

Cecil Brower plays the melody on double-stops. Calhoun's extended solo includes long chromatic runs and a few rakes at the keyboard. Brower's "weeping fiddle," a favorite effect, makes its first appearance at the end of his solo and also concludes the recording.

5. Oh! You Pretty Woman
Vocal: Milton Brown; harmony: Derwood Brown and Ocie Stockard
Take-offs: Brower
Writer: Dan Parker
Notes: The first of four label appearances by the mysterious "Dan Parker," of whom nothing is known. It is possible that the name was a pseudonym for Eli Oberstein or an assistant at the recording session. The song was later recorded by Bob Wills in 1941 (Okeh 06640).

6. My Precious Sonny Boy
Vocal: Milton Brown
Take-offs: None

Writer: Milton Brown
Notes: Written for Derwood Brown's son, Milton Thomas, then six months old. The correct title of the song is "Precious Little Sonny Boy."

Milton sings the verse, and then delivers the first of his lyrical recitations. Al Jolson recorded a different song in 1928 entitled "Sonny Boy" (Brunswick 4033) that featured another moving, emotional recitation. Milton had a versatile vocal style, and adapted easily to a wide variety of tunes. However, his most obvious models were probably Jolson, Ted Lewis, and Cab Calloway.

7. Swinging on the Garden Gate
Vocal: Milton Brown; harmony: Derwood Brown and Ocie Stockard
Take-offs: None
Writer: Milton Brown
Notes: Brower plays strictly melody, trading off with Milton's vocal, also incorporating "The Old Gray Mare" into his performance. The song resembles many children's play-party songs, such as "The Green Grass Grows All Around."

8. Do the Hula Lou
Vocal: Milton Brown
Take-offs: None
Writers: Credited to "Dan Parker," but actually written by Milton Charles, Wayne King, and Jack Yellen.
Notes: A 1924 vehicle for Sophie Tucker, "the Last of the Red Hot Mamas," who was then starring in "Earl Carroll's Vanities." She recorded "Hula Lou" with the Arcadia Peacock Orchestra of St. Louis in January 1924 (Okeh 40129). Milton may have learned the song from Fred Calhoun, who was particularly fond of music from the twenties. Most of Milton's songs were contemporary hits.

Milton's foot-tapping can be heard throughout the song, which includes repeated vocal "end-breaks" (a device where all the instruments stop playing for two bars while Milton sings).

9. Garbage Man Blues
Vocal: Milton Brown; answers: the Brownies
Take-offs: Brower, Stockard, Derwood Brown, Calhoun
Writer: Sid Barbarian
Notes: The song was originally recorded by Luis Russell and his Burning Eight as "The Call of the Freaks" (instrumental performance: Okeh 8656, January 15, 1929), and later by Luis Russell and his Orchestra (vocal performance: Okeh 8734, Columbia 35960 and various foreign issues, September 6, 1929). See Brian Rust, *Jazz Records: 1897-1942,* 4th ed. (New Rochelle: Arlington House, 1978), p. 1345. The version that most resembles the Brownies' recording is "Call of the Freaks" by the Washboard Rhythm Kings, who were billed as "the Rhythm Kings" (recorded June 4, 1931, released on Victor 23279, Bluebird B-1848 and B-5028, and Sunrise S-3114).

The record begins with three beats on a snare drum to simulate the knocking of a door (Milton raps six times on Derwood's guitar for the same effect), followed by a spoken interchange (nearly identical in the two versions). Milton is the first voice saying "Lady, get out your can, here comes your garbage man." Stockard responds in falsetto, "Gittaway from here, man, I ain't got no gobbidge!" Fred Calhoun then introduces the song, playing ninth chords on the piano. This throws Milton off and he sings the entire first verse in the wrong key. Brower's take-off is in the correct key and the remainder of the tune proceeds well. Aside from the horrible gaffe, it is one of Milton's best vocal performances. The Cab Calloway call-and-response "hi-de-ho" interplay was also used on the Rhythm Kings' recording. The Brownies' record again gave composer credit to the fictional "Dan Parker." Charles Wolfe reports another possible antecedent for the Brownies' recording, the Tennessee Ramblers' 1928 Brunswick version, which was their most successful record.

10. Four, Five or Six Times
Vocal: Milton Brown; answers: the Brownies
Take-offs: Brower, Stockard (on tenor guitar).
Writers: Byron Gay and Marco H. Hellman (1927).
Notes: Written as "Four or Five Times," this song was originally recorded by Jimmie Noone's Apex Club Orchestra (Vocalion 1185, Varsity 1026, Melotone M-12543, Brunswick 80025, May 16, 1928), featuring Earl Hines on piano. Other performances of the song Milton may have heard include records by the Chocolate Dandies, McKinney's Cotton Pickers, the Hotsy Totsy Gang, and King Oliver and his Dixie Syncopators.

"Four or Five Times" is one of many black tunes brought into white string band tradition by Milton Brown. Bob Wills's pianist, Al Stricklin, claimed that Brown sang it during the KFJZ audition for the Light Crust Doughboy program. After the Brownies' Bluebird recording became popular, other fiddle bands recorded it, including Bill Boyd's Cowboy Ramblers and Bob Wills's Texas Playboys.

The Brownies' version again features the Cab Calloway call-and-response refrain. Writer credit is given to "Dan Parker."

11. Where You Been So Long, Corrine?
Vocals: Milton Brown; harmony: Derwood Brown
Take-offs: Calhoun, Brower
Writers: J. Mayo Williams and Bo Chatman (1928 or 1929).
Notes: Familiarly known as "Corrine Corrina," this tune was recorded by Bo Chatman (correct spelling: Chatmon) on October 31 or sometime in early November 1928 for Brunswick. His accompanists included Charlie McCoy and Mississippi Sheiks' co-member Walter Vinson (Vincson). The original issue (Brunswick 7080) was popular and was reissued in 1933 on Vocalion 02701. Despite the fact that the Vocalion record may have been readily available in Fort Worth, it is more likely that Milton learned the song from Cab

Calloway's version, which was recorded on November 18, 1931, and issued on the ARC labels (Banner 32340, Oriole 2396, Perfect 15551, Regal 218, Romeo 1766). Tampa Red and Georgia Tom also had an early recording of the tune, made December 23, 1929 (Vocalion 1450). "Corrine Corrina" became a hit for Red Nichols and his Five Pennies in 1931 featuring Benny Goodman on clarinet and Wingy Manone on trumpet and vocal.

Milton and Derwood Brown sing the words in harmony while Cecil Brower and Ted Grantham play the melody. With a "take it away!" Milton introduces Brower's take-off. Fred Calhoun's triplets provide a tasteful background for the vocals.

12. Talking about You
Vocal: Milton Brown; answers: Derwood Brown and Stockard
Take-offs: Brower, Calhoun, Brower, Calhoun, Brower
Writer: Unknown
Notes: The source for this song was probably Memphis Minnie and Kansas Joe's "I'm Talking about You," recorded February 21, 1930 (original issue: Vocalion 1476). Again, the dime store issues were probably more easily found at Kemble Brothers than the scarce Vocalion disc. The song was reissued on the ARC labels (Banner 32556, Oriole 8165, Perfect 0214, Romeo 5165) backed with "I'm Talking 'bout You—No. 2" (recorded July 8, 1930). Bob Wills learned this song from Milton and sang it for his last vocal recording, made for Kapp in 1969.

Cecil Brower's inclusion of "Chicken Reel" and the subsequent couplet by Milton: "Makes no difference just how you feel / You can always dance that chicken reel" was copied by Bob Wills on his 1936 recording of "What's the Matter with the Mill," a song that also originated with Memphis Minnie. Milton Brown sang that song at dances but never recorded it.

13. Just Sitting on Top of the World
Vocal: Milton Brown
Take-off: Brower
Writer: Walter Vinson of the black string band the Mississippi Sheiks credited himself with composing "Sitting on Top of the World" on the morning after playing a white dance in Greenwood, Mississippi. In the liner notes to *Stop and Listen Blues,* a collection of Sheiks recordings (Mamlish S-3804), album annotators Stephen Calt, Michael Stewart, and Don Kent contend that Tampa Red composed the melody. Regardless, the song became a staple in western swing bands after Milton Brown recorded it for Bluebird.
Notes: The Brownies' version is nearly identical to the Sheiks' recording, issued originally on Okeh 8784. Even Brower's solo resembles Lonnie Chatman's on the original record.

14. Take It Slow and Easy
Vocal: Milton Brown
Take-offs: Brower, Calhoun, Brower

Writer: Unknown
Notes: Milton Brown's vocal performance on this song is a good example that shows his use of his voice as a jazz instrument. After stating the melody, he improvised around it in subsequent couplets, just as any of the other soloists would do. See also "One of Us Was Wrong" (41 below) and Derwood Brown's performance on "Sweet Georgia Brown" (46 below).

15. Get Along, Cindy
Vocal: Milton Brown; harmony: Derwood Brown
Take-offs: None
Writer: Traditional
Notes: The song dates back at least to 1840 in American folk tradition, as both a folksong and a fiddle tune. Derwood Brown's bass runs are especially evident on this tune, reminiscent of Riley Puckett on similar numbers. Milton can be heard singing falsetto during the instrumental breaks.

16. Trinity Waltz
Vocal: None
Take-offs: None
Writer: Cecil Brower
Notes: This pretty waltz is similar to two traditional Texas fiddle tunes, "Kelly Waltz" and, to a lesser extent, "Wednesday Night Waltz." The Cartwright Brothers (Bernard and Jack) recorded "Kelly Waltz" on December 2, 1927 (Columbia 15220-D). W. Lee O'Daniel and his Light Crust Doughboys recorded it on April 8, 1934 (Vocalion 02727). Bob Wills recorded it as "Dreamy Eyes Waltz" on November 28, 1938 (Vocalion 05161). It also became a popular number in the repertoire of the Sons of the Pioneers. The Brownies' version was renamed in honor of the Trinity River, which runs through Fort Worth, so named because of its twin forks that merge into one.
   As on most waltzes, Wanna Coffman used his bow on this recording. In later sessions, Wanna dispensed with the bow altogether, even on waltzes.

17. Loveland and You
Vocal: Milton Brown; harmony: Derwood Brown
Take-offs: None
Writer: Written as "I'd Love to Live in Loveland (with a Girl like You)" in 1910 by English vaudeville entertainer W. R. Williams, who went by the pseudonym of Will Rossiter. Williams was purportedly the first person to advertise his songs in theatrical papers. Milton may have learned this song while performing with his vocal group in the 1920s.
Notes: The Brownies' performance features another moving recitation from Milton.

18. This Morning, This Evening, So Soon
Vocal: Milton Brown; answers: Derwood Brown and Stockard
Take-offs: Brower and Calhoun trade off three solos apiece.

Writer: Traditional
Notes: This song is known by several alternate titles, including "The Craw-dad Song," "I Had a Little Mule," "How Many Biscuits Can You Eat," and others. In black tradition, it was sometimes called "Dis Mornin', Dis Evenin', So Soon." Milton Brown also sang this song with the Light Crust Doughboys. It has been suggested that the source for the Brownies' recording could have come from the Carolina Tar Heels' version of "There Ain't No Use Workin' So Hard" (Victor 20544, recorded February 19, 1927); however, since Milton Brown listened to so few hillbilly records, it would more than likely have come from Jesse Ashlock.

Cecil Brower "rocks the bow" in his second chorus. Crystal Springs bouncer Blackie Brinkley occasionally sang this tune with the Brownies at dances.

19. Girl of My Dreams
Vocal: Milton Brown
Take-offs: None
Writer: Written in 1927 by trombonist/composer Sunny Clapp, "Girl of My Dreams" was the "B" side of Gene Austin's 1928 hit recording of "Ramona."
Notes: Milton sang this song with his trio in the late twenties.

20. Loveless Love
Vocal: Milton Brown; harmony: Derwood Brown
Take-offs: Brower, Calhoun, Brower
Writers: Written by W. C. Handy and Spencer Williams in 1921 as "Careless Love." Most western swing versions that followed the Brownies' used "Loveless Love" as its title. The song is similar to "I'll Be Glad When You're Dead (You Rascal You)."
Notes: This was the last recording of the Brownies' Victor sessions.

21. Put on Your Old Grey Bonnet
Vocal: Milton Brown; harmony: Derwood Brown
Take-offs: Brower, Calhoun, Bob Dunn, Brower, Calhoun
Writer: Written in 1909, with words by the Irish-born Stanley Murphy and music by ASCAP charter member Percy Wenrich. It was recorded by many artists, including Glen Gray and his Casa Loma Orchestra in 1931 (Brunswick 6100), a possible source for the Brownies' version.
Notes: On this, their first recording for Decca, the Brownies were still settling into the studio in Chicago and were probably a little nervous. Milton tried loosening them up by encouraging Fred Calhoun during his break ("Aw, beat it out, Freddy!"). Bob Dunn was apparently too far from the microphone and his solo sounded distant. He was moved closer as the session progressed.

22. Pray for the Lights to Go Out
Vocal: Milton Brown; harmony: Derwood Brown

Take-off: Brower
Writer: Arkansas pianist Will E. Skidmore
Notes: The song was made popular in 1917 by minstrel show comedian George O'Connor, who recorded it for Columbia (A-2143). It was also recorded by Joe Haymes in 1932 (Victor 24040).

Stockard and Derwood Brown introduce Milton by using his alter ego on KTAT: "Sing it, Brother Parson Brown!"

23. In El Rancho Grande
Vocal: Brower and Derwood Brown
Take-offs: None
Writer: Mexican composer Silvano R. Ramos (1934). English words were later added by Bartley Costello.
Notes: Cecil Brower only sang two songs on Brownies' records, both in Spanish with Derwood providing harmony (the other song was "Cielito Lindo"). However, he also sang "The Martins and the Coys" as a specialty number at dances and on radio. Cecil plays melody on violin with Bob Dunn providing the harmony on steel guitar.

24. Down by the O-H-I-O
Vocal: Milton Brown; answers: Derwood Brown and Stockard
Take-offs: Brower, Derwood Brown, Calhoun, Stockard, Dunn
Writer: Sam Fried. Taken from the Washboard Rhythm Kings' recording of "I'm Gonna Play down by the Ohio" (recorded October 18, 1932; Victor 23364 with reissue on Bluebird B-5028).
Notes: A showpiece tune that the Brownies performed only on radio, this was one of several songs that displayed the Brownies' musical expertise. Cecil rocks the bow with élan, followed by Derwood's single-string chorus on guitar. In introducing Calhoun's solo, Milton sings the word "piano" fourteen times. During Ocie Stockard's solo on tenor banjo, Milton says, "Play it, Rattlesnake, play it, boy!" referring to Stockard's radio nickname.

25. I Love You
Vocal: Milton Brown
Take-offs: Calhoun, Dunn, Brower
Writer: Written in 1923 by Harry Archer with French lyrics by Paul Combis. The English translation was composed by Harlan Thompson. The song was written for the musical play *Little Jessie James*.
Notes: Milton probably learned this song when his vocal group was active. Bob Dunn's solo is played entirely on the bass strings, emulating the sound of a trombone. Milton's vocal comes almost as an afterthought, after the three extended take-offs by Calhoun, Dunn, and Brower.

26. Sweet Jennie Lee
Vocal: Milton Brown; harmony: Derwood Brown
Take-offs: Calhoun, Dunn

Writer: Written in 1930 by the prolific tunesmith Walter Donaldson, some-time partner of Gus Kahn. It was a hit for the orchestra of Isham Jones late that year. The song's melody is similar to that of Milton's composition "Sun-bonnet Sue." Many people have confused these two songs, and have mistak-enly recognized the melody of "Sweet Jennie Lee" as the source for the Brownies' theme song.

Notes: Bob Dunn's take-off on this number was his best yet. Also note the feedback from Bob's amplifier, which indicates that studio personnel may have initially moved Dunn too close to the microphone. In later songs, Dunn either reduced the volume on his amplifier or readjusted his seating.

One of Dunn's frequent musical motifs was introduced during his take-off, a four-note phrase known to the Brownies as "the musician's call." During intermissions at Crystal Springs, the Brownies would be called back to the bandstand by Dunn, who would play this phrase on his steel guitar, the only instrument that could be heard above the din of the crowd.

27. A Good Man Is Hard to Find

Vocal: Milton Brown

Take-off: Calhoun

Writer: Written in 1918 by Eddie Green, this song was made famous by "the Empress of the Blues," Bessie Smith. Ted Lewis, Marion Harris, and Wilbur Sweatman also had successful recordings of it.

Notes: The lyrics were restricted to the refrain, which was sung by Milton Brown only at the end of the record (see "I Love You").

28. St. Louis Blues

Vocal: Milton Brown

Take-offs: Brower (using "flutter bow"), Dunn

Writer: W. C. Handy's classic, written in 1914, became one of the Brownies' most popular dance tunes, due in part to the arrangement, which saw the tempo increase during the number.

Notes: Bob Dunn's take-off includes the melody from the sacred tune "When the Roll Is Called up Yonder." At dances at Crystal Springs, the Brownies of-ten played "St. Louis Blues" twice nightly, each performance lasting up to fifteen minutes.

29. The Object of My Affection

Vocal: Milton Brown

Take-off: Dunn

Writer: A contemporary pop tune, written in 1934 by the team of Pinky Tomlin, Coy Poe, and Jimmie Grier. It was recorded by Jan Garber, Glen Gray, Grier, and others.

Notes: Milton and Mary Helen often sang this together while driving in their car.

30. Love in Bloom

Vocal: Derwood Brown

Take-offs: None
Writer: Known today as the theme song of comedian Jack Benny, this was also a contemporary hit, having been written in 1934 by Ralph Rainger and Leo Robin. It was made famous by Bing Crosby.
Notes: Derwood Brown gives an affecting performance of the song, without appearing maudlin.

31. Chinatown, My Chinatown
Vocal: Milton Brown
Take-offs: Calhoun, Dunn, Brower
Writer: Words by William Jerome, music by Jean Schwartz (1906). The song was featured in the 1910 Broadway musical *Up and Down Broadway,* featuring Eddie Foy.

32. Copenhagen
Vocal: None
Take-offs: Stockard, Brower, Derwood Brown, Calhoun
Writer: Music by Charlie Davis (1924). A popular jazz standard of the 1920s, this song was recorded by many bands, including exemplary versions by Fletcher Henderson's Orchestra (featuring Louis Armstrong and Coleman Hawkins) and the Wolverine Orchestra (featuring Bix Beiderbecke).
Notes: Cecil Brower plays the melody and utilizes two of his favorite motifs in his take-off: the "weeping fiddle" and the ubiquitous "rockin' the bow," which by this time had become a staple of Texas string bands. It was also used by Jesse Ashlock, Thurman Neal, and others. The Brownies' recording was chosen by Decca to be simultaneously issued on the label's Mexican series ("Baile en Mi Rancho," Decca 10097).

33. Brownie Special
Vocal: Milton Brown
Take-offs: None
Writer: Jimmie Davis
Notes: Davis recorded the song on May 26, 1931, as "The Davis Limited" (Victor 23601). With a harmonica imitating the sound of a train engine, Davis played the part of a railroad conductor, sonorously announcing the names and local attributes of towns on the railroad line from Atlanta, Georgia, to Shreveport, Louisiana. The Brownies' version features Cecil Brower playing a breakdown, as Milton Brown repeats Davis's patter, changing the railroad line to that of the I.G.N., which ran from Fort Worth to San Antonio, Texas. Along the way, Milton calls off the names of the towns of Waco, Belton, and Austin, and shows off his ability to duplicate Jimmie Rodgers's "human train whistle." The Brownies performed this selection only on their radio programs and never at dances.

34. Some of These Days
Vocal: Milton Brown
Take-offs: Calhoun, Dunn

Writer: Shelton Brooks (1910). Noted as the theme song of "the Last of the Red Hot Mamas," Sophie Tucker. Sophie's original hit recording was from 1911. In 1927 she recorded a new version with Ted Lewis, which became an even bigger hit than the original. It was also recorded by Bing Crosby in 1932.

Notes: Fred Calhoun rakes the piano keys in his chorus and Bob Dunn again uses the "musician's call" motif. Milton sings only the refrain, near the end of the record.

35. Wabash Blues
Vocal: Milton Brown; harmony: Derwood Brown
Take-off: Dunn
Writers: Words by Dave Ringle, music by Fred Meinken (1921).
Notes: Milton Brown sang many songs performed by Ted Lewis, including "Dinah," "The Lonesome Road," "Somebody Stole My Gal," and "The Darktown Strutters' Ball," in addition to "Wabash Blues." For the first time, Bob Dunn plays chords in his take-off instead of single strings. This song concluded the first day of the first Decca session.

36. Beautiful Texas
Vocal: Milton Brown; harmony: Derwood Brown
Take-offs: None
Writer: W. Lee O'Daniel
Notes: In 1932 W. Lee O'Daniel wrote a poem paying tribute to the state of Texas and set it to the tune of "Just Because," which was already a radio favorite. The earliest appearance of "Just Because" on record appears to be a recording by Nelstone's Hawaiians (Hubert Nelson and James Touchstone), recorded on November 30, 1929 (Victor V-40273). With Milton Brown's help, O'Daniel slowed the tempo of the song down and changed its meter from 4/4 to 3/4 waltz time. Although Milton helped O'Daniel with the new lyrics, he received no credit. Milton sang the song while he was still with the Light Crust Doughboys although the Doughboys were the first to record it, in 1933, with vocal by Leon Huff. Dave Kapp wanted the Brownies to record the tune on the second day of the Chicago session, so Milton telephoned W. Lee O'Daniel for permission to do so.

37. Just a Dream
Vocal: Milton Brown
Take-offs: None
Writer: Milton Brown
Notes: A pretty, sentimental melody that Milton often sang at dances.

38. Cheesy Breeze
Vocal: Milton Brown
Take-offs: Calhoun, Dunn, Derwood Brown, Brower
Writers: Words by Milton Brown, music by Cecil Brower.

Notes: Probably the most bizarre song in the Brownies' recorded repertoire, not only because of the lyric content but also due to the blatantly jocular mood of the instrumental breaks. None of the Brownies revealed what the "cheesy breeze" was, but they all snickered when questioned about it. I leave the possibilities to the reader's imagination.

Calhoun's take-off is especially unusual, laden with rakes and Chico Marx-like attacks at the keyboard. Brower's take-off includes a blues riff listeners might recognize in some of Bob Wills's later recordings, such as "Bob Wills' Special."

39. When I'm Gone, Don't You Grieve
The only Musical Brownies track that remains unissued. They recut it in New Orleans in 1936 (see 78 below).

40. Who's Sorry Now
Vocal: Milton Brown
Take-offs: Calhoun, Dunn, Brower
Writers: Words by Bert Kalmar and Harry Ruby, music by Ted Snyder (1923). A hit in 1923 for Isham Jones, Marion Harris, and the Original Memphis Five.
Notes: Bob Dunn emits feedback during his spirited chorus.

41. One of Us Was Wrong
Vocal: Milton Brown; harmony: Derwood Brown (1st verse)
Milton Brown (2d verse)
Take-off: Calhoun
Writer: Al Goering, longtime pianist-arranger with orchestra leader Ben Bernie, wrote the song in 1923. It was recorded by Ted Weems, with whistler-extraordinaire Elmo Tanner, on December 2, 1931 (Victor 22877), a possible source for the Brownies' rendition.
Notes: After Milton and Derwood's straight-ahead first verse, Milton sings one of his best "hokum" recapitulations of the melody in the second verse.

42. The House at the End of the Lane
Vocal: Milton Brown; harmony: Derwood Brown
Take-off: Dunn
Writers: Alfred Solman and Bernie Grossman
Notes: Roy Lee Brown still sings this song in a medley combined with the Fred Howard/Nat Vincent composition "(By a Window) at the End of the Lane."

43. My Mary
Vocal: Milton Brown
Take-offs: None
Writer: Stuart Hamblen
Notes: Milton Brown's most popular song, the one most fans remember him for, and also the one that helped popularize West Coast performer Stu-

art Hamblen. Hamblen made the first recording of it on November 13, 1931 (Victor 23685). A different version was cut by Jesse Rodgers, cousin of the famous Jimmie Rodgers. Jesse covered Hamblen's pairing of "My Mary" and "My Brown-Eyed Texas Rose" at his April 2, 1934, recording session for Bluebird in San Antonio (the Brownies would record there two days later). The song became so well identified with Milton Brown in the Southwest that many thought he had written it himself, possibly as a love song for his wife, Mary Helen. However, Milton had been singing "My Mary" before he met his future bride, possibly while he was still with the Light Crust Doughboys. It was recorded by W. Lee O'Daniel and his Light Crust Doughboys on October 6, 1934 (Vocalion 02872), with vocal by Leon Huff. Milton's heartfelt recitation is still effective today. This aspect of Milton Brown's vocal style was inspired in part by Ted Lewis's similarly sentimental talkovers.

44. You're Tired of Me
Vocal: Derwood Brown
Take-offs: Calhoun, Dunn
Writers: Vernon DeSylva and Lloyd Bryer
Notes: This was one of Derwood Brown's all-too-infrequent vocal solos. Fred Calhoun and Bob Dunn each take one of their best improvised solos, with Dunn practically exploding the strings of his steel guitar.

45. I'll Be Glad When You're Dead You Rascal You
Vocal: Milton Brown; answers: Derwood Brown, Stockard
Take-offs: Brower, Calhoun, Dunn, Brower
Writer: Charles "Cow Cow" Davenport (1931), well-known writer of jazz and novelty numbers such as "Mama Don't Allow It." Original title: "You Rascal You." Popularized by artists such as Louis Armstrong, the Mills Brothers, and Cab Calloway. The song was also recorded by Bob Dunn's idol, Jack Teagarden, in 1931.
Notes: Jimmie Davis adapted the song in 1932 as "Davis's Salty Dog" (Victor 23674). Milton probably heard it as the flip side to the Rhythm Kings' "Call of the Freaks," the source for "Garbage Man Blues" (Victor 23279). The Brownies' version begins with the melody to W. C. Handy's "Loveless Love." Milton's verses get more and more innovative as the song progresses. Bob Dunn is noticeably more relaxed on this second day of recording in Chicago. Brower tries to rush his "rockin' the bow" chorus, but the rhythm section holds him back.

46. Sweet Georgia Brown
Vocal: Derwood Brown
Take-offs: Calhoun, Brower
Writers: Words and music by Kenneth Casey, Ben Bernie, and Maceo Pinkard (1925). Bernie was the vaudeville performer who popularized the phrase

"Yowsah, yowsah!" that Milton Brown used on some of his recordings and at dances. "Sweet Georgia Brown" was a hit instrumental for Bernie in 1925. It was Bing Crosby's version released in the summer of 1932 that Milton and Derwood Brown heard.
Notes: Derwood does a good job performing this number as Cecil Brower provides an exuberant "rockin' the bow" chorus for the recording.

47. Shine On, Harvest Moon
Vocal: Milton Brown; harmony: Derwood Brown
Take-offs: Calhoun, Dunn, Brower
Writers: Words by Jack Norworth, music by Norworth and Nora Bayes (1908). Featured in the Broadway musicals *Ziegfeld Follies, Miss Innocence,* and *Ziegfeld Follies of 1931.* The 1931 revival of the song was spearheaded by Ethel Waters's recording (Columbia 2511).
Notes: Milton Brown chose to utilize the familiar chorus of the tune rather than include the relatively obscure verse. Later in 1935, Ray Lackland sang the verse in a recording with Dallas's Roy Newman and his Boys (Vocalion 03272).

48. You're Bound to Look like a Monkey When You Grow Old
Vocal: Milton Brown; answers: Derwood Brown, Stockard
Take-offs: Brower, Calhoun, Dunn, Brower
Writers: Phil Baxter and Bob Miller (credit is sometimes given to Alex Hill and Clarence Williams).
Notes: Two 1930 recordings of this jazz novelty record could have been sources for Milton's inspiration. Both featured two members of Clarence Williams's Novelty Band—clarinetist Cecil Scott and banjoist Ikey Robinson. As the Hokum Boys, Scott, Robinson, and pianist Alex Hill recorded it for Columbia on May 1, 1930. Three weeks later, on May 22, Herman Chittison replaced Hill on piano, and Clarence Williams was added on jug and vocals, as Williams's band recorded the song again (Okeh 8798). This extremely rare disc was not reissued during Milton Brown's lifetime. It is therefore likely that Milton heard the song performed on the radio.

49. Wheezie Anna
Vocal: Milton Brown; answers: Derwood Brown, Stockard
Take-offs: None
Writer: Leslie Sarony (1933)
Notes: Barry Hansen reports a possible source as a 1933 recording by the New Mayfair Orchestra, led by British dance band leader Ray Noble and released in the United States on the flip side of a Paul Whiteman record (Victor 24287). Writer Leslie Sarony was a popular British comedian of the thirties. Sarony himself recorded it for the English Imperial label in 1933 (issue #2831). Milton may have heard the song on a network radio broadcast over WBAP, Fort Worth's NBC affiliate.

50. Taking Off
Vocal: None
Take-offs: Dunn, Calhoun, Brower, Dunn
Writer: Bob Dunn
Notes: Bob Dunn's only recorded showpiece with the Brownies and a tune that became popular on the Brownies' radio program as well as at dances. The song is a bouncy number that gives Dunn ample opportunity to show off his stylish and playful embellishments. The song so inspired the late Alabama bandleader Hank Penny that in 1938, at his first recording session for Vocalion, Penny put words to the chord progressions from "Taking Off." The lyrics resulted from a sign Penny saw in the recording studio advising performers to "Back Up a Little Bit." In 1987, when Hank Penny appeared as a guest on my Los Angeles radio program, I surprised him by playing the Brownies' 1935 recording of "Taking Off." Without missing a beat, Penny sang the words to "Back Up a Little Bit" along with the record. He remarked afterward, "I always wanted to sing with Bob Dunn!"

51. Darktown Strutters' Ball
Vocal: Milton Brown; harmony: Derwood Brown
Take-offs: Calhoun, Stockard, Dunn, Brower
Writer: Shelton Brooks (1917)
Notes: A hit for the Original Dixieland Jass Band in 1917, this song was revived by Ted Lewis ten years later. A likely source for the Brownies' version is Tiny Bradshaw's 1934 Decca recording, which had just been released, backed by "The Sheik of Araby." Bob Wills and Tommy Duncan duplicated Milton and Derwood's vocal duet in their September 1936 recording session for Vocalion.
    Ocie Stockard takes a rare chorus, sticking closely to the melody.

52. Crafton Blues
Vocal: None
Take-offs: Brower, Dunn, Brower
Writer: Ocie Stockard
Notes: Named for Ocie Stockard's hometown, the song was written while Stockard was learning to play fiddle in the 1920s. He later taught the tune to Cecil Brower. Stockard recorded an unissued version with the "Texas High Flyers" for Brunswick on November 28, 1930. On this recording, it was probably Clifford Gross who played fiddle while Stockard played tenor guitar.

53. Black and White Rag
Vocal: None
Take-off: Brower
Writer: George Botsford (1913)
Notes: Botsford was a charter member of ASCAP. The song has been adapted easily into jazz as well as country tradition. The selection is a showcase

for Cecil Brower. It was released as "Blanco Y Negro" on the Decca Mexican series (Decca 10097).

54. In the Shade of the Old Apple Tree
Vocal: Milton Brown; harmony: Derwood Brown (verse 1)
Milton Brown (verse 2)
Take-off: Brower
Writers: Words by Harry H. Williams, music by Egbert Van Alstyne (1905)
Notes: Duke Ellington revived this chestnut with an instrumental recording in 1933.

Milton and Derwood sing a duet on the first verse with Bob Dunn providing chimes on his steel guitar in the background. Milton sings the second verse by himself, improvising around the melody.

55. Little Betty Brown
Vocal: Square dance calls by Derwood Brown
Take-offs: None
Writer: Traditional
Notes: Derwood Brown attended many square dances with his father and was an adept square dance caller, although he muffed his lines at one point on this record. When square dances were performed during Brownies' dances, a member of the audience did the calls. Possibly learned from a recording by the Kessinger Brothers (Clark and Luches).

56. Going up Brushy Fork
Vocal: None
Take-off: None
Writer: Traditional
Notes: The Brownies' Chicago session was completed with this breakdown featuring Cecil Brower. The melody is similar to "Cripple Creek." Like "Little Betty Brown," this tune was recorded by Clark and Luches Kessinger.

57. Somebody's Been Using That Thing
Vocal: Milton Brown; answers: Derwood Brown, Stockard
Take-offs: Dunn, Cliff Bruner, Calhoun, Brower, Dunn, Calhoun
Writer: Unknown
Notes: First recorded by the Hokum Boys on June 27, 1929 (Paramount 12796, Broadway 5060). Another early version was by Georgia Tom Dorsey on July 8, 1929 (Gennett 6933, Champion 15794, Suprtone 9512, and Varsity 6039). However, the version Milton Brown most likely heard was by the Famous Hokum Boys with Big Bill Broonzy, Dorsey, and Frank Brasswell (recorded April 8, 1930, and released on Banner 0712, Oriole 8010, Perfect 150, Romeo 5010, and Jewel 20010). The song was on the flip side of "Eagle Riding Papa," which was also covered by the Brownies. It was later recorded by Tampa Red on June 14, 1934 (Bluebird B-5572).

The Brownies kicked off their New Orleans session with this tune, and the difference in Bob Dunn's attitude is instantaneously apparent. He virtually explodes into his first chorus. Wanna Coffman's bass slapping is more evident in this session. He can be easily heard behind Fred Calhoun's piano solos. Coffman learned to pick up the rhythm that was lost when Calhoun took a chorus. Milton can be heard saying "Papa CAL-houn" for the first time, although it is nearly inaudible.

58. The Sheik of Araby
Vocal: Milton Brown; harmony: Derwood Brown
Take-offs: Dunn, Calhoun, Bruner
Writers: Words by Harry B. Smith and Francis Wheeler, music by Ted Snyder (1921). A popular western swing vehicle, this song is still performed today. Musicians often answer each line with the phrase "got no pants on!" Two hit instrumental versions were released in 1922 by Ray Miller and his Orchestra and the Club Royal Orchestra. The song became especially popular with English dance bands. A possible source for the Brownies' inspiration was the version recorded by Tiny Bradshaw and his Orchestra (Decca 194, recorded September 19, 1934). This version had the lyrics included and featured another Brownie cover, "Darktown Strutters' Ball," on the flip side.

This time, Milton hollers "Papa CAL-houn" audibly. He uses it many times in the ensuing three-day session. On the New Orleans selections, it is usually Cliff Bruner who plays the melody, with Cecil Brower playing harmony.

59. Beale Street Mama
Vocal: Milton Brown
Take-offs: Dunn, Calhoun
Writers: Words by Roy Turk, music by J. Russell Robinson (1923). Recorded as "Beale Street Papa" by Bessie Smith on April 11, 1923.
Notes: This song about Memphis's red-light district is arguably Milton Brown's finest hot vocal performance. Bob Dunn plays chorded triplets in his startling solo, urged on by Milton, who exclaims, "Oh, pick it, Mr. Dunn!"

60. Mama Don't Allow It
Vocal: Milton Brown; harmony: Derwood Brown
Take-offs: Stockard, Bruner, Dunn, Calhoun, Coffman
Writer: Charles "Cow Cow" Davenport (1929)
Notes: The Brownies were in a groove after Milton's powerful performance on "Beale Street Mama," and were given an opportunity to strut their individual talents in eight-bar breaks. Cecil Brower gives way to Cliff Bruner on this tune for the fiddle take-off. Wanna Coffman takes a booming, slapping chorus, which threatens to blow out woofers even on today's speakers.

61. Our Baby Boy
Vocal: Milton Brown
Take-off: None
Writer: Milton Brown

Notes: The song Milton dedicated to his infant son Buster Lee was all the more poignant, for it was recorded the day after Milton and Mary Helen's divorce was finalized. We can only imagine Milton's emotions when he sang the line, "And when your mother takes you from my arms . . ."

62. Mexicali Rose
Vocal: Milton Brown; harmony: Derwood Brown
Take-off: Dunn
Writers: Words by Helen Stone, music by Jack B. Tenny (1923)
Notes: This popular cowboy standard was not easily adapted for jazz improvisation. Nevertheless, Bob Dunn makes an attempt to play the melody in a somewhat mocking verse. Maybe he too wished that there was more to work with on the song. Tunes such as this were used to help pace a dance and let a crowd cool off before stepping up the tempo for another number. Many patrons preferred slower songs to dance to. Most western swing bands performed this tune. Gene Autry helped bring it to national audiences.

63. Stay on the Right Side Sister
Vocal: Derwood Brown
Take-offs: Brower, Dunn, Calhoun
Writers: Words by Ted Koehler, music by Rube Bloom (1933). Original title: "Stay on the Right Side (of the Road)"
Notes: This was one of Derwood Brown's best vocal performances. The song was better suited for him than Milton because of Derwood's ability to reach the lower vocal register. This is not to say that Milton could not have handled the tune himself. However, Derwood became adept at singing gutsy, jazzy songs of this type. It is Derwood who exclaims, "Yes, Brother Brower!" during Cecil's take-off.

64. If You Can't Get Five Take Two
Vocal: Milton Brown; harmony: Derwood Brown, Stockard
Take-offs: Bruner, Dunn, Calhoun, Brower
Writers: Joe Davis, Andy Razaf, and Paul Denniker
Notes: This song was recorded at least twice before the Brownies' version. The first time was by a New York jazz band led by Beth Challis, who went by the name of Peggy Johnson on Bluebird (B-6097, recorded July 18, 1934). The second recording was by Chicago blues shouter/pianist Georgia White, who recorded the song on January 21, 1936 (Decca 7149). It is possible that the Brownies heard Georgia White's version, although it may not have even been released by the time they went to New Orleans to record (a little more than five weeks after Georgia's session). Sometimes, Decca executives would forward sheet music or about-to-be-released discs to artists before recording sessions. This may have been done with the song "Too Long," which the Brownies never recorded.

65. Cielito Lindo (Beautiful Heaven)
Vocal: Brower; harmony: Derwood Brown (in Spanish)

Take-offs: None
Writer: Quirino Mendoza y Cortez (1919)
Notes: This pretty Mexican waltz served as a pleasant change of pace for the Brownies. Cliff Bruner and Cecil Brower lead off the tune with a charming twin fiddle rendition of the melody. Bob Dunn does not play on this song, or else he is inaudible in the background.

66. The Waltz You Saved for Me
Vocal: Milton Brown; harmony: Derwood Brown
Take-off: Dunn
Writers: Words by Gus Kahn, music by Wayne King and Emil Flindt (1930).
Notes: This was the theme song of Wayne King, "the Waltz King." It is a sentimental tune that Milton and Derwood performed well together. Again, Bob Dunn tries to do something with the uncomplicated melody after playing third harmony behind the twin fiddle lead. Tommy Duncan also sang a splendid version with Bob Wills in 1938.

67. The Eyes of Texas
Vocal: Milton Brown (1st chorus)
Milton Brown; harmony: Derwood Brown (2d chorus)
Take-offs: Dunn, Calhoun, Bruner
Writers: Words by John L. Sinclair (1903); music, anonymous. Melody based on "I've Been Working on the Railroad" and other late-nineteenth-century tunes. Sinclair wrote the words for a minstrel show at the University of Texas. It is still the university's fight song. In anticipation of the centennial celebration of 1936, Fort Worth violin teacher Wylbert Brown copyrighted Sinclair's lyrics. Brown gave Cecil Brower violin lessons in the 1920s.

68. I Had Someone before I Had You
Vocal: Milton Brown
Take-offs: Dunn, Calhoun, Brower
Writers: Jack Stanley, Harry Harris, and Joe Darcy. The song's complete title is "I Had Someone Else before I Had You (and I'll Have Someone Else after You're Gone)." It was recorded by Art Gillham, "the Whispering Pianist," in 1924. Milton probably learned it while he had his vocal group in the late twenties.

69. I've Got the Blues for Mammy
Vocal: Milton Brown; harmony: Derwood Brown
Take-offs: Dunn, Calhoun
Writers: Hy Heath and William Dougherty
Notes: The Brownies never performed this song before they recorded it in New Orleans. Cliff Bruner recalled being asked if he knew any songs the band could record and he remembered this tune from his years performing in south Texas medicine shows. Composer Walter Henry "Hy" Heath was a comedian in musical comedy, vaudeville, minstrelsy, and burlesque shows for three decades. Much of his material was used by early western swing

bands and also show bands such as the Shelton Brothers. After a few minutes of rehearsal, the Brownies recorded the song flawlessly, with Milton reading the lyrics that Bruner had scrawled on a sheet of paper. Milton's Jolson-tinged recitation of the chorus was delivered as if he had been performing it for years.

70. Texas Hambone Blues
Vocal: Milton Brown
Take-offs: Dunn, Bruner, Calhoun, Brower, Dunn
Writer: Unknown
Notes: Recorded as "Old Weary Blues" by Jess Young's Tennessee Band (Columbia 15493-D), this song came from black tradition. It was adapted by Milton to pay tribute to "Cowtown," a term for north Fort Worth, site of the city stockyards. Note Brower's intricate fills on the fiddle to imitate the sound of a train whistle after Milton's line: "Oh, yonder comes a train comin' down the track." Cecil would record the song (under the title "Blues Is Nothing") with Bill Boyd and his Cowboy Ramblers on October 27, 1936 (Bluebird B-6772).

71. Easy Ridin' Papa
Vocal: Milton Brown; answers: Derwood Brown, Stockard
Take-offs: Dunn, Calhoun
Writers: D. Ling and W. Benton Overstreet
Notes: This song was adapted from "Eagle Riding Papa" by the Famous Hokum Boys (Big Bill Broonzy, Georgia Tom Dorsey, and Frank Brasswell), recorded April 9, 1930 (Banner 0712, Oriole 8010, Perfect 148, Romeo 5010, Jewel 20010). Milton Brown substituted the word "easy" for "eagle" in the Brownies' performances of the song. It became the basis for the theme songs of the Aladdin Laddies, the Light Crust Doughboys, and Bob Wills's Playboys. Milton copyrighted the theme song while he was a Doughboy but allowed Bob Wills to customize the tune for his new group in Waco. Texas Playboy bands continued to use the song as their theme. Upon leaving the Doughboys in September 1932, Milton wrote his own theme song, based on his composition "Sunbonnet Sue."

"Eagle Ridin' Papa" was first recorded by Georgia Tom on July 8, 1929, for Gennett (Gennett 6919, Champion 15834, Supertone 9508, Varsity 6035). These issues most likely would not have been available to Kemble Brothers due to their scarcity.

72. Am I Blue?
Vocal: Milton Brown; answers: Derwood Brown, Stockard
Take-offs: Dunn, Calhoun
Writers: Words by Grant Clarke, music by Harry Akst (1929)
Notes: Ethel Waters sang the song in the musical film *On with the Show* and had a best-selling recording of it for Columbia in 1929. More great fills from Brower can be heard underneath the vocal.

73. The Wheel of the Wagon Is Broken
Vocal: Milton Brown
Take-offs: Dunn, Bruner, Brower
Writers: Elton Box, Desmond Cox, and Michael Carr (1935)
Notes: Recorded by George Hall and his Hotel Taft Orchestra with vocal by Johnny McKeever (January 31, 1936, Bluebird B-6267). This was one of three western-oriented songs the Brownies recorded in New Orleans. The others were "The Yellow Rose of Texas" and "Carry Me Back to the Lone Prairie."

74. Memphis Blues
Vocal: Milton Brown
Take-offs: Dunn, Calhoun
Writers: Words by George A. Norton, music by W. C. Handy (1912)
Notes: The song was initially an instrumental; words were added by Norton in 1913. Alternate lyrics were written for the political campaign of Memphis political boss Edward H. Crump.

A 1927 recording by Ted Lewis would have been a likely source for Milton's inspiration. Milton hollers, "Swing it, Brownies, swing it!" prior to the ensemble finish.

75. Somebody Stole My Gal
Vocal: Milton Brown
Take-offs: Dunn, Calhoun
Writer: Leo Wood (1918). The theme song of English bandleader Billy Cotton.
Notes: This was another hit for the ubiquitous Ted Lewis in 1931. Milton sings his final break accompanied only by Wanna Coffman's bass fiddle.

76. Under the Double Eagle
Vocal: None
Take-offs: Bruner and Brower, Derwood Brown, Bruner and Brower, Calhoun, Dunn
Writer: Josef Franz Wagner, to commemorate the United States' centennial in 1876.
Notes: Recorded by John Philip Sousa's band in 1909, the song became a popular march as well as an instrumental breakdown for fiddle or guitar. Derwood plays the melody on the Brownies' version. This was one of the few times a Brownies record had been previously recorded by another western swing band, in this case Bill Boyd and his Cowboy Ramblers. The Ramblers' 1935 recording (January 27, 1935, Bluebird B-5945) became their most popular number.

77. Washington and Lee Swing
Vocal: None
Take-offs: Dunn, Bruner, Calhoun, Brower

Writers: Music by Thornton W. Allen and M. W. Sheafe (1910). C. A. Robbins is occasionally credited as well.

Notes: With lyrics added by Thornton Allen, this became the school song for Washington and Lee University. The melody is similar to that of "Chinatown, My Chinatown."

78. When I'm Gone, Don't You Grieve
Vocal: Milton Brown; harmony: Derwood Brown, Stockard
Take-offs: Dunn, Bruner, Calhoun, Brower
Writer: Traditional
Notes: For some reason, the Brownies' previous recording of this song in Chicago was never released. In New Orleans the following March, they recorded it again. It is one of their more playful, exuberant numbers, with possible origins as a traditional play-party song. Barty Brown used to sing it to his children.

79. The Sweetheart of Sigma Chi
Vocal: Milton Brown
Take-offs: Dunn, Brower
Writers: Words by Byron D. Stokes, music by F. Dudleigh Vernor (1912)
Notes: Recorded by Fred Waring's Pennsylvanians and Gene Austin. Milton Brown may have been familiar with Ted Lewis's version (Columbia 1296-D, recorded November 18, 1927).

During Milton's vocal, Cecil Brower clamped his tremolo mute on his violin. He had purchased it at Sparks's Fiddle Shop in Fort Worth. Wylbert Brown had used the device during his vaudeville career, and both Brower and fellow student Kenneth Pitts learned its use. Brower used it only on slow, sentimental numbers. It is rarely employed today.

80. An Old Water Mill by a Waterfall
Vocal: Milton Brown
Take-offs: Dunn, Calhoun, Dunn, Bruner and Brower
Writers: Words by Charles Tobias and Jack Scholl, music by Murray Mencher (1934)
Original Title: "An Old Water Mill"
Notes: Recorded by sweet-band leader Vincent Lopez. On the Brownies' recording, Bob Dunn attempts to play the melody, but one can hear him straining to let loose with a hot chorus. His second solo consists entirely of chords.

81. The Hesitation Blues
Vocal: Milton Brown; answers: Derwood Brown, Stockard
Take-offs: Dunn, Bruner, Calhoun, Brower
Writers: Billy Smythe, Scott Middleton, and Art Gillham
Notes: The introduction to this song is similar to the Brownies' version of "Somebody's Been Using That Thing." Alabama string band leader Hank Penny copied the Brownies' version at his first session for Vocalion in 1938.

82. Avalon
Vocal: Milton Brown
Take-offs: Dunn, Calhoun, Bruner and Brower
Writers: Words by Al Jolson and Buddy DeSylva, music by Vincent Rose (1920). Based on Giacomo Puccini's aria "E lucevan le stelle" from *Tosca*. Puccini and his publishers were awarded $25,000 in damages and future royalties as a result of a lawsuit based on the musical "borrowing."
Notes: Al Jolson's hit recording came in 1921.

83. Sadie Green (The Vamp of New Orleans)
Vocal: Milton Brown
Take-offs: Dunn, Calhoun
Writers: Gilbert Wells and Johnny Dunn
Notes: The source for this song, recorded by a variety of jazz bands in 1926, was probably Fred Calhoun. Dallas's Roy Newman recorded the song before the Brownies, in September 1935, with vocal by Earl Brown.

84. Show Me the Way to Go Home
Vocal: Milton Brown; harmony: Derwood Brown (Verse 1)
Milton Brown (Verse 2)
Take-offs: Dunn, Bruner, Calhoun, Brower
Writers: "Irving King" (pseudonym for the team of Reginald Connelly and Jimmy Campbell) (1925). The title was taken from Archie Morrow's "Show Me the Way to Go Home, Baby" (1901).
Notes: A hit for Vincent Lopez in 1926. The Brownies' version became popular when Milton sang the second verse "tipsy," complete with hiccoughs, tacking on a portion of "How Dry I Am."

85. The Yellow Rose of Texas
Vocal: Milton Brown; harmony: Derwood Brown
Take-offs: None
Writer: A traditional tune dating back to 1858, this song is also known as "The Song of the Texas Rangers."
Notes: Cowboy songs were a little out of Milton Brown's element. However, with the centennial approaching, the Brownies offered their version of the western classic, which had been recorded by Gene Autry in 1933.

86. The Roseland Melody
Vocal: Milton Brown
Take-offs: None
Writers: Words by Milton Brown, music by Cecil Brower
Notes: Milton was at his best when interpreting his own material. This sentimental melody was enhanced by Cecil Brower's use of Wylbert Brown's tremolo mute. Roy Lee Brown and the late Mineral Wells, Texas, fiddle player, Tommy Camfield, often duplicated the Brownies' performance in various Texas settings in the 1980s. According to Fred Calhoun, Brower was try-

ing to play "The Naughty Waltz" when he inadvertently arrived at an entirely new melody.

87. My Galveston Gal
Vocal: Milton Brown
Take-offs: Dunn, Calhoun, Bruner
Writers: Words by Phil Harris, music by George "Buzz" Adlam (1933)
Notes: The melody is similar to the instrumental "Dill Pickle Rag." The breathy, word-packed lyrics were appropriate for Phil Harris's frenetic style. Milton had his work cut out for him in handling this deceptively easy tune.

88. Yes Sir!
Vocal: Milton Brown; answers: Derwood Brown, Stockard
Take-offs: Dunn, Bruner, Calhoun, Brower
Writers: Edgar Dowell and Andy Razaf
Notes: Recorded by the Washboard Rhythm Kings as "Yes Suh!" on December 14, 1932 (Vocalion 1731, Brunswick 01504). With Derwood and Ocie Stockard acting as the agreeable answer-men, Milton sings the song in his best Ben Bernie "yowsah" delivery backed by Wanna Coffman's slapping bass. This recording, more than any other, demonstrates the Brownies' rhythmic superiority and shows why they had no need for drums. The ensemble ending is one of the Brownies' most spirited Dixieland finishes, with Milton joining in, yelling, "ha-ha-HAA." The Brownies' recording had a tremendous impact on north Texas musician Dave Stogner, whose 1957 recording of "Yes, Sir!" also for Decca, rivaled the Brownies' for enthusiasm.

89. La Golondrina
Vocal: None
Take-offs: None
Writer: Music by Narciso Serradell (1883). Words later added by L. Wolfe Gilbert.
Notes: Cecil Brower slows down the hectic pace set by the previous tune and plays the Southern Melody Boys' old theme song using his tremolo mute, much as he might have done before he joined the Brownies early in 1933. The song was usually played as an instrumental by early western swing bands. Note that Wanna Coffman had totally abandoned his bow by this time, even on waltzes. The song was used by Bob Wills in a 1940 medley of Spanish waltzes, which also included "Lady of Spain" and "Cielito Lindo."

90. When I Take My Sugar to Tea
Vocal: Milton Brown
Take-offs: Dunn, Calhoun
Writers: Words by Irving Kahal and Pierre Norman, music by Sammy Fain (1931). Featured in the Marx Brothers film *Monkey Business,* in which it was played on the piano by Chico Marx. The Boswell Sisters had a successful recording in 1931.

91. Song of the Wanderer
Vocal: Derwood Brown
Take-offs: Dunn, Calhoun
Writer: Neil Moret (1926)
Notes: A popular song for hotel orchestras, vocal versions of the song were later recorded by Art Landry and Annette Hanshaw, among others. Bob Dunn seems uncomfortable on his take-off. The long second day of the New Orleans session was coming to a close. The Brownies were to record twenty-two selections that day, the most productive day of their recording career.

92. Right or Wrong
Vocal: Milton Brown; harmony: Derwood Brown (Verse 1)
Milton (Verse 2)
Take-offs: Dunn, Calhoun
Writers: Haven Gillespie, Arthur Sizemore, and Paul Biese (1929)
Notes: Recorded by Emmett Miller on January 19, 1929 (Okeh 41280), this song was a favorite of both Milton Brown and Bob Wills. Milton sang it when he was vocalist with the Light Crust Doughboys. After Milton left to form his own band, Wills added it to his own repertoire. Emmett Miller rerecorded the song in June 1936, for Bluebird, followed by Wills's own recording that September. However, it was the Brownies' version that initiated the song into the western swing repertoire. Milton and Derwood sing the first verse together and begin to sing the second together as well. But Derwood drops out, realizing it is Milton's hokum chorus.

93. Chinese Honeymoon
Vocal: Milton Brown; harmony: Derwood Brown
Take-offs: Dunn, Calhoun, Bruner
Writers: W. L. Shackley and Charles Hausman
Original title: "Hong Kong Honeymoon"
Notes: Recorded by W. Lee O'Daniel's Hillbilly Boys in 1937 as "On a Chinese Honeymoon" with vocal by Leon Huff.

94. Alice Blue Gown
Vocal: Milton Brown
Take-offs: Dunn, Calhoun, Brower
Writers: Words by Joseph McCarthy, music by Harry Tierney (1919), featured in the Broadway musical *Irene*.
Notes: First popularized by Broadway star Edith Day in a 1920 recording (Victor 45173).

95. Fan It
Vocal: Milton Brown; harmony: Derwood Brown, Stockard
Take-offs: Dunn, Calhoun, Brower
Writers: Frankie "Half-Pint" Jaxon and Dan Howell
Notes: The diminutive Jaxon recorded the song for the ARC labels on November 28, 1928. The Brownies were the first to introduce this number to

other western swing bands, including Bill Boyd's Cowboy Ramblers and Bob Wills's Texas Playboys.

96. Tired of the Same Thing All the Time
Vocal: Milton Brown
Take-offs: Dunn, Calhoun, Brower
Writer: Bill Gaither (Leroy's Buddy). Gaither recorded the song for Decca as "Tired of That Same Stuff All the Time" (Decca 7141) on December 15, 1935.
Notes: Similar to other blues performed by western swing bands: "Weary of the Same Ol' Stuff" (Wills), "Gittin' Tired" (Rambling Rangers), and "Louise Louise Blues" (Derwood Brown).

97. I'll String Along with You
Vocal: Milton Brown
Take-offs: None.
Writers: Words by Al Dubin, music by Harry Warren (1934)
Notes: From the musical film *Twenty Million Sweethearts,* starring Dick Powell and featuring Ginger Rogers, the Mills Brothers, and the Ted Fio Rito Orchestra. Fio Rito performed the song in the film and on record (Brunswick 6859) with vocal by Muzzy Marcellino. Cecil Brower, who played the melody using his mute, joined Fio Rito for several years in the late thirties.

98. Goofus
Vocal: Milton Brown
Take-offs: Dunn, Bruner, Stockard, Brower
Writers: Words by Gus Kahn, music by Wayne King and William Harold (1930)
Notes: An instrumental hit for Wayne King in 1931. Gus Kahn's words were added and Dick Robertson sang them with Red Nichols and his Five Pennies the following year. Cecil Brower starts off the tune with a lively display of the melody. Fred Calhoun helped work out the sophisticated coda.

99. "Ida," Sweet as Apple Cider
Vocal: Milton Brown
Take-offs: Dunn, Brower
Writers: Words by Eddie Leonard, music by Eddie Munson (1903). Featured in the 1919 Broadway musical *Roly Boly Eyes.* Instrumental hit recording by Red Nichols in 1927. It was also the theme song of musical comedian Eddie Cantor.
Notes: This was the first song Bob Dunn ever played with the Brownies, during his on-air audition on KTAT when he borrowed Wanna Coffman's unamplified steel guitar.

100. When It's Harvest Time, Sweet Angeline
Vocal: Milton Brown
Take-offs: Dunn, Calhoun, Bruner and Brower

Writer: Harry Tobias
Notes: Bill Boyd and his Cowboy Ramblers recorded this tune before the
Brownies ("Harvest Time," Bluebird B-5894, recorded January 27, 1935)
with Bill singing lead and brother Jim singing harmony. Like fellow WRR sta-
blemates Roy Newman and his Boys, Bill Boyd learned many tunes for his
radio band from Brownies broadcasts, sometimes even beating them to the
recording studio. In the beginning a four-man cowboy group, the Cowboy
Ramblers developed into a ten-piece western swing band, utilizing many of
the components initiated by the Brownies (Cecil Brower recorded with Boyd
while he was on staff at WRR in 1937).

101. Carry Me Back to the Lone Prairie
Vocal: Milton Brown
Take-offs: None
Writer: Traditional folksong, copyrighted and adapted by Carson Robison
(1934).
Notes: A contemporary cowboy number sung by Milton with Brower and
his tremolo mute in the background.

102. A Thousand Good Nights
Vocal: Milton Brown
Take-offs: Dunn, Brower and Bruner
Writer: Walter Donaldson (1934)
Notes: This song would have made a fitting close to the intensive three-day
recording session in New Orleans, and a wistful farewell for Milton, who
had only six weeks to live. It conveyed all of the honest emotion that made
him a beloved figure in the Southwest. However, there were still three songs
left to record. "A Thousand Good Nights" was recorded by dance band leader Don Bestor (March 14, 1934; Victor 24587), backed with "Little Dutch
Mill," a song Milton Brown sang but never recorded.

103. Keep A Knockin' (but You Can't Come In)
Vocal: Milton Brown
Take-offs: Dunn, Calhoun
Writer: Perry Bradford, musical director for Mamie Smith and other "classic
blues" performers in New York City during the 1920s.
Notes: Another popular western swing standard later recorded by Bob Wills
with vocal by Tommy Duncan.

104. Baby Keep Stealin'
Vocal: Milton Brown
Take-offs: Dunn, Calhoun, Bruner
Writer: Unknown
Notes: Recorded by the Mississippi Sheiks as "Baby Keeps Stealin' Lovin' on
Me" (Okeh 8843, recorded June 12, 1930). This was another song from the
family of "Bring It On Down to My House."

105. The Old Grey Mare
Vocal: Milton Brown; harmony: Derwood Brown
Take-offs: Dunn, Calhoun, Stockard
Writers: Words possibly by Gus Bailey, music arranged by Frank Panella.
Based on J. Warner's 1858 "Down in Alabam," also known as "Got Out (Get
Out of) the Wilderness." The song was used in Abraham Lincoln's 1860 pres-
idential campaign with new lyrics, entitled "Old Abe Lincoln."
Notes: The final song Milton Brown sang on record was recommended by
Dave Kapp as an afterthought. The Brownies stumbled through it even
though they had never performed it before. Milton can be heard whinnying
during the recording. They were obviously enjoying themselves but were
understandably light-headed after their long three-day ordeal.

Derwood Brown and His Musical Brownies

106. Confessin' (That I Love You)
Vocal: Ocie Stockard
Take-offs: Calhoun, Lefty Perkins
Writers: Words by A. J. Neiburg, music by Doc Dougherty and Ellis Reynolds
(1930). Original title: "I'm Confessin' That I Love You."
Notes: Ocie Stockard assumed Milton's vocal chores on this number, which
was a hit for Guy Lombardo and Rudy Vallee in 1930. Stockard's voice had a
rawer edge than Milton's rounded tones, but Ocie was better suited to sentimental songs than Derwood Brown, who preferred up-tempo jazz and blues.
The difference between the pre– and post–Milton Brown Brownies is immediately noticeable with the smooth twin fiddle introduction by Buck
Buchanan and Johnny Borowski. Lefty Perkins's steel guitar solo consisted
entirely of dizzying triad chords.

107. The One Rose (That's Left in My Heart)
Vocal: Derwood Brown
Take-off: Perkins
Writers: Del Lyon and Lani McIntyre (1929). Popularly revived in 1937 by
Bing Crosby, Larry Clinton, and Art Kassel.
Notes: Hawaiian tunes made a resurgence after Milton Brown's death, with
Hawaiian bandleader Lani McIntyre as one of the genre's leaders. Bing Cros-
by's "Sweet Leilani" and "Blue Hawaii" were both recorded with McIntyre's
orchestra. Derwood Brown gives a credible performance but is obviously
struggling with the song. Lefty Perkins's Hawaiian solo passage is played single-string.

108. Bring It On Down to My House
Vocals: Derwood Brown, Stockard, Buchanan, Derwood Brown
Take-offs: Perkins, Calhoun, Buchanan
Writer: Unknown
Notes: Three of the Brownies switched off in singing the humorous two-line

couplets on this popular western swing standard, patterned after songs such as Memphis Minnie's "What's the Matter with the Mill?" Derwood's recording was a popular seller, and when Decca inaugurated its postwar 46000 series, this song was issued, backed with Milton's "'Ida,' Sweet as Apple Cider." However, Derwood's recording was mistakenly labeled as by his late brother. This was one of five songs from this session that Ocie Stockard recorded in September with his band the Wanderers for Bluebird.

109. Louise Louise Blues
Vocal: Derwood Brown
Take-offs: None
Writer: Johnnie Temple, recorded November 12, 1936 (Decca 7244)
Notes: Derwood puts his all into this slow blues, backed by Lefty Perkins's steel fills.

110. How Come You Do Me Like You Do
Vocals: Derwood Brown, Stockard, Buchanan
Take-offs: Perkins, Calhoun
Writers: Gene Austin and Roy Bergere (1924). It was a hit for 1920s vocalist Marion Harris that year.
Notes: Another song featuring the twin fiddle lead of Buchanan and Borowski, duplicated in Ocie Stockard's recording for Bluebird later in 1937.

111. High Geared Daddy
Vocal: Jimmie Davis
Take-offs: Perkins, Calhoun, Buchanan
Writer: Buddy Jones
Notes: Jimmie Davis recruited the Brownies for two songs during the February 1937 session. Davis's friend, Buddy Jones, adapted this risqué blues for Davis's use. According to Lefty Perkins, Davis required an assistant to cue him when it was his turn to sing, due to the future governor's faulty timing.

112. Honky Tonk Blues
Vocal: Jimmie Davis
Take-off: Calhoun
Writer: Jimmie Davis
Notes: This song is not the same as the one made popular by Hank Williams. Instead, it was the Shelton Brothers' "Deep Elem Blues" with new lyrics by Davis. Jimmie Davis met Milton Brown on several occasions at Crystal Springs, joining the Brownies as their guest vocalist.

113. Long Long Ago
Vocal: Ocie Stockard
Take-offs: Perkins, Calhoun
Writer: Thomas Haynes Bayly (1833). It was also the basis for the 1942 Andrews Sisters hit, "Don't Sit under the Apple Tree (with Anyone Else but Me)."

Notes: Lefty Perkins delivers a fiery chorded solo in this number, the third song from the session that was later recut by Ocie Stockard. Perkins was not around for that session. His place was taken in the Wanderers by trumpet player/grocer Harry Palmer.

114. I Can't Give You Anything but Love
Vocal: Ocie Stockard
Take-offs: Perkins, Calhoun
Writers: Words by Dorothy Fields, music by Jimmy McHugh (1928). Featured in the Broadway musical *Blackbirds of 1928*. The idea for the song came when Fields and McHugh eavesdropped on a poor couple window-shopping in front of Tiffany's in New York City. The two composers raced home and wrote the song in an hour.
Notes: Billie Holiday revived the song in a performance with Teddy Wilson's orchestra in 1936.

115. There'll Be Some Changes Made
Vocal: Derwood Brown
Take-offs: Calhoun, Buchanan
Writers: W. Benton Overstreet and Billy Higgins (1921). Featured in the Broadway musical *Bubbling Brown Sugar*.
Notes: Earl Brown sang the first western swing recording of the song in 1935 with Roy Newman and his Boys for Vocalion. Again, Buck Buchanan's melodic, sophisticated twin fiddle introduction helped usher in a new, more stylish era for western swing. The intro is identical to that of "Kickin' the Cat" by Joe Venuti's Blue Four (Okeh 40853, recorded June 28, 1927). Buchanan and Borowski later duplicated the intro on Ocie Stockard's swinging version for Bluebird with the Wanderers.

116. Rose Room
Vocal: None
Take-offs: Perkins, Calhoun, Buchanan
Writer: Art Hickman (1918). Lyrics later added by Harry Williams.
Notes: The only instrumental recorded by Derwood Brown and his Musical Brownies is one of the best tracks of the entire session. Led by Buchanan and Borowski's twin fiddle lead, the song churns along, thanks to the potent rhythm section of Calhoun, Coffman, Stockard, and Derwood Brown. This tune had been a staple of the Milton Brown-led Brownies as well.

117. Cross Patch
Vocal: Derwood Brown
Take-offs: Borowski, Buchanan, Borowski, Calhoun
Writers: Words by Tot Seymour, music by Vee Lawnhurst (1936). Recorded by Fats Waller and his Rhythm on April 8, 1936 (Victor 25315).
Notes: Derwood Brown was a big Fats Waller fan and clearly enjoyed himself on this tune. It also gave Johnny Borowski a chance to play his "hot pen-

ny whistle," which was probably an ocarina. Considering the regular string band instrumentation of the previous songs in the Brownies' repertoire, hearing Borowski's solo comes as a shock.

118. Everybody Loves My Marguerite
Vocal: Derwood Brown
Take-offs: Perkins, Calhoun, Buchanan
Writers: Harry M. Woods, Jimmy Campbell and Reginald Connelly
Notes: A good vocal performance by Derwood Brown, his last on record. This recording also features a spiraling Bob Dunn-inspired take-off by Lefty Perkins.

119. I Just Want Your Stingaree
Vocal: Ocie Stockard
Take-off: Perkins
Writers: Williams and Jones or Georgia White
Notes: The Brownies took their version from Georgia White's Decca recording of the tune, made May 12, 1936 (Decca 7199). Dallas blues singer Blind Lemon Jefferson recorded many songs in this style as well. Tommy Duncan sang a similar song with Bob Wills, entitling it "Honey, What You Gonna Do?" In September 1937, Ocie Stockard reprised his powerful performance on Derwood Brown's recording, changing the title to "Turn Your Lights Down Low."

*   *   *

Before traveling to New Orleans for his final recording session, Milton Brown sent a list of songs the Brownies were prepared to record to R. N. McCormick, manager of the Dallas, Atlanta, and New Orleans branches of Decca. Twenty of the forty tunes were recorded in New Orleans. The remaining songs are listed below. The titles are presented just as Milton typed them.

Alabama Jubilee
Beele Street Blues
Chinese Honey Moon (Waltz)
Deep Elm Blues
Dinah
Ding Dong Daddy from Dumas
I Got Mine
In the Blue Hills of Virginia
Little Mother of the Hills
Moonlit Waters
The Music Goes 'Round and Around
My Blue Bird's Back Again
Roll Along Prairie Moon

Sally Goodin (breakdown)
Sally Johnson (breakdown)
San
Thousand Mile Blues
Tiger Rag
What You Need is Some One to Love
When It's Harvest Time in Peaceful Valley

In addition to the recorded canon by Milton Brown and his Musical Brownies, there were other songs in their repertoire that were performed regularly yet never recorded. Band members, family, and friends of Milton and Derwood Brown mentioned the following song titles in the course of conversations and interviews:

(By a Window) At the End of the Lane
About a Quarter to Nine
Back on the Texas Range
Bugle Call Rag
Clouds
Coney Island Washboard
Easy to Remember
How Many Times
I Never Knew
I'm Putting All My Eggs in One Basket
Lady in Red, The
Little Dutch Mill
Nagasaki
Over Sixty (and Feeling Sweet Sixteen)
Pagan Love Song
Roll Along Kentucky Moon
Running Wild
Sidewalks of New York
That Little Boy of Mine
Twelfth Street Rag

Index

Duncan, Tommy, xxv, xxvii, 59, 68, 74, 93, 226
Dunlap, Tommy, 94
Dunn, Avis, 108-9
Dunn, Bob: steel guitar style, xxii, xxvii, 71-72, 86, 262n10; Jack Teagarden fan, xxii, xxvii, 196; importance of, xxxii, 112-13; early life, 108, 256n13; amplifies steel guitar, 108-13; auditions for Brownies, 109-10; personality of, 111-12; drinking exploits, 148, 163, 171; influences musicians, 164, 213, 215; hired by MB, 166; at Chicago recording session, 173; leaves Brownies, 212; later years, 225, 256n14; mentioned, xxiv, xxv, 132, 134, 140, 147, 171-74 passim, 176, 177, 180-81, 189, 205, 222, 226
Dunn, Silas, 108
Dunnam, John, 36-38
"Dusty Skies," xxvii

"Eagle Riding Papa," 38, 46, 75, 94, 247n14
Eagles Hall (Fort Worth, Tex.), 39, 42, 43, 116
East Front Dance Hall (Fort Worth, Tex.), 42-43
"Easy Ridin' Papa," 299. *See also* "Eagle Riding Papa"
Echols, Tommy, 28
"El Rancho Grande." *See* "In El Rancho Grande"
"Eleven Cent Cotton and Forty Cent Meat," 53
Ellington, Duke: meets Brownies, 173; mentioned, 193
Erath County, Tex., 1-2, 3, 5, 22-23, 221, 243n2, 244n8
Erath, George B., 1, 243n1
Everett, Jimmy, 217
"Everybody Loves My Marguerite," 310
"Eyes of Texas, The," 57, 298

Fagan, Ellis, 23-26
Fair Park (Dallas, Tex.), 83
"Fall in Line with the NRA," 91-92, 254n11
Famous Hokum Boys, 38, 46, 63

"Fan It," 304-5
"Farewell Blues," 213
Farr, Hugh, 218
Farr, Karl, 218
Federal Radio Commission (FRC), 50
Ferguson, Buster, xvii, 217, 222
Fiddle: dominance in western swing, xxiii; contests, 32, 34; style of Cecil Brower and Kenneth Pitts, 57-59; tremolo mute, 57-58, 250n11; "rockin' the bow," 104, 256n8; "beating the straws," 263n17
Fio Rito, Ted, 177, 223
Firecracker String Band, 36
"Fisher's Hornpipe," 153
Flying X Ranch Boys, xv, 226
Foley, Red, xxxi, 223
Ford, Glenn, xxvi
Fort Worth: early television, xv; string bands in, xvi; in the 1920s, 10, 14, 16, 21, 29, 244n2; as oil boom town, 12-13; radio stations, 14, 48, 50, 92-93; and the Depression, 30, 69-70; radio personalities, 64; mentioned, 18, 51, 52, 56, 66, 71, 73, 80
Fort Worth and Rio Grande Railroad, 2, 243n3
Fort Worth Chamber of Commerce, 50
Fort Worth Doughboys, 62-64, 272. *See also* Light Crust Doughboys
"Fort Worth Doughboys from WBAP, The," 62
Fort Worth Frontier Centennial. *See* Texas centennial
Fort Worth Press (newspaper), xxiii, 26, 46, 68, 72, 77, 170, 176, l95, 198, 199, 201, 216
Fort Worth Radio News (supplement), xxiii, 92
Fort Worth Star-Telegram (newspaper), 13, 14
"Four, Five or Six Times," 283. *See also* "Four or Five Times"
"Four or Five Times," 78, 99-100. *See also* "Four, Five or Six Times"
Fowler, Harry, 10, 194, 203
Fowler, Maebelle McBride, 10, 16, 194-95
French, Elizabeth Mauldin, 18
Frizzell, Lefty, xxxi

CARY GINELL is a music consultant for the motion picture and television industry. His interest in western swing stems from conducting oral histories with Texas musicians in preparation for his master's degree in folklore, which he received from UCLA. His first book, *The Decca Hillbilly Discography* (1927–45), was published in 1989. Ginell resides in Thousand Oaks, California, with his wife Gail and son Brian.

ROY LEE BROWN is known to many as a walking encyclopedia of western swing and its pioneers. A native of Fort Worth, he has been a rhythm guitarist/vocalist since the age of fifteen. He has had his own bands throughout his lifetime. For thirty-five years, Roy Lee was a fire fighter, retiring as a district chief and resuming his musical career on a full-time basis. He lives in Aledo, Texas, with his wife Ellen.

Books in the Series Music in American Life